Media Regulation, Public Interest and the Law

Second Edition

Mike Feintuck and Mike Varney

Edinburgh University Press

© Mike Feintuck and Mike Varney, 2006

First edition published by Edinburgh University Press in 1999.

Edinburgh University Press Ltd
22 George Square, Edinburgh

Typeset in 10.5/13 Sabon
by Servis Filmsetting Ltd, Manchester, and
printed and bound in Great Britain by
Biddles Ltd, King's Lynn, Norfolk

A CIP record for this book is available from the British Library

ISBN-10   0 7486 2166 0 (paperback)
ISBN-13   978 0 7486 2166 8 (paperback)

The right of Mike Feintuck and Mike Varney
to be identified as authors of this work
has been asserted in accordance with
the Copyright, Designs and Patents Act 1988.

Published with the support of the
Edinburgh University Scholarly Publishing
Initiatives Fund

Media Regulation, Public Interest and the Law

Contents

Preface to the Second Edition

Any book focused on as fast-moving a subject as media regulation inevitably risks being rapidly overtaken by events. Since the first edition of this work appeared in 1999, trends in technological development and convergence and media conglomeration have continued apace and have in particular continued to offer threats to traditional public service values in broadcasting. In an attempt to address such developments, regulatory regimes have been substantially reformed, at both the national and European levels.

This greatly revised and expanded second edition seeks to review the implications of such changes, but, in the spirit of the original work, focuses predominantly on broad underlying themes rather than fine detail. These themes have remained almost entirely unchanged and their relevance has remained as great as ever, or perhaps, in light of developments discussed, they may have acquired even greater significance. Certainly, it was interesting for us to note the extent to which the Puttnam Committee's scrutiny of the UK's Draft Communications Bill emphasised the relationship between media regulation and citizenship around which this book revolves.

Though retaining their original structure and thematic focus, Chapters 1 to 3 have been updated by both authors to reflect recent and ongoing developments. Chapter 4, though retaining coverage of the position prior to 2003 by way of important historical context, now has a substantial body of new material, written by Mike Feintuck, dealing with the position under the Communications Act of that year. Chapter 5 is in essence entirely new, and Chapter 6 largely so; both written by Mike Varney, they offer more detailed studies of aspects of UK regulation and of the significance of the relationship between different tiers of regulation in Britain and Europe. Chapter 7, rewritten by Mike Feintuck, offers conclusions which reflect the work's original focus but incorporate also the new material.

There is no more of an effort to be comprehensive in coverage in this edition than in the first. Indeed, in the interests of keeping the work within a reasonable and accessible length, we have had to lose much of the comparative element provided in Chapter 6 of the first edition. However, we hope that this second edition will continue to serve the book's original purpose of exploring thematically and in their modern context the rationales for regulation of the media, and the mechanisms and outcomes of regulation. We hope that it will continue, in the Reithian spirit, to inform, educate and perhaps even entertain. While any study of media regulation must inevitably, to a degree, be a historical snapshot, we hope and believe that by virtue of its emphasis on themes and principles, this book will remain useful and continue to inform debates in the area for at least a few years.

We are happy to take the opportunity to thank Sarah Edwards and all those at Edinburgh University Press for their assistance in the production of this work, and for their patience regarding our production of the typescript. We would also like to thank our colleagues here at the Law School of the University of Hull, who continue to strive to bring about an environment in which a wide range of legal scholarship can flourish. We extend particular thanks to Kirsten McConnachie for her work in her brief period as a Research Assistant, which contributed significantly to Chapter 4. Finally, but most importantly, we must thank our families and friends, with whom we have inevitably spent less quality time than we would have liked while working on this project.

Neither of us have ever worked on a joint venture of this kind or scale previously, nor indeed have either of us worked before on a second edition. There have been times when the production of this second edition has seemed harder than writing the first, but we are happy now to take joint and equal responsibility for all the strengths and weaknesses of the finished work.

Mike Feintuck and Mike Varney
Hull, January 2006

Abbreviations

API	applications programming interface
ASA	Advertising Standards Authority
BBC	British Broadcasting Corporation
BBFC	British Board of Film Classification
BCAP	Broadcast Committee of Advertising Practice
BDB	British Digital Broadcasting
BFI	British Film Institute
BRTF	Better Regulation Task Force
BSC	Broadcasting Standards Commission
C4C	Channel 4 Corporation
CAP	Committee of Advertising Practice (ASA)
CAS	conditional access system
CRS	computerised reservation system
CSPL	Committee on Standards in Public Life
DCMS	Department of Culture, Media and Sport (formerly DNH)
DNH	Department of National Heritage (now DCMS)
DTH	direct to home (satellite broadcasting)
DTI	Department of Trade and Industry
DTN	Digital Television Network
DTT	digital terrestrial television
ECHR	European Convention on Human Rights
EFD	Essential Facilies Doctrine
EPG	electronic programme guide
FCC	Federal Communications Commission (US)
FOIA	Freedom of Information Act
FTA	Fair Trading Act 1973
GDP	gross domestic product
GII	global information infrastructure
HRA	Human Rights Act 1998
IBA	Independent Broadcasting Authority (now ITC)
ICSTIS	Independent Committee for the Supervision of Standards of Telephone Information Services
IPPR	Institute for Public Policy Research

ITC	Independent Television Commission (formerly IBA)
MMC	Monopolies and Mergers Commission
NHS	National Health Service
NRF	New Regulatory Framework (EC)
OCPA	Office of the Commissioner for Public Appointments
Ofcom	Office of Communications
OFT	Office of Fair Trading
Oftel	Office of Telecommunications
PCC	Press Complaints Commission
PCMLP	Programme for Comparative Media Law and Policy
PEB	party election broadcast
PI	public interest
PSB	public service broadcasting
PSP	public service publisher
RA	Radio Authority
RSS	Really Simple Syndication
SMP	significant market power
TVWF	Television Without Frontiers Directive
USO(s)	universal service obligation(s)
WTO	World Trade Organisation

1

Regulating the Revolution

∽

1.1 INTRODUCTION AND OVERVIEW

Our view of the world is arguably influenced more by the media than our personal experience. We rely to a large extent on both the broadcast and printed media as communicators of politics, of culture and of 'information', and, as such, the media exercise great power in our lives.

Though both the 'popular' and 'quality' press continue to exert influence, increasingly the broadcast media of radio and especially television have come to the fore. As long ago as 1967, it could be seen that 'television can be shown to stand out among mass media in its influence on our lives' (Blumler and Madge 1967: 5) while thirty years later television was said to have become 'the defining medium of the age' (Herman and McChesney 1997: 2). While technological and commercial developments continue to change our viewing habits, there is little doubt that television viewing remains the central media experience across the globe. There is a real sense in which some combination of 'reality TV' and live news feeds has truly come to represent reality for many viewers. With this in mind, it is both inevitable and proper that the focus of a study of media regulation should be pre-eminently on television, though, as will become apparent, even television exists in an increasingly multimedia and cross-media environment.

Television enjoyed a meteoric rise to its present position of cultural supremacy. In Britain sixty years ago, radio continued to be the dominant broadcast medium and cinema was hugely significant, with television, controlled entirely by the BBC, being viewed largely as an intersting and slightly amusing experiment. This position soon changed dramatically, given impetus especially in 1953 when the BBC's live coverage of the coronation attracted the first genuinely mass audience for television and sales of television receivers soared. The power of the BBC both in radio and television had, however, reached its zenith, and the arrival of commercial television in 1955 marked the end of the Corporation's broadcasting monopoly.

The arrival of ITV, though seen as revolutionary and clearly a severe threat to the BBC's domination of broadcasting, in the longer term resulted only in a power-sharing arrangement, with public-service values coexisting reasonably happily with the degree of commercialism introduced. As recently as 1981, before the advent of Channel 4, television in Britain was still in effect a comfortable duopoly, with power shared between the BBC and the ITV companies. In the years since then, however, a fifth terrestrial channel has come on-stream, and much more significantly, new technologies, including cable, digital terrestrial and especially direct-to-home (DTH) satellite broadcasting, have changed the nature of British television.

New broadcasting technology has permitted not only a rapid and large expansion in the number of channels available, both in mainstream and niche markets, but has also contributed to a fundamental shift in the dominant philosophy underlying British broadcasting. From a position of public service dominance, which continued from the BBC's inception through the arrival of ITV and Channel 4, the last twenty-five years have seen an increasing prominence for commercial values in broadcasting, to the extent that public service values are now at risk of marginalisation. In the mid-1950s, the arrival of ITV may have seemed to challenge the public service ethos; however, the way this 'competition' for the BBC was regulated ensured that it stayed clearly within the public service tradition. Fifty years later, the cleavage between public service broadcasting (PSB) and commercial television is much sharper, and it is increasingly apparent that consideration must be given to viewing the BBC, ITV and Channel 4 as a public service whole if there is to be an effective defence against the growing dominance of truly commercial broadcasting. We will consider in Chapter 2 the challenges to the BBC's traditional position which underlie the 2004–5 review of the BBC's Charter and funding arrangements, and which, we will argue, represent a particular threat via the adoption of a perspective informed more by considerations of 'market failure' than by any vision of public service values. The statutory reforms of the Communications Act 2003, to be considered in some detail, in Chapter 4 in particular, may be thought to tell only part of the story.

While the last twenty years have seen a growing presence for new media developing via information technology (Internet services, RSS feeds, pod-casting and the like), these have not yet challenged the ongoing dominance of television, and indeed do not necessarily share the characteristics associated with true 'mass media'. The dominant influence and reach of television is certainly not threatened as yet by such developments.

Indeed, it seems clear that new media, at least in the short to medium term, do not replace but merely supplement and coexist alongside pre-existing media. Just as book reading was not entirely replaced by radio listening, so books and radio have not ceased to exist with the advent of television, CD-ROMs and net-surfing.

Indeed, the oldest form of mass media, newspapers, continue to sell at commercially viable levels in Britain and elsewhere. Whether any one newspaper has ever 'won' a British general election, as *The Sun* (11 April 1992) famously claimed, is debatable, but the continued use of this medium by those selling their wares, whether political or commercial products, and the continued existence, even under financial pressure, of a wide range of national daily and Sunday titles, should be sufficient to convince of the perceived ongoing power of the press.

In 1945, Britain had nine national daily and eleven Sunday news-papers, controlled by twelve different companies (Humphreys 1996: 77). However, Curran and Seaton (2003: 76) note the 'rapid surge of national press concentration in the early post-war period', followed by the development of increased joint ownership of daily and Sunday papers in the more recent period. By 1995, twelve national dailies (including Scottish titles) and ten national Sunday titles were shared between seven owners (DNH 1995a: Annexe 2). While total choice of title had therefore changed only slightly, the number of different owners had diminished markedly, and still more significant is the fact that five of these seven owners controlled only ten titles between them, leaving the remaining twelve titles in the hands of two controlling groups (DNH 1995a: Annexe 2). By 2002, 70 per cent of national daily circulation and 79 per cent of national Sunday newspaper circulation was in the hands of three corporations (Curran and Seaton 2003: 76).

The structural change over the last fifty years in the television and newspaper sectors sketched above, though important, tells only a small part of the story of change relating to the media market as a whole. Probably more significant, at least in the last twenty years, has been the ongoing technologically driven convergence of media, which has led increasingly to the blurring or breakdown of conventional sectoral divides between media, with digitalisation also rapidly eroding the demarcation between the media and telecommunications industries. Technological convergence has been mirrored by changing ownership patterns, with the development of giant cross-media empires cutting across the traditional divides between broadcast and print media. The influence of Rupert Murdoch, as controller via his *News Corporation* of more than one-third of British newspaper circulation, a large stake in book and magazine publishing and total dominance of the British DTH broadcasting market via *BSkyB*, is the obvious and familiar example of this phenomenon.

Even this does not, however, indicate the full extent of change to date for, just as news gathering and distribution, and cinema, especially in the English language, are now global enterprises, so cross-media empires now span not only sectoral but also national boundaries. For example, Murdoch's influence extends not only throughout Britain and his native Australia, but also into the massive North American market (Tunstall and Palmer: 1991). The ability offered by satellite technology to transmit readily across long distances, whether intentionally or in the form of overspill of transmission, often has the appearance of rendering national boundaries irrelevant. In the European context, this inevitably suggests a potential for the EU to play an active role as transnational regulator. Yet, as we will consider later, especially in Chapter 6, the market paradigm in which the Union operates combined with the lack of a single vision as to the extent of its constitutional powers render its regulatory role in this field more limited and uncertain than might be expected.

The three ongoing phenomena already identified – technological convergence, globalisation and horizontal and vertical integration – form the vital context for discussion of media regulation in the modern era. However, descriptions of and commentaries on these developments are relatively plentiful and will not be reproduced here. Rather, this book focuses on the responses, actual and potential, to the challenges posed by these ongoing changes to the regulation of the media in the context of liberal-democratic theory and practice.

A fundamental distinction between democracy and other political systems is the expectation that arises from democracy that power will not be unlimited. Those who exercise political power are expected to be accountable to those who elect them, to their peers, and to the courts, and should be subjected not only to giving an account of their actions, but also be liable to sanction if their behaviour exceeds limits established by the constitution. It can also be argued, however, that those who exercise significant 'private' power, for example employers or corporate owners, will also, legitimately, have their powers limited by the state (Parkinson: 1993), and such arguments should apply especially in situations such as those discussed by Hertz (2002) or Monbiot (2000), where corporate entities acquire powers traditionally associated with public, state bodies. Given the degree of power that the media exercise by, in Blumler's words, providing 'the informational building blocks to structure views of the world' (quoted in Negrine 1994: 2), it is reasonable to expect that they too should be accountable, that their activities should be regulated. Yet simultaneous with the acquisition of power in private, corporate hands runs the parallel trend of the abandonment by the state of many functions and activities historically associated with a vision of legitimate public activity. If Marquand's thesis on the decline of the public domain is accepted (Marquand 2004) then we should be increasingly troubled by the absence of any authority exercising countervailing powers to those of modern corporations.

The centrality of the media to democracy, as the primary information source, cannot be overemphasised, and the very fact that democracy requires citizens to be informed if they are to act effectively as citizens, serves as a *prima facie* justification for regulation within a democratic context. However, that the media are regulated is, assert Herman and McChesney (1997: 11), true in all states. Whether it is through the kind of direct government control associated with Communist or Fascist regimes, or through apparently powerful state-authorised agencies such as the Federal Communications Commission (FCC) in the US, or through quiet accommodations such as under the D-notice or lobby systems in Britain, the state at all times ensures a degree of control or influence over the media. The range of regulatory techniques adopted at different times in different places will be considered in passing at various points, but the main thrust of this work is an argument that while regulatory techniques are continually being refined and reformed, a lack of attention has generally been paid to crucial prior questions.

In essence, it will be argued in this book that the rationales for regulation ('Why regulate?') and the objectives of regulation ('With what end in mind?') have been insufficiently addressed, with the consequence that regulatory techniques, no matter how sophisticated, do not have clear targets or a clear value system underpinning them. To some extent, success or failure of regulatory activities may be assessed by reference to the degree to which the regulatory regime achieves identified objectives or outcomes. Where clear objectives have not been set, perhaps as a consequence of failure to argue and articulate adequately the underlying *raison d'être* of the regulatory regime, success or failure becomes difficult to measure.

In the context of rapid technological and structural change within media industries during the 1990s, the existing institutions of regulation, and their legitimacy, came under increasing, and possibly terminal, challenge and strain. We will consider in due course the factors that led to the creation of Ofcom and the powers it has been granted, though our position is largely sceptical as regards whether the reforms have incorporated and reflected adequately our vision of the underlying issues. The perspective adopted in this book is that the important public interest values which continue to justify regulation have often been weakly defined and protected in the past, and may well seem not to be adequately recognised or protected even under the new arrangements. A major concern of this book is therefore to develop a theoretical and institutional framework both for meaningful discourse regarding these values and for the consideration of policies which are effective in asserting and furthering values thus determined.

At the most practical level, it will be argued that success or failure in relation to public service and public interest agendas for the media cannot be measured simply by reference to viewing or listening figures. Even if viewing figures for public service television decline significantly in the face of competition from commercial broadcasting in the multi-channel context, there may still ultimately be sound democratic arguments for maintaining a strong PSB presence. While the economics and statistics of broadcasting may tend to emphasise and value the measurable, it is necessary also to measure and protect what is democratically valuable in the PSB tradition.

Arising out of this agenda, the book has four primary objectives:

1. to identify rationales for media regulation and challenges posed to them by the ongoing media revolution;
2. to identify the values underpinning these justifications for regulation, and in particular to seek clarification of 'the public interest' in the context of media regulation;
3. to examine past and present structures of media regulation, assessing performance against democratic criteria; and
4. a synthesis of the second and third objectives, to identify values and institutional features that must be built into any future regulatory regime.

Thus, Chapters 1 to 3 establish the conceptual framework for media regulation, laying the foundation for studies of particular aspects of the British regulatory regime in Chapters 4 and 5. Chapter 6 goes on to consider understandings of regulation in this context, by way of establishing the framework for the discussion of different levels or tiers of regulation relevant to the media, considering international, national and sub-national interventions, and in particular the role of the EU, before overall conclusions are drawn in Chapter 7.

In essence, attempts to regulate the rapidly changing media environment can be equated to undertaking a somewhat hazardous journey through unknown and shifting terrain. Before commencing such an expedition, the prudent traveller will want to be clear about their desired destination, will need a map showing, as far as it is known, the lay of the land, will want a compass with which to orient themselves and the map, and will need to consider the most appropriate mode of transport. This book attempts to equip the traveller with sufficient information to allow informed choices to be made in respect of all these aspects of the journey. In discussing the objectives of media regulation, a range of destinations will be considered and an attempt made to help in ascertaining which are the most desirable in terms of democratic values. The map will be provided in the form of a discussion of current and projected future changes in the media and their regulation, hopefully indicating a way through this difficult terrain to desirable destinations. By discussing the principles which underlie decisions to seek a particular destination, a compass is provided, a means of orienting ourselves and maintaining direction towards an ultimate objective. Finally, the discussion of various regulatory techniques comprises a range of choice as to modes of transport from where we are to where we might like to be.

This book seeks to offer a range of choice in respect of all of these travellers' requisites, and though it does suggest that some destinations may be more desirable than others, and some routes and modes of transport more appropriate than alternatives, it is primarily concerned to inform the decision-making process over these aspects by identifying the dangers in the terrain and the principles which may help to avoid pitfalls. It is, on the whole, a map and compass rather than a prescriptive guidebook, though like any such guide it does, quite properly, offer the authors' particular perspective – in this case one deriving from fundamental democratic expectations. In its capacity as a map it does not attempt to illustrate every hump and hollow but rather indicate the general contours and most significant landmarks. The ultimate decisions as to the destination and the techniques to be used to get there lie with policy-makers and regulators, though it is to be hoped that their choices will be informed by the matters discussed and approach adopted in this book.

Though this book is written by academic lawyers, the study of the law relating to media regulation will not be an end in itself. It is obvious that the law is implicated heavily in the process of regulation; however, its various roles and functions stand in need of close analysis. Clearly, the legality of the actions of those who regulate derives from their empowerment through law and their adherence to limits imposed by statute or other legal devices. However, of particular significance in the context of this book, is a concept which encompasses, but extends beyond, legality, namely 'legitimacy'. This relates to what can be considered as a set of requirements and expectations of an arguably 'higher order' than the legal limits on power established by statute or case law. It relates to adherence to a set of values or expectations which, in the UK and other jurisdictions which will be touched upon, derive from a liberal-democratic heritage. The accountability of those who exercise power, a crucial theme of this book, has aspects of both legality and legitimacy: claims of legitimacy frequently rely heavily on claims of being account-able, though such accountability may be as much through political and social mechanisms as through the potential for legal challenge.

As will be discussed later in this chapter and in Chapters 6 and 7, fun-damental values can generally be discovered within the constitutions of individual states, or indeed of transnational bodies such as the EU. In countries such as the US, or indeed the vast majority of Western democ-racies that have modern, written constitutions, it is likely that many of the values enshrined can, at least superficially, be gleaned fairly readily from examination of constitutional documents, including perhaps a Bill of Rights. Though they will always remain subject to contemporary rein-terpretation, these values provide a clear starting point when seeking to evaluate the legitimacy of subsequent action. In Britain, almost uniquely, the absence of a modern, written constitution renders this task more difficult, though not necessarily impossible, and the arrival of the Human Rights Act, substantially an incorporation into domestic law of the European Convention on Human Rights (Jowell and Cooper 2000; Lester 2004; Feldman 2004), goes some way to assist in this respect, at least as regards individual liberties. Certain significant aspects of the HRA will be picked up in Chapter 5. In the interests of understanding how systems of media regulation operate and the roles that the law plays, it will be necessary to examine the range of constitutional fundamentals that inform systems of media regulation in different jurisdictions under different constitutional arrangements. It is argued in this book that an awareness of the constitutional context is crucial, both in terms of under-standing and assessing how the system of regulation operates, but also in providing a basis for the establishment of rational, meaningful and clear justifications and objectives for the regulatory enterprise.

The remainder of this chapter seeks to develop a little further each of the themes identified above. By way of completing the context for this work, it is necessary to consider the power of the media and the sig-nificance of the claim of freedom of communication, a fundamental expectation in liberal democracies, though only briefly given the exten-sive literature which already exists in these areas. The phenomena of globalisation of media and media empires and the implications of technological convergence will also be examined, and the tension between commercial imperatives and public service values in the media will be opened up, an important theme to be explored more fully in Chapters 2, 3 and 4. From there, preliminary consideration will be given to the rationales, objectives, techniques and outcomes of various regulatory approaches, laying the ground for more detailed discussions in Chapters 4, 5 and 6. Finally, this chapter will introduce the vision of the legal and constitutional context for media regulation which will inform much of the rest of this book.

1.2 COMMUNICATION AND POWER

1.2.1 Freedom of communication

Claims of freedom of communication and resistance to regulation have historically formed both the theoretical basis on which much of the power of the media has been built and also the primary dynamic which determines the relationship between the state and the media. McQuail (1992: 9) establishes a historical progression in the relationship between restriction and freedom of the media, tracing it from suppression (by the state and religious authorities) and selective prohibition, to limited permission 'in the name of liberty and business', to, in the modern era, prescription in pursuit of educational objectives and, finally, to libertarianism in what he refers to as 'a market-based claim to unhindered freedom of operation'. Though not by itself particularly revealing as to the theoretical underpinnings for claims of freedom of communication, this historical progression needs to be borne in mind, especially when considering Keane's thesis that present-day arguments for media freedom largely remain based on the philosophies and issues of the revolutionary period of the late eighteenth century focused on obtaining freedom from historical state repression. The very different political, social, economic and technological context in which debates over media regulation take place at the start of the twenty-first century may, in the absence of new or at least explicit philosophical underpinnings, allow the claims for freedom of expression, so central to liberal thought in eighteenth-century Europe and America, to be subverted to the interests and purposes of the corporate giants who control the modern media (Keane 1991).

The ability to communicate beliefs, ideas and views is held to be central to democracy, yet in all democracies limits are placed on the freedom to communicate. Even in the US, where the First Amendment's guarantee of freedom of expression has the appearance of supreme authority, the courts have stated a willingness, albeit in very limited circumstances, to prevent those wishing to publish material from so doing. Although the *Pentagon Papers* litigation (1971) resulted in a majority of the Supreme Court bench finding against the executive's desire to prevent publication by the *Washington Post* and *New York Times*, the court made clear that there may be circumstances in which they would uphold such a claim to 'prior restraint' (Rudenstine 1996).

Prior restraint – the formal prevention of publication – appears the most severe of restrictions on communication. However, in Britain, a wide range of other significant restrictions exist, ranging from general laws of obscenity, blasphemy, defamation and incitement to racial hatred, through to media-specific measures such as the non-statutory regime of cinema censorship enforced by the British Board of Film Classification (BBFC), the Video Recordings Act 1984 and the notorious temporary ban on broadcasting the voices of members of proscribed Irish organisations under powers granted by the Broadcasting Act 1990. In addition, those working in the news media must remain aware of the laws of breach of confidence (central to the *Spycatcher* litigation), contempt of court and, of course, the reformed but still wide-ranging Official Secrets Acts (see Birkinshaw 2001).

The technicalities of these laws are not of concern for the moment, and it is sufficient to note that, despite the rhetoric of freedom of speech, there exists a wide range of limits on what can be communicated either by the media or individual citizens. Though the Human Rights Act may have changed things somewhat, and will be returned to in Chapter 5, it has not wholly reversed hundreds of years of British history during which freedom of communication has existed, like many other 'fundamental' liberties, merely as a residual liberty; what is not unlawful by virtue of statute or case law is permissible, with no special protection or privileges attaching to the media in Britain. We will touch on this issue in Chapter 5, but for the moment we can note that this stands in stark contrast with the position in the US where the starting point is the guarantee of freedom of speech contained in the First Amendment to the Constitution and any abridgement of it must be specifically justified. McQuail (1992: 36) illustrates the American judicial attitude to the press and its regulation with a quote from a US Supreme Court judgement (*Associated Press v US* (1945) 326 US 1) where Judge Frankfurter stated that:

> In addition to being a commercial enterprise, it [the press] has a relationship to the public interest unlike that of any other enterprise for profit . . . The

business of the Press . . . is the promotion of truth regarding public matters by furnishing the basis for an understanding of them.

Such an awareness of the role of the media in democracy has not entirely prevented the US state from regulating media activity, and particularly broadcasting, though regulatory intervention has been limited essentially to structural and economic matters rather than control of the content of media output, which continues to enjoy First Amendment protection. Indeed, even the pornography industry, historically heavily restricted in Britain, continues to enjoy a degree of constitutional protection in the US (cf. Abel 1994 and Itzin 1995). Of course, such national variations in relation to matters such as access to sexually explicit material must now increasingly be viewed in the context of an international information technology infrastructure.

The transatlantic difference in norms pertaining to freedom of communication can in part be explained by reference to the late eighteenth-century struggle for freedom from colonial rule in the US and the post-revolutionary constitutional settlement which reflects the values of its time and contrasts markedly with the British model established by the victors of the 'Glorious Revolution' one hundred years earlier. The degree of difference is still remarkable, however, given the shared philosophical heritage deriving from mainstream liberal democratic thought.

Barendt (1985) presents three different lines of justification of freedom of expression from within this paradigm. Though best viewed as 'ideal types', and clearly faced with some difficulty when confronted by the kind of issues and events relating to racist material and pornography discussed by Abel (1994), Barendt's identification of distinct theoretical justifications is helpful in identifying different threads of thought which may be hidden within or beneath general claims of freedom of expression.

The first category that Barendt considers is 'arguments from truth', which he associates closely with the utilitarian philosophy of John Stuart Mill. According to such arguments, open discussion is crucial to the discovery of truth, and thus, if speech or communication is restricted, the discovery and publication of true facts and accurate judgements will be stifled or limited. The value of such discovered truth may be inherent and autonomous or its value may derive from utilitarian arguments regarding the general development of society. Barendt notes a difficulty here, in relation to an assumption that the truth of beliefs and claims is capable of objective verification. However, this problem may not necessarily be seen to undermine the line of argument entirely if it is interpreted in terms of a consideration that most contentious beliefs can be categorised as 'possibly true' or 'probably false'.

Leaving this issue aside, a further essentially utilitarian line underlying arguments from truth can also be discerned. This is the idea that defence of freedom of expression in pursuit of truth helps to ensure that no single set of values is allowed to dominate society; the constant potential for challenge to dominant values demands continuous rational justification of such values by those in power. However, it must be questioned whether the publication of any possibly true statement is always to be defended as a result of adherence to arguments from truth. For example, there is the *possibility* of truth in overtly racist literature, though such material may be caught by laws regarding incitement to racial hatred or the like, which appear to 'trump' the basic claim to freedom of expression. Similarly, while publication of leaked government documents might appear to be justified via arguments from truth, as they clearly contribute to the amount of knowledge or truth in circulation, they may still be restricted in the name of some overriding national or public interest. Justifications for such restrictions tend to be based around a utilitarian concept of a broader public good that is furthered by them, and may be bolstered by secondary claims that protection for freedom of expression continues to exist because of the ongoing potential to debate and challenge the restrictions via democratic institutions.

Arguments from truth can be seen to rest on a faith in the efficacy of a competitive market in speech or ideas, and it is readily apparent that, like all markets, it must be regulated or manipulated if effective communication and therefore the market benefits are to be realised. At its simplest, if two competing speakers talk simultaneously, it will be difficult to understand fully what either has to say: neither will contribute to effective or meaningful debate or ascertainment of truth. Thus the freedom, to be effective, must be regulated by some agency. Similarly, if, like many markets, the 'market' in speech tends towards monopolistic or oligopolistic capture, then regulation will be necessary if the perceived benefits of the operation of the market are not to be lost.

The second approach to freedom of expression identified by Barendt appears to derive from an individualistic rather than utilitarian approach: 'arguments from self-fulfilment'. The basic argument here is that restrictions on expression inhibit individual growth, as individuals will not develop unless free to formulate beliefs and political attitudes through discussion and criticism. This might appear to be a justification of broader application than only to freedom of expression; a case can be made for its extension to include other prerequisites of effective citizenship such as decent housing or education. One perceptible limitation of this line of argument is that it can readily take on the form of a negative freedom: liberty 'against the state' rather than a positive claim. It then becomes rather more of a hostage to fortune, being highly susceptible to judicial interpretation, though hopefully within the context of overarching constitutional standards. In the modern context, as will be discussed in due course, the question must be asked as to whether freedom of communication also includes liberty from the imposition of limitations by the exercise of corporate, private, as opposed to state, power.

The third distinct line of argument identified by Barendt is described as 'arguments from citizen participation'. Especially in the context of debates involving the US First Amendment, he finds it often argued that the primary purpose of freedom of expression is to enable individuals to understand political issues, thereby empowering them to participate effectively as citizens within the processes of democracy. Though this argument is generally expressed in terms of citizens' rights, which may seem to represent an apparently individualistic model, Barendt notes that it is 'firmly utilitarian in spirit' (Barendt 1985: 20), being based around the good that will accrue for the majority of society from pursuit of this policy. He goes on, however, to indicate some specific problems that may flow from this.

Within the context of a primarily representative (as opposed to participatory) model of democracy, this approach appears to allow elected representatives, with a temporary hold on power, to impose restraints on expression 'in the public good', an issue we will return to in Chapter 5. The only obvious response to this problem seems to be that certain 'rights' such as freedom of expression are so important that they cannot be overridden easily by a government temporarily in power. Such repressive action might, especially with the aid of support from clear constitutional terms, readily be viewed as illegitimate and/or illegal. Alternative responses to this dilemma appear to fall back on either the individualistic, self-fulfilment argument or, possibly, a return to arguments from truth.

Clearly, none of the three lines of argument is without its problems, though they persist, often in varying combinations, as the key lines of argument justifying freedom of expression. Judicial decisions in both Britain and the US can often be found to contain elements of all three, though tend to rely most often on concepts of 'citizen' or 'human rights' most closely associated with arguments from self-fulfilment and citizen participation. Whatever combination of any or all of the three lines of argument is or are accepted, the centrality of freedom of communication to liberal democratic beliefs is demonstrated, though disputes over its precise nature and extent continue. Ultimately, all three share an underlying belief in the value of allowing individuals and groups to have access to a wide range of information (both political and cultural), whether from the point of view of society ascertaining truth, or individual self-fulfilment, or citizens participating effectively in society. However, in modern, large-scale societies, this must be viewed primarily as an issue of mass rather than individual communication, and both transmission and receipt of effective mass communication, even in an era of international networks of personal computers, will require access to the mass media.

In light of the power of the media, discussed below, certain other values may compete with the claim to freedom of expression. In particular, claims to privacy, not to be harassed and the avoidance of defamation will be dealt with differently in different jurisdictions. For media regulators, however, another set of issues arises in the modern context. This concerns limiting the ability of corporate media giants to utilise the claim of freedom of communication to further their own commercial ends while acting in ways that run counter to maximising the provision of 'information' upon which the claim is premised. This is the concrete manifestation of the mismatch between the claims of late eighteenth-century philosophical underpinnings and the late twentieth-century context which Keane (1991) identifies and which is illustrated in Hertz's thesis on global capitalism (Hertz 2002). Examples of the problems created and of the generally futile attempts to resolve them via regulation are highlighted in later chapters, and confirm empirically the need, identified at a theoretical level by Keane, to develop a new and appropriate public interest justification for regulation in the modern context.

In the specific context of broadcasting, Negrine (1994: 116) asks: 'How much freedom should broadcasters have, given that they have an almost monopolistic control over the means of mass communication?' It seems appropriate to answer this question in terms of setting the limits of media freedom in such a way as to ensure that their activities further, rather than damage, the public interest. The only problem with this response – unfortunately rather a large one – is in defining the public interest, the subject of Chapter 3.

1.2.2 The power of the media

Seymour-Ure (1996: 271) states that 'A history of media could easily slip into being a history of society as a whole. This in itself reflects the centrality of media in our lives.' With this caveat in mind, it is still necessary to consider the roles played and power exercised by the media before turning to questions of their regulation.

Much of the media's activity, especially in the areas of news gathering and distribution, is justified by reference to one or more of the theoretical justifications for freedom of expression expounded by Barendt. The central role of the media in political discourse places it, or ought to place it, believe Herman and McChesney, firmly within the 'public sphere' (1997: 2–8). Habermas' construct of the public sphere and of the role of the media is summarised admirably by Dahlgren (1995: 7):

> In ideal terms, Habermas conceptualizes the public sphere as that realm of social life where the exchange of information and views on questions of common concern can take place so that public opinion can be formed. The public sphere 'takes place' when citizens, exercising the rights of assembly and association, gather as public bodies to discuss issues of the day, specifically those of public concern. Since the scale of modern society does not allow more than relatively small numbers of citizens to be physically co-present, the mass media have become the chief institutions of the public sphere. Yet Habermas' concept of the public sphere insists on the analytic centrality of reasoned, critical discourse. The public sphere exists, in other words, in the active reasoning of the public. It is via such discourse that public opinion is generated, which in turn is to shape the policies of the state and the development of society as a whole.

Tehranian and Tehranian (1995: 39) state that 'It is in the process of public communication on public policies that democratic institutions thrive', and it is clear that communications media can facilitate the objectives identified in arguments from truth, self-fulfilment and citizen participation and have the potential to further the rational discourse enterprise identified in Habermas' public sphere. However, the media's activities can also be viewed in a less altruistic light, in terms of pursuing particular political agendas and in terms of manipulating material for commercial and/or political reasons. The power the mass media wields in a large-scale society where individuals will communicate personally with only a tiny proportion of their fellow citizens is clear and, if this power is not constrained by adequate accountability mechanisms, might be thought to be in breach of fundamental constitutional expectations. While the media is constrained by both the general law and media-specific measures referred to above, commentators consistently argue that this does not significantly inhibit the power and influence of the press and broadcasters on the grand scale.

In the modern context, the media must also be viewed as a huge and increasingly global commercial market. While all markets run the risk of domination by one or more major players, media markets appear to show a peculiar predisposition towards monopoly or oligopoly; the work of both Bagdikian (2004) and Herman and McChesney (1997) testifies to this, in the former case in the context of one country, the US, in the latter on the global scale. If the media are to justify their existence and power in relation to any of the theories of freedom of communication identified by Barendt, or in terms of their contribution to the establishment and maintenance of the public sphere, then they must also establish that the commercial market place in which they operate as profit-making enterprises in turn contributes to the wider, democratic market place of ideas. The media, to continue legitimately to claim the power associated with freedom of communication and the domination of its channels, must contribute to the acquisition by citizens of a range of political and cultural 'information', from which they may engage, individually and collectively, in a triangulation process which ultimately allows them an informed view of the world. In this sense, the media may properly be viewed as a public resource. If the commercial imperative drives the media to monopoly or near-monopoly of control, and this in turn results in a more restricted range of information or views being available, where 'knowledge becomes ever less a common good and more and more the privileged possession of individual owners' (Hamelink 1995: 21), then this may be viewed as running counter to the democratic expectations on which freedom of communication is premised.

Schiller (1996) addresses the issues of the modern media context still more directly, illustrating again the inappropriateness of the claim to freedom of expression by the media where their activities appear to run counter to the democratic enterprise. Noting the increasing proprietorship of information in corporate, commercial hands, he comments that while 'Historically, the threat to individual expression has been seen to come from an arbitrary state' (43), 'What distinguishes this [present] era is that the main threat to free expression has shifted from government to private corporate power' (44). In addition, as Dahlgren (1995: 148) indicates, the institutional logic of mass media, and the television industry in particular, is not to further the public sphere but to maximise profit. This is sometimes reflected in the statement that the central purpose of commercial media is not to deliver products to audiences but to deliver the audience, as a product, to advertisers. Given the power of the media and its centrality to democratic processes, if Hutton (1995: 9) is remotely near the mark in stating a 'growing conviction that an honest hearing in the press is the exception rather than the rule unless what is being said chimes with the transient preoccupations of editors and proprietors', it is clear that the media require regulation to ensure that they act in accordance with democratic principles, that the media support citizenship and the public sphere rather than undermining them. The underlying tension between commercial and public service aspirations in the media has become an ever more prominent issue in recent years.

However, in their role as 'the fourth estate', the media also claim to play a vital role in support of democracy in acting as a counterbalance to the state or government, especially in facilitating the calling to account of government. Again, this function appears to rely upon a degree of plurality in the approaches taken by the media and, in so far as ownership relates to editorial content, upon plurality of ownership. At the extreme, were the entire media to be in the control of a media magnate broadly or wholly sympathetic with the views of the government of the day, then the likely effectiveness of the media as a mechanism of accountability would be highly questionable. The net result would not be that far removed from the kind of situation in Nazi Germany or the Soviet Union (Siebert *et al.* 1956) where the state-controlled media could be viewed as an arm of the government rather than a counterbalance to it, as anti-democratic rather than furthering democratic objectives of scrutiny and accountability. Given the quasi-constitutional role that the media take on in this sense, the need for their accountability and the justification for their regulation is further emphasised. Yet the media's relationship with democracy remains fundamentally problematic. McChesney's thesis on 'Rich Media, Poor Democracy' (1999) demonstrates how, in the context of the heavily concentrated US media market, the legal and regulatory context in which the media operate has been forged to a significant extent to reflect the corporate interests of the media oligopolists, subverting democratic values.

Blumler and Madge (1967) suggest at least four aspects of the media's political impact on citizens: at the time of elections; more generally in providing a picture of the political system; in establishing and serving group relationships and interests; and as a source of knowledge leading to civic action. The reform of housing law in Britain following the outcry created by the screening of Ken Loach's *Cathy Come Home* in 1966 provides a concrete example of the media's power to influence social reform. It would be rather pious, however, to consider the media only in the context of 'informing' and 'educating', to the exclusion of the third part of Lord Reith's formula, 'entertaining'. The media's activities must be considered in terms of both, in Corner's words 'the public knowledge project' and 'the popular culture project' (quoted in Dahlgren 1995: 37).

In large-scale societies, to the extent that we share expectations, assumptions, values and, more broadly, a 'view of the world', this is the result of the entertainment industry which overlaps with, though is far from coterminous with, the media considered here. In so far as they are commercial activities, the visual and performing arts, together with leisure industries such as participatory and spectator sports and gambling (bingo, lotteries, betting shops and casinos), form part of this entertainment industry, which, though sometimes corporately related to, cannot be considered, by and large, to be part of the mass media. The area of overlap is, however, large, taking in much of television and radio output, the cinema and video market and the recorded music industry. Of these, control of coverage of major sporting events and television premieres of movies by *BSkyB* have formed the lever used by Murdoch to force the pace of change currently to be found in British television.

Whether viewed as a force towards social solidarity, as symptomatic or causal of the atomisation of society, or as a high-tech 'opium for the masses', dulling the effects of the painful cutting-edge of capitalism, it is fair to conclude that the media, and television especially, has, over the last forty years, provided most of the experiences shared *en masse* by vast sectors of society. We have shared together in the drama of sporting triumph and defeat, in world records being broken, marathon runners in tears by Greek roadsides, the recurrent drama of footballers scoring and missing penalties, and even in 2005 English cricketers winning the Ashes! We have watched together hundreds of births, marriages and deaths (and the occasional burying and discovery of bodies under patios) on our favourite soaps. We have watched thousands of fictional and recreated crimes, natural and human-made disasters, and fights and battles lost and won. We have sometimes cried and laughed together in our thousands or millions as these events unfold on our screens (or even on our radios), and though at the time alone or in our small family or social circle, they have formed the focal point of much of our intercourse with others in the days and weeks that followed. The potential for the media to raise public consciousness and indeed mobilise the public in pursuit of acts of charity can be illustrated by Live Aid and subsequent such events or in coverage of the Asian Tsunami of December 2004. The coverage, or arguably media creation, of the 'national mourning' following the death of Diana, Princess of Wales, in September 1997 provided irrefutable evidence of the power of the media to engage vast sectors of society, and indeed, arguably, contributed significantly to actual action on the part of those who chose travel to London to 'pay their respects' under the eye of the watching media. Meanwhile, the events of 11 September 2001, and in particular the images of hijacked aircraft flying into New York's Twin Towers, are imprinted permanently on the global television audience's collective retina.

Conventional television, free at the point of reception, can be said to provide 'a cultural cohesion to the nation' (Negrine 1994: 198). The significance of the threat of cultural imperialism on a global scale posed by (US) English-language dominated media therefore becomes apparent. But, whatever the messages transmitted by the media are, and however they are understood and acted upon by individuals, groups or nations, the mere fact that commercial broadcasting is able to support itself primarily from advertising revenue is indicative of the significant power of the medium in the eyes of those who have products to sell.

Also of significance, in relation to an expectation of equality in relation to citizenship, a theme to which we will return repeatedly, is how different social groups are more or less susceptible to mass media, and more or less able to triangulate their view of the world for themselves through utilising different sources. Sharing the language of a rich/poor dichotomy utilised by McChesney, Lloyd (2004: 27) summarises part of the problem thus:

> In most countries, rich and sophisticated people are often mass media poor: they don't watch much TV. Most of the poor, and certainly the lesser educated . . . are mass media rich: they usually watch a lot of television. Conversely – a problem at the heart of our modern societies – the people who watch a lot of TV tend to be information poor, and the people who don't are often information rich.

It is not though the purpose of this book to attempt to unravel the mysteries of the power of the media, or even, by and large, the social purposes for which this power is used. It is sufficient for present purposes to note that undoubted power exists, and to note also that 'in all societies the questions of who owns and controls the media, and for what purposes, have been political issues' (Herman and McChesney 1997: 11). As such, we must expect the state and machinery of government to take an active interest in media-related activities, and in particular to respond to the media's 'capability to define and present its own role to the public' (Schiller 1996: 125). However, as Eldridge *et al.* (1997: 13) observe:

> The conceptualization of the mass media as being either 'the Fourth Estate' or 'agencies of social control' is an oversimplification. The role of the mass media at any time is shaped by factors particular to the period under consideration as well as the medium under study.

Via a brief historical account of the development of and attempts by the state to control cinema and the popular press, Eldridge *et al.* (1997: 23) conclude that only in the twentieth century did 'the market and the system of information control became central to the government's strategy to manage the media'. Though access to, and control of, information must therefore of necessity provide a significant part of the backdrop to our consideration of media regulation, it is equally important to understand the particular context in which such debates must currently take place. In the modern era, globalisation of corporate media interests combines with rapid technological change to form what is, at the very least, a challenging environment in which to develop and implement media policy. To a significant extent, this challenge, which lies at the heart of our agenda in this book, can be summarised in terms of squaring corporate trends and interests, and the dominance of market-centred ideology in modern politics, with a very different set of values historically associated with the PSB tradition.

1.3 GLOBALISATION AND TECHNOLOGICAL CHANGE

1.3.1 *The global media empire*

Over recent years, much attention has been paid to the apparent domination of national media sectors, or indeed national cross-media, by individual corporate giants. In Italy, Silvio Berlusconi came to dominate the commercial television sector, and indeed challenged the primacy of the state broadcaster in the overall television market (Herman and McChesney 1997: 170–3; Tunstall and Palmer 1991: chapter 8). In Britain, Rupert Murdoch was allowed to develop dominance in DTH satellite broadcasting while simultaneously building a holding approximating to one-third of the national newspaper market (Herman and McChesney 1997: 166–70; Tunstall and Palmer 1991: chapter 6). However, regulators must remain aware that there is more to their task than 'regulating the bogey-man' (Feintuck 1997a) for, as Keane (1991: 154) notes, 'The obsession with media magnates has little in common with a politics of maximising freedom and equality of communication'. The scope of the regulatory endeavour is bigger even than the mightiest media magnate, and any individual magnate or corporation defeated on an individual basis will soon be replaced by another, or others, pursuing the same agenda and posing the same threats. There will always be more bogey-men lurking in the woods or under the bed.

More typical than near or actual monopoly in media markets is a condition of oligopoly. In the US, as charted by Bagdikian (2004), the entire media market in television, movies, newspapers and magazines has fallen increasingly into the hands of a small number of corporate giants. While such developments in themselves pose significant challenges for national regulators, for whom ensuring diversity of ownership has conventionally been an objective, a more fundamental problem has become increasingly apparent.

While regulation of media ownership has traditionally taken place at the national level, the media market has become increasingly international, both in terms of transmission of media products across national borders and in terms of ownership patterns. The former phenomenon, significant especially for the potential it offers in terms of outflanking what was, historically, 'the ultimate [national] regulatory sanction of revocation of licence' (Marsden 1997b: 2), has largely arisen out of technological developments (which will be addressed shortly) while the latter relates more to the development of increasingly international corporate structures in media markets, an aspect, say Herman and McChesney (1997), of an increasingly global economy.

Though Seymour-Ure (1996: chapter 5) identifies the existence of a significant role for foreign capital in the British (print) media even prior to 1945, he records also the changing patterns of ownership, and particularly the rapidly changing shape of the market in the 1980s and 1990s, especially in terms of 'scope, scale, management, balance and volatility' (119). In earlier eras, only the news agencies operated in a truly international environment, while in modern times the likes of *CNN* and *MTV* are broadcast globally, and empires such as Murdoch's operate on a transcontinental scale. Such developments clearly pose problems for national regulators, given the limited significance of national affiliations for global corporations; however, they also carry a threat to conventional public service values and standards in broadcasting, given that 'the major feature of the global media order is its thoroughgoing commercialism' and the resulting centrality of advertising (Herman and McChesney 1997: 1).

The synergistic strength of cross-media corporations identified by Herman and McChesney (1997) is constantly increased by the processes of horizontal integration (within individual media sectors) and vertical integration (across-media sectors) taking place on a near-daily basis. The result of these processes is the potential for even large media players such as the American broadcasters *NBC* and *CBS* to be shut out of parts of the market by real giants such as *Disney* and *Time Warner* who can provide their own films to their own broadcast and cable television channels (Herman and McChesney 1997: 68). As yet, the potential for the total global domination of American originated images is not complete, but the corporate structure for its achievement is largely in place (see, generally, Schiller 1996).

While such trends pose a clear threat to the objective of diversity which appears to underlie much of the regulatory endeavour in relation to the media, it would be naive to believe that such developments have always run counter to the wishes of national governments. Certainly, there was no active government opposition in Britain to, and possibly even encouragement for, the involvement of newspaper groups in the early development of the ITV companies (Barendt 1995: 131) though subsequently, from the Television Act 1963 onwards, regulators were given the ability to limit cross-media ownership and control. However, Herman and McChesney (1997) argue persuasively that in many cases governments, especially those of the US and UK, continue actively to encourage the transformation of home-grown media enterprises into worldwide players, in pursuit of the perceived benefits that will accrue both in terms of the national economy and in extending their sphere of influence.

The economic significance of the media market should not be under-estimated, with Doyle (2002: 30) indicating that the media accounts for 3 to 5 per cent of gross domestic product in most Western European countries. In an increasingly global economy, it should be no surprise, however, to find that much of the truly international media is US domin-ated, though Herman and McChesney (1997: chapter 3) note that even the buoyant home US market is not entirely immune from penetration by non-American media players.

While national economic benefits will inevitably prove tempting to governments, dependent for image and re-election on economic success, allowing or encouraging local media empires to grow to a size at which they can compete effectively on the global scale carries with it the risk of them having to be allowed to grow to a position where they may domin-ate the home market, posing significant challenges for domestic regula-tion. Given the undoubted significance of the media to national political, cultural and social life, such risks should not be underestimated. The problem remains that observed by Humphreys (1997a: 19):

> The main determinant of media policy in the 1990s seems to be policy makers' perception of what is in the economic interest. Unsurprisingly, given the 'structural power' of large media corporations, the 'economic interest' conforms with the said corporations' interests.

The relationship between economic interests and broader or alternative 'public interests' will be considered in Chapter 3, especially in the con-text of debate as to competing visions of competition law. It is sufficient for the moment to note that the media industries seem particularly vulnerable to concentration of ownership and the potential problems this presents (Humphreys, 1997a; also Doyle 2002: 173). While conventionally, the primary focus of the national regulatory endeavour has been on the resolution of conflicts at the domestic level, the growth of international media empires, combined with technological developments and what Herman and McChesney (1997: 41) refer to as the 'rapid reduction or elimination of many of the traditional institutional and legal barriers to cross-border transactions', has changed the nature of the game. Certainly, the development of a global information infrastructure (GII) has a sinister appearance for national regulators traditionally charged with a public interest mandate. '[C]an the undemocratic sort of capitalism that will finance the GII in fact produce a genuine participatory democratic arrangement?' asks Hamelink (1995: 16), or will its further development simply increase the ongoing trend identified by Schiller (1996) as the privatisation of information and therefore democracy? While this may be viewed simply as one aspect of a much broader trend, the challenge to democracy posed by the forces of global capitalism (Hertz 2002), the development of this phenomenon in the media sector represents a particular and immediate threat.

Understandably, one reaction to the global media has been to shift the regulatory focus away from its traditional home in the nation state to a growth in the role ascribed to international organisations in regulating the media. However, international cooperation in a field such as this is difficult, and in Europe, as suggested earlier, though the EU appears potentially to have a key role in establishing the regulatory agenda for the region as a whole, progress has been slow and laborious when compared with the rapid pace of technological and corporate development. Though these issues will be returned to later, and in Chapter 6 in particular, it should be noted at this stage that, from a democratic perspective, the EU's activities in relation to the media may be limited by the fact that its primary focus is based upon economics rather than, say, citizenship. In addition, in the 1990s both Harcourt (1996) and Doyle (1997) drew attention to the problems of institutional inertia and entrenched perceptions of national interests within member states apparent within EU attempts to develop a coherent and effective media policy, an obstacle perhaps now heightened with the greatly expanded number of member states with a stake in such matters. For the moment, it is sufficient to note Harcourt's recent conclusion that many European policies and interventions have 'side stepped the public interest in the interest of greater European integration' (Harcourt 2005: 18).

1.3.2 Technological development and convergence

While the changing corporate structure of the media industries reflects in part a general move towards a an international or possibly global economy, the rapid change in recent years has also been related to the significant degree of technological change and development. The development of Teletext services, in which newspaper groups hold a significant stake (Peak and Fisher 1996: 167), the availability of newspapers on the Web, plus the delivery of television, interactive home-shopping and banking services together with conventional point-to-point telecommunications services via fibre-optic cable are all indicative of this process. Another obvious and current manifestation of such development was the arrival of digital terrestrial television (DTT) in Britain, which will be examined shortly. In reality, DTT has still failed to capture fully the UK public's imagination, though the reality of the forthcoming programme of analogue switch-off from 2008 to 2012 will surely force many hands in this direction. However, the degree of technological development and its impact, and especially the reduction of a wide-range of material to digital bit-streams, extends far beyond DTT and represents a fundamental challenge to our view of, and methods for regulating, the media.

The 1980s saw the advent of computerised typesetting and gradually improving quality of colour printing in newspapers, and though the former especially was viewed as revolutionary in the newspaper industry, like the introduction of 'hot-metal' or linotype production twenty years earlier, it was of relatively minor significance to the typical newspaper reader. The first significant and concrete manifestation of the technological revolution for the British media 'consumer' came with the advent of DTH satellite broadcasting.

After a false, dual-track start by *British Satellite Broadcasting* and Rupert Murdoch's *Sky*, satellite television in Britain really began after the two merged or, according to Seymour-Ure (1996: 114), the former was taken over by the latter in November 1990 to form *BSkyB*. Since then, the British viewer has grown accustomed to, if not content with, the domination of live coverage of Premier League soccer, much international cricket, major boxing events and first television showing of movies by subscription channels or, on occasion, pay-per-view facilities. Sensitivity as regards sports coverage remains, highlighted by reactions to the news that home test match series would be covered by Sky, rather than free-to-air Channel 4, an announcement made with peculiarly poor timing, coming as it did in the immediate wake of England's much hailed series victory over Australia in the summer of 2005! While the development and establishment of satellite delivery has in itself formed a significant change for British broadcasting, and signalled the final demise of the BBC/ITV duopoly, it also acted as a catalyst for further change and a fundamental reappraisal of the place of the BBC, as discussed in the next chapter.

At the same time, cable companies, offering combined telephony, television and IT facilities, have sought, with limited success, to break into the British market. By the end of 1996, there were only 1.65 million domestic cable television customers in Britain (*Financial Times*, 11 December 1996) compared with an estimated one-quarter of domestic households having access to *BSkyB*'s satellite services. Almost ten years later, in 2005, 61.9 per cent of UK households had access to some form of digital television, though with the DTT *Freeview* service accounting for the majority of the growth and digital cable accounting for less than one-sixth of the digital market (Ofcom 2005c). However, it can still be argued that in the long run it is likely to be fibre-optic cable rather than satellite broadcasting that represents the potential future for the media. Fibre-optic cable offers the potential for the delivery to individual households of television and radio, networked computer facilities and interactive services such as home-banking, shopping and video-on-demand combined with telecommunications (telephone and fax) facilities. Indeed, the ultimate potential of digitalisation, allowing the transfer of all such material down a single line, seems almost boundless. Keane (1991: 160) suggests that among the more significant aspects of digitalisation are its ability to facilitate the transfer of data between media, to decrease the relative cost of information processing and, most crucially, he states, to move away from the conventional broadcasting model to a more individualised, user-selected, 'narrowcast' model of communications.

Tehranian and Tehranian (1995: 39) describe how from the scribes attached to religious orders to the rise of the secular, scientific universities with the advent of printing 'each new communication technology in history is accompanied by the rise of a new communications elite that masters the use of that particular technology and thus assumes a leading role in developing new mediating ideologies and institutions'. An indication of the potential for the digitalised media to become dominated by the technical experts of the computing industry is provided by Marsden (1997a) in noting the attempt by Microsoft, Intel and Compaq to set the technological standards for DTT.

However, in the early days of such an era, it is difficult to predict with any certainty the final extent of the impact of technological convergence.

It may be that 'mass media' will be rendered obsolete as every individual becomes their own 'home publisher', and we will no longer want or need access to mass circulation material, choosing instead to access selectively that which we want to read or watch, the end consumer setting their own agenda or scheduling rather than depending on the newspaper editor or the television programmer.

While acknowledging the beliefs of those such as Negroponte (quoted by Herman and McChesney 1997: 106) that 'the monolithic empires of mass media are dissolving into an array of cottage industries' as a result of electronic publishing via the developing 'Information Superhighway', Herman and McChesney believe that further development in this direction depends on long-term and widespread extension of fibre-optic cable networks. Therefore, they conclude persuasively, 'the Internet and the digital revolution do not pose an immediate or even foreseeable threat to the market power of the media giants' (107). They go on to note that the future commercial potential of the Internet is likely to be maximised only by those who can best advertise their products through other, more widely accessible channels (i.e. existing big-league media players), demonstrating again the synergistic strength of cross-media empires. The same authors consider also that while access to the Internet remains limited to an elite in almost all societies, such developments will further exaggerate social stratification. The same point is raised by Charlesworth and Cullen (1996: 27) who note that the so-called information revolution may 'simply bypass some sectors of society' and may lead to 'further concentration of information access, and as a result political and social influence, with those social groupings which already enjoy a disproportionate degree of power'. Certainly, DTT packages, free at the point of use after a very small initial outlay, will not equate with the considerably more extensive and expensive packages available through cable and satellite.

Whatever the future, certain immediate consequences are already apparent. Digitalisation in television broadcasting means a final end to frequency scarcity, as will be discussed in Chapter 2, the most longstanding justification for regulation of broadcasting. The potential for digital compression to create hundreds of new channels within a spectrum previously restricted to carrying five analogue television channels, suitably separated to avoid cross-channel interference, offers the potential for either vastly increased choice or 'wall-to-wall *Pop Idol*'. If, however, access to such extra facilities comes only at a price to the individual viewer, such facilities will not be available to all, but only those prepared and able to pay. If the arrangements for broadcasting these extra television services are not free-to-air, thus exaggerating social hierarchy, the development risks undermining the degree of cultural cohesion imported by conventional mass media, especially if it leads to a reduction in the perceived legitimacy of, and therefore funding for, PSB. At the same time, if the evolving situation is not adequately regulated, the range of channels, and therefore the choice of content available, may be controlled by those who control the delivery mechanisms. While at one time the major concerns would have related to intervention by the state, increasingly it seems necessary to focus on direct intervention by media owners as to specific content transmitted through their media outlets. For example, both Murdoch's removal of the BBC from his service provided to Asia via the Star satellite (Herman and McChesney 1997: 74) and the decision in February 1998 by Murdoch's HarperCollins publishing house to pull the publication of the memoirs of Chris Patten (last British governor of Hong Kong) in order to avoid alienating the Chinese government and therefore to maintain his potential for penetrating this developing and potentially massive new media market, seemed ominous portents.

However, in the modern era, attention must, at least in part, be shifted to focus on control of the media infrastructure, discussed in Chapter 6 below. Regulators seeking to avoid adverse consequences flowing from such developments may consider the adoption or adaptation of mechanisms already familiar from other fields. In telecommunications, and following other privatisations in Britain, limited Universal Service Obligations (USOs) were imposed upon the new operators, requiring, for example, basic telephony services to be maintained in the form of unprofitable call boxes in rural areas, to cater for those who did not have the means to fund a telephone in their own home. Clearly, such methods do not provide the full benefits available to those who are able to buy in the full service, just as access, even free access, to a computer facility networked to the Internet in every public library or village hall would not provide the same benefits or access as equipping each home with such a machine. The imposition of such a USO, to supply an unprofitable service and avoid the potential for 'cherry-picking' by private enterprises, acknowledges, however, in the case of utilities, the legitimacy of state intervention in markets where 'the public interest' demands it, and a willingness, on the part even of economically libertarian governments, to make economic adjustments in pursuit of a limited form of social justice. Though the transfer of such measures to the media environment may therefore be of interest, USOs remain in practice a limited concept, arguably insufficiently focused on, or giving insufficient emphasis to, equality of citizenship. The kind of base-line services likely to be provided under USO obligations are unlikely to be sufficient to ensure that all citizens have access to a sufficiently wide range of media to enable them to participate in society as citizens.

In any case, in terms of broadcasting, a straightforward adoption of USOs in the call-box form applied to basic telephony services is not suitable. It is highly doubtful that those not owning, say, DTH satellite receiving equipment would be prepared to gather routinely in a public place to watch television, though pubs and clubs have become popular venues for occasional events, especially soccer coverage. In practice, it might be necessary to impose 'must-carry' requirements upon those controlling delivery mechanisms, demanding that they carry basic services, free at the point of use, alongside subscription or pay-per-view services. In addition, perceived threats to traditional 'publicly funded', non-commercial enterprises such as the BBC might be defended against in the new commercial environment by the imposition of 'play or pay' duties, under which broadcasters not subject to the full range of PSB requirements may be required to pay a levy to help fund the delivery of 'free-to-air' non-commercial services. These and other options will all be considered in due course, but for the moment it is helpful to note that the changed technological and commercial environment has already forced a shift in regulatory focus, towards those controlling delivery and reception of broadcast media rather than on the content of programming or the ownership of broadcasting companies. It is a move away from regulation of structure and content, towards regulation of behaviour in the media market place. Again, and this will be returned to in Chapter 3, it is necessary to consider more generally the relationship between the various concepts of competition which inform the competition law perspective, and the paradigmatically different vision incorporated in certain constructs of 'public interest'.

The forthcoming rolling programme of switching from analogue broadcasting to digital has raised questions that will remain relevant whatever form the new market takes in the future. Limited attempts to restrict the anti-competitive potential of control of technological gateways in the distribution infrastructure can be found in European and British regulatory responses discussed later; however, as will be seen, it is possible that such attempts to limit power in relation to such bottlenecks (Nolan 1997; Helberger 2002; E. C. Varney 2005) will be unlikely to prove effective unless they form part of a broader, and coherent, policy of regulation of the media market as a whole. As has been suggested elsewhere, regulating this small if crucial part of the market will be ineffective unless the shape of the media market as a whole is also regulated (Feintuck 1997b, 1997c).

Schiller (1996: 40) argues that the radio spectrum, via which conventional broadcasts have been routed, is in effect a 'public natural resource', and certainly, in an age of mass communication, this argument draws strength from the significance of broadcast media in fulfilling expectations of the public sphere. To the extent that, even in a freedom of communication culture such as the US, the state has acted to regulate broadcasting (and, as will be discussed later in Chapters 2 and 3, broadcasting has consistently been more heavily regulated than print media) this principle has been fundamental in legitimising intervention. To date, however, the information revolution, especially as manifested in the Internet, has not been claimed for the public, but has largely been left to the whim of its commercial developers and market forces. Potential legal responses will be noted shortly and considered more closely in later chapters.

It may be that the modern developments in the media sphere require a new response from regulators which takes a closer look at the private property which is held by the major corporate players in the media. Although it is possible to characterise all regulation as placing restrictions on the exercise of private property rights, it may be that the situation in the media requires a new examination of ownership structures in order to ensure freedom of communication in the future (Gibbons 1992). The exercise of the traditional 'incidents' of ownership (Honoré 1961), particularly the right to exclude competitors from the facilities required to reach the viewing public, may have to be re-examined. In the future, it may be that access to delivery networks will constitute a key barrier to the increased freedom of communication which might otherwise come with the expansion of broadcasting capacity which results from digitalisation. In Chapter 6 we note that this fact is acknowledged by the European Community's 'New Regulatory Framework' for electronic communications, where the 'essential facilities doctrine' is employed in order to ensure that broadcasters are able to gain access to networks on terms which are deemed to be 'fair, reasonable and non-discriminatory'.

It is possible to argue that while these measures might have a degree of impact, it may be necessary to take measures which step beyond just ensuring the competitive functioning of the market. We suggest in Chapter 6 that the current effort to go beyond the market constraints, the must-carry obligation, is not sufficient. If this is the case, then it may be necessary to reconceptualise the view of private property in the digital media in order to ensure that citizens feel the true benefits that might be brought from the vast increase in broadcast capacity from the recent technological advances (M. Varney 2005). One way of conceptualising this possible change could be through the device of 'stewardship', a concept that will be fleshed out more fully in Chapter 7.

As already acknowledged, it is impossible to predict with certainty the extent to which the new information infrastructure will prove central to communications in the future, but, to the extent that it does prove to form an essential part of democracy, the same 'public resource' argument must apply. Regulators will need to be empowered to act to restrict the utilisation of this medium as a commercial asset if and when the commercial imperative infringes on its democratic function. The problem, of course, is that the longer regulatory action is delayed, and the more entrenched becomes the commercial ethos for the information infrastructure, the more difficult it will become to legitimate public interest intervention and to limit the private property rights of the controlling corporations. A further problem for regulators, identified by Klingler (1996), definitional by nature, also arises out of the breakdown of conventional sector divides between traditional broadcasting to a mass audience and individual point-to-point communication, with 'narrowcasting' now forming a hybrid communications medium. Taken together with the international nature of modern communications media, such issues appear to reaffirm the need for reconsideration and clarification of the principles which underlie any regulatory intervention.

Such issues must be addressed as part of the development of what McQuail (1992: 307) terms 'a revised agenda of public interest concerns'. Part of this process must involve the reclamation of the public sphere, and the relegitimation of public intervention in matters of democratic concern. Such concerns must include rectifying 'the mistaken trust in the therapeutic powers of unbridled technical expertise' (Keane 1991: 179) if the potentially anti-democratic consequences of the market, and more specifically 'technocratic capitalism' (Tehranian and Tehranian 1995: 41), are to be avoided.

1.4 THE REVOLUTION AND THE LAW

1.4.1 A broader concept of law

It is obvious that the law is heavily involved in media regulation: it forms a network of rules which are applied or not applied; it offers mechanisms for resolving disputes and for challenging decisions; it says what is lawful or unlawful; it may prescribe and impose sanctions where rules have been broken; it is the instrument via which government policy is translated into enforceable reality; it establishes authorities and grants power to them. Law is, however, about much more than judges deciding cases and the words and interpretation of statutes, the classical subjects of much traditional legal scholarship.

The range of issues raised for the public lawyer, whose focus is upon constitutional and administrative law, are widespread in the context of media regulation. These issues include, but extend beyond, the intricacies of individual court decisions in judicial review cases involving regulatory bodies, the network of often interrelating and overlapping regulatory institutions and the role of government in relation to them and the existence of both statutory and non-statutory regimes. All of these provide obvious focal points, and it is also possible to identify readily concerns arising out of the different approaches which are likely to be adopted by national and international bodies which may approach issues from different jurisprudential, constitutional and economic perspectives.

For the uninitiated, it may therefore be surprising to find that while adequate legal commentaries are readily available (e.g. Barendt 1995; Robertson and Nicol 1992), with only limited exceptions surprisingly little analysis has been carried out by British public lawyers. Among the honourable exceptions have been Lewis (1975), Elliott (1981) and Prosser (1997 and 2005) who each focused upon aspects of the broader public law agenda in the context of broadcasting licence allocation and PSB. Hitchens (1994 and 1995a) has made a significant contribution in scrutinising recent developments and indicating the need for a more thorough and considered policy review, a process to which this book is intended to contribute. While Gibbons (1998) has taken the time and trouble to pursue a more wide-ranging analysis, his work has now been largely overtaken by the rapid pace of events. In addition, Marsden (1997a and 1997b) has begun to make a telling contribution from the perspective of competition law, which has been continued by the works of Bavasso (2003), Nihoul and Rodford (2004) and Garzaniti (2003). However, with the exception of the work of Bavasso (2003: chapters 1 and 5), it remains largely true to say that:

> [T]he net effect of these contributions, while enlightening in many ways, is to leave largely untouched the underlying issues, focusing as they do primarily upon specific developments and occurrences rather than the broader issues and rationales which underlie the subject. Put more specifically, rather like the activities of government and the media regulators, the focus of commentators has tended to be on amendments to the institutional structure, and the outcomes of regulation and proposals for its reform rather than upon giving

serious consideration to the underlying rationales for the regulatory endeavour. (Feintuck 1997c)

Such tinkering with the fine detail is unlikely to equip us adequately to address the challenges posed by the ongoing media revolution. It seems largely futile to examine regulatory policies, mechanisms and outcomes without first reflecting upon the objectives, deriving from principles in turn born of the rationales for intervention.

The range of rationales in play indicate immediately a significant role for the media specialist, political scientist, economist, sociologist and many others, but the lawyer, arguably, must justify their interest, especially given the hitherto dominant tradition among British legal academics of confining themselves to the cataloguing or chronicling of the legal rules in play in the absence of any contextual or conceptual analysis. However, a wider view of law can be applied.

While public lawyers clearly have an interest in the administrative law and practice applicable to an area such as media regulation, they must also place this in its constitutional context and scrutinise legitimacy and rationality as well as mere legality. Such an approach demands not only the examination of technical rules, but also their relationship to fundamental constitutional and democratic values. It is this more holistic approach to public law that is adopted in this book. A conventional public law analysis of the institutions of media regulation can offer much, in terms of both substantive and procedural comment. However, there is a sense in which such critique becomes vacuous if not integrated with an understanding of the values which inform any such regime.

At the heart of liberal-democratic theory is a concept of citizenship, to be discussed in the specific context of media regulation in Chapter 3. If citizenship implies effective participation in society (Barbalet 1988), in an era in which effective participation has come to rely increasingly upon access to the media as the primary arena for political and cultural communication, it can be argued that access to the media, certainly in terms of receiving its output but also arguably in terms of inputting (see Barendt 1995: chapter 7), has become a prerequisite of effective citizenship. Even if, as in this book, the focus is predominantly on citizen access to the media in terms only of *receiving* a diverse range of media output, the public lawyer, in addition to considering the nature of rules and norms existing in this field and the quality of the administrative process, must also recognise that equality of access to the media (as an aspect of equality of citizenship) should be utilised as a yardstick when examining existing and proposed regulatory mechanisms.

In the absence of adequate clarity regarding the rationales and objectives of regulation, it is unlikely that the policies, mechanisms and results of regulation can be meaningfully analysed. Therefore it can be argued that it is necessary to step back from the intricacies and specifics of institutional design and focus instead upon the justifications, principles and goals of media regulation.

The law provides standards against which the behaviour of those who govern and those who are governed can be measured, though it would be foolish to believe that the law is the whole story; lawfulness is important, but remains only one aspect of legitimacy. While the law may be changed by the government of the day provided only, in Britain, that it can command a majority in Parliament, governments are concerned not only with legality, but also legitimacy. They will usually remain within bounds established by the law, but will seek also to maintain a public perception of legitimacy in their actions. They will wish to be seen as remaining within legitimate as well as legal bounds, and the former is often both much more indistinct and far-reaching than the latter. In Britain, as will be demonstrated, where the constitution is often unclear as to what constitutes legitimate action, it may be necessary to have recourse to general fundamentals of liberal-democratic theory and to often nebulous notions such as 'the rule of law' in determining legitimacy. Thus the well-rounded public lawyer must have an awareness of both the detail of the law and the framework of institutional morality within which it operates. A broader concept of law is required.

In the mid-1980s, drawing extensively on the work of Karl Llewellyn, Harden and Lewis (1986) established a four-fold classification as the basis for their discussion of law in the context of their study of the British constitution. These four 'Law Jobs' move beyond a narrow, technical definition of 'law' into a broader, socially grounded model that will inform the remainder of this book. In essence, Harden and Lewis note that Llewellyn identified four tasks which must be accomplished for any group, large or small, to continue in existence as a group.

The first of these is probably the easiest to understand. Dispute resolution, or 'the disposition of the trouble-case', is often viewed as the archetypal law job, and is certainly the one most immediately recognised as 'legal' by the lay person. This involves the resolution of felt grievances and disputes, and may be associated closely with the classical, British, courtroom process of the resolution of a bipartite dispute by reference to a tripartite procedure with an authoritative judge adjudicating. In the modern context, the judge in robes may be replaced by a tribunal panel or an arbitrator, but the nature of the task and process remains essentially the same. That said, the kind of polycentric dispute which may occur in an area such as media regulation may not lend itself well to this model of dispute resolution.

The second law job Harden and Lewis identify is referred to as 'preventive channelling'. This involves a range of procedures and institutions, ranging from the customary to the innovatory (the latter perhaps taking legislative form) which organises individual and collective activity to produce and maintain, in Llewellyn's terms, 'a going order instead of a disordered series of collisions' (quoted in Harden and Lewis 1986: 67). Though by no means the exclusive domain of the lawyer, the establishment of norms and institutional structures for the ordering of social activity is central to their activity.

The third law job, 'the constitution of groups', concerns the establishment and allocation of authority. This establishes the location of legitimate institutional power, for example of rule-making, arbitration or executive power, and furthers the broader objective of organising social life. The final law job relates closely to but extends beyond the second and third. 'Goal orientation' involves processes for determining the desired direction for society to take, either very broadly or more specifically, for example identifying the direction to be taken by the media.

Discussion of media regulation necessarily involves the consideration of all aspects of this 'extended concept of law', but even then, it remains necessary to be aware of a broader phenomenon that is much harder to define. The kind of powers and functions envisaged by the law jobs cannot always be defined by reference to 'black-letter' law – lawyers' shorthand for the law as found written in statute and judgements. Rather, it is often possible to find examples of norms and standards being developed outside the scope of, or within the open texture of, the framework of 'hard law'. The concept of the 'living law' (identified by Ehrlich 1922) helpfully encompasses such practices, identifying them as legal (within the scope of Llewellyn's definition) despite the absence of the trappings of formal legal form.

Thus some of the regulatory power enjoyed by bodies such as the BBFC, the Advertising Standards Authority (ASA) or the Press Complaints Commission (PCC) in relation to the media has a legal nature and is clearly within the scope of the 'Law Jobs', despite the absence of any apparent legal foundation in terms of statute, as is the historical pattern of interventions in newspaper takeovers and mergers in which the development of norms and practices through the exercise of discretion has been much more significant than the widely drawn statutory measures which grant the discretion. Similarly, the influence exercised by government ministers, or the informal accommodations they reach with the 'media establishment', take on the characteristics of law in terms of the law jobs without having any black-letter law basis. The allocation of power and its exercise, often through essentially corporatist arrangements with no apparent legal foundation, are just as much the concern of the public lawyer as the courtroom process of judicial review (Birkinshaw *et al.* 1990). It is just as important that those who exercise the public power of regulation should be accountable as those who exercise the power of the media.

1.4.2 The law and the constitution

It is possible to view a constitution in at least three different ways. First, and most obviously, it can be viewed as a map of power, of utility when it is necessary to navigate the organs of the state. It allows the identification of the location of various powers, such as those of the legislature, the executive and the judiciary. In this sense, the constitution can be viewed essentially as fulfilling a 'descriptive' function. Beyond this descriptive aspect, further scrutiny of the constitution will reveal that it also contains a 'normative' element. By this is meant that in addition to identifying the location of various powers, the constitution will also establish limits on the legitimate exercise of power. For example, the constitution may specify matters on which the legislature may not make law, or establish principles which the executive and legislature must not breach. It may also lay down special procedures which must be pursued for the revision of the constitution itself, or for the revision of the make-up of the legislature. In addition to their descriptive and normative elements, constitutions contain material which is neither entirely descriptive or normative. The kind of constitutional rights enshrined in the US Bill of Rights may be considered normative in nature in that they do suggest limits on the legitimate activity of the executive, legislature and judiciary. However, they are also subject to judicial interpretation, and in carrying out this interpretative function the judiciary may appear to act in pursuit of a broad set of values which underlie the constitution. In this third sense, the constitution can be said to be 'value laden', and within all the jurisdictions which will be considered in this book, broadly speaking, a common set of familiar liberal-democratic values can be found to underlie them.

The particular form of the constitution of any state will be determined by its history, and in particular is likely to be subject to change dramatically following a major constitutional upheaval or crisis such as revolution, civil war, occupation by a foreign power or the gaining of independence from a colonial power. In Britain's case, it is peculiarly difficult to discern the precise content of the constitution, the difficulty deriving to some extent from the relative stability that has existed in British constitutional arrangements since the seventeenth century. Unlike its European neighbours, Britain has encountered no significant constitutional crisis in the last 300 years and as such has had the opportunity to avoid the necessity of significant review of the constitutional arrangements.

While the avoidance of revolution and the like might be considered to be a benefit, the resulting absence of a recent fundamental reappraisal of the constitution makes life difficult for those seeking to understand the British constitution at the end of the twentieth century. A Bill of Rights, dated 1688, may be thought to be rather past its sell-by date, given the degree of social, political and economic change in the intervening 300 years, and the effective incorporation of the ECHR into UK law via the Human Rights Act has only filled part of the apparent gap. Clearly, other Acts of Parliament, especially those such as the Freedom of Information Act (FOIA) and those granting devolved powers to the constituent parts of the UK, are relevant here and international treaties also carry constitutional significance. The European Communities Act of 1972, committing Britain to membership of the EC, resulted in the transfer to the European institutions of a degree of competence in certain areas specified by the Treaty of Rome as amended.

The FOIA is of particular interest in our present context (see generally, Birkinshaw 2001). Such a measure appears to promise improved access to information for citizens and media alike, yet ultimately it must be viewed as a potentially important adjunct to, rather than a substitute for, a pluralistic and universally accessible media: for most citizens, their information will continue to come predominantly from the media rather than directly from individual requests for information under a FOIA.

Thus the constitutional documentary picture is complex, and in addition to these statutory and international documents, judge-made law, via both statutory interpretation and common law development, serves in Britain to fill many of the gaps found in the documentary material. Indeed, it can be argued that in the British context, judicial interpretation is a more significant aspect of the constitution than elsewhere, given the greater scope for manoeuvre granted to the judiciary in the absence of a clear, modern, constitutional statement. However, on the other hand, the apparent latitude provided for judges by the flexibility inherent in the unwritten constitution may also prove problematic. The lack of clarity in their constitutional position and adherence to the principle of the supremacy of Parliament (under which British judges are unable to review the propriety of Acts of Parliament against constitutional standards) has arguably led to the British judiciary enjoying a far less buoyant position and a far less creative role than, say, their US counterparts. Traditionally, the British judiciary have shown a high degree of deference to decision-making undertaken by 'expert' bodies. Crucial to any constitutional reform agenda, therefore (and many of the reforms introduced by the Blair governments do amount to such), will be the role to be played by the judiciary, who have the power to breathe life into the reforms or leave them stillborn.

A final 'source' of the constitution in Britain is a series of unwritten, and sometimes ambiguous, constitutional norms or conventions, which can be said to illustrate and represent a manifestation of the values underlying the constitution. The central one of these is adherence to the concept of the Rule of Law, frequently identified, along with Parliamentary Supremacy, as one of the twin pillars on which the British constitutional arrangements rest. Debate over the meaning of the Rule of Law in contemporary Britain persistently starts from the writing of A. V. Dicey, whose work at the end of the nineteenth century took place in the context of very different social, economic and governmental traditions to those that predominate in the first part of this century. Attempts to clarify the concept's meaning have largely come from academics rather than judges, and although writers such as Harden and Lewis (1986) have sought to identify a contemporary meaning for it, ascribing to it the qualities of a 'principle of institutional morality' rather than mere lawfulness, the concept continues to lack clarity and specificity in use (see Jowell 2000).

Though all of the various documents and concepts identified above provide fragments of the information to be found, typically, in the constitutional documents of other states, Britain has no single, modern constitutional document. Thus the common reference to an 'unwritten constitution' is both partially accurate and partially misleading. As suggested above, many documents serve as written constitutional fragments of various shapes, sizes and vintages.

While public lawyers may be unimpressed by this brief overview of the constitution, others may at this stage need some clarification as to why this is so relevant to the regulation of the media. In essence, it is important to be aware of the normative and value-laden aspects of the constitution in that they, as the embodiment of liberal-democratic values, provide the framework within which media activity and regulatory activity takes place. Where administrative law in the form of Broad-casting Acts or Communications Acts, other specific measures and the broad delegations of powers to regulators exists, so this law operates within the parameters established by the constitution. At a broader level, and especially where regulation takes place without the presence of explicit 'hard law', the values, or expectations, and hence the objectives of the regulatory regime(s), though specific to the media, must derive from more general norms and expectations of an essentially constitutional nature, and legitimacy of action must be measured against these standards. In particular, as identified above, legitimacy (as opposed to mere legality) of action presupposes limited (as opposed to unlimited) power and accountability in the exercise of power, which are in themselves fundamental assumptions attaching to the exercise of power in a liberal democracy,

Chapters 4, 5 and 6 will all consider specific examples of media regulation in which the law is implicated. It will be treated in the context described above, and will address both procedural law (related to *how* decisions are made) and the substance of decisions. Judicial review actions in Britain tend to focus on procedure, with judges traditionally being reluctant to strike down administrative action on substantive grounds. However, it can be argued that an exclusively, or even predominantly, procedural approach to review, as important as procedures are, may not reflect adequately the underlying values and expectations that should inform regulation in an area such as the media. In Britain, such principles may need updating to mesh successfully with the expectations and environment of the modern era. It seems likely that a clarification and reassertion of broad constitutional values must be combined with specific, statutory measures (both substantive and procedural) in pursuit of defined goals if media regulation is to be a worthwhile enterprise in the current climate. As will be discussed in Chapter 3, developments in the field of competition law, though important, may have strictly limited positive impact in terms of a public interest agenda for the media, by virtue of their primarily economic rather than social orientation.

As commentators such as Barendt (1995) and Humphreys (1996) illustrate, it is necessary to view apparently narrow aspects of media regulation in their constitutional context, as it is invariably the case that historical circumstance, combined with constitutional form and tradition, will have established the environment in which media regulation takes place. When consideration is given to media regulation in other jurisdictions and comparisons are made, it becomes especially important to remain aware of the different constitutional backgrounds and traditions to regulatory activity.

Certain key themes and issues have emerged in the course of this introduction. Central to these is the need to identify and articulate with clarity the underlying rationales for media regulation, for without such definition reform of the regulatory system is likely to achieve little of substance in relation to preserving or furthering democratic values. In practical terms, this seems to imply a resolution of the central tension identified earlier between commercial values and those of PSB, and specifically a resolution in favour of the latter. The degree and pace of change in the media identified in this chapter indicates the need to break with the tradition of ad hoc, incremental and reactive reform, and to move beyond what Negrine (1994: 97) refers to as 'prescriptions . . . set out in previous eras'. Reponses may take the form of structural or financial reform, such as considered in the review of the BBC's Charter and funding arrangements, or, it may take the form of substantial legislative reform, as under the Communications Act. However, it remains true to argue that the extent to which such measures prove effective in terms of ensuring that the media fulfils its democratic function is likely to depend on conceptual clarity, especially in relation to the particularly nebulous and slippery issue, 'the public interest'.

2

The Market, Public Service and Regulation

2.1 THE MARKET AND PUBLIC SERVICE

Underlying the foregoing discussion has been a tension that will run through the rest of this work, namely the struggle within broadcasting between market and public service values. A failure to identify, acknowledge and address this tension is likely to undermine any attempts to regulate. The public service tradition in Western Europe has served to insulate the media partially from what are perceived as the worst excesses of market forces. Certainly, European (and especially British) television output as a whole has historically been generally compared favourably, in terms of diversity and quality, with the US equivalent which has developed in the absence of a strong PSB tradition. That the insulation from market forces in Europe has been only partial, however, is evidenced by the experience of Italy, where the rise to dominance in the 1980s of Berlusconi in commercial broadcasting occurred in a regulatory vacuum which allowed the marginalisation of the public service tradition, representing what Humphreys describes as 'a case of market *faits accomplis* in the absence even of formal or symbolic regulation' (Humphreys 1997). A similar, though less marked trend is perhaps also suggested by the arrival of the then Channel 5 in Britain in the 1990s (now known as Five), though the latter example must be viewed alongside the continued existence of four other channels which remained essentially within public service traditions.

It can be argued that the British experience reveals some ambiguous evidence as regards whether the arrival of a competitive market in broadcasting brings identifiable benefits. The experience of the BBC/ITV duopoly suggested that the arrangement resulted in positive outcomes in terms of producing an enviable range of quality programmes, even if it remained within a culturally 'mainstream' tradition, subsequently extended somewhat by the arrival of Channel 4. Though the modern multi-channel era, with its apparently wider range of choice on offer, may seem attractive from a consumerist perspective, it may also seem to pose substantial challenges to the citizenship-oriented values of the previously dominant public service tradition. Such a situation, though perhaps appearing or being presented as a matter of technological and commercial determinism, must also properly be seen as embodying a significant degree of political choice.

The potential for privatising the BBC, the archetypal public service broadcaster, was actively considered by the Conservative administrations of the 1980s, alongside the privatisation of other utilities such as gas, electricity, water and telecommunications (see Chapter 5). While the evidence of some of these privatisations suggests that benefits may have accrued to citizens (at least in their limited capacity as consumers) as regards extended choice, reduced costs and even improved quality of service provision, there seems every chance that no such benefits would accrue from a wholly privatised broadcasting system, at least unless substantial and effective regulation were to accompany such a reform. In particular, in relation to the media, a particularly high premium is placed on diversity of output, and though there is no reason in principle why a privatised broadcasting system should not continue to provide a range of diverse, high-quality products, such an outcome would not be assured by market forces. Indeed, the opposite, in the form of homogenous, lowest-common-denominator programming has largely been the outcome of the American experience of minimalist regulation.

The commercial potential of broadcasting is clear and in countries such as the US has been acknowledged from the earliest days of radio. In the UK, however, broadcasting remained an entirely 'not-for-profit' enterprise until the introduction of commercial television in the mid-1950s. Until that time, British broadcasting, in the form of the BBC, had been unashamedly imbued with a particular, Reithian, set of 'public service' values: to inform, educate and entertain. While the introduction of ITV merely replaced a BBC monopoly with a duopoly, with commercial broadcasters still heavily constrained by public service requirements imposed by the legislation and regulation of the time, the more recent flourishing of national and local commercial television and radio, and the further expansion of channels provided by the introduction of satellite and cable broadcasting, has posed severe challenges to the public service ethos which used to predominate. There is a sense in which this is nothing new, given, for example, the launch of BBC Radio 1 as a direct response to the popularity of off-shore 'pirate' pop music stations in the 1960s, and although pirate broadcasting did not come to be legitimised in the way in which Italy's 'pirate' local commercial television channels eventually were (Mazzoleni 1992), the role of unlicensed, commercial broadcasters in forcing the pace of change upon official, national, public service broadcasters is closely paralleled. It is legitimate to ask what role remains for the BBC, or a broadcaster of that kind, in an era where the range of channels is potentially unlimited and an increasing number of viewers may see little point in funding an organisation via a licence fee when they can instead choose what they want to watch (and pay for) and, via video-on-demand or near-video-on-demand, when they want to watch it from the range of commercial channels on offer. Certainly, as will be discussed shortly, the BBC has faced some difficult struggles in justifying and defending its position in the context both of the review of its Charter, and in its attempt, starting in autumn 2005, to make a case for an increased licence fee.

In the past, the quality of commercial broadcasting in Britain has been guaranteed to some extent by regulation, demanding a minimum range of programmes and imposing limits on advertising time, but also, arguably more significantly, by the ITV companies having a monopoly over television advertising revenue. The absence of competition for this source of income has allowed the ITV companies, though arguably producing more 'populist' programming than the BBC, to maintain high production standards and to compete directly with the BBC in the 'medium-brow' markets and in sports coverage. It is not the purpose of this book to consider the quality or relative merits of programming as such, though it is important to take on board that the predominance of cheap, down-market programmes is a consequence feared by many who view with trepidation the increasing commercialism seen and predicted in television.

As has already been noted, television is a central, arguably *the* central, entertainment medium for most of the British and indeed the Western world's population. To the, presumable, delight of those who are entertained by chat shows, quizzes, soap opera and sport, an era is upon us in which this diet is constantly available, uninterrupted by news, current affairs or 'serious' programmes with informative or educative intentions. With the assistance only of a remote control, the British viewer can watch continuously, all day, every day, carefully avoiding any programme which aspires to anything more than straightforward 'entertainment'.

However, in an environment in which an increasing number of commercial broadcasters must compete between themselves for advertising revenue, and assuming that the potential amount of such revenue does not grow proportionately to the number of commercial broadcasters, the battle for slices of the advertising cake is likely to become increasingly hard-fought and destructive. Audience maximisation will be the key to attracting advertising, and if what holds or increases audience share is soap opera, violence, topless darts or chat shows, then that is what commercial broadcasters will offer; if such programming is cheap to produce, so much the better from the broadcasters' perspective. For particularly unique products with wide-ranging popular appeal, such as major sporting events and movie premieres, commercial broadcasters will be able to increase revenue both as a result of associated advertising and increased receipts from subscribers or pay-per-view users. Such charging at the point of use will mean, however, that the product will be available only to those with the means to afford it.

There may well remain niche markets for broadcasters offering more wide-ranging and challenging cerebral fare, but simple economics suggest that they will prove expensive for the viewer if supplied on a subscription basis, given the likely relatively small take-up. Given their limited appeal, it may seem difficult to justify their funding or support from the public purse. The end result of this process is that while cheap populist programming will be relatively readily available, informative and educative programming, and broadcasting of 'special' events will only remain available to those who can afford to pay premium rate subscriptions. Access to the media will therefore reflect and reinforce social stratification. Meanwhile, the switch-off of analogue transmission, scheduled to be completed by 2012, will mean that all viewers will need some form of digital decoding equipment to view any television transmissions. Even the relatively small bundle of additional channels available through *Freeview* via DTT will inevitably have some further impact in terms of reducing the audience share of conventional public service broadcasters, and hence will further increase pressure on the BBC to justify its public funding.

None of this should be taken as arguing that all viewers should be forced to take in an unremitting diet of wholesome, informing, educating and entertaining programmes as provided by the BBC in its monopoly years. This appears, to modern eyes, overly paternalistic, and also to ignore the realities of the digital age. Now that we have multi-channel technology available, there is, to borrow one of *BSkyB*'s old advertising lines, 'No turning back', and if PSB is to survive, it must do so in the context of a mixed media economy. However, if those charged with regulating the media do not wish to end up at the market-driven destination just described, with the broadcast media simply a buttress to social hierarchy and furthering 'social exclusion', offering choice only to those who can afford it, then they must consider the way forward carefully, looking at the map and compass and the alternative roads ahead, if they are not to find themselves following an itinerary that inevitably leads them to a destination that few would voluntarily visit.

Before turning to look in more abstract terms at principled arguments regarding the regulation of the media and justifications for regulation, it is necessary to look in slightly more detail at some more practical realities associated with the future of the institution at the heart of the UK's PSB tradition – the BBC.

2.2 THE BBC AND THE CHARTER REVIEW

The BBC Charter Review may offer an insight into future policy on PSB. It is widely acknowledged that the increasing pressures on commercially funded public service broadcasters, *i.e.* ITV, Channel 4 and Five may jeopardise their ability to deliver high-quality public service programming in the medium term (Ofcom 2004b: 4.10–4.17; DCMS 2005: 104–6). The increasing pressures on the commercially funded operators with public service obligations comes from the expansion of competition in the television advertising market. For the present, as we have just noted, it is evident that the limited number of players present in the analogue terrestrial television market are likely to secure significant advertising funding, but this is unlikely to continue as the number of 'multi-channel' homes with access to digital television increases (PriceWaterhouse Coopers 2005).

The BBC is in an unusual position, in the sense that, unlike other public service broadcasters, it is in receipt of considerable sums of public money, estimated at £2.4 billion from the licence fee in the period 2003–4 (BBC 2004a: 109). Although other broadcasters which are subject to public service obligations gain significant advantages through the provision of free broadcasting spectrum and other advantages provided by regulation, none benefit from the same degree of public support and funding as the BBC (Ofcom 2004b: chapter 3). We will return to consider modes of regulation informed by a competition perspective in the next chapter but should note here the fact that the peculiar position occupied by the BBC in the UK market means that, from this perspective, it can be argued forcefully that it should be subjected more strictly to competition law regulation in order to ensure that it does not abuse the market power bestowed upon it by the considerable public support it receives (Cave *et al.* 2004).

These issues arise alongside some evidence that viewers are dissatisfied with aspects of the BBC's service (Ofcom 2004a: chapter 2) and the aftermath of the Hutton Report (Hutton Report 2004), where the role of the

BBC's Governors, as regulators of the BBC's output, seem to have been called into question (Lloyd 2004). Though highlighted in the wake of the Hutton Inquiry, questions of independence, trust and accuracy in relation to the BBC go back much longer and extend much wider (O'Neill 2004). All of these issues form part of the backdrop for the BBC's Charter Review, the outcome of which will form the basis of the BBC's Charter and Agreement for the period from 2007–16. It is not our aim to enter into a detailed analysis of the Charter Review process, not least because the current state of the proposals necessitates a degree of speculation over the eventual outcome. Despite these caveats, it is evident that the process illuminates certain elements of the government's thinking on the issues of 'why', 'how' and 'to what end' in media regulation.

2.2.1 Why regulate the BBC?

In a sense, the discussion of 'why' regulate the BBC is somewhat odd – in many instances the BBC regulates itself, so it may be more fruitful to consider why the BBC exists and what goals have been created for it to pursue. There are a number of reasons put forward for the BBC's existence, familiar from the outline analysis we have already offered. The main one, according to the government, is that 'broadcasting can contribute to societies in ways that other media do not' and, furthermore, 'as citizens, we wouldn't get everything that we have come to expect from broadcasting if we relied on commercial providers alone' (DCMS 2005: 1.1). The wide impact of broadcasting on society and, more technically, the fact that some elements of broadcast content might be viewed as 'merit' goods, *i.e.* those goods which 'society, operating through the government, deems to be especially important or that those in power feel individuals should be encouraged to consume' (Lipsey and Chrystal 1999: 312), have often served as primary justifications for the existence of PSB.

It is possible, however, that these rather general justifications for PSB appear to run the risk of understating the real weight and depth of justifications for it. Historically, it has been unfortunately the case that there has been no developed and constitutionally accepted definition of PSB in the UK. Relatively few coherent models of PSB have been offered, although Curran and Seaton have helpfully identified some elements of the concept in their work on the British media (Curran and Seaton 2003: 401–4). Curran and Seaton suggest that PSB has three main features: the independent and impartial coverage of news and current affairs, the setting and maintaining of high programme standards and the ability to bind together diverse groups in society (Curran and Seaton 2003: 402).

While Curran and Seaton's work is undoubtedly most valuable, it may not offer a set of principles which would be immediately useful to lawyers and regulators. Born and Prosser (2001) appear to have offered an account of the principles of PSB which may appeal more from these perspectives. They offer a conception of PSB based on the three principles of citizenship, universality and quality. These principles may serve as a useful checklist for the future activities of the BBC, and could be used to encourage or inform the development of a more coherent regulatory policy towards the development of a model of PSB.

It is notable that Parliament has made some endeavour to offer a definition of PSB in the Communications Act 2003. Section 264(4) of the Act states that the 'purposes of public service broadcasting are' the provision of programming which deals with a wide range of subject matters and the provision of programmes 'which (having regard to the days on which they are shown and the times of day at which they are shown) is likely to meet the needs and satisfy the interests of as many different audiences as practicable.' The two further purposes identified by section 264(4) are the provision of programmes which are 'properly balanced, so far as their nature and subject matter is concerned, for meeting the needs and satisfying the interests of available audiences' and the provision of programming which 'maintain[s] high standards', particularly in regard to the content of the programmes, the 'quality of programme making' and the 'professional skill and editorial integrity applied to the making of the programmes'. Section 264(6) of the Act then moves on to the nature of programming which might be thought to satisfy the public service remit.

Though we will return to consider issues arising from this definition in Chapter 4, for the moment we can observe that, in the sense that Parliament has spoken on the issue, one might describe this definition of PSB as the one which prevails in the constitution of the United Kingdom at present. Prosser has recently argued that:

> For the first time . . . we have a definition of the public service remit applying to all UK public service broadcasters, and one which goes well beyond the market failure model to appeal to a much broader cultural conception of what public service broadcasting requires. (Prosser 2005: 228).

As already noted, the traditional mandate for the BBC was that created by Lord Reith, first Director General of the BBC, which was that the BBC should inform, educate and entertain the public (Curran and Seaton 2003: 149–150; BBC 2004: 2). While this purpose can be argued to have served the public well in previous years, there is some evidence that the generality of these purposes may have allowed the BBC to stray from its core role. The consultation process leading to the Green Paper for Charter Review suggests that some public constituencies are not satisfied with the way in which the BBC's services have become increasingly designed to mimic those offered by commercial broadcasters in order to compete for viewers (DCMS 2004: 1.23; Ofcom 2004a: 59).

The Green Paper for Charter Review argues that 'The BBC should aim to complement what is available on commercial channels, rather than competing directly against it.' (DCMS 2005: 1.23). In its review of PSB, required by section 264 of the Communications Act 2003, Ofcom has identified six characteristics which it suggests are typical of public service content. The characteristics are that programmes should be high quality, original, innovative, challenging, engaging and widely available (Ofcom 2004b: 2.13). The government has taken up this definition of public service content in the Charter Review Green Paper, suggesting that:

> All BBC programmes should aim to contribute in some way to at least one public purpose or to display at least one of the characteristics of excellence and distinctiveness set out [in Ofcom's characteristics]. The set of purposes and characteristics should form the basis for a new, more rigorous system of regulation and performance measurement. (DCMS 2005: 1.21)

In addition to the identification of the programme characteristics outlined above, the Green Paper also identifies a number of 'public purposes' which the BBC should aim to serve. These purposes include 'sustaining citizenship', 'promoting education and learning', 'stimulating creativity and cultural excellence', 'reflecting the UK's nations, regions and communities' and 'bringing the world to the UK and the UK to the world' (DCMS 2005: 31–46).

The difficulty with this approach is that it seems to reflect, and perhaps emphasise, certain realities associated with what can be described as the 'market failure' model of PSB. If the new Charter and Agreement focus the BBC's role on supplying programming that might otherwise be undersupplied by the market, there seems to be a real risk that if the BBC

> avoids commercial activities and runs down popular and mainstream programming on its channels then it may be accused of marginality and of taking the route of 'market failure' provision, simply filling the gaps left by its commercial rivals. (Born and Prosser 2001: 658).

It seems, then, that the provision in the Green Paper, suggesting that the BBC should move to complement the services offered by its commercial rivals, would push the BBC precisely down the route highlighted above. This would seem to be counter to the definition of PSB offered in section

264 of the Communications Act 2003, which expressly provides that PSB should provide drama, comedy, music and feature films which will always be the among the mainstays of free-to-air commercial broadcasters. Such an approach is also in contrast to the rather richer conception offered by Born and Prosser.

If the BBC is to be aligned with the 'market failure' model of broadcasting then there seems to be a risk that 'universality' could be placed at risk. It was noted above that there is strong evidence that commercial PSB is likely to diminish as digital television continues to expand. When this occurs, it seems likely that the BBC will be the primary provider of PSB as competition for advertising revenues becomes more fierce. In the recent review of PSB Ofcom have suggested that within the commercial sphere:

> TV channels would rely more on lower cost programming, although higher production-value content would still exist . . . It is possible that high-cost programming would be released first on pay channels, only reaching free-to-air channels some time later. (Ofcom 2004b: 4.15)

If this is the case, then it seems likely that if the BBC is shifted towards a 'market failure' model, the notion of universality in PSB will be placed under severe pressure. The BBC has faced criticism for pursuing the expensive rights to relatively recent Hollywood blockbusters or major sporting events (Broadcasting Policy Group 2004: 4.4–4.6), yet this could reasonably be viewed as an element of the universality that PSB should be aiming towards. It is evident that if the BBC's mandate is limited in such a fashion as to discourage or prevent it from pursuing such rights, then those without the ability to pay for subscription-based channels are likely to suffer a significant diminution of their ability to access content which is attractive to the operators of subscription-based services.

Some might seek to argue that under these circumstances, even if the BBC was based on the 'market failure' model, then at this point it would be able to intervene. Unfortunately, this would not amount to 'market failure' as economists would describe it. Rather, such developments would simply be the result of the market operating freely; premium content would be of far greater value to providers of subscription-based services so they would purchase it at the expense of those broadcasters funded by advertising. Such services would be provided by the market, but, of course, would only be provided to those with the ability to pay for it.

If the BBC was to be based on the 'market failure' model, providing what could be described in the main as 'merit good' content, then it would be unable to act in these circumstances, as premium content, unlike educational programming and other niche output, could not correctly be described as 'merit goods'. So, if PSB is a 'rich' concept of the nature that Born and Prosser describe, it seems unlikely that the approach suggested in the Green Paper is desirable. If PSB is to rest on the key concepts of citizenship, universality and quality, a version of it which meshes closely with the account of the 'public interest' that we offer in Chapter 3, then the government's proposal that the BBC should move away from genres offered by commercial broadcasting seems to place such values at risk in the future.

From the Green Paper, it seems that the goals of the BBC, and thus the focus of regulation of the BBC's activities, may well shift somewhat in the next Charter and Agreement. Public service goals seem likely to be more closely defined and rigorously enforced, although it is not entirely clear how the 'public purposes' and 'characteristics' set out in the Green Paper relate to the definition of PSB offered in section 264 of the Communications Act or more broadly in the literature. It is evident that the government would prefer to see the BBC operate under a 'core' set of values, offering distinctive, challenging content to audiences which is complementary to that offered by the commercial sector.

In a sense, it is possible to argue that the new Charter might focus the BBC more specifically towards the nation's needs as citizens, obliging the BBC to produce content which focuses on filling the gaps left by commercial broadcasters. A number of authors have challenged the necessity of such a mandate in the digital era, as some suggest that the public would be better served if a number of different bodies received public funds in order to make these 'merit good' programmes (Broadcasting Policy Group 2004: chapter 1). Others argue that much of the BBC's current programming does not deserve 'merit good' status and so the BBC should be shifted towards a model based on subscription (Cox 2004: 22).

If however, one takes a broader conception of citizenship values, such as the one we offer in Chapter 3 or indeed that offered by Born and Prosser, it is evident that the shift towards the 'market failure' model is unlikely to serve citizens effectively, as many of the social aspects of citizenship could be left unserved and the universality which has always been offered by public service broadcasters might be placed under threat. The 'public purposes' and 'characteristics' offered in the Green Paper, which seem to be an effort to ensure that PSB might be measurable in some way, may not allow the BBC sufficient freedom to deploy its resources to meet these ends. It may, however, still be preferable to base the Charter on values such as those of citizenship, universality and quality combined with quotas for programming where these are considered to be necessary rather than trying to create more specific criteria for the measurement of output.

Either method of setting out the BBC's mission will create difficult challenges for those designated with the task of ensuring that the BBC's output meets the criteria laid down in the 'characteristics' and 'public purposes' laid down in the Green Paper. Much like the effort to ascribe financial value to PSB, determining whether certain output meets with the criteria laid down could be a difficult and controversial task.

The creation of the 'public purposes' and 'characteristics' in PSB may lead to enhanced accountability within the BBC. Many public lawyers see rule-making which confines the discretion of those exercising public power or spending public money as a positive development (Davis 1971; Baldwin 1995: 16–17). It may be that the open-textured nature of the 'public purposes' and 'characteristics' may lead to little more effective scrutiny than the current mandate contained in the Charter and Agreement as it stands. The Governors and their ultimate replacements who are charged with ensuring the BBC's attainment of the mandate may see the 'public purposes' and 'characteristics' as being flexible tools and may prefer to adopt the approach taken by Curran and Seaton (2003: 226) when they observe that 'Good broadcasting . . . [is] not easy to measure – though we might feel quite secure about identifying [it] when we see [it]'.

At present, it is not entirely clear how these more tightly defined obligations will be manifested and policed in practice, but the effectiveness of these changes is likely to rely in turn on the effectiveness of the mechanisms and structures put in place to ensure compliance with these more specific goals. It is to this issue that we now turn, as the Charter Review has plenty to say about 'how' the BBC should be regulated in the future.

2.2.2 How to regulate the BBC – still too many cooks?

The BBC is currently the subject of regulation from a number of sources. Prior to the Communications Act 2003, the BBC's Governors were primarily charged with the regulation of the BBC's activities. The Governors are, according to the BBC's most recent report and accounts, 'the trustees of the public interest. They supervise the BBC and ensure its independence from political and commercial interference' (BBC 2004a: 6). The current Charter (DNH 1996a) and the Agreement prior to its 2003 amendment (DNH 1996b) place the greatest focus on the role of the

Governors as a self-regulator of the BBC's activities. This self-regulation extended to programme quotas, programme standards and governance issues, including audit (Barendt and Hitchens 2000: 70–82; Gibbons 1998). It is notable that the Governors are even designated a role to play in the BBC's compliance with competition law, under the terms of the BBC's 'fair trading' commitment (DNH 1996a: clause 7.1(b)).

The BBC was, prior to 2003, also subject to the jurisdiction of the Broadcasting Standards Commission, and under section 119 of the Broadcasting Act 1996 could be required by the Commission to broadcast a statement where the Commission felt that its Codes on fairness, privacy and standards (such as taste, decency and sexual portrayal, etc.) had been breached. Furthermore, the BBC is, like any other body, subject to *ex post* regulation by the Office of Fair Trading where breaches of competition law are found to have occurred. The Director General of Fair Trading was also under a duty to report on the BBC's fulfilment of the requirement that 25 per cent of its programme purchases should be 'independent productions' under section 186 of the Broadcasting Act 1990 (now repealed by the Communications Act 2003). Other than these inputs and the role of the government at the time of Charter renewal, and leaving to one side the potential for, or actuality of, informal pressure from government from time to time, external regulation of the BBC's activities was relatively minimal.

The coming into force of the Communications Act 2003 has changed this landscape somewhat. Section 198 of the Communications Act 2003 opens up the BBC to Ofcom's powers in a wide range of circumstances, and the Agreement (DCMS 2003) has been modified in order to open up the BBC to a greater degree of regulatory intervention from the sector-specific communications regulator. The first notable alteration is that the BBC is now bound, like all commercial broadcasters, to a more stringent system of regulation of programme standards. It was noted earlier that the BBC was previously subject to the BSC's jurisdiction and its codes on fairness and privacy and programme standards. In effect, although the broadcasters took the BSC's adjudications seriously, the penalties for breach were weak, requiring only publication of an adverse adjudication.

The BBC is now subject to almost all aspects of Ofcom's Broadcasting Code (Ofcom 2005d) and, under authority given by section 198(3) of the Communications Act 2003 and Clause 13 of the amended Agreement (DCMS 2003), may be subject to financial penalties for breach in the same way that commercial broadcasters might be. There is a notable exception to the BBC's subjection to the Broadcasting Code, as the

Governors retain responsibility for the BBC's compliance with the accuracy and impartiality requirements for its output. The BBC argues that this is 'entirely appropriate, as the BBC's independence is crucial in this area' (BBC 2004b: 126). There are evidently inconsistencies and perhaps some difficulties with such an approach: it seems to be somewhat unsatisfactory to be willing to allow the BBC to be governed by Ofcom's Broadcasting Code in relation to all other matters, yet leave the issues of due accuracy and impartiality in the hands of the BBC Governors. It is evident that the government appreciates this issue and although the Green Paper seems to support the status quo on this issue in the short to medium term (DCMS 2005: 5.34), there is to be a further review when the scheme under the new Charter and Agreement have operated for five years.

Ofcom have broadly supported these proposals by the government but have noted that a common regulatory approach where Ofcom takes responsibility for all matters of programme standards

> could provide greater clarity, and enable the application of common high standards across the sector. Such a system is entirely compatible with the Trust [the BBC's new governing body, to be discussed below] assuming responsibility for maintaining the BBC's editorial standards. All other news providers retain their own responsibility for editorial standards in the face of regulation by Ofcom . . . (Ofcom 2005e: 3.33)

It seems that the current regulatory system in place constitutes an unfortunate half-way house for the regulation of the BBC's programme standards. Indeed, given that Ofcom is responsible for applying the whole of the Broadcasting Code to all other broadcasters, it seems likely that greater clarity and consistency of approach might be achieved if the BBC was subject to the Code in its entirety. The Code is likely to be adjudicated on very frequently by Ofcom and is therefore likely to be forged rapidly in the furnace of experience, shaped where necessary by intervention from the courts if judicial review of any of Ofcom's decisions is sought. In this respect, there seems to be no logical reason why the BBC should be treated differently from all other broadcasters just because of its different history.

Ofcom suggests that a difficulty with the current approach is that the BBC's accuracy and impartiality might be seen by the public as a 'gold standard' which no other broadcaster might reach (Ofcom 2005e: 3.31). Although this may be the case, the aftermath of the Hutton Report may have tarnished this golden image somewhat, and it could be argued that public confidence might be better served if Ofcom, as the independent sectoral regulator for the communications industry, was available to deal with complaints that the BBC had breached the requirements of due accuracy and impartiality. This point might be made *a fortiori* given that the interpretation of the issue of due accuracy and impartiality in the news seems to open up many issues pertinent to Article 10 of the European Convention on Human Rights (to which we return in Chapter 6), suggesting that Ofcom's accountability to the courts is likely to be particularly strong when it is adjudicating on these issues.

This overlap also applies in the case of programming quotas, where the BBC Governors must agree with Ofcom certain production quotas, such as those for original productions and for programmes to be made outside of the London area (Ofcom 2005e: 3.27; DCMS 2003). In the case of all other quotas, such as those for news and current affairs programming, the Governors must consult with Ofcom and take into account Ofcom's views when setting the quota (Ofcom 2005e: 3.27; DCMS 2003). Ofcom have argued in their response to the Green Paper that it may be more satisfactory to allow Ofcom to set those quotas which are currently subject to its agreement (which are essentially externally imposed quotas), but recognises that all other quotas which are concerned with programming, such as those for news and current affairs, '. . . should remain the responsibility of the BBC' (Ofcom 2005e: 3.29). Although some might argue that the issue of programming quotas perhaps comes closer to the BBC's independence and ability to determine its output than the issue of programme standards, it may still be preferable to allow Ofcom, as an independent regulator, to set and enforce those quotas such as that for original programming which are essentially externally imposed at the present time.

The main regulatory reform to be found in the Charter Review Green Paper is that the Governors of the BBC, as they are currently constituted, will be abolished and replaced with a new independent body described, for the present time, as the 'BBC Trust'. The Trust will takeover most of the functions currently held by the BBC Governors and

> will act as the sovereign body in relation to the BBC and have ultimate responsibility for the licence fee. It will be responsible for setting the BBC's performance framework and assessing performance against it; approving strategies and high level budgets; and holding the Executive Board to account for delivery. (DCMS 2005: 5.26)

Given that the main role of the BBC Trust will be a strategic one, laying out the goals and objectives and budgets to which the Corporation must adhere and assessing the performance of the Executive Board in meeting these targets, it may seem strange that the government does not plan to separate the role of regulating the BBC in relation to issues of programme standards and quotas more completely. As Lord Currie of Marylebone, Chairman of Ofcom, noted in his oral evidence to the Select Committee on Culture, Media and Sport:

> we do think that there is an important distinction between regulation and governance. Those are two functions that the BBC governors have at present been asked to combine. We think that being clear about that distinction is important. (Culture, Media and Sport Committee 2005: Q581).

It may be that it would be more satisfactory for the distinction between regulation and governance to be drawn more clearly for the BBC, in other words if the BBC was subject to Ofcom's jurisdiction in the same way that commercial public service broadcasters are in relation to programme standards, compliance with quotas and competition law. This would leave to the BBC Trust the role of governance of the BBC – setting out broad policy goals and holding the BBC's executives to account for the spending of the licence fee payers' money. It is evident that the BBC must, like all other broadcasters, have internal measures in place to ensure compliance with the externally imposed regulation, and this would be an important function for the BBC Trust. Beyond this, however, it is questionable whether it is desirable for the BBC Trust to be operating an overlapping jurisdiction with Ofcom for matters such as the governance of quotas, elements of programme standards and compliance with competition law. Such a system appears likely to open up the BBC Trust to controversy where divergent approaches are adopted, and may lead to uncertainty over which body should receive complaints for the overlapping competences.

Clearly, there are potential problems and internal inconsistencies within the regulatory regime applicable to the BBC discussed here. These will be returned to in later chapters. However, it is also necessary to consider the degree of mesh between these arrangements, and the broader context of media regulation within which the BBC must be viewed.

2.3 REGULATION: WHY, HOW AND TO WHAT END

In adopting an analytical perspective that focuses on 'the social values at stake' (Blumler 1992b: 5) in broadcasting regulation, Blumler identifies three current issues that might impact upon these values: first, a set of questions as to how and to what ends the expanding private sector in television can be regulated, and how effective such regulation can be; second, the direction to be taken by public sector broadcasters, whether and how to continue to provide a comprehensive service or to opt for a narrower range of programming; third, to devise mechanisms of accountability for both broadcasters and regulators appropriate to current conditions. These second and third concerns have been clearly illustrated in the foregoing discussion of the BBC.

Though focused on broadcasting, the issues raised in Blumler's agenda in the increasingly cross-media environment may be applied across the whole range of media. Some of the social values at stake and the threats to them have already been indicated, and the preceding section has pointed towards some issues relevant to Blumler's second set of concerns. The rest of this book is focused closely on Blumler's first and third agenda items, and the remainder of this chapter is devoted to introducing some of the issues to be addressed before they are examined in more concrete form in later chapters.

2.3.1 Why regulate?

Some of the justifications for regulating have already become apparent in the previous discussion; in particular, the threats of monopoly and of increasing commercialism should be clear. As Schiller (1996) and others have demonstrated, the privatisation of information and communication is proceeding apace, and the option for regulation merely to stand still and fail to find mechanisms to avoid the adverse consequences of commercial and technological 'progress' is not available, unless it is deemed acceptable to sacrifice citizenship and democracy to the unbridled forces of the global economy and technological revolution. The age of public service monopoly in broadcasting has long gone, and a 'mixed economy' appears inevitable. In Dahlgren's terms, 'what is needed is re-regulation, to counteract the negative aspects of market forces and optimize the positive role they can play' (Dahlgren 1995: 15).

However, at the very heart of our approach is that it seems unwise for prescriptions such as for a remodelled BBC to be considered in the absence of establishing, or re-establishing, a coherent theoretical basis. It is not sufficient to assume the existence of meaningful rationales for regulation simply in terms of reactions to perceived threats. If any regulatory regime is to prove effective in steering away from these perceived dangers and towards a more desirable position, it is crucial, in terms of both effectiveness and legitimacy, that the underlying rationales and positive objectives are spelled out with adequate clarity. In an era in which government is driven by a hands-off approach and promises the withdrawal of the state from traditional roles, it becomes particularly important to identify and establish justifications for continuing public intervention in the media market.

As Keane demonstrates admirably, censorship, or non-liberty of communication, can be carried out equally either by state power or by corporate power (Keane 1991: chapters 1 and 2) and, given that 'the dynamics of democracy are intimately linked to the practices of communication, and [that] societal communication increasingly takes place within the mass media' (Dahlgren 1995: 2), the exercise of such democratically significant power must be subject to accountability, whether regulation of communication is carried out by public or private power-holders.

The arguments for freedom of communication discussed in Chapter 1, while appearing superficially to militate against regulation, in practice lie beneath one primary justification for intervention, the implication being that effective communication depends on the effective regulation of communication. This is not as paradoxical as it might appear. Just as two people talking simultaneously does not make for effective communication, two radio stations broadcasting on the same frequency or interfering with each other's transmission is equally unsatisfactory. Thus much state regulation of broadcasting, from the 1920s until relatively recently, was premised largely on the necessity to avoid cross-channel interference via the allocation (licensing) of adequately separated frequencies within the available, finite, spectrum. As has already been indicated, this 'frequency scarcity' rationale for intervention has lost almost all of its currency in the modern era in which digital compression and developments in cable and satellite have vastly, almost infinitely, increased the potential for the number of channels. Of course, no such justification ever applied in relation to regulation of the press, and it is therefore perhaps helpful in the search for fundamental rationales for regulation to consider the typology established by Siebert *et al.* (1956) in relation to the press.

In their seminal work, Siebert *et al.* offer a typology of media systems – 'authoritarian', 'totalitarian', 'libertarian' and 'social-responsibility' – and demonstrate the historical relationship between forms of government and approaches to regulation of the press. Both Humphreys (1996) and Negrine (1994) point towards a failure in this typology, developed from an American perspective, to reflect the significance of 'public service' models in Europe when applied to broadcasting. However, equally, both testify to the significance of this work, and the approach remains relevant and valid now fifty years on from first publication.

Siebert *et al.* establish the 'authoritarian' model as relating to an essentially 'pre-democratic' era in which the press was either owned or heavily regulated by a ruling class or group. In Humphreys' terms (1996: 8) this amounts to the effective subservience of the press to the state. The 'totalitarian' model is associated by Siebert *et al.*, writing in the 'Cold War' era, as being associated with direct state control of the media, as in Nazi Germany or the Soviet Union.

The final two categories established by Siebert *et al.* are more familiar to modern, Western eyes. The 'libertarian' model represents a situation in which the media are lightly regulated and little licensing or censorship exists. This is most closely associated with a 'free market place' of ideas and views press freedom and the ability to make profit from it essentially as a property right. The 'social responsibility' model, however, emphasises instead the role of the media as a public resource in 'informing the debate'. This appears to take on additional significance in relation to broadcast rather than printed media, perhaps because of the extra power attributed to broadcasting, but also links to the frequency scarcity justification for intervention. If the (broadcast) media are to serve society effectively, they must be both diverse and regulated, thereby justifying both regulation of ownership and/or public ownership. There is a marked shift between the libertarian and social-responsibility models, the former emphasising the private property basis for press freedom, the latter prioritising the public or collective interest in the media. In the present context of technological change, and the concurrent hegemony of market economics, Humphreys (1996) identifies a switch back to the historically earlier, libertarian model of media regulation.

While the work of Siebert *et al.* is focused predominantly on the press, their work, like that of Barbrook (1995) in relation to the French media, is helpful in identifying historical trends. However, it is necessary in this connection to differentiate between the printed and broadcast media. The social responsibility model has significantly informed the development of PSB and the rather heavier regulation of broadcasting in general than is found in relation to the press. The justifications for this higher level of regulation for broadcasters are expanded upon in Chapter 3 but appear, in brief, to be premised largely upon the extra power attributed to broadcasting as a result of its accessibility, immediacy and intrusiveness. For the moment, it is sufficient to note that Barendt (1995) identifies at least part of the justification for heavier regulation of broadcasting as resulting from the relative newness of television and radio, which has presented governments with an opportunity, historically long gone in relation to printed media, to regulate actively. Thus, as Barendt goes on to demonstrate, the heavier regulation of broadcasting compared with the press is largely contingent upon historical circumstance, constitutional form and tradition, rather than resting upon clearly defined principle.

What is, evident from all the writing, however, is the truth of Herman and McChesney's observation that regulation of the media has always been viewed as a legitimate activity for government, to which we might add that only the forms of intervention, as opposed to the fact of it, change, and that, historically, significant deregulation has therefore been likely to be more apparent than real. That said, Humphreys (1996 and 1997) expounds convincingly on a claim that some recent reform, especially in European media markets, has been driven by a process of 'competitive deregulation', with jurisdictions reforming regulation so as to attract or maintain levels of inward investment (see Chapter 6). This would be consistent with what McQuail (1992: 143) identifies as 'a more general "liberalizing" and deregulatory political-economic trend', though the real extent of the withdrawal of the state should perhaps be treated somewhat sceptically; experience tends to suggest that the state never withdraws, but simply reforms, replacing, perhaps, formal regulatory powers with informal and less accountable networks of influence (see Birkinshaw *et al.* 1990). If significant deregulation might therefore be unlikely, 're-regulation', adopting new forms in line with currently dominant political norms and expectations, is much more plausible. However, this is not to say that an answer to Dahlgren's plea for re-regulation already exists. In the absence of close consideration of underlying values, principles, objectives and policies, and the analysis of outcomes, any system of media regulation, in a period of rapid change, will quickly become anachronistic. It can be argued that incremental change over the 1980s and 1990s as a result of *ad hoc* legislative responses to changes in media structure typified British and other systems of media regulation, leaving a pressing need for a more fundamental review. In Chapter 4 we consider the extent to which the UK's Communications Act 2003 has actually fulfilled this function.

Having identified a number of different historical traditions in media regulation, it is now necessary to attempt to summarise the particular justifications for regulation currently in play, all of which, in one form or another, have already been flagged up earlier in this or the previous chapter. These can be reduced, in essence, to four rationales:

1. effective communication;
2. diversity, both political and cultural;

3. economic justifications; and
4. public service.

'Effective communication' has already been discussed in the context of frequency scarcity but, more generally, the freedom of speech ideal manifested, for example, in the US First Amendment and the ECHR suggests that freedom of expression and communication (both transmission and reception) are central to democratic expectations. In the modern context, in which meaningful freedom of communication depends heavily upon access to mass media, effective communication has come to rely increasingly upon the media. Were all communication to be channelled or controlled exclusively through state controlled media this would run counter to the liberal-democratic ideal of freedom of communication. However, the same argument would seem to apply were the media to be effectively under the control of one or a handful of media owners, a situation of private monopoly or oligopoly.

Effective communication therefore appears to imply not only unobstructed communication, but also, in the interests of democracy, diverse communication. In Britain, with the pattern of concentration in the press and cross-media identified in Chapter 1, there is a clear and present threat to the diversity of views in circulation. If, in addition, the leading market players were also to control technological gateways in distribution such as those present in the digital television markets (E. Varney, 2005) then a still more virulent form of the problem is presented. Given that effective communication, whether approached via arguments from truth, self-fulfilment or citizen participation, appears to require the presentation of a wide range of views in the media, domination of the media by one or a few players who may control editorial content threatens effective communication simply because it threatens diversity in the viewpoints which can be transmitted and received, and thereby can undermine the potential for citizens to engage effectively in a process of triangulation.

This line of reasoning leads naturally into a second identifiable underlying rationale for media regulation, namely diversity. This is clearly related to 'effective communication' rationales, but may also be presented as a separate, free-standing justification which in itself contains two strands.

The first of these connects with the point just made. Political debate, supposedly the lifeblood of democracy, appears to need a free flow of ideas via which informed participation can take place. If a small number of owners dominate press ownership, and use this position to control editorial content, there is likely to be limited scope for heterodox views. In Britain, it might be thought that there exists a close co-relation between the range of views present in the leadership of the main national political parties and those expressed within national newspapers. Certainly, the marginalisation from the 1980s onwards of 'The Left' in British party politics has been paralleled in newspaper copy. Though newspapers such as *The Guardian* and *The Observer*, and perhaps *The Independent*, may at times offer views of an arguably 'left of centre' orientation, this 'alternative' perspective is increasingly rare and relates only to newspapers with small shares of circulation. This is, of course, very different to, say, the 1960s when the *Mirror* served as a high-circulation organ for the expression of campaigning views. In reality, it is now highly debatable whether any meaningful political diversity exists in the newspaper market, with a range of centrist views reflecting the narrowing of the mainstream in British politics. However, as we saw earlier, one of the justifications for having a relatively unregulated press has been that this is acceptable as a result of heavier regulation in broadcasting. As McQuail (1992: 142) demonstrates, referring to Hoffmann-Riem's writing, 'the diversity principle lies at the heart of broadcasting arrangements in Europe', at least as manifested in the various PSB traditions. In our consideration of the BBC's Charter renewal, we have already noted some challenges to this PSB tradition, and we will return to them, especially in Chapters 4 and 5.

A note of caution is needed regarding the term 'diversity', which is used here to refer to a range of perspectives reflected in media output as a whole; in this sense, 'pluralism' in content is used synonymously in this book. However, on occasion, 'pluralism' or 'diversity' of media ownership will also be referred to, and in particular when discussing possible relationships between ownership patterns in the media and the range of views reflected in output, the reader must be careful to ensure that the correct meaning is understood. As will be discussed later, there *may* be strong contingent relationships between diversity of ownership and diversity of output, or between monopoly of ownership and homogeneity of product, in terms of political perspective or lack of diversity in programme range, but the relationship remains contingent rather than necessary. In addition, care should be taken to distinguish between what McQuail (1992: 149) refers to as 'horizontal diversity' or 'the number of different programmes or programme types available to the viewer/listener at any given time' and 'vertical diversity' in terms of the 'number of different programmes (or types) offered by a channel (or set of channels) over the entire schedule'; the latter is intended throughout this book.

Political diversity in output overlaps with, but is reasonably distinct from a second strand, 'cultural diversity', where the special remit provided to Channel 4 from its inception to cater for 'minority interests' serves to identify part of the issue. There would be wide-ranging agreement that the provision of programming relevant to varying groups, based on race, gender, age, sexual orientation or other social variants, is a positive development. 'Alternative' or non-mainstream television is thought to serve a particular function in reducing social exclusion, and this in effect provides the justification for the insertion of specific requirements to this effect in Channel 4's licence. Proponents of 'choice' would presumably support variety as an end in itself, while others would identify the underlying objective as being the reduction of social exclusion. From whatever perspective, diversity in media output appears to be a positive objective.

In an international context, the cultural diversity justification for regulation takes on a further dimension, with the identification of the mass media as a crucial factor in the continuation or demise of national culture. In Britain, S4C and certain BBC services cater for the Welsh language, while abroad, for example in France, cultural imperialism, in the form of mostly US cinema and broadcast media, is viewed by some as a threat to individual national and linguistic cultures. The same phenomenon can be seen in a still more virulent form in those states positioned geographically in the US's 'back yard' (Herman and McChesney 1997: chapter 5).

This might be considered a particularly dangerous threat in developing countries, but it can also be observed in smaller, highly developed, Western states. In a small country such as The Netherlands, with a language little spoken in the wider world, the requirements of international trade and distinctiveness from mighty neighbour Germany have both contributed to a high degree of education in and exposure to English, and it is now possible that, within a few generations, Dutch may become very much a second language to English, much as Welsh is in much of Wales or still more as Scots Gaelic is in the vast majority of Scotland.

As Thomas (1995: 179) states, 'A language at a given time is kept in existence by a group of people speaking to each other in that shared set of terms; and clearly in modern conditions, a language that does not have access to the media is doomed, for the media are an extension of people speaking to each other'. He continues that the existence of media in the minority language 'normalizes the status of minority-language speakers, [and] raises their self-esteem'. Thus the high priority attached by linguistic minorities to the existence of media in their language, for example in Wales within the UK or Cataluña in the Spanish context (see E. Varney 2005), is not surprising. Thomas believes, however, that the proliferation of broadcasting channels as a consequence of digitalisation may in practice serve only to marginalise, or further marginalise, minority-language services, given the degree of investment that will be required to establish services in the new, digital medium.

While the French demonstrate more resistance than most to Anglophone cultural imperialism (Americanisation), somewhat hesitant steps have been taken by the EU towards a cross-European response to this phenomenon (see Doyle 2002; Harcourt 2005). The 'Television Without Frontiers' Directive of 1989 (Directive 89/552), in addition to seeking to establish common transmission across member states, also required Member States to ensure that broadcasters transmit a proportion of European-produced programmes, and indeed a 'predominance of European work'. The Advanced Television Standards Directive (Directive 95/47) added to this in terms of seeking to harmonise technical standards for television receiver equipment, an agenda now taken forward by the New Regulatory Framework (NRF). Inevitably, however, in as linguistically fragmented an organisation as the EU (even discounting non-recognised, minority languages), and given the cultural diversity across Europe, a meaningful internal market in broadcasting probably remains something of an ideal rather than a reality. As we will discuss in later chapters (see especially Chapter 6) more recent developments, in particular the suite of Directives issued in 2002, can be considered to be more far-reaching in their potential consequences and have certainly been influential in the development of national policies and legislative frameworks, as is apparent in the UK's Communications Act 2003.

Before leaving diversity as a justification for regulation, it is necessary to note the potential tension between this justification and intervention premised on paternalistic concerns regarding the nature of material, especially as regards sexually explicit and violent material. The range of material which may be broadcast in any jurisdiction may be significantly limited, as in Britain, by reference to concerns regarding 'taste and decency' or, in particular, protection of minors. Though such issues will be returned to in our discussion of standards in Chapter 5, it seems clear that such censorship can be viewed as cutting across the objective of diversity, and it should therefore be expected that such a power will be exercised accountably.

In addition to the 'effective communication' and 'diversity' rationales for intervention, a third thread in current justifications for media regulation can be clearly identified. Defences of the market economy, and the competition law intended to support it, are based upon perceived benefits that accrue from the operation of competitive markets. It is claimed that markets are efficient when compared with other delivery mechanisms at delivering what society wants or needs. However, the demands of profit-producing cost-efficiency may run counter to expectations of 'social justice'. This factor, in relation to public services, and especially those services to which all have an entitlement or need as a prerequisite of effective citizenship, may require heavy intervention in markets, or even the replacement of market mechanisms for the delivery of those public services which can be characterised as 'public goods'. The application of competition law in relation to the media will be addressed directly in Chapter 3 but it is sufficient to note for the moment that the extent to which broadcasting in an age of payment-card facilities for subscription or pay-per-view services meets the definition of a public good is debatable. However, there remains also, as discussed shortly, a significant public service element attached to the media, and especially broadcast media, which appears to justify continued intervention in media markets.

As has been suggested earlier, the perceived economic benefits which accrue to the country as a whole from flourishing media industries also appear to be influential in determining government policy towards media regulation. Thus a recurrent theme in both the British Conservative government's 1995 White Paper (DNH, 1995a) and New Labour's approach to the Communications Act 2003 was the national economic interest in allowing and encouraging British media players to develop in the international media market, to develop national 'champions' equipped to compete in the international tournament. However, this growth of British-based media giants large enough to play effectively on the international stage must in turn be viewed with caution given the threat this phenomenon may pose to diversity in the British market. It must be expected that, whether referred to explicitly or not, such matters must remain central to the agenda of any UK government, no matter how ideologically non-interventionist it may profess or appear to be (see Feintuck 2003).

Historically, the tensions between different versions of economic rationales for intervention, for example between the nurturing of national champions and the preservation of domestic competition, were evident in the legal framework, and in particular the media-specific measures which supplement or modify the underlying general framework of competition law. In essence, the thrust of these measures could be seen as the amelioration of the effects of commercial activity in so far as these impact adversely upon the perceived public service values of the media, and in particular broadcasting. The same tensions appear in the relationship between the EU's initiatives, in particular the 2002 NRF, and member states' responses to them, discussed in Chapter 6. The lightening of regulatory touch under the UK's Communications Act 2003 arguably indicates the clearest shift towards a faith in market forces to deliver and, despite its establishment of a definition for PSB, a distinct move away from the traditional UK public service model.

Humphreys (1996: chapter 4) demonstrates clearly how different versions of PSB have existed across Europe, indicating that the Reithian model is not the only manifestation of a public service ethos. Certainly Price and Raboy (2003) indicate ongoing debate and a wide range of alternative understandings and emphases absorbed within the concept. The lowest common denominator across these various models appears to be a commitment to delivering 'a wide-ranging quality service to the whole population' (117), though Humphreys also identifies non-commercialism as an essential common aspect of PSB systems. This is not to say that PSB may not include a commercial element: the British experience of ITV demonstrates that, as opposed to the audience maximisation model of the US, it has been possible to have a commercial television service competing with the archetypal public service broadcaster (the BBC), but competing in terms of quality of programming rather than audience maximisation. As discussed earlier in this chapter, the foundation of this historical arrangement has been challenged in the recent review of the BBC's Charter arrangements. Whether ITV programming will retain its quality and range in the face of increased competition for advertising revenue is also a question that has already been raised.

Whether a viable model of PSB can be developed that will continue to flourish in an increasingly commercial environment supported by the politically dominant market-oriented views of the age is a key matter for debate. As Blumler notes, public service broadcasters may be torn between two equally risky options: 'On the one hand, they may be tempted to try to offer a fully comprehensive service, even when diminished resources could limit their chances of doing that well. On the other hand, they will not wish to slip into the marginal role of merely filling whatever gaps are left untended by the commercial broadcasters' (Blumler 1992b: 4) – what we identified earlier as a 'market failure' vision of the BBC's role. However, this debate must in itself be placed in the context of competing underlying rationales for state intervention in the media.

The ongoing replacement in broadcasting of a public service ethos by a clear commercial imperative provides, arguably, a justification in itself for regulation though, as Negrine (1994: 200) suggests, 'once the changes are being implemented, it will be too late to retrace our steps and recapture the Reithian ideal'. However, though it is implausible to propose a return to a pre-1950s model as a viable objective for regulation, it is not necessarily the case that 'public service' values must be discarded in their entirety or consigned to the margins of broadcasting as in the US.

The Labour government, elected in the landslide victory of May 1997, committed itself to the reduction of social exclusion, in particular via improvements in the education system. Presumably, in this context, education is seen as a key to effective citizenship. But the government must, logically, acknowledge also the significance of the media in this citizenship agenda: even the well-educated citizen will have difficulty in participating effectively in society in the absence of accessible media. Yet, as will be seen in Chapter 4, the Communications Act 2003, introduced in New Labour's second term in office, may be thought to protect narrow consumer interests to a far greater extent than it does the much broader interests of citizens.

As with the still broader concept of 'the public interest', the extent to which public service values are clearly identified and articulated is likely to be a key to whether meaningful objectives can be established for the regulatory regime. It is clear from the foregoing that there are inherent tensions both between and within the four basic rationales for media regulation. In particular, conflicts exist between the economic imperatives and the important public service objective of diversity. Though now ten years old, it still seems worth noting the conclusions of Congdon *et al.* (1995: 7) that 'Profit-maximisation and political pluralism are different and not necessarily complementary objectives', and 'there can be little confidence that unregulated commercial broadcasters are much concerned to maintain pluralism . . .'

It is unlikely that these tensions and conflicts can be neatly resolved; however, it is essential that the problems are addressed rather than ignored. Government, on behalf of society, must make clear its basis for intervention and state which rationales for regulation will be prioritised, if meaningful objectives for regulation are to be defined, and if regulators are to act consistently in the pursuit of clearly defined objectives and effectively in their capacity as 'stewards' of the public interest in the media.

2.3.2 How to regulate?

If, and only if, meaningful rationales for regulatory intervention can be determined is it possible to move on to a policy-making process which identifies objectives, and establishes techniques for achieving them.

The recent history of media regulation and its reform has occurred in the context of a perceived breakdown of the public sphere (Dahlgren 1992; Blumler and Gurevitch 1995; Marquand 2004), and the intertwining of state and civil society (Keane 1991: 107; Harden and Lewis 1986). The environment thus created has allowed the growth of corporatism, or 'Government by Moonlight' (Birkinshaw *et al.* 1990) in which government and powerful private entities reach accommodations and symbiotic relationships in a secret world, hidden from public scrutiny and outside the scope of traditional accountability mechanisms. The effects of such powerful but unaccountable relationships in an area such as the media, which touches so acutely on democratic concerns, cannot readily be quantified given the inevitable lack of transparency in their operation. It is quite possible, however, that apparent withdrawals of the state from regulatory roles may in reality merely be the replacement of public, overt, regulatory activity by hidden, unaccountable, corporatist influence, and the secret furthering of symbiotic interests by government and the media establishment. At the national level, the risk is that identified by Monbiot (2000) in terms of corporate takeover, while at the global scale, the dominance of the forces of global capitalism are well illustrated by Hertz (2002).

As is the general case in Britain, the policy-making process relating to the media and its regulation has not been transparent. Indeed, it can plausibly be argued that no recognisable policy-making process has existed; certainly, Hitchens (1995a) indicated the highly reactive nature of policy decision-making in recent years, reflecting Elliot's analogy of 'chasing the receding bus' made some fifteen years earlier (Elliot 1980). Goldberg and Verhulst (1997) noted some limited moves by the British government towards addressing technological convergence in the early 1980s, but also a very clear reversion to a sectoral approach, and a strong deregulatory approach to both broadcasting and telecommunications from 1984 onwards.

Despite the publication of numerous government White Papers in recent years – three in 1995 alone (DNH 1995a, 1995b, 1995c) plus the New Labour White Paper of 2000, in both cases presaging major legislative reform – these have invariably amounted primarily to statements of government policy rather than rigorously argued discussions of alternatives. The review undertaken prior to the 1995 White Paper on media ownership (DNH 1995a) was correctly viewed by Hitchens (1995a) as being located firmly within the incrementalist tradition. Certainly, no clear vision of an overarching media policy along the lines suggested by Negrine (1994: 203) was developed in this period, and it may well be that Britain indeed found itself in the same situation described by Klingler (1996: 69) in relation to the US, of seeking to apply regulatory structures and devices from the 'Bronze Age of information services' (the 1930s to 1970s!) in this 'information moment'. However, the absence of clearly or rationally identified objectives did not prevent the rise and fall of a range of regulatory institutions with an interest in the media.

The second half of the 1990s saw what might be thought to be a particularly complex picture. On a statutory (if often discretionary basis), the generalist competition authorities (such as the MMC, OFT and the Secretary of State) carried out regulation generally triggered by structural thresholds being met, alongside both the relevant Directorates General of the European Commission with their more behavioural focus on competition and specialist British media-related bodies such as the ITC and the Radio Authority (RA) who exercised powers under the Broadcasting Acts. In addition, behavioural and content regulation was carried out via a range of bodies which included the ITC, the Radio Authority, Oftel and the Broadcasting Standards Council, while the courts had the power to intervene in relation to statutory and common-law matters involving secrecy and breach of confidence, obscenity, blasphemy, defamation and contempt of court. Beyond such black-letter law-based mechanisms for regulation, and in addition to the market forces that regulate the structure of media markets, a further range of non-statutory or hybrid bodies also regulated behaviour and content in this period, many persisting into the present. These included the self-regulatory PCC and ASA, the Royal Charter-based BBC (though the BBC was also confined by the terms of its Licence Agreement) and the BBFC, which acted as censor on a non-statutory basis in relation to the cinema but exercised statutory powers over home-video classification under the terms of the Video Recordings Act 1984, the latter being in itself a prime example of highly reactive regulation introduced in response to an unproven outcry, including judicial statements, regarding the impact of 'video nasties'.

The late 1990s saw cries for reform from a range of sources, and in particular calls from various quarters for a degree of rationalisation and perhaps unification of regulatory structures. While Collins and Murroni argued for the development of a single regulator, which arrived in the form of Ofcom, the first edition of the present work argued in addition for the identification of a clearer rationale for regulation. While the Communications Act 2003 may have provided us with a super-regulator, it may not seem to have offered much in relation to the second area. As should become apparent when we focus more closely in Chapters 4 and 5, there still seems to be no adequate unifying legitimatory basis for the range of structures and regulatory interventions which comprise the UK's media regulation scene.

Hoffmann-Riem (1992a: 175) establishes a bipartite model of regulatory techniques, referring to 'imperative' regulation or the imposition of specific standards and requirements on the media, and 'structural' regulation which attempts to reflect in ownership patterns and market behaviour certain public service values. It is perhaps more helpful, however, for the moment, to adopt a tripartite classification consisting of 'structural', 'behavioural' and 'content' regulation, as this better illustrates the range of distinct approaches to regulation. In shorthand, 'content regulation' refers to limitations being imposed on what cannot, or must, be broadcast or published, while 'structural regulation' refers to limits on the extent of that which can be owned within any market by any one corporate entity and, in effect, 'behavioural regulation' generally serves to limit how property held can be used in relation to its impact on actual or potential competitors.

Certainly, a confusing array of regulatory approaches was in evidence. EC competition law concentrates directly on effects, or behaviour, with Articles 81 and 82 of the EC Treaty prohibiting, respectively, agreements which have as their object 'the prevention restriction or distortion of competition' and behaviour which constitutes an 'abuse of a dominant position'. British competition law now largely mirrors the position under EC competition law, as the Competition Act 1998 endeavours to implement the scheme of EC competition law into UK law. It is possible for this system of competition to apply *ex post* to any firm operating in the market if there are competition law concerns, although the 'Access Directive' (Directive 2002/19/EC [2002] OJ L 107/8), in Articles 9–13 permit *ex ante* regulation to be imposed on the activities of those market players deemed to have 'significant market power'. This has been taken forward in sections 78–93 of the Communications Act 2003. Despite the fact that the new regulatory scheme, born from EC competition law, attempts to avoid the use of structural analysis, we can see that a player is only likely to be considered to have 'significant market power' if its share of the relevant market is greater than 40 per cent (European Commission 2002a: para. 75). The concentration on structural rather than behavioural solutions to market power which traditionally blighted UK competition law is now avoided in the main, although such a possibility remains in existence for newspaper mergers under section 58 of the Enterprise Act 2002. Further discussion of the current regime can be found in Chapters 3 and 4. While it is clear that markets require constant regulation if they are to provide the benefits attributed to them, the restrictions on ownership and use of market power established by competition law, however, only form part of the bigger regulatory picture.

The apparent objectives of different parts of the regulatory regime for the media therefore vary between prevention of monopoly (or perceived abuse of market power), the protection of differing versions of 'public service' values, the provision of choice in terms of product, political viewpoint and cultural diversity, and the application of essentially paternalistic censorship. In practice, however, it seems that the debate over objectives has increasingly been focused on consumer choice of media product at the expense of broader, citizen-oriented, expectations such as those underlying the public service tradition in broadcasting or the imposition of Universal Service Obligations (USOs) in relation to utilities. This produces not only an undue emphasis on a particular version of one rationale for regulatory intervention, but also, in so far as it really allows consumer choice to determine the ultimate shape of the media market, may create a high degree of uncertainty as to outcomes. For example, it is unclear whether, given real choice, the consumer would ultimately be tempted most by the charms of DTT or satellite services or broadband cable facilities. Traders in each might ply their wares, but ultimately this may result in an undesirable trade war, replicating in a new forum the battle of formats in the early 1980s between *VHS* and *Betamax* in the home video market, a battle which resulted in much consumer uncertainty and dissatisfaction before *VHS* finally won out. The present government is following the decision of its predecessor to facilitate the development of DTT, and is now effectively tied into this policy as a result of the rolling programme of switching-off of analogue transmission to be completed by 2012. However, it is by no means certain that this is what the consumer market, let alone citizens, would or will prefer. If serious about the creation of market choice, a government may find itself, as Marsden (1997b) suggests, with no logical alternative to regulating for a range of acceptable, alternative delivery platforms, though even this must be carried out in such a way as to integrate the regulation of control of platforms alongside transmission, production and conditional access systems (CASs) as part of the larger media market.

Content regulation is also widely used, and in Chapter 5 we will consider the role of Ofcom's 'Content Board' under the settlement established by the 2003 Act. In terms specifically of standards in British PSB, the key mechanism employed has been the insertion of positive programme requirements into broadcasting licences. In addition to considering programming proposals in the process of franchise allocation (see Chapter 4) and general statutory requirements regarding political impartiality and balance, the ITC had historically been required to ensure that the broadcasters it licences provide 'for example, original programmes, children's programmes, religious programmes, programmes "of high quality", programmes which will appeal to a wide variety of tastes and interests' (DNH 1995: para. 2.11). That said, in the 1990s Curran and Seaton (1997: 303) noted that symptomatic of a shift in attitude towards and change in the status of PSB was the fact that although the arrangements under the Broadcasting Act 1990 for the allocation of Channel 3 licences required 'quality programming', 'not only was this undefined, it only occupied two paragraphs in the Act', while 'By contrast, conditions governing the financial arrangements for the auction of franchises took up fifteen pages'. In the modern context of a mixed economy in broadcasting, such a statutory focus is perhaps inevitable, though the consequent dangers of losing sight of the underlying public service ethos must be recognised. Ofcom's role, and the challenge posed to public service values by the emphasis on 'light touch' regulation under the Communications Act 2003, is discussed in later chapters.

Congdon *et al.* (1995: 70) note that 'The aim of regulation of market share is primarily to restrict influence, but it ought, within a general competition framework, to provide the necessary – though not sufficient – condition for access and for content diversity'. This is important, both in highlighting the absence of any necessary, direct, connection between regulation of market share and ensuring diversity of content, and at the same time emphasising that regulation of market share serves only as a surrogate for regulation focused unashamedly at the ultimate objective, freely available and diverse content.

It may be advisable for a degree of regulatory emphasis to be shifted to focus on market structure, and perhaps behavioural aspects of control of delivery mechanisms, given the significance of technological 'gateways' in the new, digital markets. However, when focusing on this new area, the regime must remain aware of the broader market and public service contexts and be informed by clearly identifiable objectives, arising out of clearly defined rationales for intervention. To intervene is not necessarily to deny market forces, but to give effect to them in pursuit of a modern regulatory agenda. Almost nowhere does a market survive which is not regulated, and in an area such as the media, which shows such clear tendencies towards monopoly, regulation is the necessary partner of market forces if the perceived benefits of the market are to accrue. The application of different modes of regulation, structural, behavioural and content, is not in itself unreasonable, but unless coordinated by reference to clearly articulated guiding principles, may lead to confusion, uncertainty and a lack of direction for the regulatory system as a whole.

2.3.3 *The outcomes of regulation*

It seems reasonable to assess the success or failure of regulatory policies by comparing the outcomes achieved with whatever objectives for regulation may be derived from the underlying rationales for regulation. Regardless of regulatory output (for example, evidence of increased regulatory activity) if the results or outcomes of regulation are not consistent with the policy objectives established, and with the identified rationales for regulation, then the regulatory regime stands in need of fundamental review.

In terms of the four rationales for media regulation set out earlier (effective communication, diversity, economy and public service), some preliminary conclusions can now be drawn, focused for the moment on the second, diversity, and here 'diversity' will be used to refer both to pluralism of ownership and its contingent relationship to diversity in the political orientation of media output. From this perspective, it might be concluded that regulation in Britain has to date failed, at least in relation to the press.

Noted earlier were both the increasing concentration of ownership and decrease in political pluralism in the British press in the postwar era (see Humphreys 1996; Negrine 1994: chapter 3; Seymour-Ure 1996: chapter 3). Humphreys (1996: 76) demonstrated that by the mid-1990s, in Western Europe, if the proportion of the market controlled by the largest two newspaper publishers in each country was applied as the indicator of concentration, only the French language press in Belgium and the Irish press demonstrated concentration of ownership as great or greater than the British press. He accounted for this largely in terms of national characteristics, that is, in particular, the view taken on the role of the state in relation to the media, which in turn derives from variations in constitutional and state tradition.

However, bearing in mind concentration not only within the press sector but also on a cross-media basis, what becomes apparent, within the British market, is an example of expansion towards a point of dominance, not only within individual media markets such as the press or DTH satellite television, but also across the overall market. Clearly, based on the experience of the British press, if dominance of this kind is permitted, there is absolutely no guarantee that more media will result in more or even existing levels of diversity, in either a political or a cultural sense.

A similar phenomenon can be seen in action in other jurisdictions. The accounts of the US market offered by the likes of Bagdikian (2004) and McChesney (1999) illustrate this vividly, while in Italy, the growth of Silvio Berlusconi's Fininvest empire was believed to be connected with Berlusconi's ultimate rise to the position of the country's premier. The Italian experience should serve as a warning as to the necessity of ensuring that regulation moves beyond the 'symbolic-ritualistic' function which Hoffmann-Riem (in Blumler 1992a: 198) associates with Italy.

It would be wrong, however, to assume that any of the above demonstrates the total failure of the media regulation regime in Britain. Certainly, there is little evidence of diversity being extended, and growing concentration of ownership appears to pose a significant threat to perceived economic benefits attaching to markets. In addition, as access to media output via satellite and cable technology becomes increasingly significant, so the risk of social exclusion from the democratic benefits presented by the media increases. However, though this latter threat is increasingly imminent, much of mainstream broadcast cultural and political output is still at present and for the next few years at least effectively 'free at the point of use', and the range of programming available amounts to a reasonably good standard in terms of public service values. There must be significant doubts, however, as to whether the regulatory structure will withstand the further shocks of increased technological development and convergence and greater corporate conglomeration across-media sectors. It is clear though that the track-record to date should not necessarily inspire optimism in this respect. A potential merger of mobile phone operator Virgin and cable and broadband provider NTL/Telewest, proposed in December 2005, could be seen either positively as the welcome arrival of a new giant competitor challenging the status quo or negatively as simply evidence of continuing trends towards cross-media conglomeration, with the consequences which have been noted.

The nature of the ongoing media revolution appears to demand a reorientation of the regulatory endeavour towards structural and behavioural objectives. In addressing this issue, however, regulators and policy-makers must remain aware that if the ultimate objective is a freely available citizenship-enhancing diversity in media output, it is democratically legitimate (and probably necessary), if deeply politically unfashionable, to employ the kind of imperative, content-oriented controls to which Hoffmann-Riem refers. There is no doubt that structural and behavioural modes of regulation fit more easily with the dominant market paradigm, yet in relation to citizenship-related objectives, they should only ever be viewed as a surrogate for devices aimed directly at the true goal – diversity.

3

In Search of the Public Interest

༄

3.1 THE COMPETING VALUES

The various rationales and objectives for regulatory intervention outlined in Chapter 2 may seem contradictory and inconsistent. They appear
to start from different bases, pull in different directions, exhibit tension
between each other and reach conflicting conclusions. In part, these contradictions are merely an accident of history, a reflection of the piecemeal
way policy has responded to the historical development of different
industries as opposed to 'the product of rational differentiation between
media within the framework of an integrated plan' (Curran and Seaton
1997: 329). However, the very fact that no planned, medium- or long-
term media policy or planning process has existed (Hitchens 1995a)
appears to arise out of the failure to resolve inherent tensions and identify, if not a specific desirable destination, then at least a general direction in which to travel. The central thrust of this chapter is to seek to
assist in attempts to identify a meaningful, overarching rationale for
regulation of the media, to clarify – or replace – what has been the nearest
thing as yet to serve as a guiding principle, the concept of 'the public
interest'.

Much regulatory activity, not only of the media, but also, for example,
of the utilities, is justified by reference to a claim of the public interest. It
might be expected that this basic justification would be clarified by reference to objectives that are deemed to further this concept. However,
where the concept is itself inadequately defined, it is difficult to identify
objectives with adequate specificity and still more difficult to assess
whether outcomes are meeting the various criteria which may be embodied in 'the public interest'.

The term 'public interest' is used in relation to the entire range of
media regulation issues. From particular issues such as privacy and
media intrusion through to general matters of the relationship between
the state and the media, something called 'the public interest' appears to
have informed the policy of all British governments. Even in terms of

a fairly specific issue such as privacy, as will be seen in Chapter 5, it is not easy to be certain what the public interest demands, though the concept is certainly not coterminous with what the public, or certain sectors of it, might be interested in.

McQuail (1992: 3) provisionally identifies the term 'public interest' in the media context to refer to 'the complex of supposed informational, cultural and social benefits to the wider society which go beyond the immediate, particular and individual interests of those who communicate in public communication, whether as senders or receivers'. As he acknowledges, however, this remains 'both vague and contentious' and requires further attention. Indeed, definitional problems appear to be major obstacles to the development of a meaningful construct of the public interest, though even where attempts have been made to define the concept, they tend to incorporate rather than resolve tensions between competing versions of it. An example may be helpful here in demonstrating the inherent contradictions that may be contained within the 'public interest' as recently applied in legislation.

Under the terms of paragraphs 9–13 of Schedule 2 to the Broadcasting Act 1996 (considered more generally in Chapter 4), the ITC and the Radio Authority were charged with applying a test of public interest when considering the acquisition of commercial broadcasting licences by cross-media corporations already controlling one or more newspapers. The criteria to be applied as indicative of the public interest as set out in paragraph 13 included:

a) the desirability of promoting –
   i) plurality of ownership in the broadcasting and newspaper industries, and
   ii) diversity in the sources of information available to the public and in the opinions expressed on television or radio or in newspapers,
b) any economic benefits . . .
c) the effect of the holding of the licence by that body on the proper operation of the market within the broadcasting and newspaper industries or any section of them.

In effect, this paragraph incorporated all the various rationales for regulation identified in the previous chapter, and the tension and conflict between these competing public interest claims is obvious. The regulators would have to balance potential economic benefits against the values of plurality and diversity and the effects on competition, thus incorporating the competing interests and leaving to the largely unstructured discretion of the regulator the choice of which to prioritise.

The same tension had been revealed in the Conservative government's 1995 White Paper on media ownership (DNH 1995a: 16). Described by Curran and Seaton (2003: 387) as 'a monument of social market thought', the paper sets out the government's position as follows:

> Television, radio and the press have a unique role in the free expression of ideas and opinion, and thus in the democratic process. The main objective must therefore be to secure a plurality of sources of information and opinion, and a plurality of editorial control over them. Another important objective is to provide an environment to enable United Kingdom broadcasters, equipment manufacturers and programme makers to take full advantage of major market opportunities.

Discussion later in this chapter and in the next will suggest that the Communications Act 2003 has left many of the underlying tensions and difficulties unresolved, despite the reform of the institutional structure via the introduction of the super-regulator, Ofcom. As was suggested in the previous chapter, it remains the case that plurality may have to be compromised to allow British media corporations to grow sufficiently to allow them to compete effectively with other players in an increasingly global market. However, it is not just at the national level that such tensions are revealed. In the EU context, as Doyle (1997 and 2002) demonstrates, the objective of pluralism, implying diversity of output, has, for pragmatic reasons, given way to a competing approach, in which regulation of ownership or control, an easier concept to define than diversity of output, is at the heart of the regulatory enterprise. This approach meshes with a range of other measures targeted at the Union's fundamental agenda of permitting or facilitating development of a pan-European media market alongside other goods and services. The public interest appears therefore a concept subject to ready capture and reinterpretation.

To a certain extent, the somewhat schizophrenic approach to regulation demonstrated by these examples perhaps reflects the split personality of the media in claiming to serve simultaneously both the advertiser and the audience, whose interests will certainly not always coincide (Keane 1991: 55; Blumler 1992b: 2). Tensions between competing elements of the portmanteau concept 'the public interest' must be resolved and decisions taken regarding which element or version should win out. Allowing different areas of regulation to give preference to different versions of the concept will produce inconsistency, and failing to identify and justify the grounds on which one version of the concept is preferred to another will render the process opaque. However, if consistency and transparency are to be achieved, it seems necessary to reinvent 'the public interest' in terms of an overarching principle which will guide regulators towards consistent outcomes.

Of the problems identified between the existing models, the most fundamental tension appears to be in the relationship between the media and the state. The public service tradition in the regulation of British broadcasting has already been identified as being a version of the 'social responsibility' model (Siebert *et al.* 1956) for regulation of the press. As such, this implies a significant role for the state in establishing the framework within which the media will operate. However, Curran and Seaton (1997) demonstrate not only that the conception of public service has been susceptible to change, but also that the relationship between state and media has also been subject to fluctuating pressures and differing identifications of the public interest, and, differing conceptions of the extent of legitimate state activity.

As was discussed in Chapter 1, McQuail (1992: 9) traces the conflict between state authority and media freedom through suppression and prohibition, to permission and then prescription, before a recent shift to more libertarian values. It is clear that the public service tradition in broadcasting is historically associated most closely with the prescriptive epoch yet exists today in a more libertarian environment. While it is important to be aware that the public interest in media is not synonymous with PSB, the public interest is given probably its most concrete manifestation in the form of PSB in the Western European tradition, of which the BBC is perhaps the paradigm example.

Attitudes towards the BBC, subject to a broad, supportive consensus around the Reithian tradition in the 'prescriptive' 1940s and 1950s, continued, if not unhindered then ultimately unbroken, by the arrival of strictly regulated commercial television. However, the position changed markedly in later years, and the Annan Committee Report (1977) is generally considered a landmark, tending to favour a more restricted, less interventionist role for public bodies such as the IBA (Negrine 1994: 106), and favouring the pursuit of a range of programming, catering for the interests of the diverse groups in society rather than 'seek[ing] to offer moral leadership' (Curran and Seaton 1997: 304). In discarding large parts of what remained of the Reithian, paternalistic inheritance, the Annan Report moved the basis for British broadcasting and its regulation from relatively familiar to uncertain and unstable ground. In Curran and Seaton's terms (2003: 365):

The Annan Report's reinterpretation of public service unintentionally left British broadcasters defenceless against the threats posed by recent technological developments. By so transforming public service it left no grounds to manage or control the impact of the inevitable introduction of cable, video or satellite broadcasting.

As is suggested in our discussion in the previous chapter, in shifting the orientation of PSB so that, in effect, it began to take on the characteristics of 'a poor mimicry of the market' (Keane 1991: 155), the distinctive character of PSB began to be lost, and with it perhaps the understanding of why it had existed. While the basis for public intervention in broadcasting therefore became uncertain, broader concerns regarding the relationship between the state and the media were amplified. A somewhat shrill clamour, largely from government, for broadcasters to ensure political balance or impartiality mounted in the 1970s and 1980s, with programme producers and BBC Governors finding themselves under increasingly direct pressure. On the one hand, this indicated a need for the media to be protected against the interference of the state, enabling it to fulfil its role as 'The Fourth Estate', while on the other, it suggested the need for active regulation to guarantee pluralism in media output.

To some extent this dilemma was avoided rather than resolved by an increasing application of consumerist logic to the media. The provision of pluralism would be ensured, it was argued, by the operation of market forces through which consumer choice would demand and, facilitated by ongoing technological developments, would be supplied with diversity. Whether consumer choice is likely to deliver on this promise will be explored shortly.

The inconsistencies in state/media relations abound. On the one hand, British governments have consistently refused to fund newspapers in order to promote diversity of output. On the other hand, Channel 4 was created in part specifically to enhance diversity and funded by a levy imposed upon other commercial broadcasters. The attempts to revive the ailing British film industry associated with Channel 4's remit was part of a long sequence of *ad hoc* interventions seeking to bolster British cinema, on cultural, economic and especially employment grounds. The Eady Levy, introduced in the late 1940s, through which cinema box-office takings were taxed to enable support to be given to the British film industry was an attempt to fund support via a levy on the most successful, mostly American, films. This essentially protectionist measure survived until 1984, even though, as Curran and Seaton (2003: 382) note, by then it was mostly supporting 'British' films being produced by notionally British companies that were essentially American. From 2000 to 2005, lottery-funded Film Council grants totalling £100 million were distributed to UK film-makers, and though, by way of a sample year, the industry produced a £95 million trade surplus in 2003, hidden within that figure was a £10 million trade deficit in relation to the US (*Guardian*, 14 November 2005). The difficulties for the UK film industry in relation to US global domination of the market appear to be mirrored on the larger European stage, where, as Curran and Seaton observe (Curran and Seaton, 2003: 399) despite EU funding for European film production, the American film industry has continued to increase greatly its share of the European market. The logic of such interventions in the film industry, in both economic and cultural terms, seems decidedly suspect (Grantham 2004: 190), though governments of all hues continue to remain attached to such policies. There seems to be a substantial amount of national, and possibly national*ist*, pride and symbolism attaching to national film industries, and it may seem to governments better to be seen to be doing something rather than nothing.

The willingness of governments to intervene in relation to cinema and broadcast media has, however, in recent times never been paralleled by a willingness to regulate the press. Though Broadcasting Acts and the Annan Report have frowned upon foreign holdings in British broadcasting, foreign ownership and control of British newspapers has been permitted on a grand scale. At the same time, while broadcasters have, in Britain, been constrained in their activities by licence requirements or in the BBC's Charter terms, governments have invariably been shy of intervening in relation to the activities of the press, declining to impose statutory standards in relation to privacy (DNH 1995b). As we will see in Chapter 5, reform in relation to matters of privacy, in so much as it has impacted the media at all, has originated in the much broader context of the Human Rights Act. Equally, UK governments may have shown a sound sense of self-preservation, but ultimately may be accused of something of a dereliction of duty, by refusing to act decisively to halt the promotion of one medium (satellite broadcasting) via another (newspapers) owned by one cross-media group (Barendt 1995: 135; Sadler Report 1991).

The apparent contradictions between governmental approaches to printed and broadcast media can be explained on a number of different grounds. The limited scope permitted to the BBC to cover hard news in its formative years in response to the press industry's anxieties regarding competition led, claim Curran and Seaton (1997: 329), to broadcasting being seen 'as a medium of entertainment for which "cultural" and not "political" standards were appropriate'. Such a justification appears weak in the modern era where news content in television and radio appears to grow at a similar rate to the concurrent reduction of 'hard' news in popular newspapers such as *The Mirror* and *The Sun*.

Another version is that while changing patterns and degrees of regulation of the press have occurred over a long historical period, broadcasting has a much shorter history, and has developed in an era in which the state, at least until very recently, has in general played a more active and interventionist role. Thus the history of the broadcast media cannot be traced through the phases of development identified by Siebert *et al.* (1956), but has been, from its earliest days in Britain at least, been regulated within the social responsibility paradigm – identified as a public resource and therefore legitimately the subject of state intervention.

Barendt (1995) identifies at least four different perspectives from which the differential regulation of broadcast and print media may be justified. The first of these is the familiar, if now outdated, 'frequency scarcity' type argument referred to in Chapter 2. The need to ensure adequate and clear access to the airwaves for state services such as the police and military initially formed a justification for intervention and state regulation, permitting the state to allocate frequencies.

This is a particular version of a second, 'public resource', argument. However, in an era in which other services and utilities previously identified as 'public resources' such as the utilities have been privatised, there seems little to stop the state, as in the US (Schiller 1996: 83), selling off blocks of redundant analogue frequencies as new technologies takeover. Though proposing to reform the charging basis for the radio spectrum, the Conservative's 1996 White Paper (DTI 1996) did not at that stage envisage a secondary trading market developing in spectrum. As yet it is unclear whether the rolling programme of switching-off of analogue television transmission to be completed by 2012 will lead directly to such an occurrence and the government is certainly not emphasising this as a policy, but in many ways it seems an inevitable outcome. However, in any case, even full-scale privatisation would not necessarily result in the government abandoning entirely the regulatory endeavour, but rather would be likely to see government distancing itself from regulation via the creation of statutory regulatory agencies such as those introduced for the privatised gas, electricity, water and telecommunications industries. Indeed, the role ascribed to Oftel in relation to DTT under the Broadcasting Act 1996 (see Chapter 4) suggested that steps were already being taken in this direction even ten years ago.

A third theory expounded by Barendt, like the first, derives from historical circumstance and draws upon the work of Bollinger (1990). Barendt suggests that as the printed media are relatively unregulated, it has become necessary, in order to ensure a degree of diversity and plurality in media output, to regulate more heavily the arguably more influential newcomers to the media world, the broadcasters, subjecting them, for example, to requirements of political impartiality. This is related to the logic of what is the fourth, and arguably the most clearly articulated reason for heavier regulation of the broadcast media, stated by the US Supreme Court in the *Pacifica* case (*FCC v Pacifica Foundation* (1978) 438 US 726). The majority of the Supreme Court bench in *Pacifica* justified greater state intervention in relation to television broadcasting on account of the medium's peculiarly pervasive and intrusive potential. The immediacy and, in relation to children and the vulnerable especially, the accessibility of television, together with its direct reach into the home, provides one strand of reasoning underpinning the heavier regulation of broadcast rather than printed media.

There is an essentially paternalistic line apparent here, reflecting the kind of roles performed in the UK by the BBFC and Ofcom (historically the BSC) in relation to sex and violence in the cinema and television respectively, which is at odds with more libertarian approaches towards the role of the state. Technological developments such as 'parental locks' designed to restrict children's access to such material may have an impact on this argument, especially in the current essentially deregulatory libertarian era. However, the relative difficulty of controlling access to similar material available via the Internet, if not the subject of similar 'censoring' devices, may provide an argument for similar restrictions on computer-generated material, though policing of such purported restrictions would appear to be nightmarish in terms of practicalities, the identification of a responsible originator of material and jurisdictional issues being among the problems.

However, it seems likely that the print media will continue to be more lightly regulated than broadcasting. Newspapers will continue to point towards their historically hard-fought and won freedoms, while the broadcasters, born into an age of state regulation of 'public resources' have no such historical credentials. The practical reality is that governments have had, and have taken, the opportunity to regulate broadcasting in a way which has not been available or perceived as legitimate in relation to the printed media in the modern era. What Barendt demonstrates is that the justifications for heavier regulation of broadcasting are largely contingent – contingent upon historical circumstance and constitutional form and tradition rather than resting upon clearly defined principles. Though the move to 'lighter touch' regulation, emphasised in the Communications Act 2003, apparently reduces the potential for state intervention in media markets, it seems far-fetched to expect any government to relinquish entirely its influence over such matters. There is an aspect here of a phenomenon referred to earlier, of the state rarely if ever withdrawing entirely, but rather reforming. The reality here relates to some extent with Daintith's distinction (Daintith 1979), to which we return in Chapter 6, between *imperium* and *dominium*. The apparent withdrawal from direct rule through legal instrument (via *imperium* powers) may mask ongoing potential for exercise of *dominium* via economic and political mechanisms, tax incentives, subsidies, allocation of public contracts and the like.

That said, while views may differ as to the extent to which state intervention in media markets is legitimate, both paternalists, who seek a 'properly informed' public, and libertarians, who emphasise choice, share an objective of diversity in media output. The common ground is that diversity is desirable, the difference is in response to the question 'why?' Put simply, diversity of media product is viewed, respectively, as a function of a well-informed public, equipped to participate effectively in society, or as a function of a citizenry endowed with the maximum of choice as an end in itself. If diversity in media output is universally valued, and if it cannot necessarily be guaranteed without regulation, then media regulation targeted at diversity appears to be justified.

However, this conclusion is likely to be disputed by those associated with a belief in the efficacy of market forces to respond to the wishes of individuals and provide the range of products that they wish for (see Veljanovski 1989); if market forces can deliver choice then no or minimal regulation will be prescribed. The problem from this perspective is that if markets do not deliver a range of choice that fulfils these demands, then it may be necessary to intervene to produce the necessary diversity.

Veljanovski (1987), in considering the regulation of cable television in Britain in the 1980s, succinctly summarises the weaknesses in the traditional, paternalistic concept of public service associated with broadcasting in Britain and epitomised by the BBC. Veljanovski dispenses with the frequency scarcity argument for regulation, identifying it as 'an artificial one created by government' (276) and claiming that a viable alternative would be the identification of broadcasting frequencies as private property, to be traded at will, with disputes to be resolved by private litigation.

He then went on to discuss what he considered the only remaining plank of the concept of PSB, the maintenance of standards in programming via, in Hoffmann-Riem's terms, 'imperative' regulation. Veljanovski doubts and questions the validity of both the paternalistic line 'that people should not be given what they want but what they need', and the 'market failure' approach that 'there are inherent structural defects in markets for television programming and distribution which necessitate government involvement' (Veljanovski 1987: 277).

This latter argument appears to revolve around the claim that, for commercial television, the essential purpose of broadcasting activity, profit-making, is heavily dependent upon supplying audiences to advertisers who in turn provide revenue to the broadcasters. The role for the regulator in this context is to avoid a battle for audience maximisation resulting in lowest-common-denominator programming which drives down programme standards and diversity. Veljanovski's point here though is that the end-product of the regulatory system that produced the BBC/ITV duopoly in Britain in reality resulted in direct competition for audience share between the BBC and the commercial broadcasters, and a resulting homogeneity of product, despite the two schools of broadcasting not having to compete for advertising revenue. Why? Because, says Veljanovski (1987: 278), 'Parliament will not increase the licence fee if the BBC is not seen to offer a significant proportion of the viewing public what they want', and therefore the BBC is forced to engage in a ratings war despite not being driven by the advertising revenue imperative.

If Veljanovski's argument is sustainable, then regulatory failure on the grand scale is observable. In so far as the public service ethos associated traditionally with British television can be defined, then, if Veljanovski's conclusions are correct, it is not being furthered by the regulatory approach adopted.

Without diverting from our agenda too far, it is necessary to consider whether this is indeed the case. Certainly, there is significant overlap in programme type; ITV's *World in Action* and BBC's *Panorama* were for many years broadly comparable, and it is true that ITV companies produce serious news programmes and, as has been demonstrated in relation to Formula 1 motor racing, are perfectly capable of producing sports coverage of as high a quality as the BBC. In addition, the previously distinctive voice of *BBC2* is increasingly comparable with the output of Channel 4. One exception to this pattern of similarity in conventionally regulated television is, however, without doubt Five, which appears to produce an unremitting diet of 'down-market' programming. A clearer contrast emerges, however, in the context of radio, where the five national BBC channels currently available as analogue services supplemented by a range of additional digital services continue to provide a varied, high-quality output catering for popular and minority tastes and interests. Though local and national commercial radio stations seek out and appeal to, with varying degrees of success, niche audiences, neither individually nor collectively do they provide the range of output, and particularly the in-depth analysis and news coverage, offered by BBC radio.

There is here, perhaps, an analogy which needs to be considered when reading Veljanovski's conclusion (1987: 279) in relation to cable television, that 'The direct link between consumer and cable operator afforded by pay-cable ensures that the programmes shown cater to a greater extent for the preferences of viewers (rather than those of the regulator or advertisers)'. Pay-television, whether delivered via cable, DTH satellite or DTT devices, certainly caters for niche interests, and the growth of consumer attraction to *BSkyB*'s channels in Britain can undoubtedly be attributed to its delivery of extensive and exclusive sports coverage (especially live Premier League soccer) and television movie premieres. The EC brokered break-up of the Premier League soccer rights package into six separate packages of matches sold by the FA Premier League is of questionable utility in ensuring any significant reduction of Sky's market power. Indeed, Cartlidge and Mendia Lara (2005: 1882) have argued that 'The settlement clearly does not prevent one broadcaster from acquiring more than 50% of the live rights. It is widely expected that Sky will use its financial muscle to buy up five of the six live rights packages.'

The outcome of this move, while being intended to ensure greater value and availability of football rights both for broadcasters and football fans who purchase the right to view such content, may have achieved precisely the opposite effect. Cartlidge and Mendia Lara (2005: 1882) helpfully identify the difficulties as being, in the main, that 'fans may require multiple subscriptions to whichever broadcasters obtain the rights (e.g. satellite and cable subscriptions) in order to view the matches from 2007 onwards.'

Undoubtedly also, on a global scale, *CNN* began some years ago to change the face of television news coverage and has indeed forced the BBC to introduce, in its twenty-four hour news service, a development which can be viewed as mimicking the *CNN* approach. However, there is no evidence to suggest that any single programmer's broadcasting via the new delivery mechanisms have as yet produced, or are likely to produce, anything to compare with the range of services and in-depth analysis and informative or educational content of the services offered by the regulated, public service broadcasters. Truly commercial programmers may well choose, predictably and reasonably enough, to focus on the most profitable, audience-maximising product, to the exclusion of more 'worthy' fare which may become marginalised or only available as niche products at relatively high prices which may exclude some viewers.

There is undoubtedly a market demand for the kind of product offered by *BSkyB*, but there is also a strong claim that the public would regret the passing of an age where, in addition to such programming, the quality and range of product associated with the BBC and also conventional, regulated, commercial television in Britain was universally available. This view will inevitably be ascribed the pejorative epithet 'paternalistic'; however, if television is viewed as anything more than simple entertainment, and if it is recognised that television is our primary source for a view of the world, then it seems legitimate to intervene to ensure that it continues to fulfil this function effectively, and that the unquestioned value of entertainment is not allowed to predominate entirely over the potential informative and educative aspects of the medium. If a viable basis for universally accessible PSB is not maintained alongside commercial niche broadcasting, television will be relegated to a medium of pure entertainment, with the broader democratic values currently enjoyed sacrificed on the alter of consumerism.

It is important to heed the lesson Keane draws from an analysis of the press, that it is dangerous to be 'too sanguine about the capacity of market competition to ensure the universal access of citizens to the media of public communication', as such an attitude can too easily fail 'to grasp the many ways in which communications markets *restrict* liberty of the press' (Keane 1991: 46, original emphasis).

Though the case just outlined for the defence of PSB seems persuasive, it could be rendered still more so if it were possible to identify with reasonable clarity precisely what the public service ethos in broadcasting amounts to. In making comparisons with regulation of the privatised utilities, Prosser (1997: 253) noted that in both cases the regulation of the industries is underpinned by 'social obligations'. He states, however, that 'PSB is a far more developed concept than the other forms of public-service obligation' (241), and as such it might be expected that the concept would be more readily identified.

In considering the institutional structure and approach to independent broadcasting, Prosser (1997: 255) rightly acknowledged, however, that 'the concept of public-service broadcasting is extremely difficult to define'. He went on to adopt what was then 'the nearest thing to a definition': a list of principles drawn from the Home Affairs Committee report 'The Future of Broadcasting' (1988), which includes:

> [U]niversal service, freedom of broadcasters from direct governmental intervention, provision of a service which should inform and educate as well as entertain, and programmes which should cover a wide and balanced range of subject matter in order to meet all interests in a population.

This list is helpful, but in itself requires the addition of a point which Prosser makes when considering specifically the interplay between media specific and general competition law structures in the context of the regulation of broadcasting. He emphasises that 'it must always be borne in mind that the aim of these controls is not simply maintaining fair competition but also maintaining diversity of information' (Prosser 1997: 253). Though not stated explicitly, this agenda also appears to require an acknowledgement of the potential for public service media to alleviate the risk of unregulated media contributing to social exclusion. As we saw in the previous chapter, the Communications Act 2003 goes much further than any previous instrument in offering an 'official' British definition of PSB, though we are still left doubting whether the values are adequately protected in practice, and whether citizenship values are adequately prioritised among the values or principles established.

That said, in adopting as a statement of principle the kind of model envisioned by Prosser, apparently paternalistic arguments in favour of PSB or of regulation of broadcasting in the public interest are bolstered by reference to a fundamental democratic expectation. Namely, that full and effective participation in society, or citizenship, is dependent upon universal access to adequate sources of information. There is no evidence to suggest that an unregulated, truly commercial market in broadcasting would fulfil this promise. Though some might suggest that computer technology and the Information Superhighway will in due course supersede the presently limited information provided by broadcasting, the realisation of this dream still appears some way off at present. Though such developments must be monitored and taken account of when regulating communications as a whole, they do not as yet undermine the case for effective PSB, given the still extremely hierarchical access to such hi-tech alternative services at present and in the foreseeable future.

What is helpful, however, in considering high-tech responses to access to information is that they draw our focus outwards, to the realisation that the issue must be viewed in a regional, international or arguably global context. Satellite broadcasting and measures such as the EU's 'Television Without Frontiers' Directive (89/552) and the Council of Europe's Convention on Transfrontier Broadcasting (see Coleman and McMurtrie 1995) have for some time served as marginal challenges to national sovereignty in this area of regulation. The EU's 2002 Directives, to be discussed later in this chapter and in Chapter 6, may prove to be much more significant. Likewise, as Curran and Seaton (2003: 395) note, more general global initiatives on trade, in particular the World Trade

Organisation, may also have an impact on regulatory, or more likely deregulatory, initiatives. Such moves are unlikely to present any obstacle to the commercial reality discussed by Herman and McChesney (1997) that technological convergence has combined with corporate restructuring to provide the potential for domination of media markets on a global scale by unashamedly commercial (US) English language-dominated and often American financed media giants. Vertical and horizontal integration and technological convergence mean that not only domination of individual, national media sectors is threatened, but that these genuinely cross-media or multimedia giants may dominate not only broadcasting in terms of programming, but also in terms of delivery mechanisms. It is therefore right for regulatory responses seeking to defend public service values to be pitched not only at the national level, but also, as Chapter 6 will demonstrate, at the international.

3.2 COMPETITION LAW AND THE PUBLIC INTEREST IN MEDIA REGULATION

It has already been noted that media markets, if unregulated, appear to have strong tendencies to fall into oligopolistic patterns. That said, in practice of course, broadcasting in most Western countries (the US being a major exception) has been subjected to partial state monopoly for much of its history. As Whish (2003: 10) states, generally 'It might be that social or political value judgements lead to the conclusion that competition is inappropriate in particular economic sectors', and this was indeed the case for broadcasting and most of Britain's nationalised utilities until the Thatcherite 'revolution' of the 1980s. Specifically in relation to the media, Barendt (1995: 121) states that public monopolies may in practice provide the best guarantees of plurality in media output. However, the regulatory landscape relating to the media has come to be increasingly dominated by the rhetoric and practice of deregulation and competition-oriented provisions.

Given that the threat of market domination is traditionally the stuff of competition law ('anti-trust' law in the US), it might be expected that competition law would derive from a particular economic model, and that it would therefore offer a vision which embodies a clear model of the public interest. Even here, however, a survey of the legal provisions and the principles underlying them reveals a range of objectives and orientations which may militate against a clear vision. Almost inevitably, therefore, competition law can be seen to have had a varied impact on the regulation of the media.

Historical accounts of the development of competition law render it apparent that pursuit of economic efficiency has not always been the central goal of such law (Motta 2004: chapter 1). Even in the present environment, though the increasing Europeanisation of competition law has created a significant degree of harmonisation throughout the EU's member states (Birkinshaw 2003: chapter 12), it is clear that few if any systems of competition law are oriented solely towards the pursuit of economic efficiency. The most common definition of 'economic efficiency' offered by economists is that of 'allocative efficiency' or 'Pareto optimality'. In this state of affairs, society's resources are deployed in the optimum manner, and it is impossible to reallocate resources and make one person better off unless another person is made worse off (Lipsey and Chrystal 1999: 286–8).

Allocative efficiency is the product of the operation of 'perfect markets' – economic parlance for markets which foster 'perfect competition'. A number of requirements must be met before a market can be said to be 'perfect': all firms must be producing homogenous products; customers must have perfect information about products being sold and prices being charged by all firms; each firm must be relatively small; all firms must be 'price-takers', i.e. the market must determine the price of the goods sold by the firm and the firm must not be able to influence the price by its behaviour; and there must be freedom of entry and exit to markets (Lipsey and Chrystal 1999: 140–1). In reality, such conditions seldom, if ever, exist (Whish 2003: 6) and the pursuit of such market conditions is unlikely to be successful.

Given that the pursuit of perfect markets is rarely if ever likely to be successful, a number of other efficiency-based goals for competition law have been suggested. In a seminal article, Clark (1940) argued that competition policy should act in pursuit of 'workable competition' – a concept which has been described by Whish (2003: 14) as a structure which might be 'expected to have a beneficial effect on conduct and performance, and therefore be worth striving for and maintaining'. A number of other concepts have been suggested, such as the theory of 'contestable markets' which places emphasis on freedom of entry to and exit from markets (Whish 2003: 15 and Jones and Sufrin 2004: 14). The concept which has seen the greatest emphasis in EC competition law is that of 'effective competition' – a phrase contained in both Article 82 EC and Article 2(3) of the EC Merger Regulation (Regulation 139/2004 [2004] OJ L 124/1). The concept of 'effective competition' has never been the subject of a definition, either by the European courts or the Commission itself. Bishop and Walker have argued that:

The practical application of competition law ought to be interested less in outcomes that are desirable in some theoretical, abstract, sense and more in outcomes that are feasible for regulatory intervention to achieve . . . To draw this distinction requires analysis of the various economic models of competition and the implications each type of model has for consumer welfare. (Bishop and Walker 2002: 2.10)

Here, Bishop and Walker are suggesting that competition law should be designed to maximise the 'welfare' or 'surplus' of consumers. This will generally, although not always, lead to the same outcome as the pursuit of 'total welfare' (Motta 2004: 19). These observations have led Motta to argue that competition policy should be defined as 'the set of policies and laws which ensure that competition in the market place is not restricted in such a way as to reduce economic welfare' (Motta 2004: 19). Motta's definition seems to accord with some of the observations of the European Commission, which, in a recent communication, argued that competition policy should be:

Characterised by . . . improvement of the regulatory framework for competition which facilitates vibrant business activity, wide dissemination of knowledge, a better deal for consumers, and efficient economic restructuring throughout the internal market . . . (European Commission 2004a: 2)

The existence of monopoly power is argued by most authors to have a deleterious effect on economic welfare, be this general welfare or consumer welfare. In reality, monopoly power in its pure form (where there is only one seller and a multiplicity of buyers) exists only rarely, but oligopolies, where there are only relatively few sellers and many buyers, exist much more frequently (Stroux 2004: 17–35). The market power of market players in monopolistic and oligopolistic markets may lead to the transfer of wealth away from consumers and to the firms with market power. In many cases, monopolists will exercise this market power in a way which harms efficiency and consumers, but the picture in relation to oligopoly is markedly less clear, with much greater disagreement between economists over whether an oligopolistic market structure necessarily leads to anti-competitive behaviour (Stroux 2004: 10–35; Posner 2001: 53–60; Viscusi *et al.* 2000: 101–13).

The key modern debate in the economic analysis of anti-competitive behaviour has been between the 'Harvard' and 'Chicago' schools of analysis. The 'Harvard' school suggest that market structure is the key indicator of whether the firms in a particular market will behave in a competitive manner or not (Stroux 2004: 11; Jones and Sufrin 2004: 21–2). There are evident merits in this approach, and many economists still support the central tenets of the 'structural' account, although the 'pure' account of the structuralist argument has been placed under pressure by the observations of the 'Chicago' school. Lawyers who are adherents to the 'Chicago' school's system of economic analysis (Bork 1978; Posner 2001) suggest that it is the behaviour of market players, rather than market structure, which often causes anti-competitive conduct to arise. As Jones and Sufrin (2004: 22–3) have argued:

> The fundamental Chicago view is that the pursuit of efficiency, by which is meant allocative efficiency as defined by the market, should be the sole goal of antitrust. The school does not support sentimentality for small businesses or the corner store but places trust in the market.

Competition policy in the European Union appears to serve a fusion of goals (Motta 2004: 26–30, Whish 2003: 18–23), although it is evident that modern competition law in the EU (and therefore the UK, as the Competition Act 1998 aligns UK competition law with EC competition law) is shifting towards alignment with economic analysis. This is reflected by the European Commission's recent Communication, where it states that:

> Competition policy is adapting to recognise both the teachings of modern economics and the constantly evolving dynamics and the necessary industrial development of Europe. Economic analysis is central because competition policy shapes fundamental economic decisions on investment, consolidation, pricing and therefore economic performance. It shifts the focus firmly to the economic effects of firm behaviour or of government measures. (European Commission 2004a: 7)

The Commission report suggests a degree of clarification over the nature of EC competition law and policy, with an increased focus on the economic effects of particular practices and behaviour of firms when determining whether sanctions under competition law should be imposed. It is notable that the communication hints towards a distinctly 'Chicagoan' approach – with the main emphasis being placed on the behaviour of firms rather than the structure of markets. It would be incorrect to suggest that the Harvard School structuralist approach should be ignored completely, because, as Jones and Sufrin (2004: 22) note, 'Although mainstream economists no longer believe that structure dictates performance, it accepts that structure is important to the ability of firms to behave anticompetitively.'

The above discussion has sought to demonstrate that although competition law has aimed to pursue a confusing plethora of goals over the past century, it appears that the analysis is becoming more firmly rooted in economic analysis and the pursuit of economic efficiency in the manner espoused by classical economics and, more recently, by the Chicago School. However, some would see this development as a negative one, as it suggests that the multiplicity of other goals that have been pursued in the past might be eschewed in favour of an approach that is more firmly centred on economic analysis.

The media industry has provoked a great deal of interest from economists and competition lawyers alike. What is immediately apparent, however, is that, in Marsden's terms, the communications industries must be acknowledged as 'a uniquely sensitive industry prone to market failure' (Marsden 1997b: 2). Traditionally, analogue terrestrial broadcasting had the ingredients which amounted to a classic case of market failure. First, we can see that due to the existence of 'spectrum scarcity', where interference between broadcasts would render the analogue broadcasting spectrum useless to all unless some form of government regulation intervened, the industry is necessarily destined to have a monopolistic or oligopolistic structure. Meanwhile, Ogus (1994) identifies the public interest grounds for regulation in terms of both economic criteria and, in particular, the problem of addressing 'public goods' (referred to in Chapter 2), with traditional, analogue terrestrial broadcasting certainly being in essence a 'public good'. In order for an economist to classify a good as a public good they must be both non-excludable and non-rivalrous (Lipsey and Chrystal 2003: 293), *i.e.* it is impossible to exclude those who have not paid for provision from access to the good and that one person's consumption of a particular good does not exclude consumption by another. It is evident that my watching of BBC1 at a particular time does not prevent my neighbour from doing so and, furthermore, if I have a television set then I may watch television regardless of whether I have purchased a television licence. In reality, although the lack of a licence may deter some viewers, many continue to watch without a licence.

The outcome of this market failure was that most European countries adopted a strict system of licensing for broadcasters, combined with strict 'public service' requirements to imbue media output with a degree of pluralism and diversity that would not be provided by the highly limited market (Humphreys 1996; Barendt 1995). These circumstances resulted in a very limited role for competition law in analogue terrestrial broadcasting. This situation has now changed considerably, with competition law playing a pivotal role both in the regulation of electronic communications networks (covered in more detail in Chapter 6 of this book) and of maintaining competition in the markets for the provision of broadcast content.

Competition law is not concerned with the pursuit of pluralism or diversity in the media as a central goal. In some cases, economic analysis will lead to a situation where a merger or other concentration which may reduce pluralism is prevented, but in many cases mergers have been permitted to proceed, albeit subject to certain conditions. Ungerer has recently argued that:

> [A]pplying strict competition controls to the [media] sector and the related upstream and downstream markets is a necessary pre-condition for achieving effective and sustainable pluralism. This does not mean that competition controls of market development can replace in all cases media specific controls. In many cases specific controls will still be needed to secure media plurality. We will have to keep the balance of competition controls and media specific regulatory controls in mind. (Ungerer 2004a: 16–17)

Many of the recent decisions have centred on the 'upstream' portion of the market, with great emphasis being placed on premium content such as football and film rights. The most recent competition investigations have centred on football rights, with UEFA (COMP/C.2–37.398 – *Joint Selling of the Commercial Rights of the UEFA Champions League* [2003] OJ L 291/25) and the UK's Premier League (COMP/C.2–38.173 and 38.453 – *Joint Selling of the Media Rights of the FA Premier League on an Exclusive Basis* [2003] OJ C 115/3) both coming under scrutiny for their joint selling arrangements. One of the major issues to come out of both of these cases has been the provision of rights to 'new' forms of media delivery, such as broadband Internet and mobile telephony – this seems to be a priority area for the Commission, with Ungerer suggesting that '[m]edia is content. This means that intellectual property rights are the name of the game' (Ungerer 2004b: 7).

Mentioned earlier was the EC-brokered partial unbundling of broadcasting rights for English Premier League soccer, while the UEFA decision and the FA Premier League decision both show the Commission's willingness to impose conditions on content providers in order to facilitate access to rights for new media players and, in the case of the UEFA decision, to offer greater opportunities to free-to-air broadcasters. Although these decisions may have some impact on the development of greater competition and plurality in the media sector, the majority of UEFA and the Premier League's current practices were approved as being the most economically efficient way of conducting the sale of sports rights, so the *status quo* will, on the whole, be maintained.

The *Newscorp/Telepiù* (Case COMP/M.2876 [2004] OJ L 110/73] decision, which concerned the acquisition of two digital satellite broadcasters by Newscorp in order to create a single digital satellite broadcaster, demonstrates that competition law will always be concerned with the economic evidence rather than with the pursuit of pluralism and diversity *per se*. In this case, the Commission decided that the merger would be permitted to go ahead, although the parties were required to enter into a number of divestments and undertakings designed to ensure availability of premium content to companies wishing to broadcast on alternative delivery platforms (such as DTT or cable) and agree to further restrictions on its ability to exploit its links with Telecom Italia, its partner in the merged entity.

It is evident that such a merger does reduce inter-platform competition as after the merger there was only one digital satellite provider in Italy, but the effect on intra-platform competition, *i.e.* competition between channels delivered to viewers by means of the digital satellite, may not be significantly worsened. In essence, the issue of inter-platform competition is largely determined by the effectiveness of the law and regulation designed to ensure access to networks and associated facilities for channel operators. As we will scc, this regulation is largely premised on the 'essential facilities' doctrine and general competition law, the effectiveness of which is not entirely clear.

Ultimately, in the *Telepiù* case, the Commission determined that there were advantages to be gleaned from the merger and, given the extent of the undertakings offered by Newscorp, the merger was not likely to strengthen a dominant position. Under these circumstances, the merger was permitted to proceed. While one should not read too much into this decision, as its impact on the diversity of delivered content may not have been hugely significant given that undertakings had to be given which guaranteed intra-platform competition, it still demonstrates that where there are economic benefits to be gained from a concentration, competition law will not necessarily prevent it. The result of this observation seems to be that modern competition law places less emphasis on *market structure*, which has been the traditional concern of media-specific measures, but will place greater emphasis on the *behaviour* of market players. Given that this is the case, if we are satisfied that pluralism and diversity can only be secured in the media through structural controls, then the current economic thinking which underpins competition law is unlikely to offer a solution to these concerns. In the context of EU competition law Amato has argued that:

> What ought . . . to be dropped is interference in the antitrust area from policies of other types which have so far influenced it. From this viewpoint the

times are, and are beginning to be seen as, ripe for attention to be paid (as has not yet been done) to the new framework set for us by the Maastricht Treaty. On the one hand there is the autonomy of the principle of protecting competition in relation to other principles and to sectoral policies; on the other is the new conception it adopts of industrial policy, seen no longer as a derogation from competition but on the contrary as a promotion of competitive markets. (Amato 1997: 116)

In terms of positive regulation for diversity, however, Doyle (1997) noted some years ago how in practice the EU's agenda appears to have been watered down from originally focusing on pluralism to a new and more limited emphasis on ownership, and it might be thought that the 2002 Directives do not fundamentally alter the direction of this trend. It is submitted that it would be somewhat better for media regulation if Amato's perspective was adopted. Competition law as a tool may, on occasion, lead to a desirable result for the promotion of pluralism and diversity in the media, but this should not be one of its goals. Ultimately, competition law and competition policy will be most effective if they are oriented towards the pursuit of economic efficiency, and in some cases this will lead to concentrations being permitted which we might consider to be undesirable for the maintenance of pluralism and diversity in the media. If this is deemed to be undesirable, then it may be necessary to acknowledge that measures should be adopted which interfere with the normal operation of competition law in order to achieve other goals which are socially beneficial. As Prosser has recently argued:

To accept that such considerations may exist is, however, to beg the question of what values may justify such restrictions on the normal operation of competition law. (Prosser 2005: 27–8)

We discuss some practical outcomes and issues of the approval of the 2003 Carlton/Granada merger on the public service landscape in the next chapter. Even though this merger took place before the UK's 2003 legal framework was fully in effect, the principles involved and issues raised remain constant; only the legal relationships and formal allocation of powers as between government and regulators changes. Implicit in our discussions so far on the tensions between commercial and public service imperatives in the media has been an indication of certain citizenship-related values which might underpin some regulatory measures and interventions which could run counter to the general principles and direction of competition law. The Enterprise Act 2002, as amended by the Communications Act 2003, appears to acknowledge the need to depart from competition law principles in certain cases. Part III of

Chapter 2 of the Enterprise Act 2002, as amended by section 375 of the Communications Act 2003, permits the Secretary of State for Trade and Industry to intervene in the 'public interest' in media mergers. Section 58A of the Enterprise Act 2002, inserted by section 375 of the Communications Act 2003, offers a definition of what is a relevant media merger.

The actual procedure for such an intervention under Part III of Chapter 2 of the Enterprise Act 2002 is complex and has been covered in excellent detail elsewhere (Whish 2003: 898–900), but it is notable that by virtue of section 54(7) of the Enterprise Act 2002 the Secretary of State is not entitled to interfere with the findings of either the OFT or the Competition Commission (CC) findings on the competition aspects of the merger. If the case is referred by the Secretary of State then both Ofcom and the Competition Commission are required to report on the 'public interest' issues which arise from the merger. If the Secretary of State determines that there are legitimate 'public interest' grounds to interfere in the merger then section 55 and Schedule 7 of the Enterprise Act 2002 give the Secretary of State an extensive range of powers to remedy the adverse effects on the 'public interest'.

There is little that the media like better than a story about the media, and following the Draft Communication Bill's publication in May 2002 widespread newspaper coverage was given to two possible consequences of the proposed legislation: the potential for a single owner to dominate Channel 3 (which the Carlton/Granada merger has now essentially achieved) and the possibility of Rupert Murdoch extending his already substantial UK media interests (Feintuck 2004: 113). The substance behind the headlines was that a complex range of provisions applicable specifically to the media, mostly originating from Schedule 2 of the Broadcasting Act 1996 and establishing maximum holdings and intervention thresholds, were to be swept away by the reforms identified above. As the legislation emerged, sections 369–72 of the Communications Act granted Ofcom concurrent powers with the OFT under these Acts, with the potential for further grants of power by the Secretary of State. Under sections 373 and 374, the provisions of the FTA that had historically provided specific measures applicable to takeovers and mergers in newspapers are replaced by the general provisions of the Enterprise Act.

A particular point of interest here is the language used both in the Enterprise Act and Communications Act, where reference is made, respectively, to 'Public Interest Cases' and 'Media Public Interest Considerations'. Section 42(1) of the Enterprise Act allow reference by the

Secretary of State to the OFT via an 'intervention notice' where a public interest consideration is relevant to a merger situation. Incorporated into section 58 of the Enterprise Act by section 375 of the Communications Act are really quite detailed specifications of what constitutes 'the public interest' in relation to mergers between newspapers, between broadcasters and in relation to mergers which cross the two sectors.

These provisions were added late in the Parliamentary process as something of a concession in the Lords and, as Ofcom notes, are 'often described as the plurality test' (http://www.ofcom.org.uk/ media_office/ latest_news/nr_nr_20040105). Ofcom summarises the public interest criteria as follows:

In the case of a newspaper merger, the public interest considerations, as defined by the Act, are:

1. the need for accurate presentation of news in newspapers;
2. the need for free expression of opinion in the newspapers involved in the merger;
3. the need for, to the extent that is reasonable and practicable, a sufficient plurality of views expressed in newspapers as a whole in each market for newspapers in the UK or part of the UK.

In the case of a broadcasting merger or a cross-media merger, the public interest considerations as defined by the Act are:

1. the need for there to be a sufficient plurality of persons with control of the media enterprises serving that audience in relation to every different audience in the UK or a particular area/locality of the UK;
2. the need for availability throughout the UK of a wide range of broadcasting which (taken as a whole) is both of high quality and calculated to appeal to a wide variety of tastes and interests;
3. the need for persons carrying on media enterprises and for those with control of such enterprises to have a genuine commitment to the attainment in relation to broadcasting of the standards objectives set out in section 319 of the Communications Act 2003 (for example, governing matters of accuracy, impartiality, harm, offence, fairness and privacy in broadcasting).

Though at one level these seem quite detailed elaborations of the principles underlying the powers, it is clear that the precise way in which such broad provisions will be interpreted remains subject to substantial discretion on Ofcom's behalf and, ultimately, 'It is in essence for Ofcom to objectively consider whether the new company would have too prominent a voice across all sectors of the media' (Stewart and Gibson 2003: 358).

This regime is interesting because the new system of competition law is based almost entirely on economic considerations and the procedure under Part III of Chapter 2 is the only part of the Enterprise Act 2002 which bestows a significant role on the Secretary of State. By preventing the Secretary of State from interfering with the competition findings of the OFT and CC it forces the engagement of arguments from the 'public interest' – a concept which is not elucidated clearly by the Enterprise Act 2002 or, indeed, any other source of UK law (Feintuck 2004: chapter 3). The DTI has produced an extensive document (DTI 2004) which offers some illustration of the considerations that the Secretary of State will take into account in such situations, although it offers little indication of the relative weight that will be placed on the various factors discussed in the document. Especially in the early years of the new regulator exercising this jurisdiction, companies involved in actual or proposed mergers will require guidance as to how the powers will be used, and Ofcom moved quickly after taking up its powers to indicate how it would go about offering general advice as regards proposed mergers. In essence, Ofcom's advice (http://www.ofcom.org.uk/codes_guidelines/ ofcom_codes_guidance/pi_test/pi_legal) mirrors the DTI guidance, but in reality amounts to little more than a restatement of the provisions summarised above and identifies its role as being one of applying the tests and reporting the results to the Secretary of State with a recommendation as to whether the merger should be referred to the Competition Commission for further consideration. Our essential position on this aspect of the new regime has been set out previously:

> Though Ofcom only plays one part in a process which is triggered and concluded by the Secretary of State, and with the Competition Commission playing a significant role, Ofcom's advice will surely be influential. While suspicions have been voiced by some media owners, that the provisions continue to permit an unhealthy degree of political influence over the sensitive issue of media takeovers and mergers, in fact the range of public interest criteria established under section 375 and subsequent sections do outline some key factors which might usefully form the basis for a meaningful version of the concept in this context and which may establish a framework against which decisions must be justified. Though there is clearly scope for interpretation in individual cases, they do provide a structure to the regulator's discretion. However,

one is left with a feeling that, although the Secretary of State, will now operate within the context of more transparent advice from the Competition Commission, the political role will indeed remain significant, just as it did under the former FTA provisions regarding takeovers and mergers in the newspaper sector. (Feintuck 2004: 115)

Clearly, it is not the case that the apparent objectivity suggested by economics and competition law, or the independence of regulation from government promised by the appearance of the super-regulator Ofcom, have actually occurred in this context. As critics of the new regime can argue:

> Ofcom's public interest test cannot be applied in every takeover because its inquiries can only be triggered by the Trade and Industry Secretary. This means that a government, of whatever hue, can decide which bidder should undergo such a test and which should not. That decision will, of course, be subjective. However remote the possibility, it allows a government to make a political judgement about referral which could be based, not unfeasibly, on a bidder's attitude towards its administration. (*Guardian*, 12 January 2004)

There are also some further, potentially serious, technical-legal difficulties in establishing competition rules in relation to media markets which are relevant here. In particular, problems of market definition (see, for example, Carter 2001) and measuring market share (for example, comparing readership and audience on national and local bases) which form prior questions to scrutinising dominance within a market comprise serious obstacles to a rational and predictable system.

A balanced view here must surely lead to the conclusion that the degree of transparency imported into the regime under the new provisions *may* make a substantial difference in adding credibility and legitimacy to the system. Clearly, in addition, the new merger provisions do go some way towards identifying a public interest test for takeovers and mergers in the media. However, the same balanced account must also highlight the fact that the approach is not one that will be applied in every case, that it is not as objective as might be thought or expected, and it should also be emphasised for the avoidance of any doubt that these public interest criteria apply *only* to that part of Ofcom's brief which relates to takeovers and mergers.

It is, however, clear that the 'public interest' procedure contained in the Enterprise Act 2002 is an exceptional one, which permits the Secretary of State to depart from economic analysis where this is deemed to be necessary. At the present time, no interventions have been made into media mergers under the 'public interest' procedure (http://www.dti. gov.uk/ccp/topics2/mergerspi.htm), so it is not possible for us to see how the Secretary of State will put flesh onto the bones of the guidance in the context of an actual case. The 'public interest' procedure reflects the contents of the EC Merger Regulation (Regulation 139/2004/EC [2004] OJ L 24/1), under which Article 21(4) permits Member States to apply their own law in order to protect 'legitimate interests', including 'plurality of the media'. Once again, the Merger Regulation renders it evident that Article 21(4) is an exceptional measure which permits the departure from competition law in order to protect interests which Member States consider to be important.

In summary, this section has argued that while competition law has been employed in pursuit of a number of conflicting goals in the past, EC competition law, and consequently UK competition law under the Competition Act 1998, has come closer to pursuing the goal of economic efficiency as a sole aim. An examination of some of the recent cases in the media sector appear to demonstrate that the application of competition law will lead to desirable outcomes for pluralism and diversity in some cases, but this is by no means guaranteed. As such, both EC competition law and UK competition law have acknowledged that it may be necessary to depart from economic analysis where the public interest so demands, although the precise extent of the permitted departure is unclear. There also remain a further range of underlying issues rendering the application of competition law problematic in relation to the media. In particular, significant difficulties exist in relation to market definition, especially as regards industries such as the media in which both the outer boundaries (for example, where 'media' meet telecommunications) and internal sectoral divides are increasingly blurred by technological convergence and corporate conglomeration. However, account must also be taken of the fact that in addition to pursuing the outcomes associated with 'perfect' or 'workable' competition, there may be a range of other objectives which are explicitly or implicitly embodied in competition regimes. Such matters would include assisting governments in achieving policy objectives in terms of regional employment or price inflation policies and, at the international level, protectionism or, particularly significant in the case of the EU, the pursuit of an integrated single market.

However, what is clear is that competition law, and the regulatory framework for media regulation more generally, is not based solely upon foundations of economic theory of competition. It appears at times to incorporate, if not to acknowledge fully, the existence of social objectives beyond competition as an end in itself and does not simply assume that market forces will deliver all that democracy expects of its media; in Whish's terms, competition law does not operate in a vacuum, and may have a range of objectives beyond those identified in the economic model. A strict adherence to competition theory raises difficulties in relation to externalities (social costs) and, in particular in relation to media regulation, these must include, crucially, the consideration of ensuring the maintenance of 'that variety of sources of information which is necessary for an effective democracy' (Barendt 1995: 122).

It could be concluded that competition law appears to have absorbed rather than clarified the inherent contradictions and tensions between the competing strands that comprise 'the public interest' in media regulation. Beyond such a position, some may regard competition law's increased focus on economic efficiency as an undesirable development. It is possible, however, to argue that this actually serves to clear the waters in the case of media regulation. If competition law is now focused on economic efficiency, then this obliges us to acknowledge that if we are to pursue pluralism and diversity as explicit goals, then this must be supported not from the values inherent in competition law, but by reference to the broader legal and constitutional framework which exists in EU and UK law. Though this may appear to pose challenges in the British context, establishing connections between constitutional principle and competition in the media sectors is not necessarily impossible. Just as competition law does not operate in an environment free of everything but pure economic theory, so also regulation of the media should not be free from constitutional input. Barendt sets out examples, from Germany, Italy and the US, of the constitutional courts stepping in to support legislative attempts to further media pluralism. Most notably, he refers to the role of France's Conseil Constitutionnel in establishing constitutional status for the principle of plurality of sources of information (Barendt 1995: 127). The extent to which constitutions make either a potential or actual difference to regulatory outcomes in relation to the media is very much the subject of Chapter 6; however, there appears, from Barendt's account, evidence to suggest that clarification of the underlying rationale(s) for media regulation might best be achieved via a consideration of the constitutional fundamentals. Unsurprisingly perhaps, however, nowhere are these fundamentals likely to be more nebulous than in the UK, where the public interest in media regulation is not spelled out and is, as will be demonstrated later in this chapter and the next, largely subject to potential definition only by the executive rather than any higher constitutional authority.

3.3 THE SEDUCTIVE CHARMS OF CHOICE

It has already been noted that the privileging of choice offers attractions, not only to libertarians on grounds of principle, but also as a pragmatic solution to the dilemma of state intervention in the media identified above. While digital broadcasting technology appears to offer the potential for almost unlimited choice of channel, critics of unmitigated market forces note that 'channel abundance is no guarantee against concentration of ownership or against homogeneity of content, which can result from competition for the same mass audience' (McQuail 1992: 175).

Choice is certainly significant in liberal-democratic theory, though whether as an end in itself or instrumentally as a means to achieving or fulfilling other ends is open to debate. What is not open to question, however, is that choice in this context must be informed choice. Choice based on inadequate information cannot be considered choice in any meaningful sense. Equally, meaningful choice must be between a range of attractive, desirable, differentiated options; the choice between fifty or a hundred remarkably similar options is scarcely worthy of the name.

Given that the media provide essential elements of our view of the world, the role of the media in facilitating meaningful choice must not be underestimated. In order for citizens to make considered choices based on adequate information, it is generally considered necessary for the media to deliver a wide range of perspectives – media plurality as a prerequisite of meaningful choice. The argument must now become 'how, by what structures and mechanisms, can media plurality be maximised and ensured?' Not surprisingly, the hegemony of individualism in British politics from the 1980s into this century has emphasised individual choice, but also supported market mechanisms as the best means of facilitating it.

Clearly, law can have an important instrumental role to play in ensuring such choice, and a relatively rare consideration of the relationship between 'Choice and the Legal Order' is provided by Lewis (1996). The present authors focus on choice specifically as instrumental in pursuit of citizenship rather than the more general goal of human agency pursued by Lewis, though this difference in emphasis renders Lewis's approach no less relevant.

Lewis (1996: 114) states that 'The market order is . . . a system of free exchange governed by rules which governments enforce, but it should not be subject to arbitrary and coercive intervention by government in relation to the details of exchanges between individuals.' In essence, Lewis is claiming that choice, in a democracy, is not confined to 'high politics' but to everyday relations, and that the law has an important facilitative as opposed to coercive role to play. He goes on to note the potential benefits and risks of market competition and the roles of government in this context. Processes of privatisation, contracting out or market testing in relation to what were previously public services delivered by public monopolies have introduced a degree of competition into such areas and, claims Lewis, 'All these experiments chime with the logic of choice, diversity and experiment and many of them are to be welcomed at face value' (1996: 120). He accepts, however, that the evidence from consideration of such reforms to date has been mixed in relation to the extent to which choice has been extended. In some areas, for example the introduction of quasi-market forces into state-funded schooling, there is little doubt that the range of measures originating from the Education Reform Act 1988 have in reality done little or nothing to enhance meaningful choice and have also, in practice, moved the decision-making power largely out of zones of accountability via conventional democratic mechanisms, relocating the power to choose not with 'consumers' but with those delivering schooling who may be subject only to the flimsiest accountability mechanisms. There is also evidence in this area to suggest that the exercise of such choice as exists has been uneven, tending to reproduce or heighten social hierarchy (Feintuck 1994). Despite such concerns, the *zeitgeist* appears to demand the ongoing pursuit of such policies as a matter of political principle. Indeed, market principles are now far more embedded in UK public services than ten years ago, when Lewis was writing on the subject. The New Labour government's 2005 White Paper (DFES 2005) on education makes it clear that their education policy is driven by the same principles, and looks likely to replicate the same issues and problems as were introduced by their Conservative predecessors.

The apparent failure of some such experiments does not, however, prove that the underlying logic of choice and diversity through competition is fatally flawed. It does though serve to illustrate usefully that whatever constitutional value is attached to choice *per se* must be weighed against competing values such as accountability and equity. The sort of liberty and citizenship envisaged in liberal democracy includes choice, but not to the exclusion of other values.

Lewis goes on to conclude that, in relation to the consideration of the role of choice in Western societies, 'What has been missing is a clear and public philosophical programme grounded in a contemporary catalogue of human rights operating alongside a set of congruent social and economic objectives interpreted through processes of institutional fact-finding and dialogue' (1996: 126). This is undoubtedly correct and, for better or worse, the media has a crucial role to play in this process. If citizens, diverse as they are, are to make meaningful inputs into this process, they require access to a media which is in itself diverse, allowing them to absorb and triangulate information provided from a range of perspectives. In the absence of access to media, citizens will not be in a position to exercise informed choice. Given its essential nature in relation to democracy, the media cannot be treated like a commodity; the democratic premium on diversity and universal availability means that these features cannot be left to chance. We will return in the concluding chapter to arguments concerning the protection of, after Stewart (1983), 'non-commodity values'. However, such arguments seem increasingly marginalised in an increasingly economics-driven political debate. In the modern, market, context, Schiller (1996: 126) observes that 'Substituted for . . . elemental human aspirations is the promise of consumer choice – a choice that is not genuine – and a hopelessly narrow standard of production efficiency.'

While the role of choice in media markets is, at one level, uncontested in that choice should be maximised for all citizens, at another level a crucial question remains as to how best to deliver this choice. Would a laissez-faire media market best deliver this plurality or diversity, or are alternative, interventionist, regulatory mechanisms required?

Lewis (1996: 123) states that 'Regulation is almost always a second-best enterprise', but goes on to accept that 'There are many reasons for regulating desired goals into existence' (124). He states that 'There is no denying the pace of continued regulation. What is more evasive is a clear unifying philosophy' in the context of 'the untheoretic, pragmatic approach to regulation in the UK' (125).

While 'the principle of freedom of communication presupposes an abundance of channels and choices as desirable conditions of a free and democratic society' (McQuail 1992: 175), the strong tendency of media markets towards oligopoly has already been noted and the potential risk to diversity in media output thus indicated. It seems therefore that a valid case for media regulation remains; freedom for media market players, though apparently desirable in principle, is clearly an area in which it is necessary, in Lewis's terms, 'to regulate desired goals into existence'. What those desired goals might be, and how best to achieve them, is very much the focus of this book. If meaningful citizen choice is given a high priority and this requires access to a diverse range of media, then it will be necessary to limit the freedom of those who play in the media market. The form and structure of such regulation, especially in terms of whether its focus will be primarily structural, behavioural or content-oriented, can only be chosen meaningfully when the goals are adequately clarified.

It should be noted, however, that in so far as behavioural regulation is adopted this will imply the restriction of the property rights of those who own or control the media infrastructure, a theme to be returned to in Chapter 7. If justification is required in relation to the restriction of property rights in the media, it can be found in the fact that in relation to many commodities, the consequences of market forces will not have fundamental, democratic repercussions while in relation to others, including the media, which have characteristics and significance extending beyond their market value, a minimum standard of service will be deemed essential in the interests of citizenship. In relation to services such as power and water, such interests receive a degree of protection via the imposition of USOs, although even here a high premium will be placed by citizens on price and service efficiency in relation to what is a largely undifferentiated product; I may choose between gas suppliers, but the product will remain essentially the same. In relation to the media, however, the universal availability of a wide range of 'products' has, in itself, the status of a democratic prerequisite, and the same 'product' will not necessarily be available from a range of suppliers. Thus both the commodification of media, pointed towards by Schiller (1996) and many other commentators, and the associated handing-over of media distribution to unmitigated market forces must, in the name of democracy, be resisted.

3.4 RESOLVING THE TENSIONS BETWEEN COMPETING RATIONALES: THE CURRENT STATE OF PLAY

The existing oligopolistic situation in the British media suggests that attempts to date to ensure plurality and diversity have failed, at least in so far as pluralism in ownership is concerned. That said, at present, a fair diversity of product, in broadcasting at least, is still available to all via existing PSB mechanisms. Monopoly control of major sporting events and movie premieres, though in itself significant, is somewhat marginal to the overall scheme of things, though is perhaps significant as a portent of things to come.

Various forms of competition law both media specific and general, have, as discussed earlier and as will be seen throughout the next two chapters, become increasingly significant as mechanisms of media regulation. While it might be expected that the objectives of such mechanisms would be primarily economic, given the theoretical foundation of competition law, in practice, intervention in the name of competition is used as a tool available to government to be applied in the pursuit of a range of objectives, sometimes to do with national economic objectives (for example, addressing price inflation), sometimes with international objectives (for example, protectionism, or integrationism in Europe) or sometimes with broader social/political objectives (for example, the preservation of jobs by allowing newspaper takeovers where the alternative would be closure). The problem, of course, with this latter approach is that the employment objective may cut across the objective of plurality of media ownership. Earlier in this chapter, examples were provided of how both government policy documents, and their manifestation in legislation, have incorporated rather than resolved potentially conflicting objectives.

Intervention via competition law might be, on occasion, resisted by those commercial enterprises whose growth or sales are affected by limits on expansion imposed and enforced by the competition authorities; they may claim, in the media context, that such restrictions run counter to their right to free expression. Though the US courts have addressed this issue, it may prove more difficult in the UK where constitutional principles are less clear. Certainly Barendt (1995: 166) demonstrates that American courts have identified this as a matter of limiting property, or profit-making rights, rather than an issue of freedom of expression, and sought to privilege plurality of media above these claims. That said, Marsden's analysis (Marsden 1997a) of US regulation of the pay-television market suggests that regulatory interventions have derived from a strongly consumerist paradigm, which may be thought ultimately to accept rather than challenge the commodification of media. It would not be surprising if this were also to prove the basis upon which any future EU initiatives were also to be based, with any resulting benefits for citizens as citizens being purely contingent upon benefits granted to them in their more limited capacity as consumers.

The application of consumerist rhetoric to media markets and the potentially perverse results it may produce have been noted. If choice of product is an objective, either as an end in itself or as a prerequisite of citizenship, then the media market must be regulated against the operation of free market forces which, by themselves, would be likely to produce oligopoly or monopoly and therefore run counter to an objective of plurality or diversity. In addition, from a different perspective, free market approaches to media markets raise issues which, while not of significance to proponents of consumerism, appear to fall within general constitutional expectations. Equality of citizenship appears to presuppose a degree of equality of access to media output and, if a significant part of the range of media product is available only to those with the means to buy it, the principle of equality of citizenship appears to be breached. The question of where the line should be drawn, where something akin to USOs need be applied and where they need not, is returned to in Chapter 7.

It is therefore apparent that, short of the adoption of a totally laissez faire approach to media markets and an acceptance of the likely inegalitarian, anti-democratic consequences, intervention will take place in pursuit of economic or social objectives, though overt adoption of the rhetoric of social objectives remains, even under 'New' Labour, somewhat unfashionable, being associated with active attempts at social engineering in the tradition of 'Old' politics. The combination of the application of New Right consumerist rhetoric and 'New' Labour's shyness over identifying and pursuing social objectives has allowed the development and continuation of a retreat away from traditional public service ideals in the media, and in broadcasting in particular. Certainly, it would now be unimaginable to find senior politicians supporting anything approaching a public monopoly, or even a publicly regulated duopoly, in broadcasting, a situation which persisted not so very long ago.

Alternative devices for intervention and regulation, such as the imposition of levies or granting of cash aid by government, have generally in Britain been considered inappropriate, at least in relation to the newspaper industry. Unlike in relation to the cinema industry, which we touched on earlier, concern over being associated either with state control or state censorship has seemed to underlie government's reluctance to become involved in financing the newspaper market in pursuit of diversity. This is so despite the fact that it would be perfectly possible, as in The Netherlands and Scandinavia (Humphreys 1996: 105–6) to engage in such a practice, perhaps through an intermediate body, without adverse inferences necessarily being drawn. Admittedly, though, differences in state and constitutional traditions would need to be addressed.

Ultimately, the devices utilised to regulate the media and the conception of the public interest which they have been intended to pursue have been arrived at on a pragmatic, inconsistent, and historically contingent basis. As such, it is difficult to discern a common thread running through these regulatory devices other than a commitment to ensuring, to a minimum extent at least, a degree of diversity in sources of information. Though the diversity objective is often found in combination with competing objectives, all of the mechanisms for intervention identified so far contain diversity or plurality as one aspect. Even the consumerist, anti-interventionist, rhetoric assumes and takes on board the concept of diversity of product in its privileging of choice as the key objective.

It can be debated whether the existing situation of oligopoly fulfils the demands of diversity. Whatever the answer to this question, however, the ongoing processes of technological convergence and development of cross-media empires suggest that the status quo will be unlikely to remain in place. The forces of convergence and conglomeration imply a great threat even to such diversity as presently exists, and for those who instinctively have a problem with this likelihood some rational basis for regulation towards other ends must be found.

This lowest common denominator in existing regulation may prove helpful in considering the basis for a new construction of the public interest. Diversity of output appears to be central to all the regulatory approaches, though at times can be countered by other objectives in opposition to it. What appears to be needed is a clearer understanding of *why* diversity of output is the common element across all the regulatory approaches before a meaningful rationale can be discerned and, in turn, a structure of objectives and institutional arrangements for their attainment can be established. It can reasonably be expected that this rationale will have something to do with the needs of democracy and of citizenship.

3.5 CITIZENSHIP AS THE PUBLIC INTEREST?

When the French Conseil Constitutionnel, considering the 1986 Broadcasting Bill, in effect gave constitutional status to the principle of plurality of sources of information, and when the Italian and German courts have ruled also that competition law applicable to commercial broadcasting should be sufficiently strong as to safeguard 'plurality of opinion' (Barendt 1995: chapter 6), the constitutional significance of media regulation is highlighted. It appears to be constitutionally necessary to protect, in Barendt's terms, 'that variety of sources of information which is necessary for an effective democracy' (122). At this point, unfortunately, many commentators leave the argument, apparently content in having identified the public interest. However, this plurality of information sources should not be viewed as end in itself in this context, but rather, according to Barendt's typology (Barendt 1985), as a means to achieving truth, self-fulfilment or effective participation in democracy by citizens.

McQuail (1992: 22), however, does take this further, identifying, after Held (1970), a tripartite typology of public interest theories. The first of these, 'preponderance theory', identifies the public interest with the preferences of a simple majority of the public, appearing to be consistent with market logic but failing to reflect what McQuail (23) refers to as 'the broader notion that public interest means something more than the sum of individual preferences'. The second approach, 'common interest' theory, refers to 'cases where the interests in question are ones which *all* members are *presumed* to have in common, with little scope for dispute over preferences' (original emphasis). Typical examples provided by McQuail of areas in which such theory may be applied include utilities and matters such as defence and policing, which commonly fall under the classification of 'public goods' discussed earlier. The difficulty identified by McQuail in relation to this approach is that while it facilitates the assertion of certain general objectives as legitimate, including access to media as channels of public communication, it 'does not demonstrate the necessity (or demand) for meeting any particular claim'.

The third of Held's categories discussed by McQuail (1992: 23), the 'unitary theory', he states amounts to 'the assertion of some absolute normative principle, usually deriving from some larger social theory or ideology'. In this connection, McQuail notes that unitary theories in relation to the public interest in the media can derive from quite different bases, for example from an ideological belief in either public or private ownership of media, or from claims to education, protection of minors, or of national language and culture. While acknowledging the weaknesses associated with the application of unitary theory which McQuail notes, in particular potential 'insensitivity to popular wants' and even more problematic, he states, 'their frequently authoritarian, paternalistic or ideologically contestable character' (25), it seems reasonable to state that a unitary approach to media regulation based explicitly upon citizenship as its organising ideal would not, within liberal-democratic theory, be inappropriate or encounter the other potential problems he identifies.

Thus it can be argued that, of Barendt's three lines of argument for freedom of expression, the third, citizen participation, is the most pressing, relating most closely to our fundamental democratic expectations and implying a unitary theory of public interest based upon citizenship. It also, as it happens, chimes with the rhetoric, if not necessarily the policies, of the Major and Blair governments. Addressing inequalities of citizenship, or 'multiple deprivation' or 'social exclusion', therefore becomes a central and legitimate aim for media regulation.

Admittedly, in a society which is fundamentally inegalitarian, equality of citizenship may be viewed sceptically, from the Left, as a poor surrogate for substantive equality, though it may also have attractions, in terms of proving more readily definable and certainly more likely to appear attainable within the capitalist system, and may serve as a salve for our collective, liberal conscience. In so far as the media are implicated in the delivery of this plurality of sources of information, difficult questions must be raised as to where the line is drawn as to what parts of the media output are necessary prerequisites for citizenship, and which (if any) are not. Before attempting to address this question, albeit tentatively, however, it is best first to clarify what exactly is meant by 'citizenship' and to question further its adoption in this context.

Though T. H. Marshall may be much criticised, his tripartite construction of citizenship, developed in the 1950s and early 1960s, remains a crucial landmark around which many discussions revolve and from which others depart. Barbalet (1988: 5) summarises Marshall's construct of citizenship as stating 'firstly, that citizenship is a status attached to full membership of a community, and secondly, that those who possess this status are equal with respect to the rights and duties associated with it'.

In essence, Marshall (1964: 78) identifies three 'elements' of citizenship: first, 'civil', 'the rights necessary for individual freedom – liberty of person, freedom of speech, thought and faith, the right to own property and to conclude valid contracts, and the right to justice'; second, 'political' – 'the right to participate in the exercise of political power, as a member of a body vested with political authority or as an elector of the members of such a body'; third, 'social' – 'the whole range from the right to a modicum of economic welfare and security to the right to share to the full in the social heritage and to live the life of a civilised being according to the standards prevailing in society', or, in Barbalet's terms, 'a right to the prevailing standard of life and the social heritage of the society' (Barbalet 1988: 6).

Interestingly, as Hogan (1997: 45) points out, Marshall's approach to citizenship is 'institutionally grounded', and, we might note, historically contingent:

> The specification and elaboration of each of these bundles of citizen rights was a contingent function of the differentiation and development of distinctive institutions – the law courts, parliamentary democracy, and the welfare state – at different moments in the history of citizenship.

While the institutional structure and procedural values are clearly significant in this connection, this is not to the exclusion of clearly stated, substantive values. Thus the attainment of Marshall's construct of citizenship appears to be closely associated with the full range of law jobs identified, after Llewellyn, by Harden and Lewis and referred to in Chapter 1. Though not necessarily adopting Marshall's concept of citizenship, Harden and Lewis (1986) echo parts of it, noting that 'the expectations of citizenship are unlikely to remain static' (10) and associating the institutional framework with the underlying, value-laden, precept of the rule of law (as a principle of institutional morality). They note also that 'Rule of law values . . . deny any ultimate division between the principles of citizenship and the requirements of effective government' (302).

Clearly, citizenship is central to the nature of democratic society and indeed for Ranson and Stewart (1989) is the unifying value for the public domain, though its precise definition will be subject to debate, and indeed historical capture and reinterpretation. Thus it will be necessary to be clear as to precisely what is meant when the term is used in the context of debates regarding any contemporary phenomenon such as the media.

Though presently unfashionable, if we return to Reith's tripartite definition of the BBC's function as the archetypal public service broadcaster, we find a high degree of mesh between 'informing, educating and entertaining' and the needs of Marshall's civic, political and social' aspects of citizenship. Certainly, there is a close parallel of civic and political citizenship goals in the media's 'educating and informing' functions, though the extent to which entertainment forms part of the social citizenship agenda may be more contestable. Clearly, there is the risk of this being considered grossly oversimplistic, with the definitions in themselves being too vague to be helpful. However, it is of some utility in indicating how the full range of the conventional public service remit is relevant to citizenship.

What this suggests – and this proposition will be returned to – is that if something akin to this model of citizenship is an objective, something akin to the range of products provided by the PSB model will have to be made equally available to all if anything approaching equality of citizenship is to be achieved or maintained. The problem, of course, is that not all media deliver this range, with an increasing number of niche market providers specialising in entertainment. There may be some difficulty in determining whether social citizenship demands that we all have access to live coverage of England soccer or cricket games as part of our cultural heritage, or whether the citizenship ideal is unabridged if we all have access only to highlights, while only those able or willing to pay extra for the facility may watch it live. Less controversial, however, is the question whether citizenship demands that we all have free access to a whole range of editorial views in the run-up to a general election, or whether it is sufficient that we all have access to one or two 'impartial' accounts, with more politically affiliated views available to those who wish to and are able to purchase them. The latter, of course, is the current situation, with the BBC and ITV coverage, though perhaps less heavily regulated than hitherto, in theory providing a degree of 'balance' in coverage which would not necessarily result from the market driven, privately controlled, press. The direct implication of this is a reassertion of the necessity for public service media in fulfilling expectations of citizenship.

There are, nonetheless, real practical problems which must be addressed by those advocating citizenship as a central or organising concept in debates over the current and future regulation of the media. In general, these difficulties revolve around the question 'How equal must access to the media be in pursuit of equality of citizenship?' Such problems have not, however, prevented commentators from advocating this approach, though without necessarily identifying clearly with a 'unitary' as opposed to 'common interest' concept of the public interest. Translating such sentiments or values into practical policy initiatives or law in the field of media regulation must inevitably seem well-nigh impossible when the underlying fundamental purpose is so often unclear. Yet there is no doubt that reforms of media regulation are often preceded by some effort to establish a fundamental base for the regulatory regime, though close inspection will reveal that this process is invariably more about scoring political points than about a quest to establish theoretical coherence. This is certainly true of New Labour's policies which developed into the Communications Act 2003. Unfortunately perhaps, much of the essential flavour and value which made the initial policy somewhat attractive seems to have been lost in the course of its transformation into law.

3.6 THE COMMUNICATIONS ACT 2003 AND THE 'PUBLIC INTEREST'

It is clear that the New Labour government's media policy was influenced heavily by the output of the 'think-tank' the Institute for Public Policy Research (IPPR). The media agenda developed by the IPPR emerged in the work of Collins and Murroni (1996), and showed clear links to the findings of the IPPR's Commission on Social Justice, where aspects of citizenship were emphasised and ultimately utilised to justify regulation of the media. Collins and Murroni emphasise the Commission's findings that 'the foundation of a free society is the equal worth of all citizens' (Collins and Murroni 1996: 13), and this principle is used to serve as an overarching objective for specific areas of social policy. This is translated by them into the specific context of media regulation when they state that 'freedom of access to the information necessary to full participation in economic, political and social life is a central element of citizens' entitlements in modern societies' (Collins and Murroni 1996: 76). In theory, this looks like a welcome attempt to establish a clearly principled and proactive agenda, breaking with the reactive and *ad hoc* traditions of the past, and one which recognises the centrality of citizenship concerns which has been observed in this book. It seems to relate closely to, but in some ways go beyond, the citizen participation agenda identified in Chapter 1. Collins and Murroni also very reasonably pointed towards the desirability of establishing a single 'super-regulator' to reflect the realities of the increasingly convergent and conglomerated media industries, and their proposal for 'Ofcom' became the central feature of the Blair government's 2000 White Paper.

As was argued in the first edition of this book, given the realities of modern media markets and technology, the introduction of one regulator to take on many of the functions of the then five existing bodies (Broadcasting Standards Commission, Independent Television Commission, Radio Authority, Radiocommunications Agency and Oftel) seemed eminently sensible. In many ways, the reformed structure still has much to commend it when compared to what went before. In particular, given the reality of close intertwining between delivery mechanism and product in broadcasting markets, it may well be that one super-regulator is indeed better placed to take an overview of market realities as opposed to a range of regulators focusing on different aspects. However, any welcome given to this body should not be without reservations. As has been argued elsewhere (Feintuck 2004: 107, original emphasis), 'Simply put, replacing many regulators with one does not *in itself* guarantee either more consistent or more principled regulation, or regulation which necessarily better serves objectives which might be associated with the public interest.' In addition, it should be noted that, predictably, New Labour has declined to address the perennial question of self-regulation of the press industry.

As suggested above, the real test was to be the extent to which the IPPR agenda with its emphasis on citizenship concerns was translated into legislative and administrative reality. If the central, informing concept remained undefined or inadequately specified and prioritised, there would be a great likelihood that the underlying values would be no better protected than hitherto.

A rare attempt to address such issues head on was made in 2002 in the course of scrutinising the UK government's draft Communications Bill by a joint committee of the House of Lords and House of Commons chaired by renowned film-maker and Labour-supporting life peer Lord David Puttnam (Puttnam Report 2002). Though it may be felt that the final form of the Communications Act 2003 (aspects of which are considered in Chapter 4) does not fully or adequately reflect the Puttnam Committee's findings, consideration of the Committee's report is nonetheless instructive in terms of helping to identify an agenda which reflects a citizenship-oriented approach, and which may be thought to remain absent from the current legislative framework (Feintuck 2003).

In 2000 the New Labour government in its second term in office issued a White Paper, *A New Future for Communications*. While the White Paper and the 2003 Act might properly be considered as being largely institutional in their focus, respectively proposing and establishing a large, if not quite single, regulator for the media to replace the previous somewhat fragmented structure, it can be argued that there remained a failure to address adequately underlying questions regarding principles and objectives for the regulatory system. An alternative perspective could be that the legislation as it emerged did indeed reflect a particular set of values, those of a faith in market forces characterised by reforms to competition law and an emphasis on deregulation, and the abandonment or marginalisation of a public service tradition in British broadcasting. In any case, the consequence is that the legislation failed to give any significant priority to citizenship-related factors.

It should be emphasised here that the context from which the legislation eventually emerged was not set entirely by the UK government's perspectives and priorities but was also influenced significantly, and perhaps given momentum, by a set of four Directives issued by the EU in March 2002. These Directives and the EU agenda in relation to the media will be examined in some detail in Chapter 6, but it is worth noting now that the primary orientation of these measures is towards the removal of obstacles to the creation of a single European market. Of course, though such an agenda may not necessarily be inconsistent with a citizenship-driven approach, it certainly starts from a very different point and is likely to prioritise a very different set of issues.

The Puttnam Report identified and highlighted a particular problem with the then Draft Bill in terms of how the newly created regulator, Ofcom, would prioritise competing priorities which would be absorbed into the domestic legislation from the EU's Framework Directive. Likewise, the report pointed towards the absence of any indication as to how Ofcom should prioritise some fifteen general and potentially conflicting duties set out in Clause 3 of the Draft Bill. Instead of being given clear direction, or even guidance, Ofcom was to be left to resolve any conflicts 'in the manner they think best in the circumstances', granting apparently wide-ranging and almost unfettered discretion. This was clearly mutually convenient for the government, who thus avoided substantial additional political controversy, and for Ofcom, as regulators, for obvious reasons, tend to prefer wide-ranging powers. However, it may be thought problematic from the point of view of leaving a high degree of certainty around how values, apparently fundamental to the policy, would actually be protected in practice.

The report also went on to note that a concept of 'citizen interests', which had been at the forefront of the government's White Paper and had informed the IPPR agenda which had apparently informed New Labour's media regulation policies, had failed to feature in the duties established in the Draft Bill. In perhaps the most telling of its many important findings, the Puttnam Report identified as 'an abdication of responsibility' the failure by Parliament to specify a hierarchy of duties for the new super-regulator, and recommended explicitly the establishment of a 'principal duty' embodying specifically and explicitly 'the long-term interests of all citizens' (para. 26).

The Communications Act 2003, as it finally emerged from the Parliamentary process, did incorporate some of the Puttnam Report's recommendations, and in some senses the words of section 3(1) may appear a major victory for the Scrutiny Committee:

> It shall be the principal duty of Ofcom, in carrying out their functions –
> (a) to further the interests of citizens in relation to communications matters; and
> (b) to further the interests of consumers in relevant markets, where appropriate by promoting competition.

Certainly, this reference to 'the interests of citizens' is to be welcomed. However, as we have noted elsewhere, the values will not in practice be prioritised to the extent that section 3(1) might suggest. This is because subsequent sections and subsections of the Act raise an enormous list of issues for Ofcom to consider, and without the hierarchy of duties or values which Puttnam sought:

> [T]he subsequent list of 'things which Ofcom are required to secure', and to which they 'must also have regard' totals some nineteen factors, which, under

Section 3(7), if these duties conflict, Ofcom must, in the original words of the Bill, resolve 'in the manner they think best in the circumstances'. Thus, though Section 3(6) does establish a priority for EU obligations, the clear hierarchy of duties sought by Puttnam otherwise remains absent, just as it did under the 1996 Act, leaving wide-ranging and largely unstructured discretion in the regulator's hands, and citizenship interests vulnerable to defeat by other factors. In practice, it may well be that the deregulatory agenda established by Section 6, which requires Ofcom in effect to ensure the lightest feasible level of regulation, might prove a major factor in directing Ofcom's approach to such matters, and may certainly be expected to discourage the kind of active intervention required to ensure the protection of citizenship interests. Though requirements of transparency via reasoned decision-making are imposed in relation to 'important cases', potentially contributing to the accountability of the regulator, this is not the same thing as establishing a statutory priority for citizenship-related interests. (Feintuck 2004: 109)

At the most general level, it therefore seems that the vulnerability of broad public interests in media regulation has not been satisfactorily remedied by the Communications Act 2003. That said, it may still be too early to say precisely how things will work out. It is clear though that, in general, any improvement in such respect is not guaranteed by the statutory framework, but is dependent upon the exercise of the regulator's broad discretionary powers.

Late in the legislative process, as noted above, as something of a concession in the House of Lords to pressure arising from the Puttnam Committee's detailed and telling scrutiny of the Draft Bill, section 375 of the Communications Act incorporated into section 58 of the Enterprise Act provisions relating to public interest (PI) interventions into mergers within the media industries. We noted earlier in this chapter how Ofcom's powers under these provisions do relate to a moderately clearly specified vision of the PI, focusing in effect on whether the proposed new company would have too powerful a presence across the media as a whole. However, Ofcom's exercise of these PI intervention powers will be engaged only at the instigation of the Secretary of State, allowing the possibility of party political influence and hence inconsistency in their application. More generally, it is doubtful whether these measures go any significant way towards resolving the overall lack of clarity as to understanding and application of the public interest in the context of media regulation (Feintuck, 2004: 112–16).

At the most general level, it therefore seems that the vulnerability of broad public interests in media regulation has not been satisfactorily remedied by the Communications Act 2003. The underlying problems are perhaps most clearly illustrated by Ofcom's own summary of its roles, which it states as being to:

- Balance the promotion of choice and competition with the duty to foster plurality, informed citizenship, protect viewers, listeners and customers and promote cultural diversity.
- Serve the interests of the citizen-consumer as the communications industry enters the digital age.
- Support the need for innovators, creators and investors to flourish within markets driven by full and fair competition between all providers.
- Encourage the evolution of electronic media and communications networks to the greater benefit of all who live in the United Kingdom.

(Ofcom 2004m: 19, para. 4.10)

In reality, this account of Ofcom's objectives is remarkably similar in scope to the objectives set out in the Conservative government's 1995 White Paper, incorporating much the same range of values and hence the same potential conflicts between them. The tension between democratic values and commercial, economic interests remains, with no overarching principle offering guidance as to which should be prioritised when they come into competition or conflict. Most obviously, worthy of highlighting here, however, is the term 'citizen-consumer'. It seems unlikely that the significantly different range of expectations which arise from these very different concepts can be swept away by even the most deft use of the hyphen! In terms of defining public interest values which underlie Ofcom's actions, there remains a failure to give due priority to the citizenship values which the Puttnam Committee sought. In this sense, the Communications Act 2003 can be viewed as a missed opportunity to provide a clear and legitimate statutory foundation for PI regulation, in relation to the media at least.

The Puttnam Report can be viewed as coming as close as any authoritative account ever has to identifying a clear meaning of 'the public interest' in relation to media regulation. Stating that 'there are public interests relating to the regulatory framework that are not encompassed in a consumer-driven objective', the report notes evidence given to the Committee expressing concern that 'the democratic, social and cultural interests of citizens' had not been given due weight in the formulation of the regulator's duties (Puttnam Report 2002: para. 24). Though such values may seem somewhat anachronistic, harking back to an age of a big, paternalistic state which has been marginalised in mainstream British politics since the Thatcher era, these values can be seen as informing not only the value-base of PSB tradition, but also, more broadly, should be seen as fundamental to democracy.

3.7 CITIZENSHIP, THE PUBLIC INTEREST AND THE MEDIA

While acknowledging the existence of paternalistic, educative motives underlying the pursuit of PSB, Blumler and Madge (1967: 48) identified many years ago two other premises on which claims for the media to serve citizenship objectives can be based. They refer to the majority of the public being 'spontaneously moved by a desire, however faint it may be at times, to discover more about their wider social and political environment', and, referring to our institutional political arrangements being based on a presupposition that the public are all equally qualified to participate in political processes, a resulting responsibility on the part of the media 'to provide citizens with the information and understanding that they need to play an effective part in this operation of democratic checks and balances'. Again, the link between democracy, citizenship and the media is established.

Golding (1990: 85) proposes the concept of citizenship 'as a key element in the development of a more adequate analysis of the political role of communications institutions and processes'. He goes on to ask, 'To what degree and in what ways are people denied access to necessary information and imagery to allow full and equal participation in the social order?' (98), noting that 'communicative competence and action, and the resources required to exercise them, are requisites for citizenship' (99). He makes 'a claim for the resurrection of the concept of citizenship as a critical bench-mark of enquiry in communication research' (100), to which might be added 'and media regulation specifically'.

Golding makes this plea despite being fully aware of some inherent problems, which he himself directs attention towards. He talks of the 'information gap', whereby 'the educationally and socio-economically advantaged are able to enhance their advantages via communications media, whose distribution and consumption are such as to ensure that such social division widens' (1990: 96). The reproduction or exaggeration of social hierarchy as a result of differential access to communications technology, to which the likes of Herman and McChesney (1997) and Schiller (1996) refer, is clearly a substantial obstacle to 'full and equal participation in the social order' (Golding 1990: 98). It appears that substantive inequalities in access to media may have to be addressed before something approaching equality of civic and political citizenship can be achieved. Clearly, such problems are much more likely to be heightened than resolved by the arrival of new technologies which are likely to increase inequalities of access.

Still more fundamental, however, are concerns regarding the nature of what the media *does*. Blumler and Gurevitch (1995: 98) note that 'a viable democracy presupposes an engaged citizenry', but if the media does not, in practice, offer meaningful information, education and entertainment, how can it contribute towards the attainment of citizenship ideals? Again, Golding is well aware of the problems identified here, stating that 'there can be no serious doubt that such sources as news media significantly and consistently provide *a partial and coherently weighted account* of many areas of social and political life' (1990: 85, emphasis added).

Of the various examples Golding cites in this connection, only one will be referred to here, that of Hall *et al.* (1978), where the authors consider the role played by the media in establishing, or constructing, the 'crisis' of street crime and police responses to it in the 1970s. Here, the authors identified 'a systematically structured *over-accessing* to the media of those in powerful and privileged institutional positions' (Hall *et al.* 1978: 58, original emphasis).

Though the relationship between the media and governments is complex (Lloyd 2004), structural relationships between the media and the powerful, and in particular a high degree of mutual interdependence, combines with the fact that most media are profit-oriented organisations operating in a capitalist environment to ensure that, in Blumler and Gurevitch's terms, 'the media can pursue democratic values only in ways that are compatible with the socio-political and economic environment in which they operate' (1995: 98). 'Instead of promoting a "market place of ideas", in which all viewpoints are given adequate play, media neutrality tends to privilege dominant, mainstream positions' (105). In the words of Hall *et al.*, 'The media . . . tend, faithfully and impartially, to reproduce symbolically the existing structure of power in society's institutional order' (1978: 58).

All of this might suggest some problems in advancing a concept of citizenship as an organising principle or focal point for media regulation, given the apparently symbiotic relationship between the institutions of the media and those of wider social power. However, it might also be taken to indicate the need for a clear, unitary theory of the public interest with which to challenge existing norms and practices.

Inequalities in access to the media, reflecting broader social inequalities, combine with the structural relationship and interdependence between the media and the powerful to limit the potential for genuinely impartial news coverage or reporting truly independent of the powerful ruling elite. In this light, the media can be seen as mediating, but also perpetuating, the power relationships between the rulers and the ruled. If this is the case, there appears to be a significant risk that reliance upon the media to enhance or further citizenship in any meaningful way may be no more than a pious hope. Radical critics might, of course, suggest that the nature of citizenship under capitalist liberal-democracies is such as to merely legitimise existing economic power relationships in any case, and that, as such, the pursuit of citizenship in this sense is in itself futile. Proponents of social democracy, however, may accept that existing economic inequalities do not deny the value in pursuing equality, or less inequality, in citizenship. The argument is that social exclusion is not only about economic disadvantage, but also related disadvantages across the range of citizenship criteria: multiple deprivation.

With that in mind, it is necessary to return to a consideration of whether the media can be expected to facilitate equality of citizenship. While the omens do not necessarily look hugely positive, and despite an apparently strongly entrenched position for the media, prospects for change and movement towards a more positive media influence on citizenship can be found. Though Blumler and Gurevitch (1995: 203) state that 'the political communication process now tends to strain against, rather than with the grain of citizenship', they also observe that 'Although political communication arrangements are systemically structured, they are not frozen in time but continually evolve'. The difficulty here is in identifying and taking control of the evolutionary mechanisms in order to manipulate the structure towards, rather than away from, citizen-oriented objectives.

Two factors, among others, which have tended to induce change in political communication systems are identified by Blumler and Gurevitch (1995: 204) as developments in communications technology and 'relevant changes in the structure and culture of the surrounding social and political system'. Of the first of these, the increasing predominance of television through the 1950s and 1960s as the medium for political communication is the most obvious example, while in relation to the second type of factor, one example that Blumler and Gurevitch point towards is changing patterns of media regulation, including specifically as an example 'the break-up of PSB monopolies in Western Europe' (205).

It therefore appears possible that, at a time in which technological change is occurring at a rapid pace and regulatory structures are in a state of flux, an opportunity presents itself for the communications media system as a whole to be redirected towards new goals. In this sense, the stage is left vacant for the arrival of a new conceptual focal point which pushes the media towards democracy-serving outcomes and acts as a coherent objective for the activities of regulators and the regulatory structure, though it will, admittedly, be pushing against the dominant non-interventionist spirit of the age.

Like Golding (1990), Collins and Murroni (1996) sought to make a case for citizenship serving as this key organising concept. As indicated above, the agenda developed by Collins and Murroni, and the IPPR, seems to have significantly influenced the New Labour government, at least in so far as it legislated to bring about institutional reform via the creation of Ofcom. However, though the institutional reform may seem sensible enough, there is a sense in which the legislative response has adopted the structural recommendation without the accompanying basis of principle which underpinned the proposals.

Starting from a premise that 'freedom of access to the information necessary to full participation in economic, political and social life is a central element of citizens' entitlements in modern societies' (1996: 76), Collins and Murroni consider the application of USOs as applied to date in Britain primarily in relation to telecommunications and other privatised utilities. The potential for extension of USO-type arrangements to the broader media field will be considered in later chapters, but it should be noted here, that their application depends upon the definition of a baseline level of service which is deemed adequate to avoid social exclusion and the precise level of which will be highly debatable. Just as having access to a public pay-phone is not the same as having a phone in one's own home, access to the Internet via a community resource in, say, a village hall or to satellite television in a pub or club is not the same as having on-tap access which brings the potential to develop experience and expertise and maximise the benefits on offer.

Collins and Murroni (1996: 78) go on to discuss what they call 'cultural rights' as an aspect of the citizenship agenda. A sense of collective identity can be furthered via the media, and far from resulting in homogeneity, can produce genuine diversity, as recognised for example in the strong tradition of regional programming in the BBC and Channel 3, or in the Welsh language productions of the BBC and S4C and in Scots Gaelic via the Gaelic Programme Fund initiative. These are, however, only examples of a wider phenomenon identified as 'community service obligations' which may be imposed upon public service (whether the BBC or commercial licensed) broadcasters. In general, British public service broadcasters have been required to produce a universally accessible service, free at the point of use, which fulfil the requirements, imposed via the BBC Charter or license conditions, of producing a range of programmes. Collins and Murroni conclude (1996: 79) that 'The community service obligation of broadcasting can thus be defined as viewers' and listeners' entitlement to access to a range of information, entertainment and educational programmes at affordable cost'. Of course, such public service requirements are not imposed presently upon subscription or pay-per-view services, and digitalisation promises a huge growth in such niche services.

As mentioned above, influential on Collins and Murroni's work on media regulation were the findings of the IPPR's Commission on Social Justice. This established four objectives which it was believed should influence government policy:

1. 'security' – policies aimed at prevention, or failing that relief, of poverty;
2. 'opportunity' – policies designed 'to increase autonomy and life chances';
3. 'democracy' – 'policies designed to ensure diffusion of power within government and between government and people';
4. 'fairness' – 'policies designed to reduce unjustified inequality' (or 'social exclusion').

The Commission sought to apply these as 'Benchmarks through which policy makers as well as the public can judge policy options' (Collins and Murroni 1996:14). These mesh closely with a notion of citizenship and, in the present context, it should be noted that, in particular, the last three of these may also serve equally well as criteria against which the effectiveness of the activities of media regulators may be measured: outcomes of regulation can be assessed against these standards.

Prior to the 2003 Act, regulation had been reactive, focusing on form within the sectoral and cross-media market places and largely consisting of *ex post facto* reaction to changing technological circumstances. Now, and in the future, positive regulation is required to ensure the widespread circulation of and access to a range of information and cultural products, and this must be confirmed positively as the key regulatory objective. Something akin to USOs may need to be imposed but, in terms of regulatory practice, integrated regulation of the cross-media market, including control of technological gateways, focused on outcomes is necessary if this objective is to be achieved. There is a real and disappointing sense in which the 2003 Act has failed to take the opportunity to develop a principled base for regulatory intervention.

If such regulation is to be meaningful, it must be possible to assess outcomes against known and identified criteria, and it seems reasonable in this respect to adopt the kind of citizenship-oriented principles identified by the Commission on Social Justice in the way that Collins and Murroni suggest. Collins and Murroni (1996: 13) identify the key statement in the Commission on Social Justice's work as being that 'the foundation of a free society is the equal worth of all citizens', and this can supply an overarching objective for areas of social policy, including media regulation, which can be rendered more specific by breaking it down according to, say, the benchmarks provided by the Commission on Social Justice. The key question to be asked of any media regulation policy or structure then becomes, 'Does this policy/structure further equality of citizenship so defined?'

The limitations of the concept of equality of citizenship in terms of failing to challenge and perhaps even tacitly legitimising substantive economic inequalities have already been acknowledged. In addition, there is no doubting the gravity of the problems which must be addressed by those recommending plurality of the media as a route to enhanced citizenship; the issues raised and acknowledged by the likes of Golding, Blumler and Gurevitch and Hall et al. must be taken on board. However, it is perhaps worth restating the glimmer of hope provided by Blumler and Gurevitch's analysis of the factors that are catalytic in changing the nature of political communications systems, which include technological development and changes in regulatory structures. The current conjunction of these events presents an opportunity to seize the agenda and, via a more sharply focused regulatory process, seek in the name of citizenship to maximise whatever plurality and diversity can exist.

The citizenship agenda incorporates choice maximisation, as pursued by Lewis (1996), though arguably strengthens the case by placing choice alongside other democratic expectations such as accountability and equity rather than risking unduly privileging choice at the expense of these other crucial democratic expectations. Under this agenda, plurality of the media is pursued not as an end in itself, but as a means of furthering effective choice, as a prerequisite of meaningful citizenship. As a potential quasi-constitutional principle for Britain it appears to capture the spirit of the interventions seen elsewhere by constitutional courts when seeking to ensure media plurality and diversity. It appears to reconfirm the interdependence of the media and the public sphere, railing against the threat of privatisation of communication identified by Schiller (1996), and privileges the public resource aspect of the media over competing, commercial, perspectives. It appears ultimately to justify, in pursuit of a clear concept of 'the public interest', the restriction of corporate property rights in the media.

In seeking to move towards a meaningful vision of 'public interest' in relation to media regulation, we are content still to offer an argument made previously that while vague claims of public interest or justifications for intervention (or lack of it) are open to reinterpretation or capture:

> A regulatory system overtly designed to give effect to 'furtherance of equality of citizenship' (or the avoidance of social exclusion) as the public interest . . . would be less susceptible to abuse or being ignored, and could usefully provide a starting point for the kind of rational policy-making process which Hitchens (1995a) has identified as necessary. (Feintuck 1997c)

There is therefore a high degree of reciprocity between many visions of the values inherent in the public interest and those of citizenship and, by explicitly linking a concept of public interest to citizenship, in both its individual *and* its collective sense, it may serve to offer some resistance to the increasingly dominant, atomistic vision associated with market-oriented, consumerist perspectives. However, there is an obvious question here. If the real concern relates to citizenship, and especially equality of citizenship, what is to be gained by using the language of 'public interest' rather than simply a reassertion of 'citizenship'?

One attraction of using 'the public interest' arises from the fact that, just as the legal system in this country might be said to lack any developed basis for the recognition of collective values and interests, so it also may be thought to lack any developed concept of citizenship. Though some legal definition of this term has existed historically in the context of matters such as immigration and welfare benefits, it has remained a limited notion, perhaps reflecting the historical view of Britons as 'subjects of the Crown'. Of course, debate over citizenship has been promoted in recent years via the influence of Europe, both in the context of the ECHR and also the European Union's growing influence in this area, though there is a real risk that the latter may focus excessively on a particular vision of 'economic' citizenship which does not incorporate wider values properly associated with the concept. This lack of definition for an apparently central concept such as citizenship may well relate to what has been identified as the absence of a developed concept of 'state' in Britain (Prosser, 1982), at least when compared to its continental neighbours. It may be more than coincidence that we do not see in Britain the kind of more developed body of 'public service law' that we see in countries such as France or Italy, where the concept of state is more developed and which recognise a concept of 'general interest' extending beyond the aggregation of private, individual interests (Prosser, 1997).

Of course, it may prove difficult to define 'citizen' in the absence of a developed concept of 'state' and, given the legal system's dominant individualist orientation, in so far as citizenship is recognised it is likely to be in relation to individual aspects rather than the collective aspects which link to an idea of community.

To return to the question just posed, by way of summary, what might a developed concept of the public interest linked explicitly to citizenship bring which is not already adequately covered by human rights or citizenship or existing concepts of social regulation? The arguments underlying our position have been made much more fully elsewhere (Feintuck 2004) but, essentially, three claims can be made.

First, that in making explicit the connections between law and the full set of values inherent in the political philosophy of liberal-democracy, it serves to facilitate an objective of strengthening the structural coupling of these fields of endeavour (Teubner, 1987), repairing some of the 'bifurcation' between technical legal concerns (with the likes of institutions and rule-play) and philosophical concerns and values (Minor, 1962). Second, that it gives due prominence to the marginalised values of community, transcending the pluralist fray, restraining the ongoing political trend to give absolute prominence to the values of individualism and capital and helping to address the tendency of common law systems to individualise issues. In doing so, it may serve to offer some resistance to what Marquand (2004) has persuasively described as the decline of the public domain. Third, that it provides a coherent justification for social regulation that is clearly and unashamedly independent of reliance on justifications for intervention based on market economics.

What is being suggested here is, to a large extent, the application of a developed concept of public interest as what is sometimes referred to as an 'interpretative principle' (Sunstein 1990; Feintuck 2004: 188–94). We will return to this in Chapter 7 but it is worth indicating the value of such principles here. In essence, such a principle may be of value by

> focusing regulatory and judicial activity properly on such values, and helping to avoid the risk of a technical, legal or scientific emphasis prevailing over achievement of social objectives. It may serve as an otherwise missing-link, requiring continuity of emphasis throughout regulatory practice, and offering a potential standard of review which retains a focus on the underlying democratic values rather than an otherwise disconnected set of technical legal norms which may relate poorly to the animating democratic rationales for regulation. (Feintuck 2004: 160)

Our argument here parallels closely the Puttnam Committee's approach in seeking to ensure a clear hierarchy of duties within the 2003 Act, with citizenship values at the top of this hierarchy. Given the functional centrality of formal law in implementing and enforcing such norms, it will inevitably be necessary to give the concept a legally recognisable form. Though this poses certain challenges for lawyers, it should not offer insuperable difficulties. As Bell has suggested, if legislators and judges are able to state and interpret fundamental principles of human rights, it might be expected that they should also be able to develop an enforceable and meaningful concept of the public interest which is independent of, and serves as a restraint on, the powerful (Bell, 1993: 34).

The remainder of this book examines in more detail some of the different regulatory structures and policies for media regulation applied to date, both in Britain and elsewhere. In addition to principles, structures and, especially, institutional features such as accountability and transparency must be considered. Arguably though, the central reason underlying the failure of regulatory institutions to date, and for the difficulties they are likely to face in a future uncertain in terms of technological development, is the absence of a clear, organising principle for the regulatory endeavour. As was discussed above, tensions between competing rationales for media regulation have not been articulated or resolved, but rather have been absorbed, ignored or one preferred over the other on a pragmatic, *ad hoc* basis. Pursuit of a developed concept of public interest which emphasises citizenship values appears to offer a constant and meaningful objective in itself, and a standard against which policies could be judged.

4

The Regulatory Framework Before and After the Communications Act 2003

ᴄᴏ

4.1 INTRODUCTION

Noted earlier has been a tendency for incremental and *ad hoc* reform of the regulatory regime applicable to the media. The advent of the Communications Act 2003, a massive and closely scrutinised piece of legislation, might seem to be a more radical overhaul of the UK's media regulation regime, and it certainly represents a significant landmark. However, though of great and obvious significance in terms of its reform of the institutional framework of regulation, in particular through the establishment of a new super-regulator, Ofcom, on closer inspection it might be thought that the new regulatory framework established by the Act has not adequately addressed the questions of principle, and in particular citizenship interests, highlighted in previous chapters. Indeed, the Act's emphasis on 'light touch' regulation might even be thought to serve to marginalise such interests still further.

In this chapter we offer a brief overview of the historical legal framework for regulation prior to the Act before going on to identify the key reforms and to consider their impact on power and accountability in the regulatory regime and some significant developments since. Our emphasis here will tend to be on regulatory design, the location of regulatory power and accountability in its exercise, while in the next chapter we will turn to consider the impact of the revised regulatory framework on certain aspects of the control of media outlets, of the media infrastructure and of broadcast and published media content. Our overall objective here is to consider whether the Communications Act 2003 in general represents any significant advance on what went before.

4.2 THE HISTORICAL FRAMEWORK FOR REGULATION OF MEDIA OWNERSHIP

Though the focus now turns away from the conceptual basis for regulation of the media to consider instead some examples of regulation in practice, the theoretical foundations explored in the previous chapters provide the foundation for analysis of the regulatory practices under consideration here.

Though 'behavioural' regulation is not always easily classified, regulation of the media essentially falls fairly easily into two categories: regulation of content and regulation of ownership or control of media enterprises, which approximate to Hoffmann-Riem's classifications of 'imperative' and 'structural' regulation (Hoffmann-Riem 1992a). The first considers what may be broadcast or printed, and may consist of positive programming requirements, such as under the Broadcasting Act requirements, applied for many years by the ITC, that public-service commercial television broadcasters should offer specific categories of programming. Alternatively, they may consist of negative requirements, limiting what can be broadcast, for example, on grounds of taste and decency. The second category, regulation of ownership or control, which will be the primary focal point in this chapter, may in turn be subdivided into directly structural controls (for example, prescribing the growth of an organisation in one media sector beyond a certain limit based on numbers of companies or market share in terms of turnover or audience share) and behavioural controls related to structure (for example, specifying activities or actions that would be subject to sanction, perhaps as an abuse of a position of power). Competition law, discussed in the previous chapter, whether of general application or media-specific, may be focused either on 'form', which for many years was the primary trigger for intervention in the UK, or 'effects' (essentially relating to potential or actual abuse of a dominant position) which underlies the EU approach to the subject and under the Competition Act 1998 has largely brought UK competition law into line with the EU approach.

A further, and in Britain significant, distinction must be drawn between statutory, state-imposed regimes of regulation, such as those applicable to broadcasting, and the essentially self-regulatory processes employed in relation to the advertising industry by the ASA or in relation to the newspaper industry by the PCC. Though the political rhetoric and academic language now emphasises 'co-regulation' rather than self-regulation (Marsden 2004), the same issues largely remain and will be returned to in Chapters 5 and 6. As will become apparent at various points, in relation to Britain in particular attention must be drawn to the existence of, and ongoing reliance upon, self-denying ordinances applicable, in different contexts, to government, regulators, the courts and the media, arguably the result of the absence of clear principles for regulatory intervention and perhaps symptomatic of the absence of developed and articulated principles underpinning constitutional arrangements.

In this chapter, by way of establishing the historical context in which the Communications Act 2003 must be viewed, we will discuss briefly three examples of recent regulatory practice, predominantly structural in nature, that relate to ownership or control of media. The first of these is newspaper takeovers and mergers, the area of media ownership regulation with the longest history in Britain. This will highlight significant questions of regulatory discretion, raising in turn questions of accountability. The next area to be examined is the application of media-specific competition law in the form of the Broadcasting Act 1996. An analysis will be made of the structural measures which were aimed at controlling cross-media ownership, and particular emphasis will be placed on understanding the changes made to the previous framework established by the Broadcasting Act 1990. The final subject scrutinised in the first part of this chapter also arises out of the 1996 Act but can be viewed essentially as an attempt by the state to respond to a specific technological development – the then imminent introduction of digital terrestrial television (DTT). Despite the fact that the relevant legislative framework has been substantially reformed under the 2003 Act, these examples remain instructive in terms of illustrating issues which are as relevant to the new regulatory regime as to the old.

These examples illustrate the issues raised for regulators by ongoing changes in both market structure and technology, and in particular highlight the problems arising out of the absence of a clear, principled approach to the regulatory endeavour. Though based broadly upon pluralism of ownership and competition law principles as outlined in Chapters 2 and 3, it appears that lack of conceptual clarity and a resulting lack of clear objectives risk undermining such regulatory activity, at least in relation to its aim of ensuring a diverse media output, the underlying 'public interest' justification upon which regulatory intervention is largely based. The latter two examples considered in this chapter also reveal the increasing EU influence over media regulation in Britain. The same issues must in turn be considered in relation to the reformed arrangements under the 2003 Act.

The examples considered here, however, also raise broader questions relating to the place of regulatory structures within the constitutional scheme. The role of the courts in relation to regulatory activity will be raised here, though returned to both in Chapter 5 and Chapter 6, while the relationship between national and international regulatory regimes, considered here briefly but emphasised in Chapter 6, raises questions of whether the nation state is any longer the appropriate level at which to regulate an increasingly global media economy.

Carried over from Chapter 3 and of particular significance in the context of the structural regulatory mechanisms considered here is the idea that diversity in media output via diversity in ownership is consistently presented as an objective of regulation, yet it appears necessary to view this not as an end in itself but as a mechanism for serving the needs of citizenship. Given this surrogacy arrangement and the absence of any necessary connection between pluralism of ownership and diversity in output, it is perhaps appropriate to consider and analyse structural regulation in terms of the extent to which it serves successfully as a surrogate for imperative, content-focused regulation which might be expected to pursue more directly the objective of diversity of output.

4.3 NEWSPAPER TAKEOVERS AND MERGERS

Though the press must be viewed in the increasingly cross-media context, justification for considering this sector for the moment in isolation is twofold. First, the press is the oldest of the media and, having struggled in its early history against state control and censorship, is most resistant to regulation. Second, in terms of the informative and critical aspect of media power, the press continues to claim that it fulfils these functions in greater depth than the broadcast media.

In Western Europe, the majority of broadcast media have, until very recently, been regulated in order to ensure public service standards. However, in the modern era, 'Traditionally, economic arrangements for the Press have involved a minimum of intervention by the state. To own a newspaper has been regarded as the commercial manifestation of the liberty to speak' (Gibbons 1991: 97). As such, the press retains certain sectoral distinctions, notwithstanding the current context of convergence of technology and trends towards cross-media and international conglomeration.

In Chapter 1, the high degree of concentration of ownership now present in the British newspaper market was noted. Though the issue of concentration in press ownership may appear to be particularly acute in Britain, it can also be observed elsewhere. As Bagdikian (1992: 17) noted, in the huge US market, 'a handful of corporations [have gained] control of most daily newspapers', with fourteen companies controlling half or more of the daily newspaper business in 1992, whereas the same share was controlled by some twenty companies only seven years earlier. Considering Western Europe, however, Humphreys (1996: 96) concludes in effect that, while press concentration has its own dynamic, 'oligopolistic competition is the rule' and that Britain provides the most striking example of this phenomenon.

Heightening concentration in the press market is, in the context of an increasingly global media and economy, not surprisingly an international issue, with Rupert Murdoch, in Schiller's terms, 'the Australian-English-American media mogul' (Schiller 1996: 112), being only one example of the trend towards controlling press concerns alongside other media interests on a worldwide basis (see Tunstall and Palmer 1991). Thus it seems proper to consider the regulation of press ownership as part of a broader, international media market and, given the widespread availability of newspapers via the Internet, to acknowledge the new convergent technological context in which the press operates. That said, although British cross-media ownership regulation under the Broadcasting Acts of 1990 and 1996 and then proposed EU measures sought to take the broader view by attempting to integrate newspaper ownership alongside the holding of broadcasting licences in establishing overall thresholds for regulation of cross-media ownership, a more long-standing regime existed which purported to regulate press ownership as a separate sector.

The Fair Trading Act 1973 (FTA) included specific measures controlling the takeover and merger of both national and local newspapers which went beyond general takeover and merger provisions. Under the terms of the FTA, newspaper acquisitions were subjected to scrutiny where a proprietor's newspapers, including the paper to be taken over, totalled an average daily circulation of 500,000 or more, proprietorship, either personal or through company structures, being defined in terms of holding a controlling interest. Mergers crossing this threshold, to be lawful, required the consent of the Secretary of State, which could be either conditional or unconditional. The Secretary of State in some cases would refer the matter for consideration by the Monopolies and Mergers Commission (MMC), but in a number of exceptions to the general rule *could* and, in the case of a newspaper which is not to be continued as a separate title *had to*, decide the matter without reference to the MMC. The other situations where the Secretary of State was not obliged to refer to the MMC were 'where the newspaper is not economic as a going concern and he is satisfied that the case is one of urgency if it is to continue as a separate newspaper', 'where the newspaper being transferred has an average circulation of 25,000 or less per day of circulation' and 'where the MMC has failed to make its report within the appointed time-limit' (Whish 1993: 673).

Thus the FTA provisions consisted of a mixture of specified thresholds and practices and regulatory discretion exercised by the Secretary of State. The presence of the MMC in the process appeared to offer reassurance against fears of politically motivated action by the Secretary of State, especially given that the MMC was required to take into account 'the public interest'. Unfortunately, the statutory definition of 'the public interest' in this context was so vague as to be virtually meaningless, requiring the consideration of 'all matters which appear in the circumstances to be relevant and, in particular, the need for accurate presentation of news and free expression of opinion'.

However, the reality did not necessarily match the superficial appearance of these provisions. In practice, as Whish (1993: 675–8) demonstrated, the degree of discretion vested in the Secretary of State was much more wide-ranging than at first might appear to be the case. In addition to the ability to impose conditions on newspaper takeovers and mergers, the Secretary of State also had the power to appoint members of a panel of additional MMC members who may be utilised in newspaper references. It was also the case that a large number of takeovers and mergers would fall within the exceptions to the provisions, which allowed the Secretary of State the discretion not to make a reference to the MMC and, even where a reference was made, the Secretary of State was not bound to follow the conclusions reached.

Ainsworth and Weston, writing in 1995, concluded that 'Extensive reliance on [the] exceptions (most recently in the *Guardian*'s acquisition of the *Observer* and the acquisition of the *Independent* by a consortium led by Mirror Group) has meant that in practice the majority of important newspaper acquisitions have escaped MMC scrutiny' (Ainsworth and Weston 1995: 3). Curran and Seaton (1997: 294) reported some 120 newspaper takeovers between 1965 and 1993, but the fact that the MMC dealt with only twenty-nine references regarding newspaper acquisitions between 1965 and 1994, and of those twenty-three were cleared, led Ainsworth and Weston (1995: 5) to question whether the practical effect of the FTA system justified 'the administrative burden, expense and delay that it creates', and indeed 'whether there is really any justification for continuing to treat newspaper mergers under different procedural rules than other types of merger'.

All in all, the Secretary of State enjoyed wide-ranging discretion and, given the 'fierce political argument' that Whish (1993: 677) notes in relation to some newspaper takeovers (especially the acquisition by *News International* of *The Times* in 1980 and *Today* in 1987 and repeated takeover proposals relating to *The Observer* and in particular its purchase by *Lonrho* in 1981), was, quite reasonably, subject to suspicions of pursuing party political interests and being vulnerable to 'both political pressure and the manipulation of the companies' economic strengths' (Gibbons 1991: 99). It would certainly be problematic for a Secretary of State to face Cabinet colleagues with a decision which allowed jobs to be lost as a result of a newspaper closure rather than let it be taken over, even if the takeover resulted in greater concentration of ownership. Given the relatively weak economic position of many newspapers, this is a reality which must be faced on a regular basis.

In Chapter 2, the dramatic reduction in numbers of Left-leaning British newspapers in the postwar era was noted, alongside changes in ownership patterns (Humphreys 1996: chapter 3; Negrine 1994: chapter 3). Changes in party political orientation of the national titles resulted in a situation where, by the mid-1990s, the vast majority of newspaper circulation was of a Conservative orientation, a result, states Hutton (1995: 40), 'produced not by competition in the market but by manipulation of the ownership rules by Conservative press tycoons'. In light of these trends, it is perhaps surprising to find that a regulatory regime exists at all, and to find that the question asked by the 1947 Royal Commission, 'whether such concentration as exists is on balance disadvantageous to the free expression of opinion or the accurate presentation of news' (Negrine 1994: 62), has remained an apparently important concern for government (see, for example, DNH 1995a) and commentators alike. Clearly, concentration of ownership, to the extent that ownership impacts upon editorial freedom, can inhibit the political diversity of the press though this remains an essentially contingent relationship. The precise relationship between newspaper takeovers, closures, political orientation and general market forces and trends in 'product loyalty' cannot be identified with certainty but it is obvious that, to the extent that newspapers help form public opinion or at least establish part of the climate in which public opinion is formed, control of newspapers is a highly contentious party political issue. The failure by the Secretary of State to stop acquisitions by Rupert Murdoch's group of titles (spanning the popular, quality and middle-ground markets) during the Thatcher years may not be without significance, and the mere continuation of a number of titles does not (as was noted in Chapter 2) in itself guarantee pluralism in terms of editorial line (see Gibbons 1992). Robertson and Nicol (1992: 506) described as 'understandable' the MMC's reluctance to enter into investigations into the political allegiances of newspaper proprietors, but believe that the public interest criteria established by the FTA to guide the MMC's investigations did require 'an assessment of the consequences of the transaction on the availability to the public of a reasonable variety of editorial opinion'.

With all this in mind, it seems democratically necessary (if not necessarily politically convenient for those in government) for discretion in relation to newspaper acquisitions to be properly 'confined, structured and checked' (Davis 1971), and perhaps taken out of the sphere of government influence. Whish (1993: 678) argued for the confining of the discretionary element, stating that 'there would be much to be said for removing the element of political discretion in this area by making all newspaper mergers referable to the MMC, subject to a de minimis exception', though it would probably be necessary in such circumstances to consider also making MMC findings binding. Both Robertson and Nicol (1992: 505) and Gibbons (1991: 99) in effect proposed a restructuring of discretion, requiring the imposition on those proposing newspaper acquisitions of a requirement to demonstrate that the proposed takeover or merger would not operate against the public interest, or even a burden of proving to the MMC that the acquisition would positively serve the public interest.

Another option might be to hand over such matters to the judiciary, either as part of a general or specialist jurisdiction. The potential costs and benefits of judicialising this system would have to be weighed carefully in order to assess whether any of the problems of cost and delay identified by Ainsworth and Weston (1995) in relation to the system would simply be reproduced or even heightened. In addition, any such proposal would depend for its effectiveness upon the British judiciary being able and willing to adjudicate on politically contentious issues, an area in which judges are, at least overtly, usually wary to tread.

Whish (1993: 679) stated that 'The provisions of the FTA 1973 for controlling other mergers are very different from those governing newspapers', and that in other areas of mergers and takeovers 'The system of control is benign and is essentially predisposed in favour of mergers'. The evidence presented here should, however, be enough to convince that in practice there is little difference between the predisposition of general merger controls and those specific to newspaper takeovers. The high degree of concentration of ownership and lack of pluralism in the British press was certainly not unduly restricted by the press-specific FTA provisions. On the whole, Ainsworth and Weston's conclusion that, in reality, the regime for the regulation of newspaper acquisitions rested largely upon the discretion of the Secretary of State and that the game played was not worth the candle is almost certainly correct.

The Labour government's Competition Bill brought before Parliament in October 1997 failed to amend the process relating to newspaper acquisitions, and also declined to address the specific issue of predatory pricing raised by competitors in relation to the pricing policy of *The Times*. The replacement of the MMC with a 'Competition Commission' may be thought, in itself, not to have had much more than symbolic significance.

The consistent failure of British governments to take opportunities to address competition issues in the newspaper market has in many ways been disappointing. In so far as ownership or control of newspapers is a political issue, whether in the party or broader, democratic sense, it is reasonable for the state to make special provision to protect perceived public interests in a pluralistic press. Within the permissive, discretionary structure of the FTA provisions and the application of the nebulous construct of the public interest, the statutory measures on newspaper acquisitions, in so far as they had any effect, operated simply to leave the power of determination essentially within the hands of the government of the day, a prime example of ritualistic regulation masking raw political power. The response of the New Labour administration to an extent seemed dramatic, yet might ultimately be thought to have made little difference. The apparent drama arises from section 373 of the Communications Act 2003, which simply repealed the pre-existing provisions of the FTA, applying provisions of the Enterprise Act 2002 to the context of newspapers. As we noted in Chapter 3, this has led to the publication by Ofcom of guidance as to the factors which will be considered to constitute public interest considerations in the context of newspaper takeovers and mergers, yet despite these guidelines very considerable discretion and uncertainty remains as to how they, and the provisions from which they originate, will be applied in practice in specific cases. We also noted in the previous chapter the continuing presence of and substantial role for the (party) political perspectives brought to bear by the Secretary of State, which retain great significance here, indicating not only which outcomes will be reached in particular cases but specifically which cases will be taken through the 'public interest intervention' procedures.

Thus, while the 2003 Act has changed the statutory basis on which intervention in relation to newspaper takeovers and mergers takes place, it does not seem to have had any significant impact on the problems revealed by the historical survey above. While there is an apparent statement of public interest principle in this context, the failure noted by the

Puttnam Committee to identify with adequate clarity a hierarchy of values again seems to form a significant obstacle to meaningful progress.

4.4 LICENSING COMMERCIAL TELEVISION AND REGULATING CROSS-MEDIA HOLDINGS

The focus here will be on two aspects of British competition measures specific to the media, concentrating on the interrelated issues of how licences to broadcast commercial, terrestrial, analogue television were allocated prior to the 2003 Act and how restrictions were imposed on cross-media holdings. The primary focus will be on the impact of the provisions of the Broadcasting Acts of 1990 and 1996, their intention, the procedures and principles adopted and the outcomes. While these measures have been replaced wholesale by the relevant sections of the 2003 Act, the situation which regulators now face is the product of the previous statutory framework which must be understood if the new legislation is to be viewed in its proper context. Though the media-related measures in the 1990 and 1996 Acts must be viewed alongside general competition provisions and also, in relation to cross-media regulation, measures specific to newspapers and radio, they represented the primary mechanism via which British governments sought to regulate the television market. As will become apparent, a significant issue here, noted in Chapter 3, is how markets, and hence market shares, were to be measured. Questions of 'market definition' and the difficulties in establishing 'media exchange rates' for calculating cross-media market share are highlighted in attempts to regulate and limit cross-media holdings.

As long ago as 1975, Lewis identified concerns regarding the allocation of franchises for Channel 3 by the (then) IBA. Though Lewis was writing in an era of still limited broadcasting frequencies, he observed a system with little legal control and few other institutional restraints on the wide-ranging discretion held by the IBA. He found that there was little informed public discussion of the issue and no open hearings prior to franchise allocation, that the criteria applied by the IBA were crude and not published, and that the reasons given by the IBA (when any reasons were given) were inadequate.

In 1981, Elliott conjured up the image of 'chasing the receding bus' to illustrate what he perceived as weaknesses in the approach taken in the 1980 Broadcasting Act. In the post-Annan Committee era, and with the technological revolution having now come over the horizon and clearly fast approaching, Elliott observed that the 1980 Act had simply *assumed* the desirability of government regulation of broadcasting (still substantially relying on the fast disappearing conditions of limited air-waves) and had sought to maintain the BBC/ITV duopoly, ensuring that even with the coming of Channel 4 a significant degree of government control would be retained by virtue of powers of appointment to Channel 4's management. Like Lewis six years earlier, he noted the absence of adequate institutional controls over franchise allocation procedures and no requirement to give meaningful reasons for decisions. The IBA was assumed to be the repository of the 'public interest' in such matters, but the concept remained hopelessly ill-defined. The thrust of Elliott's piece is that the 1980 Act not only failed to respond adequately to change which was already occurring, but perhaps more significantly failed to provide a framework for regulation in an era of more rapid and fundamental change which was already threatening to leave the existing regulatory structures behind.

As Barendt (1995: 13) noted, the government's apparent intention when introducing the Broadcasting Act 1990 was 'to apply a lighter touch to programme control' in relation to commercial television broadcasters, as well as reforming the licence allocation procedure relating to them. In reality, however, the procedures followed by the ITC under the Act were scarcely less controversial than those of the IBA which it replaced, containing what Hoffmann-Riem (1996: 108) refers to as 'inherent contradictions', while, as Barendt (1995: 13) notes, in practice the Act 'imposed as many new restraints on broadcasters' freedom as it lifted'.

Though its introduction was driven largely by the all-pervasive market-oriented spirit of the age which informed so-much of 'Thatcherism', the regime established ten years later by the 1990 Act appeared to offer some improvements on what went before. Admittedly, it could still be viewed as reactive rather than forward-looking, a fact to which both its failure to regulate the rise to total dominance of *BSkyB* in British DTH satellite broadcasting and the need for a further major Act only six years later bear elegant testimony. The new franchising procedure for the allocation of licences marked a shift in terminology, state Harlow and Rawlings (1997: 274), from 'contract' to 'licence' and suggested therefore a more public law-oriented approach to broadcasting which might offer some potential benefits in terms of establishing criteria for decision-making, requiring reasons for decisions and thereby increasing transparency and accountability. The extent to which these potential benefits accrued in practice is highly debatable and must be weighed against the Act's effect, described by Hutton (1995: 33) in terms of destabilising the entire ITV system.

The licence allocation system resulting from the 1990 Act took account of two criteria: a financial sustainability test and a programme quality threshold. Assuming that bidders met both criteria, franchises would normally be awarded by the ITC to the highest bidder, though the ITC retained a power, under section 17, to accept a lower bid in place of a higher one 'where there are exceptional circumstances which make it appropriate for them to award the licence to another applicant'. Thus the 1990 Act introduced a hybrid system of franchising, embodying aspects of both price bidding and public interest, the latter in this case being defined in terms of the problematic concept of programme 'quality' (Seymour-Ure 1996: 109). As Prosser (1994) observed, the fact that only half of the licence awards made in the first round of Channel 3 franchising under this new regime were to the highest bidder suggested either perhaps that 'exceptional circumstances' must have been remarkably common or that the leeway provided to the ITC was sufficient to allow them to determine matters on a very broad and largely unspecified notion of quality. Though Harlow and Rawlings (1997: 277) suggest that this outcome, in giving preference to other factors than simply the price bid, 'underscores the continuing relevance of "public interest" ', it is unclear exactly what the term was taken to mean by the ITC, and Harlow and Rawlings' other conclusion, 'that rather more discretion might have been exercised than had been envisaged in Parliament' (*ibid.*) is perhaps more telling.

Outcomes of ITC licence allocation procedures under the 1990 Act were challenged directly in the courts by losing bidders on two notable occasions. In 1992, following the first set of regional licence awards under the new regime, *Television South West (TSW)* sought to challenge the loss of their licence (*R v ITC ex parte TSW Broadcasting, The Independent* 27.3.92; see Jones 1992) while more recently a losing bidder in the contest for the fifth channel licence also sought judicial review of the decision (*R v ITC, ex parte Virgin Television Ltd* [1996] EMLR 318; see Marsden 1996).

Both cases, however, illustrated a marked reluctance on the part of the courts, in the *TSW* case the House of Lords, to interfere in relation to the substance of the decisions taken by the ITC. This should not be unexpected, and indeed, as Prosser (1997: 262) indicated, the courts were 'sensibly avoiding second-guessing the substantive decisions'. That said, the *TSW* judgement appeared to impose a requirement on the ITC to provide more in the way of reasons for its decisions on licence allocation, in particular in the circumstances of *TSW*, a holder of an existing franchise which believed itself to be the highest bidder for the new franchise. Such a move is clearly to be welcomed in terms of furthering rationality, transparency and accountability. Despite this judgement, however, a degree of lack of transparency in the ITC's procedures was revealed again five years later in the *Virgin* case.

While both *Virgin* and *UKTV* passed the financial sustainability test, the ITC determined that neither crossed the programme quality threshold test established by section 16(1)(a). Neither was therefore eligible for the licence award, and Channel Five Broadcasting (*Channel 5*) were awarded the licence in the face of one remaining application whose cash bid was much lower. In addition to (unsuccessfully) raising questions over procedures adopted by the ITC in allowing Five to amend the details of their bid to ensure that it passed the financial sustainability test, *Virgin* sought to challenge the basis of the Commission's decision relating to their programming plans.

In particular, they sought to draw attention to inconsistencies between the advice provided to the Commission in papers produced by its staff advisers and the Commission's conclusions on programming. However, Marsden (1996) notes in relation to *Virgin*'s unsuccessful challenge that 'the courts have shown no propensity to challenge the assembled expertise of the ITC in determining qualitative standards in programming', and that, given that the argument presented on this point by *Virgin* was found to be 'both impermissible and hopeless', he concludes that 'the likelihood of a successful future challenge to the quality threshold appears minimal'. Marsden questions, however, whether the regulatory role in relation to programming quality currently resting with the ITC may be about to be diminished, given their more limited role in relation to DTT, just as the role of the IBA was limited in 1984 in relation to programming requirements for cable television services which were placed under the cable authority's jurisdiction (Veljanovski 1987).

Prosser (1997: chapter 9) appears to consider the outcome of the 1992 *TSW* case to be a marked improvement on what went before. It has to be emphasised, however, that he rightly also points out that, in reality, 'in both the allocation of Channel 3 licences and the more recent allocation of those for Channel 5 the outcome was determined more by discretionary decisions on quality matters than by bidding in the market place' (266). As such, it is reasonable to expect a high degree of transparency and reasoning in such cases, and whether the decision in *TSW* is adequate in this respect is very questionable, in that the decision is limited to the situation of a highest bidder in possession of an existing licence, and is not necessarily of wider application. It can be argued that the principle of fully reasoned decisions needs to established on a general basis, not just in relation to existing franchisees, but also in relation to new applicants for licences both in terrestrial, analogue television and in similar allocation processes in relation to multiplexes in the brave new world of DTT where essentially the same issues arise. In the absence of adequate guarantees of openness in such decision-making processes it is impossible to be sure what, if any, model of the public interest has been utilised when the relevant authority reaches a decision.

Though raising interesting and important issues in itself, the allocation of broadcasting licences via hybrid franchising procedures must be viewed against the background of limits on those seeking licences who also held interests in other media. The 1995 White Paper (DNH 1995a) which preceded the 1996 Act emphasised three objectives for the regulation of cross-media ownership or control:

1. the promotion of diversity in media material and the expression of a range of views;
2. the maintenance of a strong media industry 'for the economic benefit of the country'; and
3. ensuring the proper operation of markets, including access for new entrants to markets, and the prevention of cross-media subsidies or predatory pricing,

The White Paper (DNH 1995a: para. 6.25) proposed that in relation to the television sector and cross-media holdings including television broadcasting, the ITC will be expected to balance these three conflicting 'public interest' criteria. While these are all perfectly legitimate objectives, there remains significant doubt as to whether they are sufficiently clear as to allow the existing regulators to achieve them, and in practice this suggests that wide-ranging discretion, subject still to inadequate institutional safeguards, will remain with the ITC.

It should be noted that the British government moved ahead with the 1996 Act despite the possibility of an EU Directive on the same subject being brought forward. Claims by Member State governments such as the UK that media ownership provisions should be subject to the principle of subsidiarity as a matter which is best addressed at the national level contributed to tortuous progress on this agenda. The problems of establishing common ownership regulations across Europe, even aiming only at harmonisation, always suggested that such a measure would be likely to be only at a lowest-common-denominator level, and may by themselves prove ineffective, replicating the kind of difficulties identified by Humphreys (1994 and 1996) in the federal context of Germany. For some time questions remained regarding whether EU competence extends to questions of ownership as opposed to the kind of technical issues addressed in the Advanced Television Standards Directives (1995/47) and the December 1997 Green Paper (European Commission 1997) on technological convergence, both of which were focused on internal market issues of the compatability of technology across the EU. As will be discussed in Chapter 6, the EU's 'New Regulatory Framework' for the media, established via four Directives in 2002, is significant, but remains largely focused on technical aspects of media markets.

Difficulties regarding market definition, as noted in Chapter 3, are a perennial problem for regulators seeking to ensure competition, especially perhaps in a transnational context, yet this seems to be an essential prerequisite for determining intervention thresholds, whether established by reference to a percentage market share (in terms of turnover say, or advertising revenue), the existence of a dominant position or by reference to 'market reach' or 'audience share' or degree of influence in relation to the media whether individually or as a whole. In Britain, historically, the position was peculiarly complicated as a result of the application of different thresholds based on different factors established by different pieces of legislation. In general, British competition authorities tended to show an interest when a threshold of 25 per cent of a market was controlled by one player or group. In the case of newspapers, however, the provisions of the Fair Trading Act, as noted earlier, allowed for intervention when a takeover involved circulation in excess of 500,000, equating to less than 5 per cent of the market. Huge difficulties are encountered even in relation to measuring market share in a single market, such as radio, where different bases for measuring market share may produce very different outcomes For example, 'Capital Radio's impact is twelve times higher measured by its share of time spent consuming the media than if measured by revenues' (Congdon et al. 1995: 9). Such complexities are heightened in relation to attempts to measure cross-media market shares, and clarity is not helped by the net result of measures such as those contained in Schedule 2 of the 1996 Broadcasting Act, which combined audience share with various fixed limits on ownership. While some of the additional complexities arising from the historically different emphases of EU and UK competition law provisions, noted above, have been substantially reduced following the Competition Act 1998, these were of substantial significance in the previous period and served as a further obstacle to harmonisation.

However, the EU did continue to make moves towards a Directive on media ownership, though the orientation of these measures seems rather different to that suggested ten years earlier. The first steps were taken in 1992 (see Hitchens 1994; Feintuck 1995) but progress was exceedingly slow (Doyle 2002: 162–70). In its 1996 form, a proposed Directive would have established a 30 per cent upper limit on holdings in any one media sector (newspapers, radio or television), combined with an upper limit of 10 per cent total media market share. Though acknowledging that these limits are not particularly objectionable in themselves, Doyle (1997) raised a number of practical problems in relation to both market definition and the difficulties of applying a unified formula to the very different existing patterns of ownership across the range of Member States.

The 1997 proposals for the Directive, however, as Doyle (1997) indicates, reflected a move away from an emphasis on 'pluralism' (apparently implying both ownership and output) in earlier proposals, where the legal competence of EU bodies to act might be in question, to a focus specifically on ownership in the context of the EU's internal market agenda. Doyle (2002: 166) now characterises this shift of emphasis in terms of 'Farewell pluralism; long live competition policy!' This seems to be a reasonable conclusion, Doyle (1997) having gone so far as to suggest that the change of name of the proposed directive from 'Media Pluralism' to 'Media Ownership' and the increased degree of flexibility for individual Member States were symptomatic of a change of emphasis which meant that 'the Directive is no longer about guaranteeing an equal right to pluralism (as represented by diversity of ownership) for all EU citizens, irrespective of which European markets they live in'.

Collins and Murroni (1996: 68) suggested a tiered, or stepped, approach to media ownership in combination with other proposed measures, for example guaranteeing journalistic independence by way of behavioural control over media owners. They presented a specific proposal to restrict holdings across four sectors (national newspapers, regional newspapers, television and radio) stepped down from 40 per cent to 15 per cent depending on whether a player or group has interests in one, two, three or all four sectors. While the kind of proposal presented by Collins and Murroni has many superficial attractions, not the least of which is apparent simplicity and clarity, in practice it contains implicit assumptions regarding a 'media exchange rate' and appears to understate the difficulty in establishing market share even within one sector. While, the tiered or stepped approach to setting limits on ownership within and across-media sectors is in principle an attractive one, it remains questionable whether the minimum level of diversity it would ensure across the media as a whole is adequate, and in the modern context such a measure must be expanded to factor in control of key aspects of the technological infrastructure which appears to be at least as significant as the control of production companies.

That said, the benefits of clarity and simplicity are not to be underestimated, especially when faced with the prospect of the nightmarish complexity of a journey through Schedule 2 of the Broadcasting Act 1996! While the broad 'public interest' principles included in the 1995 White Paper might be criticised on grounds of lack of detail, the same cannot be said of the cross-media measures contained in the labyrinthine Schedule 2 to the 1996 Act. Though now swept away by the 2003 Act, the 1996 measures remain worthy of consideration as regards what they reveal about the mechanisms adopted historically and the relationship, or lack of it, between the provisions and underlying rationales and objectives for media regulation. In the spirit of this book, it is intended to provide the traveller only with information regarding some of the more important landmarks to be found in Schedule 2 rather than a comprehensive descrip-tion of all its many and varied features; Gibbons (1996) provided an excellent, comprehensive commentary on the Schedule 2 provisions and their effects, and the DCMS (1998c) offered a useful summary.

The most straightforward aspect of the measures were the absolute limits on ownership. In relation to commercial (i.e. other than BBC) tele-vision, paragraph 11 of Schedule 2 established that if a person (natural or legal) controls more than a 15 per cent share of the total audience time, they may not hold two or more licences for Channel 3 and/or Five, or have more than a 20 per cent interest in two or more such licences, or provide a foreign satellite service and hold (or hold a 20 per cent inter-est in) such a licence. Paragraph 4 of the Schedule disallowed both the holding of a national Channel 3 licence together with a Five licence, and the holding of geographically overlapping regional licences. Paragraph 5 also imposed an absolute limit of three on the holding of multiplex licences for DTT, which will be considered shortly. In relation to radio, it should be noted that the Schedule did not allow the holding of more than one national licence for a radio service, whether analogue or digital.

Paragraph 11 contained the new limits on cross-media holdings which included newspapers and licensed television or radio services. It must be emphasised, however, that these restrictions did not require the break-up of any pre-existing cross-media groups and referred only to future acquisitions. Essentially, this was a liberalising set of measures, as Gibbons (1996) notes, removing many of the former upper limits on cross-ownership. Under the 1996 rules, however, the owner of a national newspaper with a market share of 20 per cent or more would not be permitted to hold a licence for either Channel 3 or Five, or a radio licence, ruling out either News Corporation or Mirror Group from an expansion into regional commercial television. The owner of a local newspaper with a local share of more than 20 per cent could not hold a regional Channel 3 licence for the same area.

As might be expected, however, the complexity of the media market does not permit its regulation to be carried out entirely by rules. Rather, a wide ranging discretion was granted (by para. 9) to 'the relevant authority' (ITC or Radio Authority) to prevent the granting of a licence for a broadcast service to a body corporate which was (or was connected with) the proprietor of a newspaper 'if the relevant authority determine that in all the circumstances the holding of the licence by that body corporate could be expected to operate against the public interest'.

The Schedule went on (in para. 13) to establish the criteria to be applied as indicative of the public interest. These included:

a) the desirability of promoting –
   i) plurality of ownership in the broadcasting and newspaper industries, and
   ii) diversity in the sources of information available to the public and in the opinions expressed on television or radio or in newspapers,
b) any economic benefits . . .
c) the effect of the holding of the licence by that body on the proper operation of the market within the broadcasting and newspaper industries or any section of them.

The tension and conflict between these competing public interest claims is, as noted in Chapter 3, obvious. The regulators would have to balance potential economic benefits against the values of pluralism and diversity and the effects on competition. This left the regulators with an unenviable task, akin to comparing apples with oranges, and, in the British context, we could not be sure that any such decision would be taken via a transparent process, or even necessarily that adequate reasons would be required or given to permit checks on the rationality of such decision-making. Thus the absence of a meaningful construct of 'public interest' permitted, or even encouraged, inconsistency in regulation, and also handed to regulators significant and largely unchecked discretionary power.

It was difficult to predict the medium-term outcomes that would result from the introduction under the 1996 Act of the combination of set limits on ownership or control, audience share criteria and the exercise of discretion by the regulatory authorities. Certainly, a minimum level of diversity of ownership would be ensured, though whether this would result in the maintenance or enhancement of meaningful diversity in programming or meaningful competition was always doubtful. To some extent, the answer given to this question would depend on whether or not it was assumed that the pre-existing settlement amounted to meaningful diversity. If it was assumed that the existing position did not maximise the diversity of media output available to all citizens, Barendt's observation can usefully be re-stated: 'Conventional competition regulation preventing, for example, new combinations without disturbing existing patterns of ownership may not be enough to achieve this goal' (Barendt 1995: 123). This could also be said to be true in relation to the limited potential for and actuality of interventions regarding newspaper ownership, discussed above.

As one of the present authors wrote shortly after the passage of the 1996 Act.

> [I]n so far as the previous regime has already allowed 63% of national newspaper circulation to be controlled by only two groups, Rupert Murdoch's News Corporation and Mirror Group, and has allowed Murdoch also to take the lead in British satellite broadcasting . . . the omens are not good. It should be expected that the best outcome now likely, from the point of view of diversity, would approximate to the present situation of oligopoly, with worse outcomes being a real possibility. (Feintuck, 1997b: 209)

It can be argued that, though focused on cross-media ownership, the measures failed to provide an integrated response to technological convergence and revised ownership patterns. Indeed, Hitchens (1995a) pointed towards a general mismatch between the regulatory forms adopted and the regulatory objectives, a mismatch deriving, she suggested, from an incrementalist approach to media regulation at a time of technological revolution; in this sense, Elliott's bus still appeared to be accelerating away. In particular, treating control of DTT multiplexes separately from other media interests appeared to fail to acknowledge that such crucial gateways formed an important new media sector in their own right, and the potential influence over the television market to be exerted by those who control multiplexes would tend to suggest that they should be included in the assessment of the size of cross-media empires. Just as the 1990 Act failed to include non-domestic satellite television in its establishment of limits on cross-media holdings, so the failure to integrate multiplexes for DTT into the calculation of cross-media holdings under the 1996 measures left the potential for powerful groups or individuals to shape the new market. A great onus was placed on the regulator to find the optimal solution, yet, as noted above, there remained room for concern regarding the extent to which regulators were sufficiently accountable, especially given the wide latitude provided to them by the courts. Perhaps the key message to come out of reviewing the operation of the 1996 Act is the apparent impossibility of future-proofing legislation in as fast-moving an area as the media – at least, that is, in the absence of establishing a sufficiently clear and strong framework of principle with which to defend against technological and commercial determinism.

4.5 REGULATING DIGITAL TERRESTRIAL TELEVISION

While satellite television had arrived in the UK in 1989 and by 1993 a greatly expanded pay-TV service was available through Sky, by the mid-1990s only a minority of UK households had adopted this new technology. In 1998 BSkyB launched its digital satellite service and by 2001 had switched off its analogue service entirely. For non-satellite viewers, the choice of channels available was expanded slightly in 1997 by the arrival of the analogue Five, available through he traditional television aerial. However, the Broadcasting Act 1996 established the legislative framework for an alternative delivery platform in the form of digital terrestrial television (DTT). Though television viewers will continue to receive the DTT signal via their conventional aerial, they will need to buy a decoder (and in some cases upgrade their aerial), though television sets with in-built decoding equipment have begun to appear on the market. Conventional analogue transmitters will be switched off in due course, in a rolling programme across regions of the UK from 2008 to 2012.

The move to digital technology promises a variety of benefits. DTT promises to bring a significant increase in the number of television channels available free-to-air while at the same time introducing better picture quality, improved stereo sound and widescreen display. This will be achieved by replacing traditional transmission of analogue signals with digital transmission via binary codes which will be unscrambled at the receiver's set through the decoding equipment. The new technology allows the content of a number of different television programmes to be transmitted simultaneously on a single frequency (via 'digital compression'), with capacity built-in to allow for channels or programmes requiring especially high-resolution images to be delivered with enhanced picture quality while other services may be transmitted at a lower quality. In addition to increasing the number of channels, digital compression also frees-up potentially valuable parts of the spectrum for sale, perhaps to the telecommunications industry (Feintuck 1997b), an agenda discussed below in relation to Ofcom's Digital Dividend Review. Blocks of the digital spectrum, 'multiplexes', sufficient to carry a wide range of DTT channels, were allocated by the ITC (ITC 1997) to licensed multiplex providers (see Feintuck 1997c).

Carrying over from the policy of the previous administration, DTT has remained central to the broadcasting policies of the New Labour governments from 1997 onwards. Though the government's consultation paper issued in February 1998 (DCMS 1998) discussed the economic impact of the introduction of DTT and stated that DTT will be part of a television market, it is clear that the government continues to view DTT as a crucial plank of the future television market (DCMS 2004a and 2004b). That said, it should be noted, however, that although DTT is the current focus of much attention, there also remains potential for the further development of satellite broadcasting, though competing for the British market with the well-established BSkyB whose market share continues to increase is likely to be considered an unattractive proposition. Of possibly still greater long-term significance, though as yet still relatively little used in Britain and dependent on a massive investment in the cable infrastructure, could be reception of television via high capacity fibre-optic cable which could integrate familiar television programming with video-on-demand, telecommunications and information technology services. November 2005 saw the arrival of UK telecoms giant BT in the cable television market, suggesting a possible renewed push for growth in this sector (*Observer*, 4 December 2005). However, there is little doubt now that beyond the full-service provision via cable or satellite involving subscription and/or pay-per-view and therefore expensive to the consumer at the point of use, customers persuaded (or forced via the imminent analogue switch-off) to move to digital reception are increasingly more attracted by the BBC-supported *Freeview* DTT service. By spring 2005, Ofcom reported that 61.9 per cent of UK households had access to some form of digital television, with by far the greatest area of growth being DTT (Ofcom 2005f: 4.2.1). By the end of June 2005, digital television penetration had reached 63 per cent. (Ofcom 2005c).

Part I of the 1996 Act was focused on the licensing of multiplex services for DTT. Though sections 40–72 made parallel provisions for the regulation of digital terrestrial radio, the focus here is on the primary broadcast medium, television. Sections 1–39 establish the statutory framework for the allocation of frequencies for multiplexes and for their regulation, inevitably not a straightforward task, especially during the transitional phase of switch-over from analogue to digital transmission. The Act anticipated that multiplex providers would deliver packages of a variety of services intended to appeal to a wide audience, though themed multiplexes are also a possibility. In addition, section 28 ensures provision of capacity via multiplexes for existing analogue service providers (the BBC and independent broadcasters licensed for Channels 3, 4 and 5) whose digital broadcast version of programmes, 'qualifying services' under section 2(2), remain free at the point of reception.

The allocation and enforcement of multiplex licences were dealt with in sections 3–17, with the Act providing for the Secretary of State to determine multiplex frequencies which were then to be allocated by the ITC. Sections 3–5 established general licence conditions, while section 12 added supplementary, specific conditions, and section 10 allowed the ITC to impose financial conditions upon the grant of a licence, essentially mirroring those in the 1990 Act relating to the financial security of the licence holder for conventional, terrestrial television. Included in the specific conditions of section 12 at subsection (1)(g) was a requirement imposing standards as to the technical quality and reliability of the multiplex service, in pursuit of the objectives established in the EU Advanced Television Standards Directive (95/47).

Section 8 established criteria which the ITC had to take into account when considering applications for available licences from would-be multiplex service providers. The criteria included the extent of geographical coverage for the proposed service, the timetable for bringing the service on-stream, the financial viability of the proposal, 'the capacity of the digital programme services proposed to be included in the service to appeal to a variety of tastes and interests', and that 'the applicant has acted in a manner calculated to ensure fair and effective competition in the provision of such services'. Thus these general conditions appeared to demand a guarantee of minimum standards of diversity in programming and the avoidance of anti-competitive practices by those controlling the provision of digital services.

While these criteria were in some respects clearer than the equivalent terms in the previous 1990 Act relating to the ITC's allocation of franchises for commercial terrestrial (analogue) licences and incorporated a similar financial viability test, it is worthy of note that the new provisions did not seem to establish a 'quality threshold' as demanding as that which must be crossed by those seeking regional ITV licences. Although the ITC retained a general brief of ensuring 'quality' in programming under the terms of section 2 of the 1990 Act, there was nothing in the 1996 Act specifically establishing such a requirement in relation to digitally broadcast services. It should be noted also that the rather vague terms of section 8(2)(f) seeking to avoid anti-competitive practices by those seeking multiplex licences had to be viewed alongside the regulatory function of Oftel in relation to conditional access systems (CASs), applications programming interfaces (APIs) and electronic programme guides (EPGs), all of which functions are now within Ofcom's remit.

Section 8 was most noteworthy though for its establishment of an overarching principle which the ITC was seemingly obliged to apply when allocating multiplex licences. The Commission had to consider explicitly whether the grant of a licence 'would be calculated to promote the development of digital television broadcasting in the United Kingdom otherwise than by satellite'. This makes clear that the government's policy at the time the Act was passed was the rapid development of DTT as the primary means of delivery, a policy unchanged by the arrival of a Labour government in 1997. Section 28 sought to further this policy by establishing a privileged position for existing broadcasters of analogue terrestrial television (BBC, regional ITV companies, Channel 4 and Five) who would have multiplex capacity reserved for them, presumably in an attempt to ensure the early development of a digital service carrying a range of 'quality' programming. Sections 19 and 31 introduced specific provisions for the protection of Welsh and Scottish Gaelic language services in DTT.

Separate to the provisions relating to multiplex licences were those for the licensing of digital programme services (i.e. the programme provider as opposed to the multiplex licensee) in sections 18–23. These were to be subject to the same conditions, for example relating to taste and decency, then monitored by the ITC in relation to conventional licensed television broadcasters under the 1990 Act. Licences would, however, be issued 'essentially, on demand' (Gibbons 1996), subject only to general requirements as to the applicant being a fit and proper person to hold such a license, terms which are not necessarily uncontentious in themselves (see Hitchens 1995b).

Section 33 addressed the medium-term decision to switch off analogue transmission, requiring the Secretary of State to keep under review the development of DTT services, the expectation being that simultaneous transmission of analogue signals ('simulcasting') would continue until such time as the vast majority of viewers are receiving DTT. Estimates as to this period varied, but were commonly in the region of 10–15 years (see DCMS 1998a), a timeframe now confirmed by the government's commitment to complete the switch-off process by 2012.

Conspicuous by their absence from the primary legislation on broadcasting were detailed measures concerning arguably the key regulatory issue arising out of DTT, namely the technological infrastructure relating to EPGs etc. This, states Gibbons (1996), commenting on section 12, reflected the government's wish not to intervene in market activity which would itself, the government believed, in time result in the emergence of an industry standard. In their ability to organise the EPG and allocate channels, an unregulated controller would have power to discriminate between broadcasters. In addition, many concerns have been voiced regarding the problems of compatibility between equipment supplied by different manufacturers and the potential for a destructive war of formats such as that experienced in the early days of home video-cassette recorders. In practice though, it might be thought that some of these concerns would be lessened if the development and marketing of decoder equipment were to be undertaken by a major multiplex provider or an established player in pay-television such as BSkyB, given that it would then be hard to imagine any other potential competitor attempting to launch alternative decoder equipment. However, while such a situation might avoid a potentially destructive battle, the viewer could need some reassurance that such a dominant degree of control over both the distribution system and technological gateway would not lead to abuse of this power. Clearly, any such abuse could impact adversely on citizens' ability to access a diverse range of broadcast material, though in the current consumerist climate, the best comfort offered at the time was probably summed up in the observation by Herbert Ungerer of the EU's Directorate General IV (Competition) quoted by Marsden (1997b) that 'Consumer benefit will result from increased possibilities of supply only if markets are liberalised and gates are kept open'. While the comment as to liberalisation may be more closely connected with the EU's economic agenda than with the kind of citizenship interests discussed in Chapter 3, on this occasion the interests of citizen-as-citizen and citizen-as-consumer appear to coincide so far as the maintenance of free movement through gateways is concerned.

Though the EU produced general statements on standardisation, interconnection and interoperability of telecommunications, information technology and other communications equipment, many of the issues relevant here were addressed directly by the Advanced Television Standards Directive (95/47). Article 4(c) establishes a requirement that:

> Member States shall take all the necessary measures to ensure that the operators of conditional access services, irrespective of the means of transmission, who produce and market access services to digital television services . . . offer to all broadcasters, on a fair, reasonable and non-discriminatory basis, technical services enabling the broadcasters' digitally-transmitted services to be received by viewers authorized by means of decoders administered by the service operators, and comply with Community competition law, in particular if a dominant position appears.

The UK government introduced by secondary legislation measures (Advanced Television Services Regulations 1996, SI 1996/3151) which implemented the Directive, Regulation 11 largely reproducing the terminology of Article 4(c). In force from the same date as the Regulations, 7 January 1997, was a Class Licence (under section 7 of the Telecommunications Act 1984) introduced by the Secretary of State to authorise the running of CASs relating to subscription services.

Though functions have become fused in one location by the arrival of Ofcom, Britain's then telecommunications regulator, Oftel, was to play a significant role in this area, both in terms of licensing the CASs and establishing guidelines for the CAS sector. In this respect, Oftel (1997c) identified four key objectives:

1. ensuring that control of conditional access technology is not used to distort, restrict or prevent competition in television and connected services, i.e. is not used anti-competitively;
2. ensuring that control of conditional access technology does not lead to consumer choice being artificially constrained both in relation to consumer equipment and the range of services available;
3. facilitating the ability of consumers to switch between delivery mechanisms; and
4. facilitating consumer choice by ensuring ease of access to relevant information.

Oftel indicated that their guidelines, within the framework established by the Regulations and the Class Licence, 'are part of a systematic effort to ensure consistency of approach to the regulation of communications networks, whether they are wire or fibre-based or wireless, or broadcast or hybrids of these' (Oftel 1997c).

The active involvement of Oftel (which had hitherto been primarily the regulator of telecommunications) in relation to the development of CASs seemed welcome at the time. It served as an acknowledgement of the convergence of media and communications technology and could be seen as pointing the way towards a future in which a unified regulatory regime would be put in place. In the meantime, however, the measurement of audience/circulation share as an indicator of strength of cross-media holdings remained inadequate given that it failed to integrate into this calculation the crucial factor of control of technological gateways. Disappointingly, while paragraph 5 of Schedule 2 to the 1996 Act established a maximum of three multiplex licences which could be held together, it did not factor this holding into the overall limits on cross-media ownership.

Thus the 1996 Act sought to establish a detailed framework for the regulation of the new DTT delivery platform. It even appeared to represent a somewhat proactive rather than reactive move. However, subsequent history has demonstrated the difficulty in establishing a legislative basis which ensures the viability of such a new service and the critical role of market forces in such an area.

The imminence of the arrival of DTT and its importance in the minds of significant media players were emphasised in early 1997 when applications were made for the first available multiplex licences. Competing with an application from *Digital Television Network (DTN)*, wholly owned by *CableTel*, Britain's largest cable television company, was a consortium, *British Digital Broadcasting (BDB)*, incorporating three of the biggest players in British commercial broadcasting: *BSkyB, Carlton Communications* and *Granada Television*. With the active cooperation of the BBC, *BDB* made an application based on proposals to provide fifteen new channels. If this application had been granted as it stood, it would have allowed Rupert Murdoch, the key figure behind both *BSkyB* (Britain's major satellite broadcasting company) and *News Corporation* (whose publications account for over one-third of the British national newspaper market), to exercise a further significant influence over the media via control of multiplexes and the associated CAS.

In June 1997, despite acknowledging the qualities of a competing bid from *DTN*, the ITC awarded control (ITC 1997) of the three commercial multiplexes for DTT to the *BDB* consortium. However, influenced in part, no doubt, by advice from Oftel (Oftel, 1997a and b), the ITC was only prepared to accept the *BDB* bid if *BSkyB* were to sell its one-third equity holding to the other consortium members, themselves both already major media players.

Despite *BSkyB*'s withdrawal from the consortium, Oftel's Director General continued to express concern regarding *BSkyB*'s likely position of dominance in relation to programme supply to the new channels, especially in the key areas of sport coverage and movie premieres. He noted that, even with *BSkyB* excluded from holding a share in multiplex licences, 'the participation of BSkyB . . . as a long term supplier of certain pay TV services, in particular sports programming, raised substantial competition concerns in the pay TV network and conditional access markets' (Oftel, 1997b). This reflects the situation described by Herman and McChesney (1997: 68) in the US, where media giants like *Disney* and *Time Warner*, who increasingly provide their own products, notably films, on a privileged basis to their own channels, can effectively shut out competitors from the market.

On the day after the announcement of the ITC's decision, it was observed that 'The BDB affair has exposed the regulatory turf war between . . . Oftel and the ITC, making it even more imperative for the Government to produce a new, more robust regulatory system for the new media technologies' (*Guardian*, 25 June 1997). A degree of tension between regulators sharing jurisdiction is inevitable and perhaps even helpful in the short term if it facilitates the articulation of clear regulatory standards. However, it was by no means clear that this would in fact be the outcome, and, in the longer term, it might have been expected to result primarily in uncertainty, and may have indeed impeded the identification and attainment of regulatory goals. It may also have led to resentment among those who felt that they had suffered at the hands of an uncertain regulatory regime, and the overall effect of this tension seems to be to confirm the logic behind the development of Ofcom.

However, in practice, the initial settlement established for DTT proved short-lived. While DTT broadcasts began in 1998, uptake of the BDB service (branded *ONdigital*) was small, despite offers of free set-top decoder boxes. In 2001 *ONdigital* relaunched as *ITV Digital*, but by the end of 2002 even this new service had closed down, having singularly failed to achieve commercial viability. Replaced by the new *Freeview* service, which incorporates a major BBC presence, the figures quoted above illustrate the major role now being played by DTT in leading the growth in digital television, suggesting that, at the third attempt, the DTT market is becoming properly established.

Of course, to a significant extent viewer uptake of digital television must be seen to be driven not exclusively by the attractions of the new service in terms of picture quality and availability of additional channels, but significantly by the policy decision to switch-off analogue transmission by 2012. The 'Digital Dividend' for viewers, in terms of the television services they may receive, is of course matched by what is perhaps a more significant, parallel dividend in terms of the freeing-up of blocks of the spectrum by the more efficient use of frequencies arising from digital compression, to be sold-off for new commercial uses. Ofcom's Digital Dividend Review, launched in November 2005 (Ofcom 2005g), indicates unambiguously the intention in this context to shift from the historic 'command-and-control' approach, via which government or its agencies allocated frequencies, to a market-led approach to be overseen by Ofcom.

The example of the infancy of DTT and its regulation demonstrates perhaps that despite attempts to establish a detailed framework in the 1996 Act, the generally reactive and marginal reform of the British media regulation regime brought about in the 1990s can be viewed as having failed to resolve underlying tensions between competing regulatory approaches and philosophies. In particular, the challenge of seeking a firm regulatory basis while simultaneously seeking to emphasise market solutions seemed to pose an almost insuperable problem in the context of DTT. Indeed, in confirming attempts to allow the coexistence of competing and potentially conflicting rationales, it might be thought to indicate a degree of ongoing complacency and myopia which was always likely to prove dangerous in the context of the ongoing media revolution. Certainly, the story of DTT is one driven by technological development, commercial pressure and governmental faith in market forces rather than an emphasis on citizens' needs or desires.

In reality, while we have now had more than ten years of government policy dedicated to the development of DTT, it needs to be remembered that DTT cannot be viewed as a direct competitor to digital satellite services. DTT does not offer the range of services offered by Sky, either in terms of the sheer number of channels or the premium subscription sports and movie services. It does, however, for a relatively small initial outlay, provide a somewhat expanded range of services, incorporating all major existing and extended PSB services, and may be thought to continue in a modern format the socially inclusive aspect of television broadcasting. In practice, once all viewers have made the initial outlay (though some social-exclusionary effect should still be anticipated here), and assuming a problem-free switchover to digital transmission, it should be expected that to some extent the arrival of DTT will serve positively in terms of raising the threshold of quantity of channels available through a baseline, free-to-air television service. Of course, it should also be remembered that the rapidly increasing uptake of this service cannot necessarily be viewed simply as a consequence of a popular clamour or desire for the new service; the lack of interest from viewers in DTT during its first few years serves as elegant testimony to this. Rather, it must also be seen in terms of viewers accepting the inevitably of the forthcoming termination of conventional analogue services. The increasing uptake of DTT has been brought about directly by government policy, though this in turn can properly be viewed as driven by a high degree of technological and market determinism.

4.6 THE COMMUNICATIONS ACT 2003 AND OFCOM'S EARLY YEARS

The government's response to the tensions and failings illustrated above was the reform package introduced by the Communications Act 2003 centred around the introduction of the media super-regulator, Ofcom. While there was clearly a pressing logic indicating such a move and it was a move favoured by influential thinkers within the New Labour fold (IPPR/Collins and Murroni), as was argued strongly by critics at the time, for example in the first edition of this work, simply replacing multiple regulators with one would not necessarily remedy long-term underlying problems relating to the lack of development, articulation and application of clear principles for the media regulation regime. Just as had previous major legislative reforms of the regulatory system, so the passage of the 2003 Act represented another opportunity to consider such fundamentals and to redesign the regulatory structure to reflect them.

As will become apparent in Chapter 6, the legislative reform was driven not only by such pressing domestic issues, but also by harmonisation-oriented developments within the EU manifested in the 2002 'New Regulatory Framework'. The UK government's White Paper (2002) certainly reflected this influence and the kinds of issues just considered in the previous section. However, as has been argued elsewhere, 'whether the real underlying issues were fully addressed is highly questionable' (Feintuck 2003: 106). As has been noted in the previous chapter and elsewhere (Feintuck 2003), despite the Puttnam Committee's best efforts, the legislation passed in 2003 seems to pay lip-service to, rather than develop and pivot regulation around, a concept of 'public interest'. Indeed, it may be reasonably suggested that the primary driver for the programme of reform related not so much to any issues specific to the media context, but rather to the UK government's ideological attachment to the efficacy of market forces, and consequently to the perceived benefits to be had from deregulation. As a result, the government's rhetoric associated with the introduction of the legislation to Parliament placed great emphasis on deregulation, or 'light touch' regulation, and in particular the intention to remove or relax the existing rules relating to media ownership introduced by the 1996 Act (Feintuck 2003: 112). The light-touch requirement is translated in section 3(3) of the Act into a requirement for Ofcom's regulatory activities to be 'proportionate . . . and targeted only at cases in which action is needed', an approach re-emphasised by the section 6 duties to review regulatory burdens. These provisions mirror the focus of other, associated New Labour legislation, as exemplified by the Enterprise Act 2002 (discussed in Chapter 3), which in turn might be seen as reflecting a high degree of continuity from the previous Conservative government's Deregulation and Contracting Out Act 1994.

The Communications Act 2003, which received Royal Assent in July of that year, is certainly a voluminous piece of legislation, with its 411 sections and 19 schedules running to a total of 590 pages in printed form! In many ways the Act's greatest significance relates to the establishment of Ofcom, the 'super-regulator', which acquired powers previously exercised by the ITC, Radio Authority, Broadcasting Standards Council, Radiocommunications Agency and Oftel, plus a range of wholly new powers. Here we seek only to highlight the measures which relate most closely to our central themes. In particular, we will reprise briefly our comments on the Act's provisions relating to Ofcom's general duties and powers before turning to focus on those relating to competition in media markets. In this latter context we will consider in particular the merger of Carlton and Granada which formed a major practical test of how New Labour would exercise power in this area. Discussion of Ofcom's role in relation to broadcast programme content, established in sections 12 and 13 of the Act, are considered in Chapter 5, while the high-profile issue of broadcasting rights relating to major sporting events is picked up in Chapter 6.

4.6.1 The public service broadcasting review

Ofcom's relationship with the BBC and the review of the BBC's Charter has already been considered in Chapter 2. However, the 2003 Act imposed on Ofcom a duty to engage in a broader review of public service television as a whole. Under section 264, Ofcom was required to engage in a review of public service television broadcasting in the UK, both from the point of view of considering the extent to which broadcasters have met existing obligations, and also, under section 264(3)(b) 'with a view to maintaining and strengthening the quality of public service television broadcasting'.

We considered in Chapter 3 how the Act sets out, in section 264(4), the purposes of public service television, in terms of a wide range of subject matter, meeting the needs and satisfying the interests of as many different audiences as possible, with a proper balance as regards nature and subject-matter to meet such interests, and providing programming which meets high general standards as regards content, quality of programme making and professional skill, and editorial integrity. Beyond these purposes, section 264(6) goes on to add expectations of public service broadcasting as a whole, including 'the dissemination of information and for the provision of education and entertainment', the stimulation of cultural activity and diversity, the facilitation of civic understanding and comprehensive and authoritative coverage of domestic and international news and current affairs, plus specifically a suitable range and quantity of programming relating to science, religion and social issues, plus sporting coverage, children's programmes and an appropriate quantity of programming made outside the London area. In some ways, this list might seem no more than the Reithian vision restated, or somewhat fleshed out.

The huge task of reviewing public service television (meaning BBC, ITV, Channel 4, Five and Teletext) in relation to these standards was undertaken by Ofcom in three phases (Ofcom 2004a, 2004b and 2004c), starting November 2003, with the findings of the final phase of the review being published in February 2005. The findings are, inevitably, voluminous, but are summarised succinctly in Ofcom's Annual report for 2004–5 on its Core Areas of Activity (Ofcom 2005h), from which we quote below. Again, we will not attempt to be comprehensive in our coverage, but will simply try to highlight some issues and findings which resonate in relation to this book's key themes.

The review brings out some telling trends. With digital take-up at 56 per cent of households, Phase 1 of the review found significant drops in the main terrestrial channels' audience share over the previous five years, with viewing figures for certain 'serious' current affairs and arts programming being 50 per cent lower in multi-channel homes when compared with households equipped only to receive analogue terrestrial. In terms of broader programming, BBC and ITV average audience shares dropped by almost 4 per cent and 8 per cent respectively between 1998 and 2003, with audience share of ITV and Channel 4 in homes with satellite television in 2004 only just over half of that in non-satellite households. The review also highlights a significant landmark, in that it reveals that in 2003–4, subscription revenues overtook advertising revenue in commercial television for the first time.

Despite such trends, and an emphasis by Ofcom on the 'promotion of more choice and competition' (Ofcom 2004c: 1.8) through a competitive market place, Ofcom found widespread public support for the idea that public intervention in broadcasting was justified and sustainable, based on a recognition that the benefits offered (associated with the characteristics of public service broadcasting identified above) could otherwise be under-provided by the market. As a result, Ofcom concluded from Phase 1 that there was a strong and enduring rationale for the continued provision of PSB, into the digital age'. However, in the course of Phases 2 and 3, Ofcom concluded that the institutional and regulatory arrangements and funding methods currently associated with public service television 'would not survive the transition to the digital age, and could erode by digital switchover, if not before'. More specifically, in the absence of any continuing spectrum scarcity justifying regulation via licensing, and given increased competition for viewers draining funding, the current model could not be sustained, with current affairs and regional programming, two key aspects of the public service tradition, thought to be particularly at risk. The position arrived at seemed to be that if change is not undertaken, one possible outcome of an increasingly competitive commercial sector was greater responsibility on the BBC in terms of delivering a public service agenda, raising substantial questions of funding, and, if the BBC acquired something like a monopoly in public service provision (whether or not strictly within the 'market failure' model discussed in Chapter 2) an absence of plurality of public service voice. Thus Ofcom points towards a need to develop a model of public service television which is sufficiently adaptable and flexible to respond to the challenges and changes which will emerge in the digital era.

An outline of Ofcom's vision of a new model is set out in the findings of Phase 2 of the review. The findings include: a 'recognition of the increasing importance of a properly funded, independent, public service-focused BBC, funded through a licence-fee model' but with substantially revised governance arrangements (see Chapter 2); Channel 4 remaining a not-for-profit, free-to-air broadcaster; a new approach to programming for the UK's regions and component nations, affecting both BBC and ITV; and a specific role for Channel 5 as a 'market-led public service broadcaster' with a commitment to domestically produced programming. However, perhaps the most interesting and controversial finding might be thought to be the proposal for 'the establishment of a new Public Service Publisher (PSP) model, using new technologies and distribution systems to meet audience needs in the digital age'. Ofcom suggested an increase in the television licence fee to cover the cost of the PSP providing public service content across a range of new media platforms, but the spending figure suggested for the PSP, £300 million per annum, seems small, representing only less than 3 per cent of the UK commercial television revenues in 2003, but, conveniently perhaps, being approximately the same amount of licence fee money currently being spent by the BBC on preparations for digital switchover.

Certainly the three-phase Ofcom review must represent the most detailed and far-reaching review of public service television in the UK ever undertaken. In combination with the unprecedented statutory enshrinement of a coherent statement of values of public service broadcasting in the Communications Act, and the contemporaneous reviews of BBC governance, Charter and licence fee, the world of public service broadcasting has come under an extraordinary amount of scrutiny in recent years. The extent to which public service values identified in these processes mesh with what might be termed 'the public interest' has already been addressed in Chapter 3, and will be returned to, though on an interim basis it can be concluded at this stage that the process of review has at least served as an opportunity for unpacking and examining some long-standing and often implicit assumptions about the basis for the historical model of public service broadcasting in the UK.

4.6.2 Ofcom's general powers and accountability

However, Ofcom exercises a range of powers extending far beyond reviewing public service television. Ofcom's general functions, powers and duties are set out in sections 1–9. As discussed in the previous chapter, though section 3(1) establishes a principal duty relating to the interests of citizens, the potential significance of this is substantially reduced by the same subsection's parallel requirement for Ofcom to 'further the interests of consumers', while later subsections of section 3 list a further nineteen factors which Ofcom is required to secure or to which it must also have regard. As already observed in Chapter 3, these potentially conflicting priorities must be read alongside the duty under section 3(6) establishing a priority for EU obligations and the duty under section 6 to pursue the lightest possible touch in regulation, minimising the regulatory burden. Combined with the section 3(7) power to resolve any conflict between its general duties 'in the manner they think best in the circumstances', it might be thought that these provisions confirm the likely relegation of citizens' interests to some way down the hierarchy of Ofcom's priorities, or at least a lack of certainty that they will receive significant priority.

Clearly the accountability of operation of a regulator with as wide a set of powers and extensive discretion as Ofcom is of some concern, and an important aspect of this would seem to be transparency of operation. The Select Committee on Culture Media and Sport in its Second Special Report (2003–4 session) noted that:

> To ensure maximum transparency in regulatory decisions, and to provide a further safeguard against regulatory capture, Ofcom should hold hearings and meetings, including board meetings, in public with minutes published promptly. Publicly funded, and theoretically publicly accountable, bodies should not operate in secrecy. (Para. 47)

In response to this approach, the government noted that 'under the Communications Act, Ofcom must, in performing its duties, have regard to the principles of the Better Regulation Task Force, including that of transparency, and any other principles appearing to them to represent the best regulatory practice' (ibid., Appendix 1). However, the government continued, 'It is for Ofcom to decide on the balance between these and operational imperatives.'

In its reply to the Select Committee on these matters, Ofcom gave an unambiguous response. Starting from a position that 'Ofcom will always strive to be transparent in how decisions are reached', the reply goes on to refer to open public meetings held around the country and further consultation on its Annual Plan. However, it continues that:

> Ofcom believes that the Board should continue to meet in private and that this will not compromise our goal of effective accountability or our commitment to transparency. Notes of the Ofcom Board meetings and other advisory committees are always published on the Ofcom website. Ofcom believes that holding Board meetings in public will inhibit the free interchange of ideas and opinion necessary for collective Board responsibility . . . Commercial confidentiality also presents particular difficulties in allowing Board meetings to be held in public. (Ibid., Appendix 2)

While it has been noted by the DCMS Select Committee (3rd Report, 24 February 2004: 12) that 'this is not the first time that the net-curtains mentality has prevailed over the Government's commitment to openness', the polemical tone of this statement should not drown out the very legitimate constitutional and democratic concerns raised by any lack of transparency in the operation of such a powerful regulator. Government, or regulation, 'by moonlight' (Birkinshaw *et al.* 1990) in the absence of the antiseptic glare of sunlight, should always trigger alarm bells for those concerned to ensure accountability – especially so where the powers involved in regulating touch so closely upon the democratically central, public interest concerns regarding the media's role in relation to citizens.

4.6.3 *Regulating Channel 3*

Historically, the regulation of commercial broadcasting as manifested by ITV/Channel 3, pursued one aspect of citizenship interests via obligations imposed on regional licence holders to provide programming tailored to the needs of viewers in their particular regions. The regional nature of the ITV structure was a fundamental feature from its earliest days. Section 263 of the 2003 Act confirms Ofcom's duty to secure compliance with such licence requirements or conditions, while section 287 specifies a requirement for regional programming 'of particular interest to persons living within the area for which the service is provided'. It is of interest, however, that section 286 also empowers Ofcom specifically to ensure that the regional programming for Channel 3 licence holders must contain a 'suitable proportion' (section 286(1)) of programmes and expenditure made outside the M25 area, which requirement is rendered somewhat more specific by the words 'a significant proportion' in section 286(6). While this could be viewed as much a matter of general industrial and economic policy as of media policy, the reality for Ofcom seems likely to be that regional commitments will have to be balanced against other commitments required of licence holders. How Ofcom interpret and enforce requirements in relation to regional programming and production raises important questions about how the regulator may in practice support aspects of public service broadcasting. It is worth quoting from the Select Committee on Culture Media and Sport's Second Special Report (DCMS 2004: para. 58):

> The protection and maintenance of regional commitments by Channel 3 licensees will be the first major test for Ofcom. It is essential that it pass this test, since faith in its decisions will otherwise be undermined. Furthermore, we see no reason why this process should not be conducted in public.

Thus the Select Committee highlights both the significance of the issues involved and, again, the need for transparency and accountability in Ofcom's decision-making. The government's response was as follows:

> The Government notes the Committee's recommendations. The Government is committed to retaining a strong regional dimension to public service broadcasting. The provisions of the Communications Act should ensure that public service broadcasting continues to reflect UK cultural traditions, and to meet the needs of diverse social and linguistic communities. This is a matter for Ofcom and . . . it must find the proper balance between transparency and effective decision-making. (DCMS Second Special Report 2004: Appendix 1)

While the government's sanguine response serves to reconfirm a commitment to regional programming, it also confirms its non-interventionist approach and the discretion invested in Ofcom in this respect, both as regards substance and transparency in procedures. While Ofcom issued guidance in April 2004 as regards how it would interpret the statutory requirements on regional production, it has now gone somewhat further, announcing in its Annual Plan for 2005–6 plans for a review of the content production sector. However, it should constantly be borne in mind that Ofcom's duties and powers in this field are subject to the overarching 'light touch' requirement of section 6. A somewhat firmer commitment to regional programming might be thought necessary, especially given the challenges posed to the traditional vision of a regional basis for Channel 3 by digitalisation and the fragmentation of audience share and advertising revenue which is likely to result, and also by the more immediate threat apparent from any unification of Channel 3 as a result of corporate mergers.

4.7 CARLTON AND GRANADA – TOWARDS A UNIFIED ITV

Despite the significance of ongoing consideration of the BBC's Charter and its licence fee, this should not be allowed to overshadow another very significant landmark event in UK public service broadcasting in recent years: the merger of the two giants of ITV, Carlton and Granada. Especially given the strong regional basis traditionally underpinning Channel 3 which has just been discussed but more generally the emphasis placed on diversity of voice within pubic service television, the consequences of this merger, if unregulated or inadequately regulated, seem to have the potential to allow commercial forces and corporate interests to reshape fundamentally the public service broadcasting landscape.

The interplay of provisions of the Communications Act 2003 and Enterprise Act 2002 establishing the legal context for 'public interest' interventions in media mergers has been discussed in the previous chapter. However, It should be borne in mind that the merger of Carlton and Granada was announced in October 2002, with Ofcom only at a nascent stage at that time and the Communications Act 2003 not yet passed. The financial powers necessary to establish the regulator had been granted by the Office of Communications Act 2002, but while the Communications Bill which set out the regulator's substantive powers had been published in May 2002, the Parliamentary passage of the Bill was not concluded until it received Royal Assent and passed into law in July 2003. Thus the merger occurred contemporaneously with the passage of the Communications Act 2003 and the new law was not applicable for the period in which the events took place, though the approach adopted by the government and the outcome achieved may be indicative of the approach likely to be taken to future cases.

As noted earlier, under the Broadcasting Act 1996, paragraph 11 of Schedule 2 established that if a person (natural or legal) controls more than a 15 per cent share of the total audience time, they may not hold two or more licences for Channel 3. The proposed merger of Carlton and Granada was to result in approximately a 19 per cent market share (Doyle 2002: 718) and would consolidate all but three of the fifteen regional Channel 3 licences. It also had a significant potential to reshape or distort the market in television advertising, allowing the newly formed Carlton/Granada group to dominate via holding a massive 51 per cent share of TV advertising revenue (Wilkinson 2003: 23). Under the existing legislation, a merger involving more than 15 per cent of audience share could be permitted, subject to ministerial approval as advised by the Competition Commission.

In March 2003, with the Communications Bill still to complete its Parliamentary passage, Patricia Hewitt, Secretary of State for Trade and Industry, referred the proposed merger to the Competition Commission for a determination as to whether it was likely to be contrary to the public interest. Seven months later, in October, the Competition Commission reported that the merger raised public interest concerns in two respects: first, in relation to the remaining Channel 3 regional licensees outside the group, and second, in relation to future competition within the market for sales of advertising time. In November 2003, however, the minister announced that the merger would be allowed to proceed, allowing the creation of ITV plc, given that signed undertakings in respect of threats to the public interest had been received. In addition, in response to the particular concerns of the advertising industry, the Competition Commission put in place the Contracts Rights Renewal process, incorporating an independent adjudicator supported by Ofcom in monitoring the system, in order to protect against unfair or discriminatory practice in the sale of television airtime by the newly dominant corporation.

Thus, in permitting the merger, recognition was given to and active steps were taken to protect certain vulnerable economic interests within the media industries. This is not to say, however, that a broader range of 'public interests', manifested in public service values relevant to citizens either individually or collectively, were necessarily adequately protected and, as was emphasised to Ofcom by Gerald Kaufman, as Chair of the Commons Media Select Committee, in December 2003, close monitoring might be required to ensure that they met the obligations arising form the undertakings given prior to the merger being approved.

Some post-merger developments and ongoing trends may seem troubling as regards Channel 3's public service remit. Despite the fact that Ofcom's review revealed that the vast majority of viewers are 'very' or 'quite interested' in programming relating to their area, local and regional programming within ITV had already been subjected to cuts in 2002 and 2003, and in October 2003, with the merger on the point of approval, ITV made public plans to cut almost 50 per cent of the workforce at Southampton-based Granada franchise, Meridian Broadcasting. February 2004 saw the closure of ITV studios in Nottingham and the announcement of restructuring in Birmingham, resulting in the loss of

400 jobs. Such moves seemed to challenge not only traditions of local programme production, but also raised concerns among trade unions as regards the production of independent programming falling to freelance contractors, leading to a likely reduction in the quality of working conditions within the television industry (O'Malley 2005). In early 2005, Ofcom determined that ITV would be allowed to halve its religious programming, with the regulator basing the decision on the 'taken together' standard of section 264(6), which means that the question of sufficient quantity of this category of programming should be judged across all public service channels (i.e. including BBC and Channel 4) rather than viewing ITV in isolation. Later in the same year, arising out of Phase 3 of its public service review, the weekly requirement for non-news regional programming applicable to ITV was cut to one and a half hours – less than one tenth of its previous peak, and with the likelihood of a further reduction still after digital switchover in 2012. Though not in themselves fundamentally challenging the basis for delivering public service television, such developments do indicate the potential within the regulatory framework for the degradation of the public service landscape. Though statistics may not always be reliable indicators of meaningful trends, the 2004–5 period saw ITV's viewing figures decline, most dramatically in relation to its 10 p.m. news slot where it competes directly with the BBC. Without claiming to offer this as a firm conclusion, it could obviously be suggested that ITV's contribution to the public service broadcasting culture is reducing.

At the same time, however, another more concrete consequence of the merger can be identified. The consolidation and centralisation arising from the merger resulted in a situation where, after its first full year of trading as a merged company, *ITV plc* announced a 57 per cent increase in pre-tax profits, arising from a combination of increased advertising revenue and savings in operating costs.

What is illustrated by the Carlton/Granada merger here is a clear tension between competing visions of public interest which should be reasonably familiar from the framework established earlier in this book, and which has historically been accommodated, if not always comfortably, within the regulatory framework for commercial television in the UK's public service model. Though not strictly a test of the new powers established by the 2003 Act, it nonetheless illustrates the significance of the matters to be determined via whatever discretionary power is granted under the legislative framework. On the one hand, we see the 'public interests' associated with the regional ITV tradition which militate against the merger. In Doyle's terms, 'a key test is what impact consolidation of radio or television ownership is likely to have on the total value these services give to their audiences. In order to favour the public interest, consolidation of ownership must be achieved without any reduction in aggregate listener or viewer welfare' (Doyle 2002: 721). On the other hand there is a different vision which, though a legitimate factor, might be thought dangerous if excessive weight or total primacy is given to it. This relates to the government's view of a perceived national economic interest in allowing media corporations to grow, both in order to achieve economies of scale and potentially to compete effectively in an increasingly large-scale global media market. If Doyle is right to suggest that 'the main impetus guiding actual changes of policy is a desire to accommodate the strategic interests and concerns for major UK commercial media players' (Doyle 2002: 715), then the broader vision of public interest historically associated with British public service television may well be under serious threat.

4.8 SAME AS IT EVER WAS?

In relation to the legislative framework and regulatory practice in place prior to 2003, it could be legitimately observed that there was a certain lack of clarity in relation to the vision of the role of the state as embodied in media regulation. Measures designed to bring about a particular model of competition were applied, though based on somewhat arbitrary fixed limits and differing approaches and in the absence of clear definition of the media market. The regulatory machine was periodically reformed, in response to the changing market and technological environment, but without the development or statement of clear objectives appropriate to new circumstances. The absence of anything approaching a serious media policy, or fundamental review of regulatory practices, was repeatedly illustrated. The approach was to an extent typified by the Conservative and New Labour governments' unswerving adherence to the rapid development of DTT as opposed to cable or DTH satellite as the primary delivery platform, with an underlying suggestion that they failed to challenge the views of DTT's proponents and exponents who, Marsden (1997b: 3) observed, presented it as 'a paradigmatic, determinist "revolutionary" policy choice'.

Though the changes to the statutory position brought about by the 1996 Act could be condemned as simply reactive, a response to the changing media market, they faced the still more serious charge of failing to iron out underlying defects in the system. In particular, the lack of clarity in regulatory objectives remained and seemed likely to be resolved pragmatically by the outcome of a possible 'regulatory turf war' between the ITC and Oftel, rather than as a result of informed, public debate.

The failure of the 1996 Act to integrate control of DTT multiplexes and infrastructure into calculations of broader market share seemed worrying, and short-sighted at the time, and no less so now. No aspect of the media market can be treated in isolation in such a fast-changing environment; forty years ago it was apparent to Blumler and Madge (1967) that 'It is essential that [the] modern communication process should be examined as a whole and not by studying certain parts in isolation'. Just as the exclusion from the relevant provisions of the 1990 Act for non-domestic satellite broadcasters allowed Murdoch's *BSkyB* to extend its overall empire, to define the shape of the British DTH satellite broadcasting market and to influence the shape of broadcasting as a whole, so failures in the regulation of DTT may have consequences not limited to that particular media sector. The implications of the spread of the *Carlton* and *Granada* empires into DTT, though not necessarily problematic in itself at the time, may now seem to have been the forerunner of the newly consolidated position in the form of *ITV plc* following their merger, even if the early involvement in DTT did not prove wholly successful.

In summary, the regulatory patterns established in relation to conventional television and DTT remained highly reactive in nature up to and including the 1996 Act, with government policy and legislation steered not in the direction of clear objectives but rather blown by the gusty winds of change. An acknowledgement that pluralism in ownership is not an end in itself but merely instrumental in the furtherance of citizenship objectives might have provided a stronger anchor for regulation in the tidal wave of change. In addition, the application of an unambiguously citizenship-oriented approach may have also helped in the interpretation of both broadly stated assertions of public interest justifications for regulation (for example, as stated in DNH 1995a), and the complex, technical provisions contained in Schedule 2 to the 1996 Act.

The difference in approach to regulating the broadcast and printed media has already been referred to in Chapter 3, and will be returned to in Chapter 5 as regards broadcast or published content. However, it is worth reiterating here that in an era of technological convergence, where both television news-type services and newspaper material is available via the Internet, such differences become increasingly difficult to justify. In addition, the increasingly international nature of broadcasting, and of press ownership, may add extra pressures to the policing of broadcast content.

However, this did not necessarily constitute a case for a move to lowest-common-denominator or minimalist regulation; the position was not such as to concede defeat from a citizenship perspective. Rather, it led authors such as Collins and Murroni (1996) and one of the present authors (Feintuck 1999) in the direction of a single communications regulator, best able to take an overview of the media market, but, crucially, structured in such a way as to ensure transparency and rationality in the exercise of its discretion. It is interesting to note that in the late 1990s even Oftel, the new arrival on the media regulation scene, showed signs of enthusiasm regarding the rationalising of regulation towards a single regulator model, though on a basis which excluded regulation of content, an exclusion which, given the underlying objective of regulation, would seem to risk undermining the utility of any such move.

Ongoing concerns persisted following the 1996 Act as regards powers such as those exercised by the ITC and BSC, or the powers of appointment and influence exercised by the government in relation to the appointments to the BBC's Board of Governors and to a lesser extent Channel 4, and it was necessary and advisable to continue to argue that they must be exercised in the sunshine of public scrutiny. Thus, in addition to substantive reforms being indicated in relation to ensuring the presence and pursuit of rational objectives for the regulatory endeavour, it was also necessary to consider a new range of procedural safeguards, especially given the historical absence in Britain of clear constitutional principles and weaknesses in the judicial system in respect of elaborating principles of general application.

In essence, it seemed to some that the regulatory system was doing little more than legitimise the outcome of market tendencies within the media, being left with more symbolic than substantive significance. Though tinkering at the margins, the 'system' continued to allow high degrees of concentration within and across different sectors of the media and demonstrated little if any likelihood of establishing and/or moving towards clear public policy objectives. The regulatory system was essentially reactive, and in respect of ownership patterns largely failed to establish an alternative agenda to that which results from the exercise of market forces, therefore offering at best flimsy protection to citizenship values. As was suggested in earlier chapters, it may be that a conceptual leap was needed, in which it is acknowledged that the essential democratic role played by the media demands that a move away from a simple model of ownership towards a model approaching 'stewardship' in which those who control the media, and especially essential facilities such as technological gateways, are placed under duties, actively enforced by regulators, to serve not only their individual or corporate interests, but also those of all present and future generations of citizens. This will be returned to in Chapter 7.

When writing the first edition of this book in 1998, it was observed that despite two opportunities in then recent years, in the form of major pieces of legislation relating to the media and the coming to power of a new party of government in 1997, Britain appeared to be likely to continue to struggle on into the twenty-first century with a system of media regulation scarcely worthy of the name, consisting of inconsistent and ineffective measures which fail to fulfil democratic expectations, including, centrally, accountability in the exercise of power. Having outlined in this chapter some of the key features of New Labour's massive Communications Act 2003, it is necessary to try to assess whether the prognosis now is any more positive than it was in 1998.

Without doubt, ongoing rapid changes in technology and in corporate structure have continued to form the context in which media regulation takes place. The question is whether they still continue to set the agenda or whether reform of the legislative framework and institutional structures of regulation has offered support for a reassertion of public service values in broadcasting, or more broadly the public interests related to citizenship associated with the media as a whole. Unsurprisingly, based on what we have set out above, our clear answer to this later question has to be 'no'. This conclusion, though regrettable, is not at all surprising given the wide range of different influences to which the 2003 Act is intended to incorporate responses. Pressures to reform and rationalise the pre-existing regulatory structure in the face of technological development, media convergence and corporate conglomeration may prove difficult to reconcile with the pressure to encourage growth in the economically important media sector. While the pressure to pursue, as a matter of government policy and ideology, a deregulatory agenda may be consistent with the latter of these approaches, this in itself may not sit easily with the pressure to comply with European harmonisation requirements, expressed in the four Directives of 2002, in pursuit of a single-market agenda. Though the removal of some of the detailed thresholds and limits established by the 1996 Act, and in particular its Schedule 2, is probably to be welcomed in recognition of the rapid pace of market change in the media, it is not at all certain that the broad deregulatory framework with which it has been replaced offers cause for confidence in terms of protecting public interests.

Without doubt, the introduction of the 2003 Act still represented a landmark opportunity to establish a sound and rational base for media regulation in the UK. Noted in Chapter 2 was a welcome given in some quarters to the development in the 2003 Act of a definition of public service television. As with the arrival of the super-regulator Ofcom, it would be churlish not to welcome this. However, it remains the case that any intention to reverse the decline of the public domain (Marquand 2004) in the context of broadcasting via this mechanism is likely to be undermined as a result of inadequate priority, or primacy, being assured for citizenship interests. Discussed in Chapter 3, the attempts by the Puttnam Committee to achieve this were not wholly successful. Though the argument was won, to the extent of having the furtherance of interests of citizens feature as the first listed duty of Ofcom, the practical outcome may well prove to be minimal, given the long list of potentially conflicting duties including those such as the interests of consumers, the promotion of competition as an end in itself (section 3(4)(b)) and in particular the overarching requirement of 'light-touch' regulation. Most significant of all though, from the perspective adopted here, is the absence from the reformed regulatory framework of the clear hierarchy of duties, with citizenship values at the top, sought by the Puttnam Committee. Thus, while the institutional structure has been dramatically, and in many ways appropriately, redesigned, it may be no better equipped to offer support for public interest values given the failure to give them adequate priority, and may be no more satisfactory in terms of the transparency and structure of regulatory discretion.

While there may be some limited value in defining public service television and in imposing a duty on Ofcom to further citizens' interests, this is not the same as establishing a framework which is focused centrally on public service values and the protection of citizenship issues. The position under the 2003 Act is that Ofcom can, while complying with its statutory framework, reduce citizens to 'citizen-consumers', with the hyphen illustrating the simplicity of subjecting democratic interests associated with public service broadcasting and citizens to the rule of commercialism and consumerism. In this sense, the Communications Act 2003 can be viewed as another missed opportunity, and perhaps the last available opportunity, to provide a clear and legitimate statutory foundation for public interest regulation in relation to the media. In this sense, with regret, the conclusion must be that the situation is very much the 'same as it ever was'.

5

Institutional Design and Accountability in UK Media Regulation

༄

5.1 INTRODUCTION

Previous chapters have considered values, objectives and some of the mechanisms utilised in regulating the media, and have noted the democratic requirement that power, whether public or private, should not be unlimited. They have not, however, in general focused on the limitations placed upon those who exercise regulatory power. In this chapter, the focus is shifted from predominantly structural regulation of media markets to focus on the activities of the media, and those who regulate them, from the perspective of accountability.

Liberal-democratic expectations such as freedom of expression and property rights may appear generally to have militated against strong regulation of the media in such a way as to override competing democratic claims for pluralism, diversity and equality of access to the media. That said, regulators have undoubtedly exercised, and no doubt in the future will continue to exercise, wide-ranging discretionary powers over the democratically significant media. The examples considered in Chapter 4 appear to suggest, however, that such powers are not always utilised in pursuit of clearly identified objectives.

In the previous edition of this book, criticisms were made of the existing arrangements for a number of regulatory bodies. The Communications Act 2003 hailed a major institutional change as a wide range of regulatory activities relating to the media were brought under the auspices of a new regulatory commission – Ofcom – which now largely exercises regulatory control over both the infrastructure of broadcasting and the content of broadcasts. In addition to Ofcom, there are a number of other bodies which still remain. The British Board of Film Classification (BBFC) still plays an important role in the regulation of films to be shown at the cinema and pre-recorded material. Self-regulators might be argued to have increased in prominence. While the Press Complaints Commission (PCC) has remained under scrutiny as regards the effectiveness of its interventions (O'Malley and Soley 2000: chapter 7; Coad 2003 and 2005), the Advertising Standards Authority (ASA) has grown in importance, now having a central role in the regulation of advertising which appears in both print and broadcast media. We will return to these examples of self-regulation (or what is increasingly referred to as 'co-regulation'), both towards the end of this chapter and in the course of the next.

While the previous edition of this book placed some considerable emphasis on the impact of the German, US and UK courts on the regulation of the media, it indicated unambiguously that the UK courts had exercised little and marginal influence when compared with their counterparts in other jurisdictions. Recent years have seen a number of developments which might suggest a greater significance for the UK courts in this respect. However, we will see that applications for judicial review have not, in fact, led to substantive outcomes which change significantly or fundamentally the way that the courts interact with specialist regulators. Meanwhile, the impact of the Human Rights Act 1998 (HRA), while not leading to radical changes, has led to some alterations in the way in which regulation is carried out. More notably, however, it is arguable that the role of the PCC, historically embroiled in complaints about the infringement of privacy, has since become somewhat overshadowed by the courts' creation of a common law right to privacy from the law of breach of confidence.

5.2 ASPECTS OF ACCOUNTABILITY

This chapter considers the extent to which those who regulate the media in Britain are adequately subjected to mechanisms which serve this end via the three processes, now familiar to many British public lawyers, of, after Davis (1971), 'confining, structuring and checking' their discretion. In essence, Davis' tripartite agenda requires discretion to be:

1. 'confined' – to that realm where discretion is preferable to rules in terms of the benefits it may offer;
2. 'structured' – in such a way as to maximise its potential benefits while minimising the risk of arbitrariness via a system of principles indicative of the manner in which it will be exercised; and
3. 'checked' – via both internal review procedures and external scrutiny by independent bodies such as the courts.

Thus, argues Davis, discretion must be 'cut back' where it is not beneficial, necessary or therefore advisable, while wherever discretion is appropriate it must be structured either via a process of 'internal rule-making' in the form of the development of publicly available codes of practice or the like or the imposition of guidelines from outside, and must be subject to scrutiny within the institutional hierarchy of the body exercising the power, in addition to the potential for external, authoritative, independent review by the likes of courts or tribunals. Though there remain potential difficulties in Davis's agenda, particularly in establishing the optimal point for the exercise of discretion (Baldwin and Hawkins 1984), the extent to which Davis's criteria are met can nonetheless be utilised as a key indicator of the degree of accountability existing in the practice of media regulation.

It should be noted that 'accountability' is used in this chapter to refer to two related but distinct ideas. The first means a requirement to give an account of one's actions, either directly to the public or via public authorities, which will often feed into but is not necessarily connected to the second, which means to be accountable in the sense of being liable to sanction if found to have acted in breach of some requirement or expectation attaching to the exercise of power. The latter, liability to legal sanction, is the traditional public lawyer's version of accountability and in particular focuses on the potential for the courts to impose sanctions upon bodies found to have been in breach of established standards. The former is, however, arguably more important, as it requires the body to provide sufficient information to render it subject to meaningful scrutiny and relates more to democratic legitimacy than the narrower basis of legality. The provision of such information may in itself be sufficient to establish accountability without the need for formal legal action. Given the expense and time involved in legal challenge, the absence of any strong duty to give reasons in English public law and real doubts regarding the ability of conventional adversarial processes to resolve satisfactorily the kind of complex, polycentric disputes often associated with media regulation issues, it becomes clear why accountability via the courts should be considered something of a last resort.

Since the previous edition of this book appeared, there have been some developments which might serve to reduce doubts relating to some aspects of accountability in regulation. Ofcom has proven to be a relatively open regulator which consults widely before adopting regulatory measures (Ofcom 2003) and generally gives detailed reasons for decisions. It is also evident that measures from other parts of government, such as the Cabinet Office's guidelines on consultation (Regulatory Impact Unit 2004) and the Nolan principles on public life (Committee on Standards in Public Life 2005a) have also led to some reforms of the practices and procedures of regulation. It is also clear that the impact of Article 6 ECHR, implemented by the HRA, has led to greater endeavours to ensure fair procedures where penalties are to be imposed. As suggested in Chapter 3, however, it still remains necessary to acknowledge significant concerns regarding the absence of a developed framework of 'public interest' principle, underlying and informing such interventions and reforms.

It is, however, important at this stage to re-emphasise explicitly that regulatory actors are not, and should not, be subject only to accountability via the courts. Indeed, it can be argued that courts might most appropriately be viewed only as a safety net or backstop in relation to accountability of media and other regulators. It is preferable that accountability should be achieved primarily via the structuring and internal checking of discretion, though with a necessarily high degree of transparency imported into decision-making in order to facilitate scrutiny. The availability of background information underlying decisions, and meaningful reasons being given for decisions are important prerequisites of effective accountability. In the absence of adequate transparency, it is difficult to subject decision-makers to meaningful scrutiny and to be sure that they are accountable in either of the word's senses. There has been some recent pressure to strengthen the involvement of the public in decision-making processes (Regulatory Impact Unit 2004), and it seems that a modern conception of accountability should reflect these concerns. The work of Day and Klein may be instructive in this respect, as they suggest that

> accountability is all about the construction of an agreed language or currency of discourse about conduct and performance and the criteria that should be used in assessing them. It is a social and political process. It is about perceptions and power. It can therefore be expected to vary in different contexts depending on the nature of the policy arena and the different organisational actors. (Day and Klein 1985: 2)

Davis's conception of discretion and its control is relatively state- and agency-centred; the reliance on 'confining, structuring and checking' of discretion is primarily viewed as being an activity which should take place internally or by courts and other public bodies. There are, however, some strong arguments to suggest that there should be a broader role for a degree of 'horizontal' accountability – with regulators being held accountable by groups in civil society (O'Donnell 1999). This need seems to be recognised by the Better Regulation Task Force (BRTF) (2003: 22) when it is argued that, 'Whilst accountability to Ministers and to Parliament is important, it is equally important that regulators are more clearly answerable both to those who they regulate and those on whose behalf they are regulating.'

In this chapter we will see that Ofcom has proved to be willing to enter into a dialogue with those parties which are subject to its regulation. In particular, Ofcom's role in the enforcement of standards in broadcasting has demonstrated a willingness to negotiate with broadcasters in order to ensure future compliance with the Broadcasting Code. Furthermore, it seems that Ofcom has been willing to take account of the views of regulated parties in the formulation of regulatory policy, and has often given a detailed response to the submissions made by broadcasters during consultation processes. A good example of this process seems to be the consultation (Ofcom 2004d), Ofcom response to the consultation (Ofcom 2004e: Annex 2) and the final Code of Practice on Electronic Programme Guides (Ofcom 2004f). Here, Ofcom showed a great willingness to engage in consultation and justify its actions in a statement issued alongside the final Code. However, in the absence of an adequately clear and developed framework of principle informing the regulatory process, it is only proper to acknowledge the very fine line which exists between fruitful negotiation between the regulator and the regulated, and the possibility of capture of the regulatory agenda by powerful lobbies within the regulated industry.

Regardless of such questions, we might well be much less confident that Ofcom is truly accountable to citizens. The first part of this book identified the tensions inherent in Ofcom's duties to serve both citizens and consumers and the difficulties this might cause. One of the authors of this book has suggested that, in this connection, pursuit of a vision of 'the public interest' should be allied to a greater use of deliberative democracy in regulation (Feintuck 2004: chapter 2). In a different approach, Black (2000, 2001) has called for a 'thick' proceduralisation of regulation based on deliberative democracy, with law providing the procedures which would allow such deliberation to take place. Black argues that

> . . . deliberative proceduralism is, should be, employed where the administration is involved in refining goals, designing laws, implementing them or adjudicating on them (regulating) and entails the direct introduction of the deliberative process into the administration. (Black 2000: 54)

There are a number of competing conceptions of deliberative democracy which have been subscribed to in various ways by a number of commentators. In essence, though, the concept always contains a number of key elements, outlined by Parkinson (2003: 180) as its insistence on some form of inter-personal reasoning as the guiding political procedure, rather than bargaining between competing interests; the idea that the essential political act – the giving, weighing, acceptance or rejection of reasons – is a public act as opposed to the purely private act of voting . . . Democratic deliberation should somehow embody the essential democratic principles of responsiveness to public wishes and the political equality of every member of the public.

The attractions of deliberative democracy are many, and there is little doubt that media regulation may serve the interests of the public more closely if such mechanisms were to be adopted. In particular, we would suggest that a deliberative approach would be of particular significance in recognising and serving a range of democratic values which extend beyond the aggregation of individual interests. A real difficulty with any implementation of deliberative democracy, however, is that it will often prove difficult to identify appropriate fora in which such deliberation can take place. A particular problem with adopting a model of deliberative democracy is that 'Deliberative decisions appear illegitimate for those left outside the forum, while bringing more than a few people in would quickly turn the event into speech making, not deliberation' (Parkinson 2003: 181). Although a variety of forums have been suggested, including the use of citizens' juries (Collins and Murroni 1996: 154–6; Smith and Wales 2000) it seems unlikely that the 'ideal type' deliberation, propounded by Black and Parkinson, is likely to come to fruition. Given that this is the case, we may have to be satisfied with a variety of 'traditional' methods of accountability, such as consultation, the giving of reasons and transparency of decision-making. This is acknowledged by Dryzek (2000: 80), when he argues that 'Democracy as discursive contestation should be compared with these real and so defective alternatives, not with some unattainable ideal of how the will of the people can take effect directly in policy-making.' This latter perspective might prove particularly helpful in moving debate beyond institutional emphasis pursued by some special-interest groups such as lawyers, who may expend great energy in arguing for a particular (interest-group serving) institutional vision, while failing to give due prominence to the significant democratic issues at the heart of the debate.

At a pragmatic, and we would argue 'realistic', level, it may be that in practice our primary objective should be to strive for strong accountability combined with a range of participatory processes. Given that outcomes which are negotiated through perfect deliberation are unlikely, we may have to be satisfied with traditional methods of participation and accountability combined with a regulator acting in pursuit of a clearly identified set of public interest goals.

It is important, however, to re-emphasise in this connection the significance of access to information and reasoned decision-making. Birkinshaw (2001: 24) argues that, 'Information is inherently a feature of power. So too is its control, use and regulation', and exclusive control of information, whether by government, or, as Schiller (1996) argues persuasively, private corporations, is in fundamental opposition to democratic ideals. Certainly, access to information is a crucial aspect of accountability, but it must be viewed alongside structural design in making an overall assessment of the accountability of a regulatory organisation. The Freedom of Information Act 2000, while by no means perfect (Birkinshaw 2005: chapter 1), has created an impetus towards the development of openness. Ofcom has a publication scheme (Ofcom no date a) as required by section 19 of the Act, and it appears to be expansive (Ofcom no date a: section D). In the scheme itself it is argued that 'Ofcom aims to be as transparent as possible and proactively to make as much information as it can available' (section E).

The duty to give reasons forms an important part of openness and access to information – and can form an important part of the appeal or judicial review process (*R v Secretary of State for the Home Department, ex parte Doody* [1994] 1 AC 531; Birkinshaw 2005: 9.128). The desirability of reason-giving has been acknowledged in a number of other cases (Fordham 2004: 62.1.6–62.1.10) and it seems important that Ofcom is willing to disclose the reasons for formulating regulatory policy and for its adjudications in individual cases. Section 19 of the Freedom of Information Act 2000, in its requirements for publication schemes, alerts public authorities to the desirability of publishing reasons for their decisions (Birkinshaw 2005: 1.194). We will see below that Ofcom's record on reasoned decision-making is generally good, both in terms of the giving of reasons for the adoption of regulatory policy and on the adjudication of individual cases.

Although these are early days in Ofcom's reign over the UK communications sector, it is fair to say that the Ofcom website contains a wealth of information about its activities, including copies of research that it has commissioned and a great deal of information about its day-to-day activities, including minutes of meetings. Although this only offers a limited snapshot of the true transparency of Ofcom's activities, it appears that the current level of openness may be worthy of the praise which was previously offered to Oftel (Graham 2000: chapter 9). The trend towards openness is a welcome development, and it may seem evident that Ofcom are making best endeavours in this area. However, it remains the case that the statutory duties which are incumbent on Ofcom, to be found in section 3 of the Communications Act 2003, are in some ways rather general and contradictory, and it is also worth recalling at this stage the questions raised in Chapter 4, perhaps as much symbolic as practical, relating to Ofcom's decision not to hold its board meetings in public.

The first part of this book argued that the absence of established and clearly expressed goals has been one of the fundamental weaknesses of the media regulation system to date. What we can confirm at this stage is that while a clear accountability agenda can be identified and that there is some discernible progress in this respect, this agenda will remain ultimately limited if the underlying value system remains inadequately defined.

5.3 FORMAL POWER AND INFORMAL INFLUENCE

It is clear that, in Britain and elsewhere, national governments will exert much power and influence over the general environment in which the media operate. Government may also play a significant role in establishing the agenda for future media development, though in recent times there is a strong appearance of corporate and/or technological determinism rather than proactive decision-making by democratically elected government. In particular, the regulatory framework for satellite broadcasting, and the acceptance and emphasis placed by both the previous Conservative and present New Labour administrations on digital terrestrial transmission as opposed to satellite or cable as a platform for the delivery of digital television, both appear to have been driven more by the development of the relevant technology by its corporate proponents than by any detailed consideration in democratic fora of the full range of alternatives. Democratic fundamentals lead us to expect, however, that such decision-making powers will be exercised within a framework of principle embodied in the constitution, pre-eminent among democratic expectations being that of accountability.

It might be expected that, consistent with their duties of party political impartiality, public service broadcasters would be insulated from government interference in relation to their output. While the BBC is notionally independent, it clearly has close relationships with government, not least because of government powers of appointment to its Board of Governors. Curran and Seaton (2003: 162) suggested that the Thatcherite reforms of the BBC were brought about in some ways by the appointment of Marmaduke Hussey and John Birt as Chair of the Board of Governors and Director General respectively. There is little doubt that the government's power of appointment is likely to have a significant impact on the day-to-day operation of the Corporation. As regards the

New Labour government's appointment of Gavyn Davies to the Chair and Greg Dyke to the Director General's post at the BBC, Wring (2005: 385) suggests that Dyke was '. . . one of the select group of associates who had funded Blair's 1994 leadership campaign', and it seems evident that both appointees had considerable sympathy for the New Labour project.

More recently, we can see a collapse in the relationship between the government and the BBC, with the events which culminated in the Hutton Inquiry demonstrating animosity between Downing Street and the BBC's senior managers (Wring 2005: 384–6). The appointment of Michael Grade to the Chair and Mark Thompson to the Director General's post at the BBC seems more difficult to gauge. It has been argued that 'Both [are] veterans of the BBC, with experience of working for Channel 4, and thus well placed to begin planning for the Review of the Corporation's Royal Charter in 2006' (Wring 2005: 385).

It is notable that the approach taken by the new Chair of Governors and Director General might be heavily influenced by the realities of the government's formal influence (through the formulation of the Charter and Agreement and decisions over funding) over the BBC at the time of Charter renewal. In Chapter 2, we noted that the Charter review process suggests a number of changes to the governance structure of the BBC, including greater independence for the BBC's Board of Governors from the management. Some of these reforms have already been implemented (BBC 2004a: 5; BBC 2005: 2–3) and Michael Grade has suggested that one of the key roles for the BBC's Governors over the next year will be to '. . . ensure a smooth transition to the new governance system out-lined in the Green Paper' (BBC 2005: 2). It is difficult to ascertain whether the Charter Review gives the government of the day too much influence over the future direction of the Corporation, but it seems crucial that, beyond the government, Parliament retains a key role in the formulation of the final Charter and Agreement, and that the process is as open and transparent as possible. The BBC Governors appear to be strongly united around one central principle – that even post-Hutton 'The BBC is not worth having if it is not editorially independent' (BBC 2004a: 2).

Ofcom is a new regulator in the structure of a regulatory commission – an approach more familiar in the USA. This approach departs from the structure adopted in many of the UK utilities sectors and which was adopted by Oftel prior to its amalgamation into Ofcom, and provides for a separate Chairperson and Chief Executive, an approach which the BRTF (2003: 25) supports as '[improving] the checks and balances on the organ-isation', and a management board, replacing the 'Director General' approach which has been more often used in previous regulatory structures. Some concerns over the informal influence exerted by the government still remain; by virtue of section 3(a) and (b) of the Act, the Chairperson and the other members of the Board of Ofcom are appointed by the Secretary of State. Such appointments are, of course, regulated by the Committee on Standards in Public Life (CSPL) and the Office of the Commissioner for Public Appointments (OCPA). Such appointments must be made in accordance with the OCPA Code of Practice (OCPA 2005: 1.05), which is intended to '. . . provide departments with a clear and concise guide to the steps they must follow in order to ensure a fair, open and transparent appointments process that produces a quality outcome and can command public confidence.'

The CSPL has acknowledged a number of imperfections and weaknesses in the current system (CSPL 2005: 2.2), but states that 'The system is undoubtedly an improvement on the pre-existing arrangements of unfettered ministerial patronage' (CSPL 2005: 2.1). Although the discretion over who to appoint ultimately belongs to the minister, the process aims to confine, structure and check the exercise of that discretion in line with the OCPA principles, which include merit, independent scrutiny, openness and transparency, and proportionality (OCPA 2005: 9). While this process may offer a degree of independence, there is still potential for ministerial fiat to play a role in appointments to the board of Ofcom. The board in turn is charged with the appointment of the chief executive and the executive members of Ofcom.

While the arrangements for the appointment of the Ofcom Board are not radically different from those which prevailed for the appointment of the ITC and Radio Authority, we can see that the OCPA Code has since been strengthened and, in accordance with the recommendation of the BRTF, the roles of chairman and chief executive have been separated and Ofcom is governed by a Board. The BRTF have argued that 'A strongly formulated Board can provide protection against political interference and be a real impetus for driving through change'. In addition to the structure of the BBC and Ofcom's governance, there is a range of other bodies which have a significant impact in the sphere of the media. The Channel 4 Corporation (C4C) has a particular mandate, now contained in section 265(3) of the Communications Act 2003, and continues the mandate which has been in place ever since the Broadcasting Act of 1980. Though still required to put out minimum total hours in respect of news, current affairs, education programmes, etc., Channel 4 has a particular brief, overseen now by Ofcom, not to aim at the same mass audiences as ITV and BBC1, but to serve 'minority' interests, or 'tastes and interests not generally catered for by Channel 3' (Peak and Fisher 1996: 166). Among other aspects of Channel 4 that distinguish it from other public service broadcasters in Britain are the fact that it does not produce its own programmes but instead buys them from independent producers, acting in effect as a televisual publisher.

In its initial years, Channel 4 was funded by a levy on the advertising revenue of regional commercial ITV companies who sold and retained the revenue from advertising on Channel 4. However, as Channel 4 established itself, both in terms of programming and, consequentially, as a locus for niche advertising, the financial safety net provided by the levy on other commercial broadcasters became less necessary and justifiable. Under the funding formula provided by sections 26–27 of the Broadcasting Act 1990 which allowed money to flow in either direction, Channel 4 was allowed to sell its own advertising, but still with a safety net to be provided by the Channel 3 companies. In the previous edition of this book it was argued that Channel 4, as a result of its innovative funding basis and unusually specific public service brief, was therefore somewhat distanced from conventional British arrangements for public service broadcasting and accountable against different criteria, and it has remained something of an exception to the general pattern. It is notable that under Schedule 3 of the Broadcasting Act 1990 it was the ITC, and not the Secretary of State, which was empowered to make appointments to Channel 4's management board. This situation continues to prevail today, with the ITC's functions transferring to Ofcom by virtue of section 1 and paragraph 4 of Schedule 1 of the Communications Act 2003, a situation which, arguably, gives Channel 4 greater independence from political influence than is the case for the BBC.

Inevitably, in an increasingly commercially focused PSB context, financial and accounting issues seem often as relevant or more so than political, legal and democratic issues of accountability. The previous funding arrangements for Channel 4, where its deficits were effectively 'guaranteed' by the Channel 3 licensees and its profits were, at least in part, distributed to the holders of Channel 3 licences, no longer prevails. Section 201 of the Communications Act 2003 repeals the previous provisions in the Broadcasting Act 1990 and leaves Channel 4 to retain its surpluses and be liable for its deficits. At present, Channel 4's financial position seems healthy: C4C made a profit of £60.3 million in 2004 (C4C 2004: 48) and C4C has launched a number of new services, including the digital only More4 in the past year. Ofcom's Public Service Broadcasting Review (Ofcom 2004a, 2004b, 2004c), discussed in more detail in Chapter 4, suggests that the future for Channel 4 could be somewhat more challenging, as competition in the advertising market becomes ever more intense.

Channel 3 licences also contain public service obligations, which could be under pressure in the future due to increased competition in the advertising market. These obligations were set as part of the licence allocation process under the Broadcasting Act 1990 and are now reviewed and controlled by Ofcom under the provisions contained in sections 264–271 of the Communications Act 2003. Section 264(4) together with section 264(6) are of particular interest, as they lay down more clearly than ever before a vision of what public service broadcasting should hope to achieve, although the remit for Channel 3 and 5 licensees contained in section 265(3) of the 2003 Act is still exceptionally vague, stating that the remit 'is the provision of a range of high-quality and diverse programming'. These provisions replace the previous definition of PSB, which was offered as part of the criteria for the award of a Channel 3 licence in section 16(2) of the Broadcasting Act 1990.

It is evident that Ofcom, under its duty to provide guidance on programme policy under sections 264(4)–(6) of the 2003 Act and under the power to enforce public service remits in section 270, can have a significant impact on the output of public service broadcasters. As such, it will be essential that any such guidance is formulated in an open and transparent manner with suitable consultation, and that any actions to enforce a public service remit are undertaken in a similar manner. Although the Secretary of State has the power to amend the definition of PSB contained in section 264 under powers granted by section 271, it is notable that the procedure contained in the 2003 Act requires an interplay between Ofcom and the Secretary of State, and also, under section 271(4), requires public consultation before any such changes are made. This may seem to offer a more significant limitation on the potential for the exercise of discretion than previously existed under the Broadcasting Act 1990.

A final important issue to consider in terms of the influence which might be exerted by the government over broadcasting through the funding and licensing process lies in the scheme for the PSP outlined in Ofcom's PSB Review, noted in Chapter 4 above. For the present time, it is difficult to determine the manner in which the allocation of funds in the PSP process will be made, although, in a paper for Ofcom, Mason (2005) suggests that there are three potential processes which he describes as 'beauty contests', 'auctions' and 'negotiations'. The main experience of such processes in the past lies in the auction for Channel 3 licences, which due to the nature of the statutory scheme fell somewhere in between a 'beauty contest' and an auction. The process for the allocation of Channel 3 licences has been the subject of considerable criticism due to its lack of openness and transparency (Prosser 1997 and 2000; Barendt and Hitchens 2000; Barendt 1995), and it is vitally important that the process for allocating PSP funding offers a significant improvement on that process, particularly given that it could have a decisive influence on the direction of PSB in the future.

In terms of direct powers to require the transmission of (or require the refraining from transmission of) specific content, the government retains power, contained within the BBC's Charter and Agreement and under section 336 of the Communications Act 2003 for licensed broadcasters, to order that an announcement be transmitted (section 336(2)), or to 'refrain from including in their licensed services any matter, or description of matter, specified in the notice' (section 336(5)). In either case, the Communications Act 2003 gives the licence holder the right to broadcast the fact that material has been broadcast, or prevented from being broadcast, by government intervention. The BBC's agreement, in section 8, permits similar directions to be given, and once again bestows a discretion on the BBC over whether or not to announce that such a direction has been given. The government has seldom used these powers, although there are some notable examples. Perhaps the best known of these arose in the context of the ban on broadcasting the spoken words of those associated with certain proscribed organisations, most notably Sinn Fein and the Ulster Defence Association, in the late 1980s and early 1990s. Robertson and Nicol (2002: 27) describe the ban as 'a plain infringement on the right to receive and impart information'. The ban was based, in relation to ITV companies, upon powers granted by section 10 of the Broadcasting Act 1990 (previously section 29, Broadcasting Act 1981), and in relation to the BBC on conditions contained in the Licence Agreement which supplements the BBC's Charter. The statutory provisions permitted the Home Secretary to order the ITC to 'refrain from broadcasting any matter or classes of matter', offering the clear potential for prior restraint of broadcasters with the only avenue of redress being to challenge the minister's exercise of discretion by way of judicial review.

When judicial review was *sought (R. v Secretary of State for the Home Department, ex parte Brind* [1991] 1 All ER 720), it became clear that the grant of discretion to the Home Secretary by statute meant that to succeed, a challenge would have to demonstrate that the minister had acted 'unreasonably'. In practice, this standard of review allows enormous latitude to those vested with discretion, on occasion requiring challengers to demonstrate in effect that the decision-maker had taken leave of their senses. In practice, of course, the 'ban' was demonstrably ludicrous, from the time that Channel 4 took the decision to dub actors' voices over pictures of spokespersons for the prescribed organisations, but the 'soft' standard of review meant that legal accountability in relation to the discretionary power was virtually meaningless, a problem compounded by the fact that, in the situation of either a party of government with a strong majority or cross-party support, accountability through Parliament is also rendered largely nugatory.

It is perhaps rather difficult to judge the response of the courts to such a ban in the context of the Human Rights Act 1998 and the right to freedom of expression contained in Article 10 ECHR which was implemented by the Act. The *Prolife Alliance* case ([2003] UKHL 23; [2004] 1 AC 185), decided by the House of Lords in 2003 and discussed below, is based on a different statutory framework concerning decisions made by broadcasters under the statutory framework which aims to protect taste and decency. In the post-HRA era, it may be that the courts would take a dim view of the use of section 336 of the Communications Act 2003 to prohibit political speech of the nature of that which was prohibited in the late 1980s and early 1990s.

While the section 336 powers are obviously significant, still more wide-ranging powers of government intervention in relation to broadcasting also exist. The BBC's Licence Agreement permits the government, in the case of a perceived emergency and where it is considered expedient to do so, 'to take possession of the BBC in the name and on behalf of Her Majesty'. Originally included as part of the government's response to the General Strike of 1926, it has never been applied to its full effect, though Robertson and Nicol (2002: 28) note that it was used during the Falklands War to permit the government to use BBC transmitters to transmit propaganda broadcasts into Argentina.

Of greater concern, we might think, is the apparently compliant response by the BBC in 1985 to government pressure not to screen the controversial *Real Lives* documentary concerning terrorism in Northern Ireland, when, they state, the BBC 'cravenly banned the scheduled programme after Mrs. Thatcher had condemned it, unseen, as likely to encourage support for terrorists'. Seymour-Ure (1996: 69) notes that the Thatcher governments, to a much greater extent than any previous government, 'seemed ready to treat the BBC and IBA governors as political placemen and women', and he gives examples of their willingness to 'interfere directly with programmes', 'accuse producers and interviewers of deliberate bias' and 'impugn broadcasters' patriotism' (see also Negrine 1994: chapter 6).

That said, it seems possible that some of these concerns might now be allayed by the stronger culture of independence promoted by the Principles of Public Life (CSPL 2005a), combined with the board structure introduced at Ofcom and the evident distancing of the BBC from the government of the day. Furthermore, applications under the Freedom of Information Act may also raise the possibility of subsequent discovery of such informal influence, so we might hope that any past excesses will be curtailed in future relationships between the government and the media. Though such incidents may come to light relatively infrequently, they acquire a high media profile when they do. Given the nature of such issues and accusations, it is inevitably difficult, however, to be clear as to the precise extent to which governments successfully exert influence over broadcasters. It is obvious, however, is that a very real potential exists for the exercise of influence in a hidden and unaccountable manner, especially when, for example in the run-up to licence or Charter renewals or reviews of the licence fee, public service broadcasters are most heavily dependent upon active government support.

5.4 COMPLAINTS AND 'STANDARDS' IN BROADCASTING

The redress of grievances or felt wrongs is one of the essential 'Law Jobs' identified in Chapter 1. One forum in which grievances may be redressed is the law courts; however, as Birkinshaw (1994) establishes, extra-judicial grievance redress is arguably of at least a great a significance in the modern day. As he rightly notes, 'a public lawyer's interest in the process of accountability and complaint resolution is not diminished simply because there is an absence of a judge or counsel, prerogative orders or writs. The pursuit of effective procedures for accountability and resolution of grievances is what counts' (24). We will now consider the resolution of complaints regarding media behaviour and output, and its importance will indeed be demonstrated despite there being scarcely a courtroom in sight. The dispute resolution processes discussed here form a potentially important part of the structures of accountability (in both its senses) relevant to the media, and whether this potential is in practice fulfilled will be the central question to be addressed.

As will be discussed shortly, complaints regarding the press are addressed largely through self-regulatory mechanisms. However, it should come as no surprise, given the pattern identified earlier of greater regulation of broadcast media, to find that complaints over broadcasting, both in relation to broadcasters' practices and the content of their programmes, are dealt with not by self-regulatory mechanisms but by bodies created by statute and with members appointed by government. It is notable, however, that significant changes have been made to the regulatory regime by the Communications Act 2003, and that Ofcom has made some alterations to the process of regulation of broadcast content.

The previous system of broadcast complaints, created under the Broadcasting Acts of 1990 and 1996 and the BBC's Charter and Agreement gave viewers recourse both to the ITC (for breaches of its Programme Code, but only in relation to licensed broadcasters) and the Broadcasting Standards Commission (BSC), which had jurisdiction to deal with two separate issues: programme standards, where the BSC had a Code on taste, decency and the portrayal of violent or sexual conduct, and another Code which dealt with fairness and privacy complaints (Barendt and Hitchens 2000: 138–50). There was significant overlap between the ITC's Code and the BSC's Codes, but only the BSC could deal with complaints relating to the BBC as the ITC had jurisdiction only over private broadcasters.

The BSC had been open to criticism on a number of grounds. In particular, its effectiveness could be questioned as a result of it being unable to give significant redress to complainants: section 119 of the Broadcasting Act 1996 provided for publication of the BSC's findings, combined with the potential for the BSC to oblige either the BBC or a private broadcaster to transmit a summary of their findings on air (Barendt and Hitchens 2000: 143–4, Robertson and Nicol 2002: 793–4). Robertson and Nicol (2002: 801) comment, reasonably enough, that 'The fact that the BSC has not been challenged in court over its "standards" adjudications may reflect . . . the fact that nobody takes BSC adjudications very seriously.' Barendt and Hitchens (2000: 150) also noted that 'It is difficult to envisage that commercial broadcasters would view a finding against them as having the same impact as one by the ITC or the RA.'

The range of sanctions available to the ITC which might be invoked against all licence holders, including Channel 4, were considerably more hard-hitting. Adherence to the ITC's Programme Code (ITC 2002) formed one of the conditions upon which broadcasters held their licence, and sections 40–42 of the Broadcasting Act 1990 allowed the ITC to impose three types of penalty – transmission of a correction or apology, imposition of a financial penalty or a shortening or revocation of a licence to broadcast. The use of these powers has been described as 'rare but severe' by Robertson and Nicol (2002: 816), meanwhile the ITC's procedure in its exercise of these powers of sanction, particularly where financial penalties were imposed, has been questioned on the basis that

'The safeguard, in every case, is merely that the licence holder must be given "a reasonable opportunity to make representations" before the punishment [was] served' (Robertson and Nicol 2002: 825).

Complaints against the output of the BBC not addressed to the BSC were dealt with internally by the BBC's Programme Complaints Unit, with the potential for an appeal to the BBC Governors' Programme Complaints Committee (Barendt and Hitchens 2000: 78; BBC 2004a: 78–9). In essence, though the BBC was not bound by the ITC Code, it applied a similar range of standards to its own output by virtue of section 5 of its Agreement. The Hutton Inquiry exposed a number of defects in the BBC's complaints handling mechanisms (BBC 2004a: 5–6; Hutton 2004: 212–14), and it is evident that the BBC have implemented a new, streamlined structure (BBC 2005) to deal with those complaints which are not addressed to Ofcom or are not under the jurisdiction of Ofcom under the terms of section 13 of the BBC's amended Agreement (DCMS 2003). Under the new Agreement, which followed the enactment of the Communications Act 2003, the BBC is bound by most aspects of the Ofcom Programme Code, but the BBC's Governors retain control over the requirements of impartiality, accuracy in news and the placement of commercial products in programmes (Ofcom no date b).

It is arguable that many of the deficiencies that the Hutton Report identified have now been addressed, but as noted in our discussion of the BBC Charter Review process in Chapter 2, it might be preferable for Ofcom to takeover control of all 'standards' complaints in relation to the BBC, although there are some arguments that the Governors should retain control over impartiality and accuracy, particularly in relation to news, in order to retain the BBC's reputation for independence and high-quality journalism. There is much to be said, however, for ensuring equal protection and application of the entirety of the Ofcom Content Code (2005d) to all broadcasters.

Under section 12 of the Communications Act 2003 Ofcom is obliged to create a 'Content Board', the purposes of which include, according to section 13(2)(a), carrying out 'functions in relation to matters that concern the contents of anything which is or may be broadcast or otherwise transmitted by means of electronic communications networks'. The precise scope of the Content Board's responsibilities seems to be unclear, as unlike the other committees of the Ofcom board, no terms of reference are available on the website. The Content Board is of particular interest given our focus, as in the Board's statement about its functions and role it states that it will 'examine issues where the citizen interest extends beyond the consumer interest, with focus on those aspects of the public interest which competition and market forces do not reach' (Ofcom no date c).

It is evident that the Content Board will play a crucial role in the regulation of broadcast content and should be expected to have a significant influence over the development and continued updating of the Broadcast Code. Sections 12(5) and 12(6) of the Communications Act 2003 endeavours to ensure that there is adequate representation of the various regions of the UK on the Content Board, but it may be thought anomalous or disappointing that the Act does not provide for similar representation for those from various cultural or ethnic backgrounds. The procedure of the Content Board is open, with details of the agendas of its meetings and notes from previous meetings made available to the public, and the fact that the Ofcom Content Board is appointed by Ofcom itself rather than by the government of the day should certainly be viewed as a positive development from the days of the BSC and ITC. That said, the fundamental question may still be whether or not the Content Board moves away from the 'paternalism' which the BBC and BSC/ITC combination were accused of in the past (Robertson and Nicol 2002: chapter 16).

The Ofcom Broadcast Code was finally published in May 2005, after an extensive consultation period which had taken place from July to October of the previous year. The Code is designed to fulfil Ofcom's duty, under section 319 of the Communications Act 2003, to produce a Code in order to set the standards in line with the 'standards objectives' outlined in section 319(2). While the detail of the rules contained in the Code lies beyond the scope and purpose of the present work, the formulation of the Broadcast Code is most interesting from a public lawyer's perspective, as it demonstrates a willingness on the part of Ofcom to be open about the way in which it formulates regulatory policy. The Code (Ofcom 2005d) was accompanied by a statement outlining the reasons for the adoption of the Code as it stands at present (Ofcom 2005j) and guidance on the interpretation of the rules in the Code (Ofcom 2005k). Ofcom has taken steps to make much of the material that informed the final version of the Code, including research, available on its website. The statement which accompanied the publication of the final Code (Ofcom 2005j) appears to serve as a positive example of regulatory practice, in the sense that it offers detailed responses to the views of those who responded to the original consultation and outlines the way in which the final Code has been altered in order to take account of these views.

It is evident that the content of the Code has been influenced by the enactment and coming into force of the Human Rights Act 1998, with the introduction stating that:

> Freedom of expression is at the heart of any democratic state. It is an essential right to hold opinions and receive and impart information and ideas. Broadcasting and freedom of expression are intrinsically linked. However, with such rights come duties and responsibilities. The setting out of clear principles and rules will allow broadcasters more freedom for creativity and audiences greater freedom to exercise their choices, while securing those objectives set by Parliament. (Ofcom 2005d: 2)

The Code has evident similarities to the old ITC Code (ITC 2002) on programme standards, but Ofcom have expressly stated that 'We wanted to draft a code that would not simply rewrite previous codes, but would be a genuinely new code, rooted in the new broadcasting legislation' (Ofcom 2005j: 1). The statutory obligations incumbent on Ofcom under section 319 of the Communications Act 2003 are not radically different to those imposed on the ITC under sections 6–9 of the Broadcasting Act 1990, and the standards themselves remain similar. Although the Communications Act 2003 has done much to clarify the duties incumbent on Ofcom when drawing up the Broadcasting Code, it will be the implementation and enforcement of the standards therein which will have the greatest impact on broadcasters.

The former ITC programme code (ITC 2002) was not accompanied by additional guidance, unlike the Ofcom Code. As such, it is evident that Ofcom has endeavoured to structure its discretion under the Code somewhat more than the ITC did in the past, but still make it clear that 'It is the responsibility of the broadcaster to ensure compliance with the Broadcasting Code' (Ofcom 2005j: 15). It is evident that Ofcom has aimed to create an environment of partnership with broadcasters, making a great deal of information available which should assist the making of judgements as to the acceptability of certain output. Ofcom also publishes a fortnightly 'Broadcast Bulletin' which outlines the complaints that have been received by Ofcom, outlines the reasons for its decisions where it upholds a complaint, and also sets out reasons for its decisions regarding certain programmes found not to be in breach even where subject to a large number of complaints.

The sanctions available to be imposed by Ofcom for a breach of the Code are, in essence, identical to those that were available to the ITC – an obligation to transmit a statement of findings (a sanction more often invoked by the BSC), the potential to impose a financial penalty and, in the most severe cases, revocation of the broadcast licence. Gibbons (1998: 258–9) has argued that the enforcement relationship between the regulator and the licence holders tends to be formalised by the range of sanctions which are available, and it is evident that there are relatively few formal sanctions available to the regulator. Much like the ITC, Ofcom has invoked its power to issue formal sanctions relatively infrequently, but, through the medium of the Broadcast Bulletin, has taken the approach of warning a number of broadcasters that they should improve their compliance procedures. Examples of such warnings include the one issued to the Hindi channel *Gangaajal*, which transmitted a film containing what was found to be excessive violence and swearing prior to the watershed, which prompted Ofcom to remind the channel that it must have compliance procedures in place (Ofcom 2005l). In many cases, the only outcome is that Ofcom will determine that a particular programme was in breach of the Code without issuing any further guidance to the broadcaster.

While such an outcome may seem to be ineffective, it is evident that the Ofcom Code is relatively new, so these decisions have the effect of building a library of adjudications which, even if not constituting binding precedents as such, will aid future interpretation of the Code. By way of example, Ofcom's decision over the BBC's scheduling of Tarantino's *Pulp Fiction* at 9.10 p.m. determined that this had been a breach of the Broadcast Code because 'A combination of seriously offensive language, graphic violence and drug-abuse occurred early in the film, before 21:30. Under the relevant Code, 18 films are not prohibited but the content should be suitable for the time of transmission. Such intense material is not normally expected so soon after the watershed' (Ofcom 2005l: 5). The BBC appealed this decision three times, but Ofcom has refused to change its decision, which may seem to constitute a decidedly paternalistic straw in the wind.

It is interesting to note that where Ofcom does decide to impose a sanction for a breach of the Code, the decision is passed to the 'Ofcom Content Sanctions Committee', which consists of members of both the Ofcom Content Board and the Ofcom Board (Ofcom no date d). It seems likely that this structure has been influenced by the requirements of Article 6 ECHR, where the difficulties of policy-makers adjudicating on their own policies caused some potential difficulties for the UK planning system (*R (On the Application of Alconbury Developments Ltd.)* v *Secretary of State for the Environment, Transport and the Regions* [2001] UKHL 23; [2003] 2 AC 295). The need for a degree of independence between those determining cases under a policy and the creators of the policy itself appears to be demonstrated by the *Begum* case (*Begum* v

Tower Hamlets LBC [2003] UKHL 5; [2003] 2 AC 430), although, much like in the *Alconbury* case, there is no doubt that Ofcom is subject to the full jurisdiction of the High Court for judicial review of its decisions. A similarly constituted committee, but this time with members drawn solely from the Content Board, is in place to determine fairness and privacy-related complaints. Furthermore, the Committee's Terms of Reference state that one of the Committee's duties is to ensure that 'where the sanction under consideration includes a financial penalty or shortening or revocation of a licence, to invite oral representations from licensees' (Ofcom no date d). While this provision may have been included to meet with the requirements of the older cases on procedural justice such as *McInnes* v *Onslow-Fane* ([1978] 1 WLR 1520) there seems little doubt that after the decision of the House of Lords in *Smith* (*R (On the Application of Smith)* v *Parole Board* [2005] UKHL 1; [2005] 1 All ER 755) that this would most likely be required in order for the sanctioning procedure to be satisfactory for the purposes of Article 6 ECHR.

Although we can see that the process through which Ofcom's Content Sanctions Committee operates has been informed by recent decisions concerning the Human Rights Act 1998, the *Prolife Alliance* case (*R (On the Application of Prolife Alliance)* v *BBC* [2003] UKHL 23; [2004] 1 AC 185) suggests that the process of judicial review of the decisions that the Committee reaches is unlikely to be radically altered. The decision of the Court of Appeal ([2002] EWCA Civ 297) suggested a different approach, particularly where political speech was at stake:

> Where the context is broadcast entertainment, I would accept without cavil that in the event of a legal challenge to a prohibition the courts should pay a very high degree of respect to the broadcasters' judgement, given the background of BA 1990, BA 1996, the BBC Agreement, the codes of guidance and the BSC adjudications. Where the context is day-to-day news reporting the broadcasters' margin of discretion may be somewhat more constrained but will remain very considerable. But the *milieu* we are concerned with in this case, the cockpit of a general election, is inside the veins and arteries of the democratic process. The broadcasters' views are entitled to be respected, but their force and weight are modest at best. ([52])

However, the House of Lords did not adopt the approach taken by Laws LJ in the Court of Appeal, and Lord Walker ([2003] UKHL 23: [124]) suggests that there should be a willingness to support broadcasters and regulators in the interpretation of the broadcast codes because:

> The broadcasters also had to take into account the special power and intrusiveness of television. They are, by their training and experience, well qualified

(so far as anybody, elected or unelected, could claim to be well qualified) to assess the Alliance's PEB [party election broadcast] as against other more or less shocking material which might have been included in news or current affairs programmes, and to form a view about its likely impact on viewers.

If this case, which raises some highly controversial issues about the restriction of political expression, resulted in the House of Lords supporting the BBC and other broadcasters in their decision to demand cuts to the Prolife Alliance's party election broadcast, then it seems that the courts will likely be willing to continue the British judicial tradition of deferring to the expertise of the regulators in the vast majority of cases and circumstances.

By the end of 2005, the Content Sanctions Committee had been called upon ten times since Ofcom's powers came into effect. The sanctions imposed in the cases vary, with one licence revocation in the *Auctionworld* case. In this case, Auctionworld was a licensed channel which breached various provisions of the advertising standards code and had previously been warned by the ITC. In the case (Ofcom 2004g, 2004h), the Content Sanctions Committee first imposed a fine of £450,000 and warned the channel that it intended to revoke its licence unless its conduct improved. Ultimately, the licence was revoked in December 2004, by which time the company was in administration. A number of financial penalties have been imposed, with three of the most notable all being given to 'adult' channels for the broadcast of 'R18' classification material, which is prohibited under the Ofcom Code (Ofcom 2004i, 2005m, 2005n) and a fourth penalty of £125,000 was issued to Piccadilly Radio in Manchester for serious breaches of the Code concerning offence and taste and decency (Ofcom 2005o). In this case, the presenter concerned had aired a number of racist views and had made a number of jokes about the killing of a British hostage in Iraq.

Although some might take issue with Ofcom's stance with regard to 'adult' material as being somewhat paternalistic, in general it seems that Ofcom are in the position described by Ayers and Braithwaite when they argue that '[R]egulatory agencies are often best able to secure compliance when they are benign big guns. That is, regulators will be more able to speak softly when they carry big sticks . . .' (Ayers and Braithwaite 1992: 19). The difficulty with this, of course, is that 'speaking softly' – stating that certain output is a breach of the Code, but taking no further action – may often have a greater 'chilling' effect on freedom of communication than taking formal action as, in essence, broadcasters may play safe, and curtail their own output in order to avoid sanction under the Code. In reality, however, it seems that to date there is very little if any evidence of Ofcom using its powers excessively or casually in this context, and indeed the regulator has usually required a number of serious breaches of the Code to occur before imposing a sanction.

The above suggests that the new Broadcasting Code offers a significant improvement over the previous arrangements. Ofcom is now the sole body with responsibility for the redress of grievances in the broadcasting sector (although, as discussed in Chapter 6, the ASA now has responsibility for complaints about advertising on television) and, as such, the plethora of Codes which used to exist have now been reduced to one. The process leading to the formulation of the Broadcast Code can be viewed largely positively, and it seems that Ofcom have made some effort to inject public participation into the process. In their enforcement of the Code, Ofcom may be seen to have stayed within the bounds of reasonableness, even if the approach may yet on occasion appear somewhat paternalistic. On the whole, it seems that there have been some significant improvements in the system of grievance redress since the previous edition of this book, although there are still some weaknesses. In particular, it may be thought problematic that the regulator still has no power to award financial redress to those who have suffered infringements of the fairness or privacy sections of the Code. Despite this, it seems that the two areas of performance we outlined above (effective redress of grievance and accountability of the regulator) have both seen marked improvements. Against these same criteria of effectiveness and accountability, the self-regulatory mechanisms employed in the form of the PCC and the ASA will now each be considered briefly in turn.

5.5 THE PRESS COMPLAINTS COMMISSION

Despite persistent, if somewhat cyclical, clamour for reform of the self-regulatory arrangements for the press over many years, there are few, perhaps disappointingly few, changes to report in this field since the first edition of this work appeared.

Self-regulation of the newspaper industry began with the creation of the Press Council in 1953 (O'Malley and Soley 2000: 58). Since then, a number of reforms have taken place, many under the shadow of pressure from the administration of the day that some form of legislation would be enacted in order to appoint a regulator if the industry could not successfully regulate itself. In 1990 Sir David Calcutt reported on the Press Council (Calcutt 1990) and recommended its replacement with a more effective regulator. This led to the industry's creation of the Press Complaints Commission, which was subject to a further review by Calcutt in 1993 (Calcutt 1993). The outcome of the review was by no means positive, with the Committee arguing that:

> The Press Complaints Commission is not . . . an effective regulator of the press. It has not been set up in a way, and is not operating a code of conduct, which enables it to command not only press but public confidence . . . It is not truly the independent body it should be. (Calcutt 1993, quoted in Curran and Seaton 2003: 356)

The PCC code has been subject to thirteen amendments since its inception in 1991 (PCC no date) but has retained its basic structure. Significant changes were made to the Code after the death of the Princess of Wales in 1997, which resulted in strong public pressure for a strengthening regulation. As such, the provisions on privacy and intrusion into grief and shock were strengthened, and the exhortatory tones of the previous code – that newspapers 'should not' contravene the terms of the Code – were replaced with a more imperative language, i.e. that newspapers 'must not' infringe the provisions of the Code (PCC no date). Despite all of these amendments, it is notable that many of the provisions of the Code are still clothed with defences based around a broad 'public interest' test, which has, as one of its constituent parts, the notion that 'There is a public interest in freedom of expression itself.'

From the perspective of many complainants, the PCC is unlikely to offer a satisfactory mode of grievance redress. Although it is free and relatively easy to contact the PCC, there is only one formal sanction available to the PCC if a breach of the Code is upheld – that of the publication of its decision (PCC 2005). It is evident that many other complaints are resolved informally, without the need for a formal adjudication, via negotiation between the newspaper, the PCC and the complainant (PCC 2005). In reality, the majority of cases result in apologies or corrections being published, but there is no power to offer financial compensation, or even to fine repeated transgressors of the PCC Code. On some occasions there is little doubt that an apology or correction, whether elicited from a formal ruling which is very rare (Culture, Media and Sport Committee 2003: Table 2) or an informal resolution of the grievance, will prove appropriate and satisfactory to an aggrieved party. There is, however, no question that the PCC is lacking the 'big sticks' which Ofcom, as the broadcasting regulator, possesses.

There seems to be little doubt that the PCC is accountable to the courts for its decisions (R v *Press Complaints Commission, ex parte Stewart-Brady* [1997] EMLR 185), but it is more questionable whether it is accountable in other ways. For instance, it may be difficult to judge whether the PCC has truly been successful in meeting its goals, as it is not entirely clear what these goals might be. Curran and Seaton (2003: 357; see also O'Malley and Soley 2000: chapter 11) argue that

> the principal deficiency of press self-regulation was not its lack of independence, nor its ineffectiveness, but its dearth of ambition . . . Unwanted by the press, it settled for being a customer complaints service, and discreet lobbyist for the industry.

Herein lies the fundamental conflict at the heart of the PCC's role and existence – is it oriented towards serving the legitimate democratic interests of members of the public, individually and collectively, who have been damaged by reckless or inappropriate use of press power, or is it primarily there to serve the interests of the press industry, forming an effective shield against the threat of harder-hitting statutory intervention? Much evidence suggests the latter: the PCC does not seem to have a clear set of identifiable goals, other than complaints redress under its code (which has not been entirely successful), and even in recent years it has not engaged in significant amounts of training and does not appear to have pursued an increase in journalistic standards with sufficient voracity. As such, critics of the PCC continue to suggest that it should be replaced with a form of statutory regulation (O'Malley and Soley 2000: chapter 11; Coad 2005). However, a recent Private Member's Bill, the Right of Reply and Press Standards Bill 2005, has not progressed to become law, and it seems that the current New Labour administration have no great desire to introduce a stronger regulatory regime for the press (Curran and Seaton 2003: 360–1).

A particular issue of some controversy for the press has been the issue of personal privacy. Scanlon (2000) argues that privacy is linked to 'prevailing ideas of personal dignity and of the aspects of one's life it is shameful or embarrassing to have others observe'. Broadcasters have been subject to relatively strict regulation on the infringement of privacy, but the press have not been constrained in the same manner. In some respects, privacy is a difficult issue for the press, as the economics of the industry render it necessary to attract readers who find much material, which might be deemed by many to be an infringement of privacy, to be of great interest.

The PCC has faced particular difficulties in controlling the newspapers' excesses in respect of breach of privacy, especially where celebrities or members of the British Royal Family are concerned. Seymour-Ure (1996: 259) identifies a range of key episodes, ranging from the so-called

'Squidgy tape' (in 1990 the publication of an apparently affectionate telephone conversation between Princess Diana and a friend) to the 'toe-sucking episode' (in 1992, photographs of the Duchess of York with her financial advisor at a poolside in St Tropez) through to the 'Camillagate tape' (in 1993, apparently pillow-talk phone calls between Prince Charles and Camilla Parker-Bowles) and the 'gym photos' (1993, photographs taken of Princess Diana while working out in her Chelsea gym). This list is, of course, far from comprehensive, and in particular does not include the 'photo-fest' covering the relationship between Princess Diana and Dodi al-Fayed in the weeks running up to their fatal accident in Paris. The extent to which these publications reflect the degree or nature of the public interest in the Royal Family, or alternatively the power of the media to create an interest, is uncertain, as is the case also in relation to the media's coverage following Princess Diana's death. More recently, we might identify the now famous *Hello!* magazine pictures of the wedding of Michael Douglas and Catherine Zeta-Jones, press investigations into the private lives of a number of famous football stars and the publication of photographs of Naomi Campbell outside a 'Narcotics Anonymous' meeting have all provoked considerable controversy.

It must be right to conclude that the PCC has failed to protect the privacy of those in the public eye (Blom-Cooper and Pruitt 1994). Even if it had the desire to do so, it is evident that the current sanctions available to it would do little to resolve the situation, as the PCC is neither in a position to prevent the publication of a particular story, nor to award compensation for an article which is deemed to have infringed an individual's privacy. As such, as the PCC is currently constituted, it is unable to offer an effective guarantee of a right to privacy. In the previous edition a quote was offered from Robertson and Nicol (1992) which stated that 'The publication of intimate details of private lives without the slightest public-interest justification cannot be the subject of legal action unless they have stemmed from a breach of confidence or some other legal wrong. There is no substantive protection for privacy in British law.' This quotation, written thirteen years ago, remains factually correct today. We still have no substantive privacy law in the UK, though since the coming into force of the Human Rights Act 1998 the courts have demonstrated a flexible approach towards the use of Article 8 ECHR to refashion the breach of confidence remedy, which was primarily a commercial remedy at common law, into a more effective mechanism to protect privacy rights. It is not necessary here to offer a detailed exposition of the law on this issue, as others have covered this thoroughly (Leigh 1999; Fenwick and Philipson 2000; Moreham 2001, 2005).

However, it should be observed that the HRA may seem to have allowed the courts to use constitutional principle in order to fill a gap left by the current regulatory regime. The decisions in cases such as *Douglas* (*Michael Douglas, Catherine Zeta Jones and Northern and Shell Plc. v Hello! Limited* [2001] EWCA Civ 353; [2001] 2 All ER 289); *A v B* (*A v B plc and Ors.* [2001] 1 WLR 2341 (QB) and [2002] EWCA Civ 337; [2002] 2 All ER 545 (CA)) and the more recent decision of the House of Lords in *Campbell* (*Campbell v Mirror Group Newspapers Ltd.* [2004] UKHL 22; [2004] 2 AC 457) all seem to suggest that the common law will continue to offer protection in certain circumstances. There is no doubt that the HRA has had a significant impact in this area, though these developments appear to illustrate and reconfirm the under-lying weaknesses in the 'front-line' regulator, the PCC.

As it presently stands, according to most accounts, the PCC is an ineffective regulator which fails to offer adequate redress in a great many cases. A recent report (Culture, Media and Sport Committee 2003: para. 84) has suggested that the remedies available to the PCC should be improved, with the potential to increase the membership fees of repeated transgressors of the PCC Code and to offer modest compensation to wronged parties in certain cases. Without these additional sanctions, it seems unlikely that the PCC will offer a genuinely effective means of redress in all but the most minor cases of infringement of the Code. That said, the cynical observer might conclude that the PCC has in practice been extremely successful if its primary objective is seen as being, in the perceived interest of sections of the press industry, to avoid the imposition of hard-hitting regulation. As ever, clarity as regards fundamental purpose and underlying values is essential before a meaningful conclusion can be reached as regards the effectiveness of regulation.

5.6 THE ADVERTISING STANDARDS AUTHORITY

Television advertising is subject to relatively stringent regulation, historically carried out by the ITC, with responsibility now passed to Ofcom under the Communications Act 2003. In practice, this task, like the regulation of all other advertising in the UK, is now carried out by the ASA. Ofcom delegated its powers (Ofcom 2004j) to regulate television broadcasting, in accordance with the powers granted to it under section 1(7) of the Communications Act 2003. Under this regime, the ASA has agreed a Code with Ofcom, (BCAP 2005a) and is now charged with the enforcement of the Code. Ofcom will not become involved with individual decisions made by the ASA, but will maintain an overview of the operation of the system. The ASA is unable to invoke additional sanctions than the ones which are already available to it, but may call on Ofcom to issue a sanction for breach of a licence condition in certain cases (Ofcom 2004j: para. 27). There are some concerns with this delegation – in particular in terms of accountability. As we will note below, the ASA is subject to judicial review in the courts, but it remains important to ensure the existence of other effective accountability mechanisms if we are to be confident that it will maintain similar standards to those generally reached by Ofcom.

Historically, the ASA has shown significant evidence of good practice; it keeps the text of individual adjudications on the Code online, and it has issued guidelines alongside its Broadcast Advertising Code (BCAP 2005b). On the whole, the ASA has proven to be an effective regulator, perhaps because of the more widespread industry support for such a regulator in this sector, and has a record of dealing with most complaints rapidly (Borrie 2005: 67). The ASA will be accountable both to the courts and to Ofcom for its performance in the broadcast sector, and it seems that there are no obvious reasons why we might object in principle to the ASA taking over the regulation of broadcast advertising.

This aspect of regulation is influenced, unsurprisingly in light of the potential for spill-over transmission across national boundaries, by European provisions. Both the Council of Europe's Convention on Transfrontier Television, and the EU's TVWF Directive (Directive 89/552, discussed in further detail in Chapter 6) seek to harmonise minimum standards, requiring the clear demarcation of advertising from programming, limiting the percentage of broadcast time given over to advertising and the frequency of commercial breaks, though Article 19 of the Directive permits Member States to impose stricter limits than those established in the Directive (Barendt 1993: chapter 9; Skouris 1994).

While television advertising is therefore closely regulated by national and international law, the rest of the British advertising industry, in print, cinema and on hoardings, is run almost entirely on a self-regulatory basis under the aegis of the ASA. This is not to say, however, that the ASA operates entirely in a legal vacuum, as advertisers are subject to general background law as to obscenity, blasphemy, defamation, etc., and to advertising-specific law relating to misleading advertisements, etc., and the ASA is subject, despite not being a statutory body, to the supervisory jurisdiction of the courts via judicial review procedures.

The ASA is, in effect, an umbrella group for the various trade associations in the advertising industry which aims to enforce the requirement of the British Code of Advertising Practice which seeks to put flesh on the

Authority's skeletal position that advertising should be 'legal, decent, honest and truthful'. Though the ASA's Committee of Advertising Practice (CAP), which draws up and revises the relevant Codes of Practice, consists of members of the advertising industry, its governing council, which has the power to approve or override CAP decisions (Graham 1994: 197), has at least half of its membership made up of persons unconnected with the advertising industry (Munro 1997: 12). In addition to handling complaints regarding specific advertisements, the ASA routinely monitors the advertising industry's output, including pre-publication scrutiny, and reports the findings of its investigations in a monthly 'Case Report'. Graham (1994: 200) identifies the release of decisions and reasons into the public domain as an important legitimating factor.

The sanctions applied by the ASA, where a breach of the Code is found, appear at first sight far from draconian but seem to be effective. The ASA will require an advertiser to amend or withdraw an advertisement found to be in breach of the code, and any advertiser who fails to comply with such a requirement will find it impossible to place advertisements in publications or sites controlled by those in the trade who are ASA members. It is at this stage that the self-regulation of the advertising industry appears to diverge from the PCC's self-regulatory activities in relation to the press. The key to the success of the ASA scheme is that it is actively enforced by those in the advertising trade, while a large sector of the press appear to be far from content to support the attempts of the PCC to impose and enforce standards. The fact that a broadly consensual approach appears to exist at this level in the fiercely competitive advertising industry does not, however, mean that disputes regarding the ASA's exercise of power do not arise.

The efficacy of the ASA regime can obviously be questioned in individual cases. For example, the Benetton poster campaigns, clearly intended to shock, in pursuit of the sale of knitwear emphasised the bind in which the ASA can find itself, as did the controversy over the Conservative's 'Demon Eyes' posters featuring Tony Blair in the 1997 General Election campaign. Should the ASA allow a 'shocking' advertisement to run and allow the public to be shocked, or does it ban the advertisement and provide the affronted advertiser with the media publicity attendant upon such a ban? It is a 'no win' situation for any regulator of the advertising industry, and it is not necessarily fair to base criticism of the ASA on such examples. Some body, whether self-regulatory or statutory, will, inevitably, have to exercise discretion over such determinations if any control over advertising is to be exercised, and the important question is not so much 'who regulates?' but rather the extent to which whoever exercises power in the supposed public interest is accountable for their actions. Accountability in the exercise of discretionary power can be facilitated by the confining, structuring and checking of discretion, and in particular through transparency in the exercise of powers and through liability to sanction, including scrutiny in the courts.

Following the decision in R. v ASA ex parte The Insurance Services plc (1990 2 Admin LR 77), it is now well established that as a consequence of fulfilling a function, which, if the ASA did not exist, would have to be fulfilled by a body established by the government, the ASA is subject to the procedural and, in so far as they exist, substantive requirements enforced by the courts via judicial review. Thus the ASA must act in good faith and follow fair procedures in reaching its decisions, and must not act illegally or irrationally (as defined in case law). In general, however, as Lidbetter (1994: 115) notes in connection with a review of both the ASA and ITC, the courts appear 'to treat the substantive decision of a body which they regard as having expertise in a given area with deference', the indication being that courts will be very reluctant to overturn decisions of the ASA on substantive grounds and are likely, largely, to confine their scrutiny to the decision-making process.

This difficulty in persuading a court to overturn the decision of an 'expert' body such as the ASA can be seen as a double-edged sword. Clearly, such a body is likely to have greater knowledge and experience of the substantive issues in question than judges and may use more appropriate mechanisms than the adversarial courtroom process. On the other hand, however, too great a degree of judicial deference to decision-makers may put off prospective challengers to decisions and allow discretion to remain unchecked. The risk is of having decision-makers potentially abusing discretion without adequate checks, though judges intervening on substantive grounds without clear, substantive principles to guide them, would seem at least equally problematic.

This situation throws up some nice problems for academic lawyers, but should not be allowed to hide an important underlying truth relating to the self-regulatory function carried out by the ASA in relation to the advertising industry. The fact is that the system of self-regulation enforced by the ASA is generally, by way of stark contrast with the PCC, considered by commentators to be successful.

Like the press, the advertising industry would seem to be an obvious target for statutory control if a government ultimately determined that standards were persistently falling below acceptable levels. In the case of the overtly commercial advertising industry, it would be more difficult for the industry to defend itself on claims of freedom of expression (whether in terms of arguments from truth, self-fulfilment or citizen participation) given that its fundamental and undeniable *raison d'être* is to sell products (Munro 2003), as opposed to the more high-minded, if sometimes far-fetched, justifications offered for their existence and claims of freedom by newspapers. Ignoring, for the moment, the fact that newspapers are, essentially, commercial enterprises and in themselves constitute a product to be sold, newspaper editors can at least (some more plausibly than others) resort to freedom of expression arguments to defend themselves from the threat of statutory control. The same argument also provides a useful way-out for politicians fearful of intervening in 'the freedom of the press' for concerns over the public opinion-forming power that the press might wield against them.

Without either the freedom of expression argument or the leverage over government available with which to defend themselves against the possibility of the imposition of statutory regulation, the advertising industries are more vulnerable and in essence just have to make self-regulation work. The advertising industry's collective will in favour of self-enforcement of regulation is therefore fully mobilised. By way of contrast, the newspaper industry, and in particular the tabloid sector, with the shield of the claim of freedom of expression available to them, appears to feel more able, in pursuit of scandal and therefore circulation, to flout attempts by the PCC to establish standards of conduct, safe in the knowledge that any government will be reluctant to intervene.

In considering the role of the ASA and its supervision via judicial review, Lidbetter (1994: 115) posited two alternative rationales for the advertising industry's preference for self-regulation. On the one hand are the benefits of 'flexibility and informality which may offer an opportunity to avoid some practical and constitutional difficulties that limit the utility of controls imposed by law', while on the other is a possibility that 'self-regulation is merely a means of industry avoiding the imposition of a statutory backed set of regulations which could go further than the controls imposed by self-regulation'. Both of these justifications are essentially pragmatic, and a preference for one over the other might ultimately depend on whether one is a lawyer or an advertising executive! That said, it is clear that there is no evidence that self-regulation inherently runs counter to public interest, or democratic, or constitutional expectations. Consideration of the ASA alongside the PCC suggests that self-regulation, provided that it fulfils basic requirements of accountability, is not in itself problematic, but rather that it is the context in which self-regulation operates that can ultimately determine whether it can provide appropriate and effective regulation. However, this elides rather than answers a crucial prior question: how do we know when it is proving effective? Readers will be unsurprised to find that we believe that it is necessary, in this respect to have recourse to a fundamental structure of values which must inform any regulatory endeavour. We will return to this theme in the concluding chapter, but in the meantime now turn to consider the important question of where regulatory power should be located in an increasingly multi-tiered and international media context.

6

Tiers of Regulation

6.1 INTRODUCTION

In this chapter we seek to offer an analysis of the framework of media
regulation in the UK which gives appropriate attention to the increasing
significance of developments emanating from Europe. We have emphasised earlier the huge changes in media regulation and its context which
have occurred since the appearance of the last edition of this book in
1999, and in that time there has been in particular a considerable expansion in the role of the EU, driven in the main by technological developments in the media sector. The same period has also seen a significant
increase in the extent of self- and co-regulation in the media. These phenomena raise a range of important issues which have come increasingly
into the spotlight over the last seven years, and demand much closer
scrutiny than hitherto.

The role of the UK courts in the regulatory process, while still relatively weak, has also expanded in the media sphere over recent years. The
impact of the Human Rights Act 1998 (HRA), particularly in relation to
the regulation of media content, has been significant. We have seen that
the promulgation of Ofcom's 'Content Code', along with a number of
other measures, have been impacted upon by the implementation of
certain of the rights in the European Convention on Human Rights into
UK law by the HRA. This inevitably builds on the examination of the
impact of the courts' role in media regulation in the UK touched upon in
the previous chapter. While we do not seek to offer a detailed or comprehensive account of what might be described as 'media law' (a field
best served by Robertson and Nicol's (2002) seminal work), it will be
necessary to highlight decisions in some of these areas which have had a
particular impact on the regulatory process as a whole.

We have already said much in previous chapters about the values
which we argue should inform the media regulation regimes. However,
before it is possible to discuss 'tiers of regulation' in this context, it is necessary to indicate more clearly what we mean by the term 'regulation'.

6.2 THE NATURE OF REGULATION

6.2.1 What might be meant by 'regulation'?

Commonplace or dictionary definitions of regulation will inevitably leave many questions unanswered. We need answers to questions such as 'Regulation by whom?', 'Regulation to what end?' and 'Regulation with what authority?' Of course, all of these questions have been addressed in detail by scholars of regulation and all we attempt here is to identify and highlight those which have informed our approach.

A number of definitions of regulation have been offered over the years. In a seminal work, Ogus (1994) discusses Selznick's (1985) definition of regulation, which suggests that regulation is 'sustained and focused control exercised by a public agency over activities that are valued by a community' (Selznick 1985: 363). This definition is very much a 'state-centred' view of regulation, with total emphasis being given to the intervention of public agencies. It is evident that many studies of media regulation in the UK (Barendt 1995; Prosser, 1997; Gibbons 1998) have all placed the greatest emphasis on public intervention. This focus is entirely unsurprising, as much of the regulation which took place in the media sector, particularly in relation to broadcasting, was intervention by public agencies such as the ITC. With the exceptions of the Press Complaints Commission (PCC) and the Advertising Standards Authority (ASA), there were relatively few instances of self-regulation in place in UK media regulation.

The potential extension of other forms of control, such as self-regulation and the likelihood of greater intervention by the courts in certain media issues post HRA means that a more sophisticated definition of regulation, which acknowledges the multiplicity of potential regulatory bodies, may have to be adopted. Black offers an account of three descriptions of regulation often propounded in the literature. She suggests that:

> In the first, regulation is the promulgation of rules by government accompanied by mechanisms for monitoring and enforcement, usually assumed to be performed through a specialist public agency. In the second, it is any form of direct state intervention in the economy, whatever form that intervention might take. In the third, regulation is all mechanisms of social control or influence affecting all aspects of behaviour from whatever source, whether they are intentional or not. (Black 2002: 18)

It has been suggested above that the regulatory strategies adopted in the media sector have most typically been characterised by the first and second definitions of regulation – specialised agencies prevailed in the regulation of commercial television and radio and the competition law functions were largely exercised by the OFT. After the coming into force of the Communications Act 2003, Ofcom has an extremely broad remit to regulate many of the activities of the media, bringing the remits of the various 'legacy' regulators under the ambit of one 'super-regulator' for the communications sector. In many areas, then, it is possible to argue that the little has changed – regulation is still manifested in practice as rules promulgated by the state and monitored and enforced by a government agency.

The funding of the BBC might be characterised as the second form of regulation, as there is significant state funding and intervention in the market for broadcasting which is demonstrated by the BBC's 'public service' remit. This type of governmental intervention is further characterised by the licensing process, last entered into under the Broadcasting Act 1990, for ITV regional licences. This process was originally intended to allocate the licences to the highest bidder via means of an auction, in accordance with Coase's vision (Coase 1959). In reality, however, there is strong evidence that this did not happen, as the ITC often used its discretion under section 16(1) of the Act to grant the licences to those broadcasters who were deemed to be offering a greater degree of 'quality' in their output (Prosser 1997: 251). These interventions have undoubtedly had an impact on the market, and seem to be examples of state 'largesse', as discussed by Reich in the 1960s (Reich 1964). Reich's argument was that:

> Government owns or controls . . . the radio and television spectrum which is the avenue for all broadcasting . . . The radio and television industry uses the scarce channels of the air . . . free of charge and all are entitled to make a profit. (Reich 1964: 743)

Although it is not possible to suggest that the analogue broadcasters are able to use broadcast spectrum free of charge as there are financial charges for spectrum use, it is evident that the benefits of such spectrum use have significantly outweighed the burdens imposed by the auction process under the Broadcasting Act 1990 and the public service obligations incumbent on such licence holders. Although there are significant questions over the sustainability of advertising-funded public service broadcasting (PSB) in the digital era (Ofcom 2004a, 2004b), it seems likely that direct state intervention in the broadcasting sector will continue to prevail through the 'public service publisher' model (Ofcom 2004c: chapter 5).

Black's final definition of regulation is evidently broader and potentially encapsulates the other two definitions which she offers. We can see an expansion of various forms of self-regulation and co-regulation, with Ofcom contracting out the regulation of broadcast advertising to the ASA. The existence of the Independent Committee for the Supervision of Standards of Telephone Information Services (ICSTIS), a self-regulator concerned with the regulation of premium-rate telephony services, is also contracted out by Ofcom. The use of 'contracted out' regulators exercising control over particular issues may become more prevalent. Ofcom has recently consulted on criteria to govern the transfer of functions to co-regulatory bodies (Ofcom 2004k).

The relevance of self-regulation in the media sphere is further exemplified by the existence of the PCC, a body which has continued to regulate the press despite continued warnings from the government that it may be necessary to impose some form of governmentally mandated regulation (O'Malley and Soley 2000: chapter 11). While this type of self-regulation is evidently not the same as the schemes which are 'contracted out' by Ofcom, it seems that the existence of such regulation would still fall into Black's third definition of regulatory endeavour.

It may be worth noting at this point that Black considers regulation to take place only if the behaviour of the regulated party changes in some way. The PCC has been subject to a range of criticism as there is some evidence that its existence has had relatively little impact on the behaviour of the newspapers that it regulates (O'Malley and Soley 2000: chapter 7; Coad 2003 and 2005). Despite its detractors, it is evident that the PCC is intended to have a regulatory function, and the exercise of these functions is designed to lead to particular outcomes. It is questionable whether the outcomes of such regulation have been positive because, as O'Malley and Soley (2000: 141) note,

> self-regulation in the UK was not a positive institution designed to promote high standards, deal effectively with complaints and protect press freedom. It was there to defend the proprietors, who funded it, from the encroachments of politicians, journalists and members of the public who wanted the press to be more responsible than the owners were prepared to allow.

Although some may find this criticism of the PCC's role and position somewhat extreme, it is evident that the PCC is often held up as an example of an ineffective self-regulator, adjudicating over a Code of Conduct which has only relatively minor impact on the behaviour of those who are subject to its jurisdiction.

The above discussion suggests that a modern view of media regulation requires a vision of regulation which is not entirely state-centred. There are significant examples of self-regulation and co-regulation currently in place, and there is the potential for the use of such bodies to be expanded in the future. As such, the discussion of the term 'regulation' in this book requires a degree of nuance: although most regulation of the broadcast media still adheres closely to the 'state-centred' models of regulation outlined in earlier works, the degree of involvement of 'private' regulators is seeing a significant expansion over time.

The examples of regulation which have been given thus far are relevant because they are examples of *sustained* regulation which is designed to achieve particular outcomes within the media sector. All of the regulators and all of the regulatory functions outlined above are designed to ensure a degree of control over the activities of the media on a day-to-day basis. It is important to note, however, that this is not the only type of regulation which could manifest itself under Black's third definition, which might be described as a most expansive definition of the concept (Black 2002: 12).

If we are to adopt a more expansive definition of the concept of regulation then it is also necessary to emphasise the way in which actors other than those identified above may have an impact on the process of regulation as a whole. It is likely that some actors might have a less sustained input into the regulatory process, but their pronouncements may still have a significant impact on the behaviour of both regulators and the regulated parties. In the previous chapter we discussed some ways in which the courts have had an impact on the regulation of the media in the UK, with privacy offering a key example of an area of regulation which has been heavily influenced by the courts since the enactment of the HRA.

In light of these many and varied forms of regulatory intervention, it is increasingly apparent that it is necessary to adopt a viewpoint which looks across and beyond state-centred media regulation. This necessity is likely to be reconfirmed by the increased growth of alternative means of broadcasting delivery, such as the Internet, where self-regulation is, and seems likely to remain, the main method of exerting control (Murray and Scott 2002). Under these circumstances it seems apposite to re-emphasise Black's (2002) point that a modern concept of regulation may require 'de-centring' from the state. As such, her article suggests that a new definition of the concept should be offered:

> [R]egulation is the sustained and focused attempt to alter the behaviour of others according to defined standards or purposes with the intention of producing a broadly identified outcome or outcomes, which may involve mechanisms of standard-setting, information-gathering and behaviour-modification. (Black 2002: 20)

It is evident that such a definition is intended to be broad. It tells us little about the values which should underpin regulation, or the nature of the outcomes to be achieved, which allows it to be a useful analytical tool in a range of different circumstances. The previous chapter, however, suggested that regulation of the media should necessarily be a value-laden endeavour – designed to pursue the 'public interest' (Feintuck 2004). The remainder of this chapter will refer to regulation within this analytical framework, that is regulation as a concept will be broadly conceived and analysed in order to determine whether the processes are likely to lead to outcomes which serve the 'public interest'.

6.2.2 Multi-level control

We have noted above that recent developments in media regulation have rendered it necessary to have a far greater appreciation both of measures adopted at the level of the European Community and also of the decentralisation of regulatory power, both to self-regulators and subnational authorities. Furthermore, it is necessary to have an appreciation of the interface between the institutions which exist at each 'level' of regulation, as the regulators themselves, government institutions and the courts are all likely to interact in order to influence the regulatory regime which is in place. Hancher and Moran (1989: 272) suggest that:

> Understanding economic regulation then means understanding a process of intermediation and bargaining between large and powerful organisations spanning what we conventionally termed the public and private domains of decision-making.

Although Hancher and Moran's analysis centres on the concept of economic regulation, it seems likely that it might also extend to other forms of regulation designed to pursue social goals (Ogus 1994: 4–5). The complex interplay between different actors in the 'regulatory space' has been further analysed by Scott (2002: 330). He argues that:

> The dispersed nature of resources between organisations in the same regulatory space means regulators lack a monopoly both over formal and informal authority. This observation draws our attention to the need to conceive of strategies of regulation as consisting of a wide range of negotiated processes, of which rule making and enforcement are but two.

We will argue below that the existence of a multiplicity of government and private actors, acting at different levels of government, be it at the European level, the national level or the subnational level, can lead to benefits but may also cause difficulties for regulatory consistency. An analysis of self-regulation requires a slightly different approach, as it is necessary to determine whether such self-regulation shares all of the characteristics of state-mandated regulation (Black 1996).

More than ever before, we might characterise regulation of the media, in particular the broadcast media, as an increasingly complex matrix of regulatory systems which are interfacing with one another in order to secure a range of sometimes conflicting outcomes. The division of competences between the EU level, the level of the Member State and subnational authorities varies between national legal systems. In the UK, the influence of subnational authorities over issues of media regulation is very limited, with most matters being 'reserved' to the Westminster Parliament. The situation in other Member States can differ significantly, with the German (Koenig and Röder 1998; Libertus 2004) and Spanish (Ariño 2004) subnational authorities having a far more significant role to play in the regulation of the broadcast media in their respective jurisdictions.

The allocation of certain tasks to self-regulatory or co-regulatory bodies appears to be an acknowledgement that these institutions may be better placed to secure certain outcomes. Difficulties arise with self-regulation, in part due to the multiplicity of definitions of the concept which exist in the modern literature on the issue. A further detailed analysis of the potential for self or co-regulation in the media sector, alongside a brief analysis of its manifestation in practice in the UK, will be offered later in this chapter.

6.2.3 *Explanations of the manifestation of multi-level control*

We have noted above that media regulation has seen a significant increase in the amount of 'multi-level' activity in recent years. It may be useful to analyse these developments through the lens of two different strands of academic literature. The first of these notes a trend towards the 'reconfiguring' of the state. Majone (1997: 139) has argued that Europe has seen a significant shift in the behaviour of states over the past few years. In essence, he argues that there is a

> reduced role for the positive, interventionist state and a corresponding increase in the role of the regulatory state: rule making is replacing taxing and spending.

Many would argue that this is nothing new in the broadcasting sector, as private broadcasting of both radio and television, subject to extensive regulation by the state, has been a feature in most European countries for some decades (Barendt 1995: chapter 4; Humphreys 1996: chapter 5). What is notable in the modern shift towards digital broadcasting and distribution of broadcasting over networks other than terrestrial analogue is that the industry is less reliant on broadcast spectrum, the grant of which always gave the state particular leverage in the exercise of regulatory control. The variety of delivery mechanisms available for broadcasting now raise a range of challenges to this traditional picture.

Networks for the delivery of digital broadcasting are all under private ownership, and the most significant delivery platform in the UK – Sky's direct-to-home satellite system (Ofcom 2005c) – is based outside the UK's jurisdiction in Luxembourg (Humphreys 1996: 168–9). These developments have placed state regulation of broadcasting under far greater scrutiny than has traditionally been the case. The New Regulatory Framework (NRF) in the EU serves as an acknowledgement of the fact that electronic communications services are becoming increasingly transnational. The activities of the media corporations which provide the content to be supplied over these networks are crossing international borders ever more often (Herman and McChesney 1997; McChesney 1999). Despite this increased internationalisation of broadcasting, we can see relatively little internationalisation of regulation, particularly in relation to issues of broadcast content.

These developments place the state's ability to exercise regulatory control under considerable strain. It is necessary to appreciate that the ability of the nation state to regulate many of the activities of the media industry is becoming increasingly limited. Regulation will have to become increasingly sophisticated, sometimes shifting towards supranational solutions, while at other times engaging with the type of negotiated outcomes described by Scott above. It seems unlikely that a strict adherence to a 'state-centred' view of regulation will allow satisfactory responses to be offered to all the multiplicity of issues raised in the ever-developing media context.

A second strand of literature which assists analysis of the current regulatory framework lies in the discussion of the subsidiarity concept. Subsidiarity is a heavily contested concept which has been the subject of a range of different analyses (Føllesdal 1998). The theoretical discussions of the concept, while important, must be tied to the debate which rages over the precise meaning of 'subsidiarity' as it is set out in Article 5 of the EC Treaty (De Búrca 1998; Scott 2002; Van Hecke 2003; Barber 2005). In many ways, it is this manifestation which may

have a greater impact on the regulatory realities in the EU. Scott offers
a helpful definition of the subsidiarity concept within the EC Treaty
when he suggests that

> The principle of subsidiarity underlies the recognition of the capacities of a
> variety of actors at different levels to effectively carry out tasks under cir-
> cumstances where the EU institutions do not have exclusive competence.
> (Scott 2002: 64)

Although Scott limits his own analysis to the principle contained within
the EC Treaty, his definition illuminates the background principle which
inheres in much of the literature. This principle may be described as the
'most appropriate level' principle. Under this conception of subsidiarity,
regulation must take place at the level which would be most effective,
considering all relevant factors. There is significant debate over whether
the principle of subsidiarity provided for in Article 5 of the EC Treaty is
genuinely intended to provide for this 'most appropriate level' principle.
There is some evidence that the European principle was introduced in
order to encourage a degree of decentralisation and return decision-
making power to the Member States (Estella 2002: chapter 3), although
it is evident that the EU has still been willing to expand its competence
into a range of areas which are shared with the Member States if this is
deemed to be necessary.

At the EU level, Article 5 of the EC Treaty links the subsidiarity principle with a version of proportionality, described by Scott (2002: 64)
as '. . . [supporting] the search for "softer forms of law" and alternative techniques of control which are less intrusive than hierarchical
controls.'

An application of the EU subsidiarity principle in the manner intended
by Member States such as the UK at its inception would seem to suggest
that many instances of regulation should be focused at the Member State
level (Cary 1993). It will be noted below that regulation of the media is
a particularly sensitive issue in many Member States, raising a number
of significant constitutional questions and issues regarding the division
of powers within Member States themselves. The German system has
seen lengthy disputes between the Bund and Länder level over the regulation of broadcasting (Barendt 1991; Humphreys and Lang 1998), and
such potential disputes within and between the Member States would
require resolution before there could be any potential for competence to
be shifted to the EU level.

Despite the considerable disagreement about the precise meaning of the
subsidiarity principle, it seems most useful for regulators to characterise

the principle as suggesting that regulation should take place at the 'most effective level'. We will see that implementation of such a system is unlikely to be simple, as there are a number of significant constitutional and political challenges to the manifestation of a system of control which would transfer all functions to the 'most effective level'. Furthermore, there is likely to be significant disagreement over which level might be the 'most effective' to implement a particular regulatory scheme. On the one hand, it is evident that the activities of large media corporations might be most effectively regulated at the supranational level, yet the importance of cultural and linguistic diversity might only be adequately represented at either the nation state or subnational level (McGonagle *et al.* 2003; McGonagle and Richter 2004).

The application of the subsidiarity principle in the sphere of media regulation may raise more questions than it answers. Even if it is possible to agree that the majority of media regulation should take place at the level of the EU, or at Member State level, or at the level of subnational authorities, or even that schemes of self- or co-regulation would be most effective, the constitutional and political realities of the current regulatory framework will prevent many potential instances of regulatory reconfiguration.

Another potential difficulty with the division of regulatory labour between actors at various levels of government and the involvement of self-regulators is that the dispersal of regulatory power may lead to fragmentation of the goals to be pursued. In our discussion of the current measures implemented at the EU level below it is evident that the economic focus of the EU's activities colours the interventions that are made at this level. If it is our objective that regulation of the media should pursue consistently 'the public interest' then there may be concerns that the differing competences and goals pursued by actors within the regulatory space may pull in different directions. The key to regulatory success in the future will be to ensure that regulatory resources are deployed in a way which will ensure that the public interest is successfully pursued.

The remainder of this chapter will examine some of the 'tiers' which impact on the regulation of the media in order to offer an assessment of the interplay between different levels of government in the regulatory space. The discussion will commence with an analysis of the interventions at the EU level before considering the likely impact on regulation at Member State level. After these sections, we will examine the role of subnational authorities and self- and co-regulators in the future regulation of the broadcast media.

6.3 THE AGENDA IN THE EUROPEAN UNION

6.3.1 *Introduction*

Though alternative frameworks could be utilised for the study of a 'European' agenda in this context, our discussion in this section will be primarily concerned with the agenda adopted by the European Union (EU) which has had a significant impact on Member States' ability to deviate from the path chosen by the EU legislative authorities in a number of fields.

The regulatory interventions made into the broadcasting media which are made by the EU might be most helpfully split into two areas. The longest-standing intervention into the broadcasting industry arises from Article 49 of the EC Treaty. In 1974, the European Court of Justice acknowledged that television channels would be construed as 'services' for the purposes of Article 49 (Case 155/73 *Italy* v *Sacchi* [1974] 2 CMLR 177). This treatment of channels as services had little impact on the UK at the time of the decision, as the technical capacity for broadcasting, and the geographical distance of the UK from mainland Europe meant that relatively few broadcasting channels from continental Europe could be received in the UK. In mainland Europe, however, it is evident that broadcasts crossed national frontiers from a much earlier stage (European Audiovisual Observatory 2004: 9).

It is notable, however, that the decision had a greater impact in mainland Europe, where the extension of the protection of Article 49 EC to broadcasting services had an impact on the ability of Member States to regulate the activities of broadcasters which were broadcasting from another Member State (Varney 2004: 508–15). In essence, broadcasting is treated like any other service and, as such, the ability to regulate services which emanate from another Member State is curtailed to those circumstances permitted by Article 46 of the EC Treaty, or where regulation might be permitted under the famous 'rule of reason' test (Case 33/74 *Van Binsbergen* v *Bestuur van de Bedrijfsvereniging voor de Metaalnijverheid* [1974] ECR 1299).

Ultimately, the treatment of broadcasting as a service caused some difficulty for the ECJ, as each Member State sought to exert regulation over the provision of broadcasting services. It is evident that social and cultural mores vary throughout the Member States and, as such, a number of cases on the regulation of broadcasters reached the ECJ (Lenaerts and Van Nuffel 1999: 4-152–4-155). We will not explore this web of case law at this juncture, but further details of these cases' impact on the manner in which Member States might regulate broadcasting can be found in a number of other sources (Varney 2004; Barendt and Hitchens 2000: 167–72). It is evident, however, that some of the controversies over the precise extent to which Member States were able to regulate broadcast content rendered it necessary for a Directive to be enacted which harmonised certain elements of Member State policy towards broadcasting (Barendt and Hitchens 2000: 173–5). The result of this was that after many years of negotiations (Wallace and Goldberg 1989: 175–8) the Television Without Frontiers Directive (Directive 89/552/EEC) was introduced, which was amended in 1997 by Directive 97/36/EC (Drijber 1999).

6.3.2 The Television Without Frontiers Directive

The Television Without Frontiers Directive (TVWF Directive) has been described as a measure which promoted deregulation of broadcasting (Harcourt 2005: 9) and, on the whole, it is evident that the harmonisation brought about by the Directive has limited the ability of Member States to regulate broadcasters which provide services from outside of their jurisdiction (Varney 2004). This is perhaps unsurprising, given the core objective of the Directive, which is described by the European Commission as

> essentially internal market policy, and is governed by internal market objectives of freedom of movement for goods . . . and the freedom to provide services. (European Commission 2003: 8)

This situation is unsurprising, given the relatively limited legislative competence available to the Community legislator. The Television Without Frontiers Directive finds its legislative basis in Articles 47(2) and 55 of the EC Treaty – measures which allow harmonisation in order to facilitate free movement of services in the internal market. As a result, the majority of the measures in the TVWF Directive are oriented towards achieving this goal. In essence, the TVWF Directive engages in a process of 'minimum harmonisation', whereby it seeks to harmonise the regulation of broadcasting content to a limited extent in order to facilitate the free movement of broadcasting services between the Member States.

The Directive obliges all Member States to permit broadcasting services which are operating lawfully in another Member State to offer their services within their jurisdiction. The Directive contains restrictions on certain advertising practices and the broadcast of content which may be damaging to minors in order to provide a minimum threshold of protection for viewers. Member States are free to impose more stringent standards on broadcasters under their jurisdiction (jurisdiction is usually determined by the place of establishment of the broadcaster). This has, to some extent, created a degree of 'forum shopping', where broadcasters have sought to incorporate in, and broadcast from, Member States with the least restrictive rules on broadcasting.

A result of this development is that Member States have, at least to some extent, seen a significant limitation of their ability to regulate broadcast content where the broadcaster is lawfully established in another Member State (Varney 2004). A further result has been that a number of Member States have assimilated their broadcasting laws in order to comply with the TVWF Directive (Harcourt 2005: 160–2). This harmonisation has been largely deregulatory in its effect, as the TVWF Directive harmonises relatively few areas of content regulation. The majority of the measures which harmonise content regulation in the Directive are concerned with advertising in its various guises (Articles 10–20), whereas the measures in Articles 2a, 22 and 22a seek to protect minors and public order.

The TVWF Directive demonstrates one of the key problems faced by all authorities seeking to regulate broadcast content – technological developments have expanded the ability to broadcast far beyond the borders of the nation state and this expansion renders many efforts to regulate broadcasters at the Member State level somewhat impotent. Article 2a of the TVWF Directive presents the possibility for a Member State to prohibit the services of a broadcaster based in another Member State where the service has infringed the provisions of Articles 22 or 22a. Article 22(1) of the Directive states that

> Member States shall take appropriate measures to ensure that television broadcasts by broadcasters under their jurisdiction do not include any programmes which might seriously impair the physical, mental or moral development of minors, in particular programmes that involve pornography or gratuitous violence.

The Directive does not seek to define what sort of content might serve to 'seriously impair the physical, mental or moral development of minors' or, for that matter, what might constitute 'pornography or gratuitous violence'. These issues are a matter for the Member State concerned (Case E-8/97 *TV1000 Sverige AB* v *Norwegian Government* [1998] 3 CMLR 18), but it is evident that the restrictive provisions in Article 2a of the TVWF Directive render it most unlikely that many cases will arise where a receiving Member State can prevent a broadcast. Article 2a of the Directive requires that the provisions in Articles 22 and 22a are infringed on at least two occasions, and the Member State proposing to take unilateral measures against a broadcaster must consult with the broadcaster, the European Commission and the Member State which has jurisdiction over the broadcaster before any such measures can be taken.

In the two years covered by the latest Commission report on the TVWF Directive the Commission notes that the procedure under Article 2a of the Directive was only commenced by one Member State (European Commission 2003: 15). It is not entirely clear whether the reason for such a limited number of actions under Article 2a is because the Member States have a relatively harmonised view of the issues at stake in Articles 22 and 22a, or whether the stringent procedure renders many disputes to be resolved by other means. It is evident, however, that cultural differences between the Member States remain, and it is therefore unlikely that meaningful harmonisation of content regulation will be achieved in the near future (European Audiovisual Observatory 2004: 28).

The TVWF Directive contains two further elements which are of interest because they are designed to further social and cultural, rather than economic, goals. Articles 4 and 5 of the TVWF Directive contain measures designed to increase media pluralism through the promotion of independent productions and productions of European origin, and Article 3a of the Directive permits Member States to impose measures which ensure that certain events of 'major importance to society' are available to a 'significant part of the public in that Member State'. Member States are not required to draw up a list of events under Article 3a, and at the time of the last report on the TVWF Directive the majority of Member States had not done so (European Commission 2003: 9–10).

Article 4 of the TVWF Directive creates a framework through which Member States are required to ensure that, 'where practicable, and by appropriate means', broadcasters reserve a majority of their transmission time for 'European works', a term that is defined in Article 6. Article 5 of the TVWF Directive seeks to secure, through identical wording, that all broadcasters reserve at least 10 per cent of their transmission time for programmes made by producers who are independent of broadcasters. These measures have a clear intention of promoting the broadcast of European programming and increasing media pluralism by encouraging the development and acquisition of independent productions. The European Commission report on the operation of Articles 4 and 5 of the Directive suggests that the measures have, to some extent, been a success. For most Member States, the proportion of European material broadcast in accordance with Article 4 of the Directive was in excess of the requirements, with 66.1 per cent of all output being 'European' in 2002. On the whole, the amount of independent material has exceeded the 10 per cent requirement by a considerable margin, with an average of 34 per cent in 2002 (European Commission 2004b: 5–8). While these figures suggest that all is well with the operation of Articles 4 and 5 of the Directive, there are many questions surrounding the success of the provisions as a whole.

At the time of its promulgation, the inclusion of Articles 4 and 5 in the TVWF Directive was highly controversial (Barendt and Hitchens 1999: 190–1). It was noted above that the legislative basis for the TVWF Directive arises from provisions in the EC Treaty concerned with freedom to provide services. At the time of the Directive's promulgation, there was nothing contained in the EC Treaty which would have suggested that the Community had competence to act in the field of culture. The Maastricht Treaty introduced a new Title into the Treaty on 'Culture', but this does not provide legislative competence for the adoption of measures to harmonise laws among the Member States. Article 151(4) of the EC Treaty provides that:

> The Community shall take cultural aspects into account in its action under other provisions in this Treaty, in particular in order to respect and promote the diversity of cultures.

However, it is evident that the legal basis for Articles 4 and 5 of the TVWF Directive remains somewhat questionable. Despite this fact, as Barendt and Hitchens note: 'Now that the Directive has been in force for 10 years, these arguments have become less significant' (Barendt and Hitchens 2000: 194). It seems that even if the legal basis of Articles 4 and 5 might be questionable, Member States have still been willing to implement the requirements into national law.

Even so, pressing criticisms might still be made regarding the effectiveness of the provisions of the Directive. As noted above, Article 4 of the Directive imposes a requirement that broadcasters should be required to ensure that over 50 per cent of output is 'European' in origin. Article 6 goes on to offer a definition of content which will be considered to be 'European', and it is notable that the definition goes beyond just that content which is produced in the Member States of the EU, and includes co-productions and productions from a state which is party to the Council of Europe's Convention on Transfrontier Television.

At first glance, Article 4 appears to have been successful. The Commission reports suggest that broadcasters have generally met and exceeded the target of 50 per cent (European Commission 2003). While these figures appear to be highly promising, it is not entirely clear that they give an accurate picture, as the mechanisms in place for monitoring the success of the provisions in the Member States have varied widely (European Parliament 2005: 5; European Commission 2005a: 3–4). However, we might be sceptical that this has led to the benefits that were hoped for when the Directive was promulgated (De Witte 1995). The Weber Report from the European Parliament argues that the vast majority of the 'European' work broadcast is in fact produced in the nation where it is broadcast (European Parliament 2005: 11). Given the linguistic divergences between the Member States this is perhaps unsurprising, but it does call into question the likely effectiveness of a provision which wishes to produce inter-state trade in European television productions. The Parliament's Report argues that 'A European Audiovisual Space [is] yet to take shape' (European Parliament 2005: 12). It may have been more apt for the Parliament to consider whether such a 'European Audiovisual Space' can *ever* be constructed. The linguistic barriers to such a development are self-evident, and it may also be that differing national preferences for programme content and genre may also act as a barrier to the construction of the European Parliament's vision (Grimm 1995).

A further difficulty faced by Article 4 is the language in which it is couched. Due to the disagreement between the Member States over its necessity, Article 4 is the product of compromise, and obliges Member States to ensure that the 50 per cent quota is met 'where practicable and by appropriate means'. This generality in wording has led to some doubt being cast over the legal enforceability of Article 4 (Barendt 1995: 235) and it is evident that the practicability of some channels meeting the requirement is now becoming questionable. The increasing number of specialised channels which are dedicated to a particular genre of content has placed great strain on the ability of broadcasters to meet the requirements of Article 4, as sufficient 'European' content to meet with the criteria is not always available (Drijber 1999: 106; European Parliament 2003: 9–10). The solution offered by the European Parliament is to reform the Directive in order to offer a definition of 'specialist' channels (European Parliament 2003: 9–10), but it is not entirely clear how such a definition would be created and effectively applied to the variety of different channels available throughout the 25 Member States.

Article 5 of the TVWF Directive is concerned with 'independent' works, a concept which is not defined in the Directive. This lack of definition has caused the most difficulty, as Member States have adopted differing definitions of the concept. The current review process acknowledges that the lack of definition over what is an 'independent production' causes considerable difficulties in determining whether the quota has been satisfactorily met in a particular Member State, and may also frustrate the purpose of the provision, as many producers may not be 'independent' in the sense that the framers of the Directive hoped for. This particular difficulty has been acknowledged by both the European Commission (European Commission 2005a: 5–6) and the European Parliament (European Parliament 2003: 12 and 2005: 18) and may be a subject for future reform.

The other measure within the TVWF Directive which is of some interest from the social and cultural perspective is Article 3a, which is concerned with the protection of certain events of major national importance for free-to-air television. This Article of the Directive aims, in some sense, to preserve an element of 'universal service' or access for national citizens to certain events of major national importance. It is notable, however, that another key aim of the provision is to subject Member States' decisions in this area to a degree of oversight by the European Commission (Craufurd-Smith and Böttcher 2002: 119). The consolidated list published in the Official Journal informs us that relatively few countries have chosen to adopt measures under the provisions of Article 3a ([2003] OJ C 183/03).

The UK did adopt such measures in the Broadcasting Act 1996, sections 98–104ZA, as amended by the Communications Act 2003. Initially, these measures were adopted prior to the implementation of Article 3a by the 1997 revision of the TVWF Directive, but the Broadcasting Act was soon amended in order to be compatible with the provisions of the Directive (Craufurd-Smith and Böttcher 2002: 115–17). A range of sporting events are covered (see Ofcom 2004a: 22), and it is evident that the provisions in Article 3a have allowed the general public to have access to a range of sporting events that may otherwise have been available only to those with access to subscription-based services. The application of Article 3a has generally been strict, with the UK banning the transmission of certain matches of the Danish football team on Danish subscription television in accordance with the reciprocal obligation in Article 3a(3) of the TVWF Directive. This occurred despite the fact that Danish public service broadcasters had shown relatively little interest or willingness to acquire the rights (Craufurd-Smith and Böttcher 2002). The ITC's decision to prevent the broadcast was ultimately upheld by the House of Lords (*R. v Independent Television Commission, ex parte TV Danmark 1 Ltd.* [2001] UKHL 42; [2001] 1 WLR 1604).

Recent reports from the institutions of the EU do not seem to suggest the likelihood of any radical reform of the TVWF Directive (European Commission 2003; European Parliament 2003 and 2005). If changes are to be made then it seems likely that these changes may endeavour to clear up some of the uncertainties in the Directive, such as the definition of an 'independent producer' and clarifying the method through which Member States are to report on the implementation of the measures. The other modifications under discussion for the Directive are mainly designed to ensure that it is able to keep pace with technological developments. Article 1(a) of the Directive defines broadcasting as '. . . the initial transmission by wire or over the air, including that by satellite, in unencoded or encoded form, of television programmes intended for reception by the public.'

This definition, while satisfactory at the time the Directive was promulgated, may no longer give the Directive sufficient scope in the twenty-first century (van Loon 2004). A particular difficulty is that the current definition of broadcasting would only cover 'linear' broadcasting services, defined by the European Commission as

> services that are scheduled, *i.e.* where there is a succession of programmes arranged throughout the day and the viewer does not control the timing of the transmission . . . These services would include . . . traditional television, web casting, streaming and near video on demand, whatever the delivery platform. (European Commission 2005b: 2)

This definition of broadcasting has been effective up until now, but technological developments, particularly those which may lead to the increased prevalence of 'television on demand' or 'non-linear' broadcasting may limit the effectiveness of the Directive. 'Non-linear' broadcasting is defined by the European Commission as 'on-demand services where users/viewers are able to choose the content they wish at any time, e.g. video on demand, web-based news services etc. whatever the delivery platform' (European Commission 2005b: 2).

At the present time, the definition of broadcasting in the TVWF Directive does not seem to embrace 'non-linear' services (Van Loon 2004: 177–9). The decision of the European Court of Justice in the *Mediakabel* case (Case C-89/04 *Mediakabel BV* v *Commissariat voor de Media*, 2 June 2005, unreported) renders it clear that there is a degree of difficulty caused by the scope of the TVWF Directive. In the *Mediakabel* case, the company concerned offered a 'near video on demand' service known as 'Filmtime'. The service operated by broadcasting a pre-selected range of films which could be viewed only by subscribers who paid a fee either by telephone or remote control. Mediakabel argued that the service did not fall within the definition of 'broadcasting' in the TVWF Directive as the films were only available to view if the subscriber requested the material and purchased an access code. The European Court of Justice rejected this argument, arguing that the 'Filmtime' service was

> not commanded individually by an isolated recipient who has free choice in of programmes in an interactive setting. It must be considered to be a near-video-on-demand service, provided on a 'point to multipoint' basis and not 'at an individual request of a recipient of services'. (Case C-89/04 *Mediakabel BV* v *Commissariat voor de Media*, 2 June 2005, unreported, para. 39)

While the decision is surely correct from the perspective of the definition of the TVWF Directive, it perhaps demonstrates the fact that techno-logical developments may have led to unintended consequences. Media-kabel were eager to avoid the 'Filmtime' service falling under the TVWF Directive because if it was considered to be subject to the Directive then the service would have to comply with Articles 4 and 5 on European and independent works. Mediakabel's service was primarily concerned with delivering popular films and the nature of its service rendered it difficult, if not impossible, to meet with the requirements. This situation may reit-erate the need for some clarification of an exception from the provisions of Articles 4 and 5 for 'specialist services'.

The *Mediakabel* decision also clarifies the fact that 'non-linear' services of the nature outlined in the Commission's definition are not currently covered by the TVWF Directive. While this may not be a concern at the present time, as such services are relatively undeveloped, it is perhaps important that certain of these services are captured by the provisions of the TVWF Directive. This is acknowledged by the Commission, which is currently suggesting a two-tier approach, where non-linear services will be subject to the provisions of the TVWF Directive which are concerned with minimum standards for content, but would not be subject to the rules in Articles 4 and 5 (European Commission 2005b). This would have the desirable effect of facilitating inter-state trade in non-linear services and clarifying the minimum standards which would apply to such services, without introducing the complexities of attempting to apply Articles 4 and 5 to such services.

Unfortunately, such a revision would not resolve the difficulties faced by Mediakabel and other such specialist or thematic services. Ultima-tely, if sufficient content is not available then they will be unable to acquire it. Given the questionable legal enforceability of Articles 4 and 5 of the TVWF Directive it may be better to allow exceptions for cer-tain channels rather than test the legal enforceability of the provisions, which may be rendered ineffective if they are found not to be legally enforceable.

The broader agenda for the revision of the TVWF Directive is relatively limited. The European Parliament has called for an expansion and strengthening of the content package contained in Articles 10–22a (European Parliament 2003), but the Commission does not seem to be in favour of anything other than a limited effort to clarify certain elements of the existing provisions (European Commission 2005b). It seems apparent that a radical expansion of the Directive or a strengthening of any of its provisions is most unlikely, particularly given the delicate political compromise on which the Directive is based. It is evident that there may be some willingness to address some of the issues, particularly in defining the scope of the Directive and clarifying certain definitions in Articles 4 and 5, but an expansion of the content element of the Directive to cover more areas seems most unlikely.

In summary, the TVWF Directive has been successful in providing a framework for the exchange of broadcasting services. It is evident, however, that the Directive has had the effect of severely limiting Member States' ability to regulate broadcast content coming from outside their jurisdiction, even where channels are specifically designed for a particular country but broadcast from another country in order to avoid certain broadcasting rules. It seems that this has been the main use of the Directive, as relatively few channels have significant cross-border appeal in much of Europe due to linguistic and cultural differences across the Member States.

We have noted above that the social and cultural provisions in the Directive have been a more questionable success. Article 3a of the Directive, which is concerned with the broadcast of sporting events, has been a relative success, but has been adopted by relatively few Member States. Articles 4 and 5 have provoked more controversy. Although the Commission reports reveal that both provisions have been a success in the sense that their targets have been met and exceeded, the lack of definition of certain crucial terms, such as what is an 'independent' production, may tarnish the apparent positive outcomes. The proposed reform process may lead to sharper definitions in this area, which may in turn lead to a clearer picture of whether Articles 4 and 5 have been a genuine success.

A final issue which is illustrated by the TVWF Directive is that the continual technological developments in broadcasting may have placed certain of its assumptions under pressure. Though the current definition of 'broadcasting' which is to be found in Article 2 of the TVWF Directive is broad enough to capture a significant majority of modern television services, including what is described as 'near video-on demand', the advent of 'non-linear' services, where viewers actually determine what content is to be viewed without any editorial decisions being made by a broadcaster, would not be covered by the current definition (Van Loon 2004; Case C-89/04 *Mediakabel BV* v *Commissariat voor de Media*, 2 June 2005, unreported). Current reform proposals (European Commission 2005b) suggest a two-tier approach to the control of such services. The TVWF Directive would apply in its entirety, including the provisions of Articles 4 and 5, to all 'linear' services where broadcasters exert editorial control over scheduled content. 'Non-linear' services, however, will only be subject to the provisions of the Directive which address content standards. Although this may seem an improvement on the current position and would serve to clarify the law for new 'on-demand' services, it would not necessarily offer an ultimate resolution to some of the difficulties posed by the developments in broadcasting.

A particular example of the current difficulties caused by the universal application of the TVWF Directive seems to be highlighted by the *Mediakabel* case. Articles 4 and 5, while undoubtedly created in order to pursue valuable social and cultural goals, may place unduly onerous requirements on the providers of specialist channels or film services, yet the scope of exceptions from the Directive is currently very unclear. The Directive needs to be amended in order to take account of this issue, but it seems to be important to ensure that if Articles 4 and 5 are to continue to have an effect then the scope of the 'specialism' exception should not be too broad.

The TVWF Directive demonstrates the EU's response to issues of broadcast content. In a sense, the area of content is one where the EU has had a more limited impact, due both to the delicate political negotiations required in order to reach an agreement and the limited competence bestowed upon the Community in relation to issues of culture and broadcast content. Such limitations are much less apparent when we turn to examine the EC's 'New Regulatory Framework', which is centred on the regulation of electronic communications networks.

6.3.3 The 'New Regulatory Framework'

The 'New Regulatory Framework' (NRF) introduced in 2002 consists of four Directives: the Access Directive (Directive 2002/19/EC, [2002] OJ L 108/7), the Authorisation Directive (Directive 2002/20/EC, [2002] OJ L 108/21), the Framework Directive (Directive 2002/21/EC, [2002] OJ L 108/33) and the Universal Service Directive (Directive 2002/22/EC, [2002] OJ L 108/51). These Directives now form the main basis for the regulation of electronic communications networks throughout the EU's

Member States. The Directives address a vast range of issues in the electronic communications sector and we will only address those provisions that have a significant impact on broadcasting; others have offered a more detailed analysis of the Directives as a whole (Nihoul and Rodford 2004; Garzaniti 2003).

As we noted above, what we must understand as 'broadcasting' has become considerably more complex in recent years. There are now a huge range of methods for delivering broadcasting (van Loon 2004) and in the UK alone there are currently services to deliver broadcasting via analogue terrestrial, digital terrestrial, digital satellite, analogue and digital cable and ADSL technologies in either the whole or part of the country (Ofcom 2005c: 4–5). These developments lead to the possibility of a large range of electronic communications networks being used to deliver broadcasting to potential viewers. As such, the NRF is largely 'platform neutral' – its rules might apply to networks regardless of the technology used to transport the broadcast signal to viewers' homes.

As we noted in the section on competition law above, the NRF is largely concerned with developing competitive markets in the electronic communications sector. This is aptly demonstrated in a speech by Mario Monti, ex European Competition Commissioner, where he stated that, 'In the electronic communications sector . . . we have now clearly moved from a mainly administrative approach to regulation, to a regulatory perspective entirely based on, and therefore clearly compatible with, competition analysis, law and practice' (Monti 2003).

As such, the majority of the provisions in the Directives are concerned with facilitating the development of competitive markets in electronic communications networks. The majority of the other provisions in the Access Directive are concerned with allowing regulators to impose certain tools and techniques of economic regulation in order to ensure that those market players deemed to have 'significant market power' (SMP) behave in a manner which is compatible with competition law. It is notable that the Access Directive permits *ex ante* regulation to be imposed on market players which are considered to have SMP, whereas competition law might apply *ex post* to the behaviour of any market player, regardless of whether they are considered to have SMP for the purposes of the Directive or not.

It is interesting that two of the measures contained in the Access Directive permit *ex ante* regulation to take place regardless of whether the operator has SMP in relation to broadcasting. Article 6 of the Directive takes what Helberger (2002) has termed to be an 'absolute' approach to the regulation of the conditional access system (CAS). The great significance of this technology was touched on in earlier chapters, but it is important to emphasise that even if a broadcaster is not wishing to offer a 'pay-TV' service it may still be necessary for them to utilise conditional access facilities in order to resolve issues of intellectual property rights which may otherwise arise if the broadcasting signal encroaches into another state (Helberger *et al.* 2000: 28–30). Article 6(1) of the Directive obliges Member States to implement the provisions in Part 1 of Annex 1 of the Directive to the CAS. In so far as is relevant, paragraph (b) of Part 1 of Annex 1 provides:

> All operators of conditional access systems, regardless of their means of transmission are to . . . [O]ffer to all broadcasters, on a fair, reasonable and non-discriminatory basis compatible with Community competition law, technical services enabling the broadcasters' digitally-transmitted services to be received by viewers or listeners authorised by means of decoders administered by the service operators, and comply with Community competition law.

Article 5(1)(b) of the Directive permits Member States to determine whether the same obligations should be imposed on operators of electronic programme guides (EPGs) and applications programming interfaces (APIs). Although the imposition in this case is not obligatory, section 74(2) of the Communications Act 2003 has extended the 'fair, reasonable and non-discriminatory' obligation to operators of EPGs and owners of APIs. It seems that from this perspective, the UK government has considered the EPG and API to be sufficiently important technologies to warrant *ex ante* regulation.

The effect of these provisions is to determine that the CAS is an 'essential facility'. The essential facilities doctrine (EFD) is a relatively controversial doctrine in competition law (Areeda 1990; Bergman 2001) and it has a relatively uncertain scope in EC law (Doherty 2001; Jones and Sufrin 2004: 475 *et seq.*; Whish 2003: 663 *et seq.*). Despite the relative uncertainty which surrounds the application of the doctrine, it has been broadly embraced by the NRF. In 1995, Herbert Ungerer noted that, 'The concept of essential facilities will become central, in parallel to and complementary with public interest legislation in the field of public networks, such as the EU Open Network Provision concept developed in the telecommunications sector' (Ungerer 1995: 69).

In fact, the NRF embraced the EFD more completely than could have been imagined at the time of Ungerer's speech. It has been argued that a great deal of the measures contained in the Access Directive are in fact concerned with the application of the EFD (Nihoul and Rodford

2004: 4.326–4.332). The motives for the relatively wide use of the EFD in the NRF have been described by Nihoul and Rodford as demonstrating

[A] political desire that the Commission shares with the Parliament and the Council to open existing infrastructure to new service providers. The purpose was initially to put an end to the era of telecommunications monopoly. It is now to ensure that the existing infrastructures are used efficiently for the benefit of consumers. (Nihoul and Rodford 2004: 4.332)

Whatever the motives for the introduction of the EFD, it is plain that it will now play a crucial role in the regulation of access to the facilities necessary for digital broadcasting. Most broadcasters will require access to conditional access services when broadcasting via digital satellite and possibly via digital terrestrial, and all broadcasters will require access to the EPG as without this viewers of digital television have no means to select a particular broadcaster's services. The applications programming interface is not necessary in many cases, but given the increasing prevalence of additional 'interactive' content being provided via 'the red button' it seems likely that many broadcasters will wish to supplement their broadcasts with such material.

Given the centrality of these technical services to the 'digital revolution' it is unsurprising that they are treated as targets for *ex ante* regulation in the NRF. The question that remains is whether the obligation to provide access on 'fair, reasonable and non-discriminatory' terms is likely to be effective. In a sense, the obligation to grant access on such terms is a peculiar fusion of public regulation and private contracting. At the European level, there is little concrete guidance as to what might constitute 'fair, reasonable and non-discriminatory' terms for access to the technical facilities necessary for broadcasting. The commentaries on the Directives draw inspiration from the case law on essential facilities for the most part (Nihoul and Rodford 2004) but there is little other material to guide the negotiations of the parties. At the present time, the European Commission has not produced any guidance to aid the negotiations of the parties, so the only guidance at present arises from the case law and the wording of the Directives and implementing legislation, along with any guidance that might be produced by National Regulatory Authorities.

It is important to emphasise at this point that the CAS has been subject to EU level regulation since 1995, when the Advanced Television Standards Directive (Directive 95/47/EC) was implemented. Unfortunately, although this 'fair, reasonable and non-discriminatory' obligation has been in place for some time, there is no case law directly on the subject of access to the CAS available to further guide us on what contractual terms will pass muster. The provision of technical services for digital broadcasting is what might be described as a relational contract (Collins 2003: 18–19), defined by Collins as:

> [A contract where] performance is likely to last for a period of time, or perhaps indefinitely, the economic success of the transaction for the parties depends upon a relatively high degree of co-operation . . . and the obligations undertaken by the parties cannot easily be confined to determinate obligations. (Collins 2003: 18).

It is evident that the contract for the provision of technical services is undoubtedly long-term, as it will need to continue for the length of time that the broadcaster wishes to offer its service on a particular delivery platform. It also seems likely that the relationship will require a degree of cooperation, as the technicalities of broadcasting combined with the constant technological developments in the sector necessitate some flexibility in the relationship between the parties. An example of this need for cooperation is the work by BSkyB and the BBC to ensure that viewers automatically received the BBC service most appropriate for their region (BBC 2003). It is more difficult to draw concrete conclusions about the determinacy of the obligations between the parties in a contract for technical services in digital broadcasting. It is obvious that certain elements of the contract will be clear and determinate – the obligation on the network operator to provide the service will be determinate, as will the remuneration to be provided by the broadcaster which is granted access. There are, however, certain to be less clear-cut issues, and the Ofcom consultation on EPGs (Ofcom 2004d) renders it obvious that the EPG operator has retained the discretion to reorder or alter the way in which the channels are displayed or allocate different channel numbers within the duration of the contract. If we turn to examine the obligation to offer access on 'fair, reasonable and non-discriminatory' terms, a number of issues arise.

The first issue relates to Davis's (Davis 1971) observations on discretion, noted in Chapter 5. Classical theories of contract have suggested that the parties are free to negotiate any agreement that they see fit (Fried 1982), although the law has long been willing to acknowledge that in certain situations the existence of an imbalance of powers between the parties might necessitate legal intervention in order to ensure a degree of fairness for the weaker party (Collins 1999). The Access Directive acknowledges that the operators of the CAS and EPG and the owner of the API are in an advantageous position and seeks to confine the discretion that would normally be available to a contracting party – not only is there no choice but to offer access to all broadcasters who request such access, but the access must also be granted on terms that are 'fair, reasonable and non-discriminatory'.

Once the contract is created, any discretion which the facility's owner retains might be confined *ex post* by general competition law, or potentially by the regulator, as it is possible to argue that if the outcome of the exercise of contractual discretion by the facilities owner is unfair, then the term must not have been 'fair, reasonable and non-discriminatory' in the first place! From a public law perspective, such regulation is unproblematic, other than where the obligation placed on regulated parties is uncertain. The 'fair, reasonable and non-discriminatory' requirement might be characterised as a rule which constrains the discretion that would ordinarily be available to contracting parties, but it may not be sufficiently well-defined to give the parties any certainty as to how the regulation should affect the outcome of their negotiations. It is rather difficult to be certain about the effectiveness of the requirements placed on the technical facilities for digital broadcasting, but it is notable that Baldwin's studies found that uncertainty over the content of a rule renders compliance less likely (Baldwin 1995: 159–60).

The above discussion seeks to demonstrate that the provisions in Articles 5 and 6 of the Access Directive, while designed with the laudable aim of ensuring access to the technical facilities for digital broadcasting, may have created a degree of uncertainty. The European legislation offers little guidance as to what terms may be unsatisfactory. This is in marked contract with the 'grey list' of unacceptable terms provided in Annex 1 of the Unfair Terms in Consumer Contracts Directive (Directive 93/13/EEC; Teubner, 1999; Fletcher 2002). It is important to note that Oftel provided some guidance over what terms might be acceptable when granting access to the CAS (Oftel 2002) and Ofcom has provided some guidance over access to the EPG (Ofcom 2004f), but this guidance is in relatively general terms and does not guarantee consistency of approach throughout the EU's Member States.

Some authors have argued there is less need to provide prescriptive terms if there is some agreement within the industry over the type of behaviour which is acceptable by the contracting parties (Collins 1999: 268–71). The consultation which Ofcom entered into over the regulation of EPGs (Ofcom 2004d) and some of the responses received (BBC 2004c) suggest that there is not full agreement between broadcasters and BSkyB over what might constitute 'fair, reasonable and non-discriminatory' terms. This appears to demonstrate the desirability of more detailed guidance at the European level, which would ensure a consistency of approach across the Member States and would serve to offer some clarification of the guidance in the case law, enabling the parties to have greater certainty in their contractual negotiations.

The second area of the NRF which has a specific and immediate relationship to broadcasting is the imposition of 'must-carry' obligations. Article 31(1) of the Universal Service Directive provides that:

> Member States may impose reasonable must-carry obligations, for the transmission of specified radio and television broadcast channels and services, on undertakings under their jurisdiction providing electronic communications networks used for the distribution of radio or television broadcasts to the public where a significant number of end-users of such networks use them as their principal means to receive radio and television broadcasts. Such obligations shall only be imposed where they are necessary to meet clearly defined general interest objectives and shall be proportionate and transparent. The obligations shall be subject to periodical review.

Recital 43 of the Universal Service Directive suggests that the provision of Article 31 in the Directive allows Member States to act 'in the interest of legitimate public policy considerations'. It is undoubtedly true that the inclusion of must-carry in the Directive permits a social element to regulation, as Article 31 renders it possible for a Member State to oblige operators of all networks used to convey broadcasting signals which are under their jurisdiction to convey the services of certain broadcasters. The realities of Article 31 demonstrate that the social aims of the provision are heavily limited by economic considerations (Varney 2004/2005). It is notable from the text of Article 31(1), which is outlined above, that a relatively large number of conditions must be met before must-carry obligations can be imposed. The network on which the conditions are imposed must serve 'a significant number of end-users' and the obligations must meet 'clearly defined general-interest objectives' and be 'proportionate and transparent'.

The European Commission produced a Working Document to accompany Article 31 and this document seems to illustrate that the Commission's interpretation of the provision is heavily coloured by economic considerations. Article 31 does not require that Member States should provide that network operators be remunerated, but the Commission Working Document argues that:

> There is no obligation on Member States to ensure a remuneration for network operators in return for must carry obligations . . . Nevertheless, the general criteria indicated under Article 31(1) . . . may imply, under specific circumstances, that some form of remuneration should be provided in order

for the must-carry obligation to be considered proportionate or reasonable. (European Commission 2002: para. 1.2.2.4)

It is evident that the Commission intends the scope of must-carry obligations to be relatively limited. In its recent Working Paper to the 10th Report on European Electronic Communications Regulation and Markets, the Commission makes it clear that it is currently investigating the measures taken by Member States to ensure that they are compatible with Article 31, particularly 'where the general interest objectives have been defined in broad terms' (European Commission 2004c: 33–4). It is evident from the Report (European Commission 2004c) that most Member States have chosen to implement must-carry obligations or had pre-existing obligations in place prior to the implementation of the Directive which the Member States have deemed to be compatible with Article 31.

The outcome of the Commission's review of must-carry will be interesting, as it is likely to give an indication of the approach to be adopted towards such social measures when they collide with the development of markets in the electronic communications sector. For the present time it is impossible to speculate on the outcome, but it seems to be important to note that the approach under the Directive and the Commission's guidance that has been issued so far both seem to envisage must-carry as a measure which should be applied to a relatively small number of channels and which, in general, should be the subject of remuneration at market rates. It is evident that this approach is entirely compatible with the development of competitive markets in the electronic communications sector, but an overly limited approach could lead to social goals, such as pluralism and diversity of media output for those citizens on the lowest incomes, being placed under threat (Varney 2004/2005).

A further criticism that might be levelled at the European must-carry provisions is that they do not provide for access to the CAS, EPG and API. As a result, even though broadcasters might benefit from must-carry requirements on the network, if the services that they provide require access to technical services then these must be the subject of negotiations between the owner of the facilities and the broadcaster. A consideration of the framework would suggest that must-carry is a relatively dubious benefit for broadcasters, as the Commission Working Paper (European Commission 2002b) appears to suggest that remuneration of the network operator at market rates should be the usual position even where a broadcaster is granted must-carry status and, beyond this, it is still necessary to negotiate access to the CAS, EPG and API with the operator of these facilities and pay for these services at the negotiated rate. Given that this is the case, it is rather difficult to see what benefits a broadcaster might obtain from being given must-carry status in any case!

As we can see from the discussion above, the NRF is primarily concerned with creating competitive markets for electronic communications throughout the EU. Although it is evident that the Access Directive seeks to regulate the technical services for digital broadcasting on an *ex ante* basis, this is essentially economic regulation – extending the essential facilities doctrine, which is adopted under the auspices of Article 82 EC, to the CAS and allowing the Member States to choose whether to extend the *ex ante* obligation to the EPG and the API. While this should, in theory, improve the position in the market for these services, the effectiveness of the obligation is called into question by the lack of clear guidance on what constitutes 'fair reasonable and non-discriminatory' dealing.

The must-carry obligations contained in Article 31 of the Universal Service Directive are a more obvious source of social obligations. In a sense, Article 31 confirms the permissibility of a practice that was already in place in many Member States, but there are significant questions over the precise extent to which it limits the discretion of the Member States to impose must-carry obligations. Article 31(1) certainly places some limitation on the imposition of must-carry obligations, and an examination of the Commission's Working Document suggests that these limitations may be relatively extensive. Such limitations may render the award of must-carry status to a broadcaster to be of limited, if any, benefit. For the present time the effect of Article 31 is unclear, as we have not yet seen any Commission action on the issue, but if the scope of the provision is very limited then this might be a source of some disappointment and concern, as the potential for Article 31 to promote pluralism and diversity in media output is likely to be heavily curtailed.

6.3.4 *The impact of state aid law*

There have been a number of significant works on the impact of state aid on broadcasting in recent times (Bartosch 1999; Craufurd-Smith 2001; Bavasso 2002; Prosser 2005: chapter 9). The relevant issues derive from Article 87 of the EC Treaty, which states that:

> Save as otherwise provided in this Treaty, any aid granted by a Member State or through State resources in any form whatsoever which distorts or threatens to distort competition by favouring certain undertakings or the production of certain goods shall, insofar as it affects trade between Member States, be incompatible with the common market.

A significant question which was the subject of some legal uncertainty in the late 1990s was whether state funding of PSB can be said to constitute state aid for the purposes of Article 87 EC. The current case law, of which the cases of *Ferring* (Case C-53/00 *Ferring SA* v *Agence Centrale des Organismes de Securité Sociale (ACOSS)* [2001] ECR I-9067) and *Altmark* (Case C-280/00 *Altmark* [2003] 3 CMLR 12) are the most significant, suggest that if the finance given to broadcasters by government serves merely as recompense for public service obligations discharged by them, then such payments will not constitute state aid for the purposes of Article 87 EC.

The approach preferred by the Commission prior to the cases outlined above had been to characterise state funding of PSB as state aid, and then to look to whether such aid was justified under the 'general interest' justification contained in Article 86(2) EC. Member States were able to argue that public service broadcasters were providing 'services of general economic interest', and therefore should be permitted to receive public funding. It is evident that in the vast majority of cases the Commission was willing to accept that such aid was justified (Craufurd-Smith 2001). If the state funding offered to broadcasters is deemed only to be compensation for the burdens imposed on those who discharge public service obligations then it seems to be evident that justifications will no longer be necessary, as Article 87 EC will no longer apply to such payments.

What is evident, however, is that the exclusion of such 'compensatory' funding from the ambit of Article 87 EC has placed an ever more intense focus on the nature of the public service mandate given to a broadcaster. In *Altmark* (Case C-280/00 *Altmark* [2003] 3 CMLR 12: paras 89–90), the ECJ argued that:

> First, the recipient undertaking must actually have public service obligations to discharge, and the obligations must be clearly defined . . . Second, the parameters on the basis of which the compensation is calculated must be calculated in advance in an objective and transparent manner, to avoid it conferring an economic advantage which may favour the recipient undertaking over competing undertakings.

The European Commission is to take steps to formalise this procedure for 'public service compensation', particularly because the Commission believes that 'in some cases the criteria laid down in *Altmark* for the setting of the amount of compensation will not be met and that such compensation will, therefore, constitute state aid' (European Commission 2005c: 3).

The outcome of this situation seems to be that whether compensation is not characterised as state aid under the decision in *Altmark*, or it is deemed to be conferred in a way which renders it as state aid, far greater attention is likely to be paid to the manner of entrustment of the public service mandate. Point 10 of the Commission's discussion paper (European Commission 2005c) is of particular interest because it states the Commission's desire to introduce a regime which requires the public service obligations to be outlined in a specific manner and for a method to be in place for both calculating and reviewing the amount of compensation to be paid. Point 12 of the Commission's document (European Commission 2005c: 3) exposes a more significant difficulty with the application of the regime to PSB. Point 12 states that:

> The amount of compensation may not exceed what is necessary to cover the costs incurred in discharging the public service obligations, taking into account the relevant receipts and reasonable profit for discharging those obligations.

It may be very difficult to determine satisfactorily what might be 'necessary' for public service broadcasters, as it seems that public service broadcasters will generally spend whatever funding is given to them on the provision of programming and services (Varney 2004: 520–6). It will be difficult to set out public service obligations in such a precise manner without curtailing the freedom and independence presently given to public service broadcasters in the majority of the Member States. The BBC Charter Review in the UK appears to be taking account of these developments at the European level, as it seems that the new Charter will contain specific authorisation for the BBC to offer an Internet service and the potential to enter into broadcasting over the Internet (DCMS 2005: 8.44–8.45), in addition to offering the range of analogue and digital services that are currently offered.

If we consider the nature of the current agreement between the BBC and the government (DNH 1996 and DCMS 2003), it is unclear whether or not the obligations contained within it are couched in sufficiently specific terms to satisfy either the test contained in *Altmark* or the Commission's document (European Commission 2005c) and draft decision (European Commission 2005d) should the funding need to be justified under Article 86(2) EC. In essence, the current agreement leaves a considerable degree of discretion to the governors over what services should be offered and how the BBC's income should be divided between the various activities undertaken by the Corporation. If this arrangement was not deemed to be acceptable from the perspective of state aid law, then it may be that this will have a significant impact on the BBC's discretion to spend the funding that it receives. Although it is impossible to say with any certainty whether the structure of the current agreement would be deemed to be compatible with the new rules, it is evident that if the mandate had to be considerably more specific, significant questions would be raised over the BBC's ability to retain independence from government.

6.3.5 Regulation at the European Level: Subsidiarity in Action?

There are obvious reasons for the adoption of regulation at the European level. It is evident that both the Television Without Frontiers Directive and the 'New Regulatory Framework' can be seen as responses to an increase in the incidence of cross-border services. The TVWF Directive aims to create a degree of what Dougan (2000) and Hatzopoulos (2000) have both described as 'minimum harmonisation'. The realities of the situation may be somewhat different, as it seems unlikely after the decision of the ECJ in *De Agostini* (Cases C-34–36/95 *Konsumentombudsmannen (KO) v De Agostini (Svenska) Forlag AB and TV-Shop i Sverige AB* [1998] 1 CMLR 32) that further regulation might be imposed on broadcasters lawfully broadcasting in another jurisdiction, at least in respect of the issues which have been harmonised by the TVWF Directive (Criscuolo 1998; Varney 2004: 515–20).

The approach taken by the European Court of Justice might be deemed to be attractive for those who believe in a strong market for cross-border television services, but also highlights a difficulty with shifting the regulation of broadcast content, even in limited spheres, to the European level. It is evident that Member States have very different cultural mores (Craufurd-Smith 2004) relevant to broadcast content, yet the TVWF Directive removes the possibility of regulation in a 'receiving' Member State in the many cases (Holmes 2004: 192–3). The package of minimum harmonisation has therefore had a more significant impact on the ability of Member States to assert their own cultural preferences for broadcasting standards than might have been first envisaged.

At a broader level, it is evident that the increasing numbers of cross-border television broadcasts necessitate some degree of action at the EC level. The TVWF Directive has done much to clarify the earlier case law on free movement of services as it applied to broadcasting. The 'positive' obligations imposed by the TVWF Directive seem to be somewhat more controversial. Article 3a of the Directive, while acknowledging the difficulties caused for some Member States where broadcasters based in another jurisdiction acquire the broadcast rights to events of national significance, has only been implemented by relatively few Member States. Where the Directive has been adopted it has demonstrated difficulties (Craufurd-Smith and Böttcher 2002), as in the *TvDanmark* case (*R (On the Application of TvDanmark1 Ltd.)* v *Independent Television Commission* [2001] UKHL 42; [2001] 1 WLR 1604) as even though neither of the Danish public service broadcasters had demonstrated a significant interest in acquiring the rights to the football matches held by TvDanmark at the time of first bidding, they were still able to oblige TvDanmark to share the rights at a later date by exploiting the provisions in Article 3a of the TVWF Directive. Although this may be deemed to have benefited the viewing public to some extent, it is evident that it imposed a heavy burden on TvDanmark in the case at issue.

Articles 4 and 5 of the TVWF Directive, which are analysed in some detail above, have evidently had an impact on ensuring that European and independent producers respectively have been protected from the import of programmes from the USA, but we might have reasons to doubt the efficacy of these rules (De Witte 1995). In particular, Barendt and Hitchens (2000: 193) have argued that:

> Article 4 determines a work as 'European' essentially on the basis of location and/or nationality. Again, a question must be raised as to how this contributes to the development of television programmes about European culture or identity.

Given the complex operations of most of the large media corporations, it seems unlikely that such quotas will prevent their influence from expanding. Intelligent use of the corporate form, including complex corporate group structures, may mean that the activities of the major corporate players in the media sector could be classed as 'European' for the purposes of Article 4 of the TVWF Directive or 'independent' for the purposes of Article 5 regardless of the fact that we might be sceptical that this is genuinely the case. The relatively limited competence available to the Community to act in the cultural sphere (Craufurd-Smith 2004), together with the need to broker agreement between Member States over the terms of the TVWF Directive (De Witte 1995), may lead us to believe that the inclusion of such goals within the Directive was always likely to be a dubious enterprise.

If we expose the provisions in the TVWF Directive to a subsidiarity analysis then it appears that the Directive has met with only limited success. The provisions which aim to provide 'minimum harmonisation' have facilitated the cross-border transmission of broadcasting services, suggesting that from the economic perspective, regulation at the European level has proven to be the most effective. If we look at this from a cultural angle, we might have far greater reservations about the substantive outcome of such regulation, as certain states have been obliged to forego their cultural preferences in order to facilitate the cross-border trade in broadcast content (Varney 2004). It is possible to offer a critique of the European conception of subsidiarity, in the sense that when considering whether regulation would be 'most effective' at a particular level, the question almost always seems to be viewed from an economic perspective.

The NRF, particularly in its impact on broadcasting, throws the previous observation into stark relief. There is evidently the need to ensure a multilateral response to the developments in the electronic communications markets, and the convergence between telecommunications and broadcasting through digitalisation renders it inevitable that such a response will have a significant impact on broadcasting. It is evident from the discussion of the TVWF Directive above that there is only limited competence for the EC to legislate on content issues. As a result, the NRF makes it explicit that its measures are not intended to impinge on the regulation of broadcast content:

> It is necessary to separate the regulation of transmission from the regulation of content. This framework does not therefore cover the content of services delivered over electronic communications networks using electronic communications services, such as broadcasting content . . . The separation between the regulation of transmission and the regulation of content does not prejudice the taking into account of the links existing between them, in particular in order to guarantee media pluralism, cultural diversity and consumer protection. (Framework Directive (Directive 2002/21/EC, [2002] OJ L 108/33, Recital 5)

Despite this acknowledgement of the vital linkages between the means of transmission and broadcast content, it is submitted that the NRF fails to ensure adequately the public interest in freedom of communication. Though the Directive provides a detailed approach to the economic regulation of the infrastructure for the delivery of digital broadcasting, it has been suggested above that the NRF pays only scant attention to issues of pluralism and diversity in broadcast content.

We have suggested above that the EC level is more likely to be effective in dealing with the cross-border issues which arise from modern electronic communications technologies but this effectiveness may well cause difficulties where a rigid division between infrastructure and content is maintained. If pluralism and diversity are to be maintained, it may be that the private property rights of infrastructure operators must be limited beyond an obligation to deal with competitors on terms that would be set in a competitive market environment. Although the NRF states expressly that it does not intend to impinge on the Member States' ability to regulate broadcast content, the situation in relation to the regulation of conditional access systems and electronic programme guides, combined with the limitations imposed on the ability to impose must-carry obligations, have placed severe restrictions on the ability of Member States to engage in regulation which might serve to increase the opportunities available to content providers to gain access to viewers.

We can see from the above that there are strong arguments from the perspective of subsidiarity to suggest that greater action at the EC level could lead to more effective control of the corporate players in the broadcasting industries. Furthermore, it is notable that the sheer quantity of cross-border activity in the broadcast media (European Audiovisual Observatory 2004) and the telecommunications sector (European Commission 2004b) render the arguments for such intervention irresistible. What is evident, however, is that this intervention, in practice, has coloured such intervention with a distinctly economic hue.

6.4 REGULATION OF THE MEDIA IN THE NATION STATE

6.4.1 *What regulatory roles remain at the national level?*

We have noted earlier that there may be some significant and increasing difficulties in relying on the nation state as a significant *locus* of power in the future regulation of the media. In previous chapters, we observed that the media's activities are becoming increasingly transnational, and in the case of EU Member States such as the UK, we can see that discretion at the national level to regulate issues of infrastructure is now substantially restricted by the NRF. That said in the European context, regulation of broadcast content, in both positive and negative guises, remains almost wholly in the hands of national authorities or, in some jurisdictions such as Germany (Humphreys 1996: 137–8; Humphreys and Lang 1998), primarily in the hands of subnational authorities. The only limited exception to this situation lies in the supranational measures, such as the TVWF Directive which is analysed in detail above, or the European Convention on Transfrontier Television, drawn up under the auspices of the Council of Europe (Hondius 1988).

In Chapter 2, we noted that the UK's policy towards broadcasting has often been considered to favour certain commercial interests, and there seems to be a risk that the increased need to woo large commercial players into a particular jurisdiction in order to reap economic benefits may lead to a 'race to the bottom' in regulation, or what Humphreys (1996) terms 'competitive deregulation'. This phenomenon is said to occur when

> regulators apply less rigorous requirements (e.g. allow higher levels of pollu-tion or enforce lower safety standards) and do so in the hope of attracting inward investment or giving certain producers advantages in the market place. (Baldwin and Cave 1999: 184–5)

It is difficult to be absolute about the real extent of this phenomenon in relation to the broadcasting sector. Esty (2000: 215) has argued that it is impossible to generalise about the existence of, or benefits which might flow from, regulatory competition in relation to a particular issue, – *i.e.* 'a consensus seems to have emerged in support of the hypothesis that benefits from regulatory competition are highly context specific.' In fact, it is noteworthy that many commentators on the issue consider regu-latory competition to be a positive phenomenon (Esty 2000; Charny 1991). In relation to corporate law rules, which have seen the most focused analysis, it has been argued that regulatory competition provides a number of significant advantages, because the process leads to 'a con-straint on the ability of any state to impose inefficient regulations and a system that efficiently matches the preferences of corporate consumers with the terms of regulation' (Bratton *et al.* 1996). The difficulty with these analyses lies in the fact that they all place great focus on the benefits in terms of *economic efficiency* which might accrue from regulatory com-petition.

It is possible to produce some evidence of a degree of regulatory com-petition in the media sector, with Humphreys and Lang (1998) adducing a degree of evidence of such competition prevailing between the Länder in Germany. We have also outlined the shift of BSkyB's satellite uplink to Luxembourg in order to pursue a more favourable regulatory regime, which also suggests that there is a degree of such competition in place within Europe. This observation appears to be further supported by cases under the TVWF, such as *De Agostini* (Cases C-34–36/95 *Konsument-ombudsmannen (KO)* v *De Agostini (Svenska) Forlag AB and TV-Shop i Sverige AB* [1998] 1 CMLR 32), that certain broadcasters are choosing to broadcast from another jurisdiction in order to avoid stricter regula-tory rules on content or certain positive obligations.

While some might see regulatory competition as a beneficial pheno-menon, and it may well be so in the context of the rules of corporate law, we might have reason to believe that it may have a deleterious effect on media regulation. The quote from Johnson, below, suggests that the pursuit of rules which might be deemed to be most economically efficient may not have a positive impact on the citizenship values which we argue should be central to media regulation. Johnson has argued that:

> What economic analysis does not do is tell us whether those who bear the costs do so 'justly' or in 'fairness,' unless efficiency in the market place is the agreed social goal. Most economists frankly confess that if the goal is other than efficiency, for example, the redistribution of wealth, their analysis can only identify the fact that the choice is being made based on non-economic considerations. (Johnson 1988: 732)

It may be that the concerns over regulatory competition in the media sector are overstated. In the case of corporate law rules of general application, it is possible to argue that there is much more freedom for legislators to amend rules and relax standards. In most European jurisdictions, the laws which regulate the activities of the broadcast media are more closely linked to the constitution of a particular country (Barendt 1991, 1995) and hence the values which inform the constitution, and therefore in many jurisdictions the potential scrutiny of amendments to media regulation is much greater than would be the case in many other sectors.

Even if we accept that the argument about competitive deregulation is overstated, it is evident that the nation state's historical position at the centre of media regulation is under great pressure. Regulatory rules which are deemed to be too restrictive by either broadcasters or viewers will inevitably lead to efforts to avoid the impact of such regulation. Murray and Scott have persuasively argued that

> broadcasters can relocate their operations to different jurisdictions to avoid national regulation (and this predates digitalisation) while listeners and viewers can relocate from the more controllable forms of delivery to satellite and Internet. (Murray and Scott 2002: 494)

For the present time, it may be that national regulation of the activities of the media is sufficiently effective. In the previous chapter we suggested that many of the recent measures adopted by Ofcom, alongside some decisions of the UK courts, have made a significant impact on the behaviour of the media. It seems somewhat less likely that this situation will continue to prevail in the future, as technological developments such as the delivery of television over broadband Internet (Ungerer 2005), combined with the liberalisation and Europeanisation of the regulation of electronic communications networks, are likely to lead to further development of cross-border activity.

If the citizenship interests outlined earlier in this book are to be effectively protected then it may be necessary for a more sophisticated view of regulation to be adopted at the national level. What responses might be offered to this increasing pressure on the role of the nation state in the regulation of the media? It is submitted that there may be three options available to national regulators. In order to combat the dangers created by regulatory competition, it may be necessary to enter into what Esty and Geradin (2001: 34) have characterised as 'interjurisdictional collective action'. The difficulty with this option is that there may be little likelihood of effective cooperation in order to protect citizenship values. We have assessed the role of the EU in the regulation of the media, and we have suggested that the majority of EU measures have, unsurprisingly given the limited legislative competence available in the EC Treaty, been primarily economic in their aims. It seems unlikely that this situation will change in the near future.

A second international forum which has some potential for media regulation is that of the World Trade Organisation (WTO). It is evident that audiovisual services and broadcasting are technically covered by the GATS agreement (Matsushita *et al.* 2004: 235–6), though the EU and its Member States have not made any commitments about the broadcasting sector. Herold (2003: 6) has argued that:

> The fact that the EU (and its Member States) abstained from according national treatment and market access to non-EU service providers led to a *de facto* exclusion of the sector from the GATS framework. According to Article XVII GATS, the EU is not bound by the principle of national treatment in the field of audiovisual services.

It is clear that there were significant concerns about the impact on cultural policy that the inclusion of broadcasting in the GATS agreement might have (Prosser 2005: 208; Footer and Beat-Graber 2000). These concerns render it apparent that the WTO is likely to prove an unsuitable forum for collective action to protect citizenship interests in the media. It is notable that the USA was pressing for inclusion of broadcasting in the agreement, but the EU and its Member States were robust in their refusal. Given that the USA's tradition in broadcasting has primarily been concerned with the facilitation of commerce (Bagdikian 2004; McChesney 1999), it seems evident that any harmonisation of laws at the WTO level is much more likely to lead to erosion of the protection currently afforded to citizenship interests rather than a strengthening of such measures.

A second option available to nation states and subnational authorities may be to exercise what Daintith (1994) identified as the *dominium* power, referred to in Chapter 3. This power can helpfully be contrasted with the *imperium* power. Daintith famously defined these powers as follows:

> I use the term *imperium* to describe the government's use of the command of law in aid of its policy objectives, and the term *dominium* to describe the employment of the wealth of government for this purpose. (Daintith 1994: 213)

We noted above that government has long exercised its *dominium* power in the broadcasting sector, with the award of licences to broadcast on scarce spectrum being one such example. However, this previously scarce spectrum has reduced markedly in value since the advent of digital networks and alternative means for the delivery of broadcast content (Ofcom 2004c). What may be indicated therefore, provided always that adequate safeguards are in place to ensure proper levels of accountability in the exercise of such power, is a more extensive use of the *dominium* power than has traditionally been the case. The existence of the BBC serves as an obvious example of the outcome of an exercise of governmental financial power, and there is, of course, a great weight of evidence indicating that the existence of the BBC has been at the heart of the historically strong PSB tradition in the UK.

The potential for the *dominium* power to be exercised in a manner which is likely to be beneficial to citizenship interests seems to be acknowledged by Ofcom, with its suggested 'Public Service Publisher' scheme (Ofcom 2004c; Mason 2005), alongside other interventions to support PSB. Although the value of spectrum has decreased, and so the impact of licensing spectrum to broadcasters is no longer such an effective means of supporting PSB, it could be that the expansion of such licensing could have a beneficial impact on freedom of communication. It is evident, however, that this particular potential aspect of the government's *dominium* power is unlikely to be exercised, given, as we noted in Chapter 4, that the government seems to be keen to exploit the 'digital dividend' by auctioning the broadcast spectrum which is released by digitalisation to commercial players (Cave 2002; Ofcom 2005g).

Although it is undoubtedly the case that state support and funding of broadcasting might have a positive impact on supporting citizenship interests and providing for freedom of communication, the limited resources available to governments combined with the operation of the state aid rules in the EC seem to render it unlikely that there will be a significant expansion of state funding for broadcasting. It is here, perhaps, that the impact of subnational governments might be the most telling, as these bodies are often willing to fund programming which caters for cultural or linguistic minorities (McGonagle *et al.* 2003; McGonagle and Richter 2004). In the UK, this is unlikely to be very significant, as most powers to intervene in media regulation are reserved to the Westminster Parliament.

Overall, we can see that the exercise of both *imperium* and *dominium* powers at the nation state and subnational level will continue to have some impact on the regulation of the media, but it will become increasingly necessary to turn to supranational responses in order to exert control over large media corporations. It is evident that, for the time being, both the EU and the WTO are far from ideal fora to which to entrust the protection of citizenship interests. Although it is evident that the operation of EC law has allowed for certain measures to be adopted which secure citizens' interests in the media, the limited legislative competence to pursue such goals prevents an expansive approach to the achievement of such goals, and any positive outcomes in relation to citizenship remain entirely contingent on their consistency with economic objectives. The WTO's role in the media is currently very limited, although this might be viewed as a positive situation given that the likely impact of an expansion of the GATS to the broadcast media would be that further economic liberalisation would ensue.

If it is not possible for a satisfactory response to be offered to the modern developments in the media through the use of *imperium* or *dominium* power at the supranational or national levels then a third alternative available to states wishing to regulate the activities of large media corporations will be to search for other means of control which are less reliant on the exercise of state power in order for them to operate effectively. The concepts of self-regulation and co-regulation have attracted some interest recently, and it is to these concepts that we now turn.

6.4.2 Self-regulation and co-regulation – a more satisfactory solution?

The concepts of self-regulation and co-regulation are the subjects of some debate within the literature so it is important to set out what we mean by these concepts at this point. Ogus has noted that 'self-regulation is a broad concept, covering a wide range of institutional arrangements', and it is evident that there are a range of perspectives on the issue (Ayers and Braithwaite 1992; Black 1996, 2000 and 2001; Baldwin and Cave 1999: chapter 10). Ayers and Braithwaite (1992: 102–3) offer a useful distinction between co-regulation and self-regulation when they suggest that,

> Co-regulation . . . is usually taken to mean industry-association self-regulation with some oversight and/or ratification by government . . . [S]elf regulation envisions that in particular contexts it will be more efficacious for the regulated firms to take on some or all of the legislative, executive, and judicial regulatory functions.

In Chapter 5, we analysed an instance of co-regulation which exists in the UK in the form of the ASA's oversight of broadcast advertising which is contracted out by Ofcom, and we also considered an instance of self-regulation in the form of the PCC where there has been almost no governmental intervention. If we return to the 'regulatory space' metaphor outlined at the start of this chapter, it seems that both self-regulation and co-regulation are an acknowledgement that industries themselves may be in the best position to contribute to the control of their activities. One reason for the favouring of self-regulation and co-regulation is that the costs of regulation, which would otherwise be borne by the state, are shifted to the industry itself (Baldwin and Cave 1999: 128). More interestingly, if states or international organisations can persuade the industry to enter into a degree of self-regulation then it may be that there is no need to employ either the *imperium* or *dominium* power of the state in order to enforce regulation. This has been seen by many as a development which may allow control to be exerted over activities on the Internet (PCMLP 2004; Marsden 2004).

It is notable that co-regulation has been somewhat more popular in the media sector than self-regulation. In his report on a European Commission-funded study, Marsden suggests that in modern co-regulation:

> The state, and stakeholder groups including consumers, are stated to explicitly form part of the institutional setting for regulation. Co-regulation constitutes multiple stakeholders, and this process results in greater legitimacy for claims. However, direct government involvement including sanctioning powers may result in the gains of reflexive regulation – speed of response, dynamism, international cooperation between ISPs and others – being lost. It is clearly a finely balanced concept, a middle way between state regulation and 'pure' industry self-regulation. (Marsden 2004: 188)

It is notable that the European Commission has demonstrated an interest in co-regulation (Scott 2002: 69; Marsden 2004: 188; McGonagle 2002; Palzer 2002), perhaps in part because adopting less formal 'Recommendations' in certain areas might encourage Member States to seek or accept harmonisation of approach in areas which are outside the strict legal competence of the EC. Although this could be perceived as an advantage, Scott suggests that the general approach of the European Commission to co-regulation has been cautious, with a preference being demonstrated for state-centred models of regulation (Scott 2002).

It is evident that co-regulation might bring significant advantages in some circumstances and may often gain a greater degree of compliance because the outcomes are in some way negotiated with relevant stakeholders, including the party to be regulated. Ultimately, however, co-regulation is backed up with the threat of some form of state-sponsored sanction. As we noted in the previous chapter, the co-regulatory regime that Ofcom has instituted with the ASA for the regulation of broadcast advertising is ultimately reinforced by the threat of statutory enforcement measures. It is very much open to question whether such measures would be effective without the threat of such state intervention. Furthermore, co-regulation suggests that the state has a particular role in setting the standards by which the regulated parties are to be judged. As such, co-regulation is attractive in the sense that the state may have some 'ownership' of the values and goals which are to be achieved by the co-regulatory regime.

We noted above that the globalisation of the media renders it less likely that individual nation states will be able to exert effective control over the activities of the media. An attraction of co-regulation, particularly if it is brought about by a degree of agreement at the supranational level, is that it may be able to offer a multilateral response to some of the issues which arise from these developments in media markets. It is much more questionable, however, whether we can rely on co-regulation to secure citizenship interests in freedom of communication. In Europe, it might be possible for co-regulation to deliver such outcomes, as there appears to be a fair degree of agreement among the Member States of the European Union over a concept of 'public service' (Prosser 2000, 2005: chapters 4–5). In addition, co-regulation may also still be an attractive option within the EU, as it appears to offer an opportunity to coordinate regulatory responses to the regulation of the activities of the media without the need to agree on an expansion of competence of the EU institutions. However, in the international context beyond the EU the likelihood of agreement over common values seems to be much more slight.

The phenomenon of self-regulation has, it has been noted above, been the subject of many different visions and definitions. The most well-known vision of self-regulation to be posited recently is perhaps that offered by Black (1996, 2000, 2001), who suggests that self-regulation should generally be seen as a reflexive method of regulation, *i.e.* 'instead of directly regulating social behaviour, law confines itself to the regulation of organisation, procedures and the redistribution of competences' (Teubner 1993: 57). While self-regulation may offer a number of advantages, particularly from the perspective of cost, flexibility and rapidity of regulatory response, there are notable difficulties with the application of self-regulation in the media sphere.

The first difficulty lies in the effectiveness of the sanctions that self-regulation might be able to offer. Ayers and Braithwaite (1992: 44) have argued that

> an important part of making self-regulation effective is to embed self-regulation in schemes of escalating interventions. In particular, we argue that retaining public enforcement (detection and punishment) of privately promulgated standards is likely to be an important component in constituting genuine private self-enforcement.

If we are reliant on self-regulation in order to ensure satisfactory standards for media content or to impose certain positive obligations, then it may be that 'pure' self regulation, without the threat of Ayers and Braithwaite's (1992) 'benign big gun' of the state to step in and take enforcement action against any repeated transgressors, will not be effective. Given that self-regulation may be seen to be a solution in many cases where state action is not possible, we might be dubious about the effectiveness of such regimes. The example of the PCC might serve as an example of self-regulation which has long been identified as relatively ineffective, but has remained extant in the absence of a credible threat of government action if the self-regulatory regime is deemed to be failing.

A second, and equally significant, difficulty with self-regulation is that the state has little control over the values to be pursued by the self-regulatory regime. In respect of the media, Marsden (2004: 191) sounds a cautionary note over the effectiveness of self-regulation when he argues that, 'Self-regulation offers a complaints procedure and alternative dispute resolution. However, there may be less protection for rights than with the protection offered by law. For example, injunctions, fines and sanctions may be unavailable within a self-regulatory regime.'

This point seems to be reinforced by Prosser (1999: 212) when he argues that the reflexive vision of self-regulation 'leaves unanswered the problem . . . of the substantive values which should underpin utility regulation.' The core argument in this book is that regulation of the media should be heavily value-laden and designed in order to pursue the 'public interest' goals we outlined in Chapter 3. Given these criticisms, we might be doubtful that self-regulation will be sufficient to ensure effective regulation of the media.

7

Conclusions: Protecting Democratic Values

∽

7.1 THE INCOMING TIDE

This book sets out to act as a guide for those wishing to view the landscape of media regulation and to offer suggested routes to desirable destinations. However, it is not easy to write a guidebook to an area when the incoming tide is in the process of changing the contours of the landscape, and perhaps even washing parts of it away. Observers are free to watch, with some combination of awe, excitement and trepidation, as waves of technological innovation and convergence, globalisation and cross-media conglomeration combine, and then appear to wash over, familiar landmarks on the media scene. The height and ferocity of the waves are clear from wherever the observer stands, but for those charged with regulating the media, watching is not an option, and instead they must intervene if the tidal forces are not simply to be allowed to take their course.

The first edition of this book, written seven years ago, concluded that the regulatory mechanisms then in place had failed to address the threat posed by the media revolution. The regulatory forms and practices applied had resulted in the trends of commercialism meeting with little resistance. In the mixed economy in which the media operated at the end of the twentieth century there was apparent a significant risk, if commercial trends were not addressed, that PSB and the values it represented would all too easily become marginalised. It was clear that the consequence of such a development would be the diminishment of citizenship.

Over the last seven years, the UK's media regulation landscape has inevitably undergone substantial change. Technology has moved forward with digitalisation making apparently inexorable progress in television, and media concentration has continued apace with the merger of Granada and Carlton as the most conspicuous example. At the same time, the regulatory framework has changed dramatically, with a much more developed European agenda now in evidence and, under the UK's new statutory framework, a number of smaller regulatory agencies have been swept away to be replaced by a shiny new regulatory edifice in the form of Ofcom. Such developments must also be viewed in light of substantial changes made over New Labour's three terms in office to the broader political and legal context in which regulation takes place. Of particular significance in relation to the media might be expected to be the impact of the Freedom of Information Act 2000 and the Human Rights Act 1998.

While the change in general climate that might be associated with the FOIA and the incorporation of the ECHR via the HRA might appear positive, it was always going to be necessary for more specific measures to be introduced in relation to fields such as the media. In doing so, it would be consistent for the government to adopt the same approach as it claims to have applied to education, namely to emphasise its impact on citizenship, and indeed to articulate the linkage between the two, identifying how one complements the other in respect of facilitating participation in society as a citizen. This, however, implies a direct and considered reconsideration of the value base which underlies regulation of the media, and even the least observant reader cannot fail to have been struck by our sense of disappointment at the failure to grasp the opportunity presented by the legislative process in relation to the Communications Act 2003, and in particular the failure to adopt fully the recommendations of the Puttnam Committee in relation to the advisability of prioritising citizenship interests as part of establishing a clear hierarchy of values and duties for Ofcom.

To a substantial extent, the issues noted seven years ago as central to media regulation remain unchanged. A fundamental objective for media regulation remains that of ensuring universal access to a wide range of quality media products, and therefore any move towards greater access to a wider range of media is apparently to be welcomed. In this sense, digitalisation, especially when offered free at the point of use as in DTT, appears to have much to offer. In addition, new technology does appear to offer the potential for increased citizen access to the media in terms of input. In this sense, it offers some attractions in terms of the potential ability of individuals and smaller groups to communicate their views directly, addressing some of the problems associated with the ability to access conventional broadcasting. Transmission via the Internet, for example, shares some of the aspects of point-to-multi-point transmission traditionally associated with broadcasting and does not have the same cost barriers to entry, but it does not, as yet, however, have the same reach as conventional mass media, and access to it is restricted largely to the socially advantaged. It does not equate with Curran and Seaton's model of 'Civic Media' (1997: 363), nor, given the absence of a genuinely mass audience, does it provide the advantages identified by Dovey (1995) in relation to 'authored' works transmitted under Community Programming obligations by existing public service broadcasters in terms of avoiding blandness and self-censorship in the traditional mass media. The key issue here is ensuring that 'access' aspects of PSB are integrated into the mainstream, as opposed to becoming marginalised in the way that the public broadcasting system has in the US (McQuail 1992: 53; Schiller 1996). From the other perspective, of receiving programming which relates to a local community, there is a real sense in which the substantial threat to the model of regional and local programming traditionally associated with the Channel 3 model in Britain (noted in Chapter 3) may be thought to diminish local identity and further the process of centralisation and potential globalisation in programming.

Of course, the potentially egalitarian aspects of electronic publishing and access to digital media more generally will occur only if gateway facilities are kept freely open and commercial interests are not allowed to dominate the new media. It will therefore be necessary to regulate the new media just as much as the old, if the potential benefits are to be reaped and the blight of domination by commercial interests avoided.

At the risk of underestimating the impact of new technology, it seems unlikely that new, interactive services routed through fibre-optic cable will, in the foreseeable future, entirely replace conventional broadcast and printed media. Rather, it seems more likely that, just as radio supplemented rather than supplanted print, and television has, though reaching an extraordinary degree of prominence, not led to the demise of other media, so networked services via the Information Superhighway are likely to create and fill a new niche alongside other existing media. There is no evidence to suggest yet that the new technology will provide the range and quality of media product associated with PSB, though it may, if used selectively, usefully serve to supplement it. However, it is clear that, conglomeration involving cable television companies and a mobile telephone specialist, such as the merger proposed in late 2005 between NTL/ Telewest and Virgin, will offer a new constellation of issues which regulators will need to address. There is a sense in which, within the competition paradigm, such developments may well be welcomed, challenging the degree of power enjoyed by Murdoch as the dominant player in the British media scene. However, the limits of the economics-oriented competition perspective, discussed in Chapters 2 and 6 and to be returned to, suggest only a limited utility from a public service or public interest perspective in the replacement of something approaching a commercial monopoly with a commercial oligopoly.

If the new technology is to be central to our media and communications systems in the future, an important first step is to recognise key aspects of national and global information infrastructures as 'essential facilities' within communications and therefore democracy, and to claim them for the public before the claims to private benefit become too firmly embedded:

> US experience suggests that once a commercial system is firmly in place it becomes difficult to challenge, and as its economic power increases so does its ability to keep threats at bay and gradually to remove all obstacles to commercial domination of the media. (Herman and McChesney 1997: 148)

This task of claiming new technology as a public resource is, however, unfortunately, much easier said than done, given the enormous power already wielded by the giant corporate bodies currently running the network with all the synergistic strength identified by Herman and McChesney (1997) and the reluctance of governments to cooperate internationally against this trend. That said, the recognition within the EU regulatory and legal system of certain aspects of the digital infrastructure as 'essential facilities' and the pursuit of 'must-carry' and universal service objectives does represent an issue where the outcomes of an agenda pursuing a competitive market have also, incidentally, furthered objectives that would be consistent with an approach driven by citizenship concerns. It is important to emphasise here 'incidentally', as it remains our argument that while regulation for competition via effective markets may *contingently* serve citizenship or public interest ends, it should not be assumed that it *necessarily* will. Such measures cannot, and should not, be viewed as an adequate substitute for measures explicitly targeted at social, as opposed to economic, purposes.

Of course, if the Information Superhighway were to replace wholesale existing media, the damage to 'cultural cohesion' would be significant, especially if its availability is limited to those with either the technical or financial ability to utilise it; the strongest forms of regulation would be indicated in such a situation. If, on the other hand, it forms only one part of the media, then it must be regulated alongside other media as part of a broader media market. This task will certainly be impeded by the international nature of the superhighway, and difficulties will be encountered, as McQuail (1992: 305) suggests, in terms of identifying 'a media originator (what used to be called the "mass communicator") who has full responsibility for public performance or who might, in principle, be held accountable to "society", according to public interest criteria'. Nonetheless, these issues must form a necessary focus for regulators in coming years, and international cooperation must take place to resist the technologically determinist arguments of those with a vested, commercial interest in the technological infrastructure. Regulation must absorb and act upon the implications of technological development and convergence and of corporate conglomeration in the media, and must replace the traditional, sectoral approach to regulation with a more holistic view of the media. As evidenced by Chapter 6 it is also clear that subsidiarity, in the sense of locating regulatory authority at its most appropriate and effective level, is an issue of some considerable importance here.

There is little doubting that, as Dahlgren (1995:148) indicates, the institutional logic of corporate media players is that of commercialism or profit rather than 'public sphering'. The extent to which the industry can be subverted, or converted, towards serving the public interest goal of citizenship, traditionally associated with PSB, remains the pressing question.

Clearly, it is no more possible or sensible to preserve the entire media landscape in its historic public service form than it is to seek to return to, and freeze parts of the countryside in, a pre-industrial agricultural era; in both cases, the tide has already come in too far, and much of what is left from previous eras and is valued perhaps with a nostalgic glow is already in the process of changing beyond recognition. In order to determine what should be sought to be preserved and what let go, a clear set of priorities must underpin any effective action. The history of media regulation to date, in Britain and elsewhere, has, however, been one of reactive, *ad hoc* response to technological and commercial innovation with a focus on the mechanisms and institutions of regulation rather than the reasons for their existence. To move beyond prescriptions from the past (Negrine 1994: 97) a radical reappraisal of the basic rationales for the regulatory endeavour is required. To avoid being left simply 'chasing the receding bus' (Elliott 1981) it is necessary to look ahead, have some idea when the bus will leave and be sure that it will take us where we want to go. Before identifying the policies and mechanisms that will be applied, clarity must be achieved as to the values and principles that lead to the conclusion that some outcomes are more desirable than others. In the absence of clearly articulated rationales and objectives for regulation, there can be no clear idea of where the process of regulation will or should lead.

Though citizenship has been heavily emphasised in this book as the primary justification for regulation, it is also clear that the genuine economic importance of the media industries, in terms of GDP and employment, also demand the industries' regulation. Measures designed to continue support for independent production via Channel 4 and the imposition of independent programme quotas, or indeed in the future via a Public Service Publisher, may prove useful both in terms of continuing to stimulate this financially important secondary market and in maintaining a degree of diversity in output. However, too great an emphasis on the economics of the industry is likely to be at the expense of the protection of its democratic significance. The application of essentially economic forms of intervention, such as the mechanisms of competition law, in the absence of measures dedicated to the support of broader public interest matters, appears to confirm rather than resist the commodification of the media.

It is clear that media output is not just another commodity but rather part of the lifeblood of democracy and therefore requires regulation going beyond the economic; this is recognised in the application of the essential facilities doctrine and the consideration of USO type measures. In Hoffmann-Riem's terms 'From the very outset, broadcasting regulation was not charged simply with the pragmatic role of "traffic police" but in addition by continual reference to a special public interest in freedom of communication' (Hoffmann-Riem 1996: 335). To place too much emphasis on freedom of communication as a justification for regulatory intervention is, however, a dangerous strategy, given its vulnerability to 'capture' by corporate interests (Keane 1991) and the fact that it may appear to serve ultimately as an impediment to effective regulation for diversity of output via positive programme requirements and the like, as in the US where the constitutionality of regulation has been challenged and in effect limited on such grounds (Feintuck 2004: 141–52).

Much regulation relating to concentration of ownership tacitly acknowledges that the purpose of intervention is the maintenance of plurality of output, though its emphasis is clearly on plurality of ownership. However, as is apparent from studies of Britain and other jurisdictions, such measures have largely failed in both senses, and even where a degree of plurality of ownership has been maintained, this in itself does not necessarily result in diversity of output. If the key objective or justification for regulation is the achievement of universal access to a diverse range of high-quality media products, then it must be acknowledged that patterns of ownership are not significant in themselves but only in their instrumental, and largely contingent, potential to result in output.

Even in the US, where the Western European PSB system is considered alien and where broadcasting has operated and been regulated from its inception on a commercial basis, the commercial outlook has justified the application of 'essential facility' and 'must-carry' doctrines which have averted the risks of the worst excesses of monopolistic power. Implicit in this approach is a recognition that the airwaves and gateways to the air comprise public rather than private assets. As has been indicated, the greater regulation of broadcast as opposed to print media can be identified as historically contingent; the development of broadcasting occurred predominantly in an era in which such activity was viewed as being legitimately within the role of the state. Since that era, however, the vision of legitimate state activity has become much narrower, and with it has come the privatisation, in various forms, of what was previously considered to be the public sphere. It is in this context that the information superhighway has developed, not in an anarchic manner as is sometimes suggested, but within the logic of the market paradigm rather than regulated in a public interest tradition.

The fact is, however, that there remains a clear public interest in regulating the media in all its forms. It derives substantially from the citizen participation approach to freedom of expression identified in Chapter 1, and is thus closely related to the citizenship rationale for regulation espoused by Collins and Murroni (1996). If individuals are cut off from mainstream media, they are denied the information necessary for them to participate in civic society, and they are denied access to an important element in the matter that holds society together *as* society. In this sense, like education, healthcare, food and housing, availability of the media becomes, in effect, a prerequisite of any meaningful construct of citizenship. For a government such as Tony Blair's, said to be concerned with multiple deprivation and which established, within months of taking office, an interdepartmental 'Social Exclusion Unit', avoiding exclusion from the media must presumably be a high public policy priority. Whether such rhetoric will be transformed into meaningful action will depend both on the degree to which the political will exists, and also the recognition that the media are an area, from the perspective of citizenship, at least as important as utilities such as power and water where regulation of the activities of private companies is considered important and justifiable. The fact that that failure to regulate can result in the privatisation of democracy, through corporate control of information flows and access restricted to those who can pay, suggests, however, that regulation of the media is still more important than regulation of other utilities and commodities.

When buying other commodities or utilities, it is usually possible to make choices based upon quality of product or service and cost. On the assumption that there is more than one supplier available, the choice is likely to be based largely on these criteria. In the case of the media, however, it is unlikely that I will have any choice over the supplier of information, given that a degree of exclusivity exists over particular products.

If only one supplier provides worthwhile news coverage, I need access to that supplier. If I am a soccer fan, and only one channel broadcasts Premier League soccer, I will want access to that channel. Of course, my exclusion from such services will not occur if, either, they are freely available or if I have the means to pay for them on a subscription or pay-per-view basis. However, once exclusive control over information exists, I am at the mercy of the owner of those exclusive rights, and, moreover, as concentration of media ownership increases, so the likelihood of exclusivity increases with it and the range of materials free at the point of reception may decrease significantly. Clearly, not all media products constitute material that can be identified as a prerequisite of citizenship. My unfulfilled desire for a channel dedicated to gardening programmes would not significantly impede my ability to operate as a citizen. That said, difficulties in defining where essentials end and luxuries begin must be acknowledged.

There is, however, enough evidence of the centrality of the media to democracy to indicate that the media require regulation, in the public interest, to a far greater degree than other commodities or services. Given the pronounced tendencies for media markets to tend towards concentration in private ownership, which presents the problems of exclusivity and, contingently, of lack of diversity of output, and given the perceived democratic and social need for diversity of content, it seems that regulation is both inevitable and desirable. It is also essential, though, that public policy interventions are premised on clearly articulated rationales.

The predominant form of regulation that has been considered is regulation of ownership and of behaviour, based upon economic, market principles. This is convenient, both in terms of the market-oriented zeitgeist and the desire of governments around the Western world not to be seen to be involved in control of content for fear of accusations of censorship. There are, however, severe limitations attaching to this approach. First, the relationship between ownership and diversity of content is contingent, and the problems associated with concentration of ownership could readily be addressed by the introduction of guarantees of journalistic and editorial independence (Gibbons 1992). Second, it is apparent that the measures adopted to date, in Britain and other Western jurisdictions, have singularly failed to prevent a high degree of media concentration, and the institutional structures require a radical overhaul if they are to meet the challenge of the ongoing revolution. The locus classicus of such failure might be thought to be the US market (see Bagdikian 2004), but markets such as Germany (Humphreys 1996) and Italy (Mazzoleni 1992) demonstrate the very clear tendency of media markets to result in oligopoly in the absence of effective regulatory intervention.

The failure of competition-oriented measures to maintain an apparently adequate level of diversity is, however, still more fundamentally problematic. In practice, the whole raft of competition-oriented provisions purport to ensure the benefits of markets while avoiding the perceived adverse consequences of monopoly. As has already been noted, it is perfectly possible for a monopoly or near-monopoly public service system, subject to adequate requirements as to programming, to provide the supposedly market-related advantages of diversity and quality, and in this sense it may therefore be misguided to seek to adhere doggedly to market-oriented mechanisms. This is highlighted by the US experience. In this context, Bagdikian (2004: 6) notes how 'competition' within the media results in imitation of the popular or populist rather than innovation, or, in Schiller's terms, 'There has been no lack of *a certain kind* of competition between the dominant three, now four, national broadcasting networks' (Schiller 1996: 85, original emphasis), but that this competition has revolved around maximising audience share and therefore advertising revenue, and has resulted in a predominantly bland, commercial, homogenous television diet. However, market forces have been for some time, and look likely for the foreseeable future to be, 'flavour of the month' on a near global basis, and as such any move to an alternative model of broadcasting seems an extremely remote possibility. The empirical evidence of the failure of the existing approach in terms of diversity appears to have done little to dampen governmental enthusiasm for such mechanisms.

While this might be considered unfortunate, it seems very unlikely that any major divergence from this policy will occur. Inevitably, national governments will seek to pursue policies which produce perceived economic advantages from a national perspective, and invariably in the modern era this means via market mechanisms. It may be that the only hope for a different approach lies with international bodies, but in Europe, where the major regional power, the EU, is premised precisely upon a market philosophy, there seems little hope of an alternative vision emerging. As we have already suggested, the EU is better placed than national governments to develop an anti-commodification agenda in relation to the media but, given its politico-economic agenda, is unlikely to act effectively in this respect.

In our estimation, this is where we truly run into what Prosser (2005) talks of as 'the limits of competition law', as even the most effective competition regime will not deliver in relation to a citizenship agenda. The media regulation regime based predominantly on a competition approach does, ironically, provide something that we have argued for: a clear hierarchy of values. Regrettably, from our perspective, at the top of the set of values come those of market players, and perhaps next down consumers, with citizen interests coming at best a very distant third. Collins and Murroni (1996: 12) summarise the dilemma thus: 'A stronger competition policy, though desirable, is not sufficient to secure the public interest in media and communications. For the economic characteristics and political importance of media and communications are different from those of steel and shoes.' What is needed, they go on to say, 'is competition policy where competition can thrive in the public interest and regulation where it cannot'. Given the unreality of reverting to anything approaching a public service monopoly position, the pragmatic use of market forces and public policy-based intervention, which Collins and Murroni advocate, a mixed economy appears the best available option. The tension revealed by this approach, between commercial values and public service values, has been the pivotal point around which almost all the debate in this book has revolved.

Marsden (1997b) appears to offer support for the use of overtly 'content-biased' policies. Here lies a problem, however, as the inherent shyness of governments to interfere overtly with media content is currently compounded by the strong belief in the efficacy of market forces. Hesitancy to exercise what, if it serves the public interest, would clearly be legitimate government power is probably the major factor accounting for the failure of governments to engage in a considered and long-term policy-making process in relation to the media. However, it is clear, as demonstrated earlier, that both overtly, for example via positive programming in PSB, and covertly, via informal power and influence over public service broadcasters and regulators, governments can and do regularly interfere with programme content.

It is not, however, the existence of such powers as such that is problematic, since in so far as such content-oriented regulation is demonstrably necessary in the public interest in terms of diversity and quality of product and in pursuit of social inclusivity for citizens the power is legitimate. Where such power is not exercised in the public interest and/or is not exercised accountably, it has no legitimate foundation and should not exist. All that remains then is to establish adequately transparent and accountable mechanisms for the exercise of that power.

In many respects, a tiered approach of the kind discussed in Chapter 6 may seem to offer a promise of a structure which is more flexible and offering a wider range of locations of regulatory power. The existence of a range of regulators such as Ofcom, technically independent from government, self-regulatory and co-regulatory responses and supranational bodies such as the EU may seem to offer a wider menu of choice as to the appropriate means of regulation. However, if such regulators are not working to briefs which emphasise values beyond those of the market, they offer no greater likelihood of protecting citizenship-related values than do traditional state-centred models of regulation. Though legal instruments of regulation and, as noted in Chapter 5, regulators themselves may on rare occasions differentiate between consumer and citizen interests, such occasional and inconsistent recognition is not sufficient in relation to what, from any meaningful 'public interest' perspective, are starkly and crucially different interests and values.

The tiered approach also implies a vision of subsidiarity, yet in practical terms it is clear, as we established in Chapter 1, that in relation to many aspects of the media it is increasingly the case that the only appropriate level of regulation will be at the supranational level. The bottom line here, to return to Schiller (1996: 121) again, is that the pursuit of competition in this context, by national governments or international bodies such as the EU, 'signifies the relinquishment of national accountability to the play of market forces'. In Leys' terms, contrary to traditional views of sovereignty, governments increasingly find it necessary, in order to stay in office while operating in the context of a global economy, 'to "manage" national politics in such a way as to adapt them to the pressures of transnational market forces' (Leys 2001: 1). In this context, while there are times when it may seem that going beyond the nation state may offer the best hope of finding a locus of regulatory power which may look beyond economic imperatives and may therefore be better placed to reassert democratic values, to look to the EU in this respect may be futile: as we established in Chapter 6, there is no doubt that the very obvious objective of the EU's 2002 New Regulatory Framework is the furtherance of a competitive market in the digital media infrastructure. The adoption of market forces is a positive policy choice, though it may be presented as a non-policy, or at least a device for avoiding government responsibility by permitting the free play of supposedly value-neutral market forces. Of course, market forces are not neutral, and indeed, as noted in Chapter 3, they tend to produce results that reproduce or exaggerate social hierarchy. Leys (2001: 3) sums up the position admirably:

> Contrary to the impression given by neoliberal ideology and neoclassical economics textbooks, markets are not impersonal or impartial but highly political, as well as inherently unstable. In the search for survival, firms constantly explore ways to break out of the boundaries set by state regulation, including the boundaries that close non-market spheres to commodification and profit-making. This is a crucially important issue since it threatens the

destruction of non-market spheres of life on which social solidarity and active democracy have always depended.

Failure to intervene effectively in media markets in pursuit of citizenship objectives leaves everything of value in the PSB tradition vulnerable to the tide of market forces. Some of the public service landscape has already been washed away. Much top-level sport has already been lost and is probably irretrievable given the need felt by most sporting bodies to maximise income from broadcasting rights and the ability and willingness of, for example, satellite broadcasters to pay large sums in order to reap the benefits of using sport as one of the levers with which to open up for themselves an established place in broadcasting. Whether or not sports coverage is considered able to claim a place as a significant element of the public interest in broadcasting is debatable, though it does seem to form an important element in shared popular culture and national, social cohesion. To some degree, this is recognised by existing legislation, though the list of sporting events given statutory protection to which free-to-air coverage cannot be denied is limited, and subject to review by the Secretary of State; failure to 'list' live coverage of Premier League soccer and the removal of protection for home test match series are obvious examples of the limitations of this measure, and the drive by sports authorities to maximise television revenue in the short term.

To some extent, the loss of such subject matter is in itself less problematic than the longer-term trend this appears to indicate. The more attractive material is provided by via pay-television, and the less the BBC and other free-to-air broadcasters have to offer, the greater the problems for the public service broadcasters in justifying their existence. Among the likely consequences of this are attempts by ITV companies to go 'down-market' in programming, competing for audience share with lowest-common-denominator fare, and the increasing difficulty for the BBC in justifying its privileged, compulsory licence fee basis for funding. As was seen in Chapter 5, the response of the BBC to intense pressure in the 1980s was to adjust itself to a more market-oriented style but, primarily, to defend itself by continuing to provide a wide range of quality programming. The Charter Review process and licence fee debate discussed in Chapter 2 and Ofcom's PSB Review covered in Chapter 4 all serve to indicate the ongoing pressures on the archetypal public service broadcaster to justify its continuing existence in anything like a recognisable form. The very fact that the BBC, and the public service values it epitomises, have been vulnerable to such potentially damaging pressure, however, suggests a failure in earlier times to articulate and legitimise adequately these values, and an ongoing risk that the best we may hope for, in the absence of strong, principled and expeditious interventions to support the underlying values, is a greatly impoverished version of PSB. This is, of course, just one example of a range of criticisms which can be levelled at the institutions of media regulation in terms of a long-term lack of effectiveness. However, as we have argued repeatedly, there is little utility or meaning in arguing about more or less effectiveness in this context, unless there is prior discourse resulting in clear answers to questions as regards values and objectives. As we saw in Chapter 5, especially in our discussion of the PCC, it becomes extremely difficult to discuss institutional success or failure in the absence of clear and agreed criteria against which 'effectiveness' can be measured.

There is therefore, in the increasingly competitive world of broadcasting, a pressing need to reinvest the public service tradition with a sense of legitimacy of purpose, and attempts to do this must be premised upon the fundamental public interest values of diversity and quality in programme-making and the pursuit of social inclusivity. Relegitimising PSB will need more than theoretical justifications, however, and an important part of the process will have to be a restructuring of the institutions of PSB, notably the BBC, its internal governance arrangements and its relationship with Ofcom, so as to ensure the maximum degree of transparency, accountability and therefore legitimacy in their operations.

The very fact that PSB has not yet withered away entirely and that the state continues to regulate (albeit rather ineffectively) in the name of the public interest (though this remains under-specified) demonstrates a recognition of the value of the public service tradition. While it is only right to welcome a reconsideration of and statutory definition of PSB in the Communications Act, such definition will assist little in defending the tradition, if the values which underlie it, its *raison d'être*, is not also spelled out with some clarity. It is the protection and service of what we might call, after Stewart (1983) 'non-commodity values' in broadcasting, values associated with citizenship not profit, or what we might call 'the public interest', which is the function which PSB has uniquely fulfilled.

To date, regulation has done just enough to ensure that a 'mixed economy' of public service and commercial broadcasting now exists, though there is no doubt in which direction the tide is running. If the public service tradition is to be defended and reinvigorated, it is necessary to move beyond tacit and slightly apologetic defences of it against the market-oriented arguments, and instead argue loudly for an acceptance of the reality that *only* the public service tradition has been *proven* to guarantee the range and quality of programming and reach all sectors of society that the public interest demands. Any other, market-driven, alternatives are likely to fail in one or all of these respects, leading to an undermining of the public interest and, ultimately, via the erosion of citizenship, the diminishment of democracy. Though the mixed economy in the media, and broadcasting in particular, is now established, this does not deny the necessity for regulators to be empowered or required to act effectively to protect and promote public service and public interest values. Indeed, regulation remains a necessity if the mixed economy is not to transform into an entirely commercial media market.

If regulators fail to intervene effectively now, the future of broadcasting, a public resource, is abandoned to the tidal forces of commercialism. It cannot be certain what will remain of the media landscape when the waters recede sufficiently to allow a view and thus, if there is anything considered worthy of protection, steps must be taken without delay.

The power of the incoming tide is immense and artificial sea defences offer protection only for a limited period. Over longer periods, coastal erosion will take its course and conservation of the landscape, be it England's east coast, the National Parks or the media 'landscape', will not be successful if attempts are made simply to preserve it at a static moment in history. Just as farming, land management practices and demography will change, influenced by wider social and technological developments originating outside the local area, so with the media, where information technology and global commercial imperatives represent forces that cannot simply be excluded or ignored. Just as the landscape of a National Park must be allowed to develop in accordance with changing wisdom on land use and tourist policies, though hopefully in a way that preserves its essential qualities, so the media cannot be insulated from technological and commercial change but, again, with good management it should be possible to maintain, in a modernised and sustainable form, those aspects of it that are most highly valued.

7.2 RISING ABOVE THE WAVES

Building new structures that rise above the incoming tide is a more attractive proposition than trying to learn to live under water. Designing new institutional structures that hold back the tide in places and rise through the waves in others is the key task now facing would-be institutional architects. The key to success in this respect is building upon foundations sufficiently deep and strong to support a structure in the turbulent waters above. In this context, it may be that the law and its constitutional basis in democracy offer a solid base upon which to build; it may be far from perfect, but may be the best available option, or indeed, in effect, 'the only game in town'. Different positions will provide observers of the incoming tide with different perspectives, rendering certain features more or less prominent. The standpoint of the public lawyer offers one view of the key management issues for those involved in media regulation in the current context of the inrushing tide.

The history to date of *ad hoc* reactive adaptation in response to developments associated with corporate and technological change, is not encouraging. The failure to legislate effectively is a result of a congeries of factors, which include not only political fashions such as adherence to market values and concepts such as the 'rolling back of the state', but also, importantly, an unfounded hesitancy to pursue unashamedly content-biased policies for fear of breaching democratic expectations of freedom of expression. This latter factor is in particular observable in the US, where intervention to achieve a minimum range of pluralism in the media (in pursuit of a particular concept of competition) is deemed lawful, but any attempt to control content would be likely to be struck down as a breach of the constitutional promise of freedom of speech.

As Schiller (1996: 43) observes, 'Historically, the threat to individual expression has been seen to come from an arbitrary state', and therefore it is not surprising that there are clear and inevitable tensions between the state and the media. The media claim to act as the 'Fourth Estate' subjecting state power to scrutiny and, in an era of mass political communication, to provide the information necessary for citizen participation in democracy. Modern-day governments are therefore understandably wary of intervening openly, especially given their heavy dependence on the media's roles in disseminating their policies and forming public opinion, raising the likelihood of quiet, corporatist, symbiotic accommodations between the media and the regulatory state. However, it is also necessary to be aware of Keane's warning (1991: 130) about how regulation premised upon freedom of expression may be utilised by corporate giants not as intended, as a shield to protect citizens from state repression, but as a sword to attack state attempts at regulation, citing freedom of expression as a just cause. Lloyd (2004) directs us towards a more general risk, that the freedom provided to the media by its relationship with government may be abused in a manner that may ultimately be antithetical to democratic expectations and, in particular, common understanding of the media's role in democracy.

The consequence of historical lack of effective regulation of the media by the state has been the modern realpolitik of media, under the control increasingly of international, corporate, profit-oriented giants, controlling information flows subject only to the vagaries of market forces. It seems unlikely that any serious commentator would argue that this is sufficient to ensure that the enormous power wielded by the media is adequately controlled to ensure the fulfilment of the fundamental, liberal democratic principle that power should not be unlimited. The fact that the media is increasingly privately owned should not blind politicians to the reality that the media, with their central place in democracy, continue to form an essential public resource and should therefore be subject to adequate accountability mechanisms ensuring that this public function is properly carried out.

Public lawyers are therefore charged with the task of devising mechanisms that ensure that the media fulfil the provision of a diverse and high-quality range of material to all in order that citizenship may be furthered. However, given the important role of media freedom in scrutinising the activities of government, other organs of the state and powerful private concerns, devices must also be put in place to ensure that the exercise of regulatory power over the media, and especially any government role in the media regulation process, is also exercised in an accountable and legitimate manner. Accountability in regulation is a particular concern of public lawyers, but is also, of course, a feature of the political system as a whole (Norton 2004).

It is first necessary to reassert, as the fundamental, democratic principle that justifies or legitimates media regulation, the objective of ensuring that a diverse, high-quality range of media are made available to all citizens in the interests of seeking to avoid social exclusion. Though this construct does not, in itself, provide practical answers to all the many issues which must be addressed, it does provide the foundations upon which answers can be built and the values which must be reflected and embodied in institutions.

One particularly troublesome issue which cannot be avoided is that citizenship implies a degree of equality, and therefore raises a question, in terms of both substantive and institutional arrangements as to the degree of equality which must be sought or protected. While there can be little doubt over the impropriety of privatisation of significant civic communication (such as election coverage) the answer is not so clear-cut in relation to popular cultural material such as soap opera or sport, though these serve an important social function and therefore seem, arguably, to form part of the public sphere. This raises a range of essentially sociological questions regarding the cultural and social significance of the media which it is not the place of this book to attempt to resolve. It is, however, reasonable to note here that, as in relation to other aspects of media regulation, the pattern of intervention by governments in cultural events has largely been typified by a pragmatic and unprincipled approach.

Though loath to interfere with market place agreements between sporting bodies and broadcasters, the British government, as was noted in Chapter 3, over many years sought to support British cinema via a levy and latterly through the presence of Channel 4 in the broadcasting field, where pursuit of the policy of independent production was intended to deliver positive financial spin-offs for the film industry with a number of huge commercial success resulting from association with Channel 4. In addition, governments have consistently subsidised 'high' but commercially unviable art in the form of opera and ballet in a way that would not occur in relation to more populist culture. If intervention in relation to elitist art is considered legitimate (in the public interest), it is consistent to argue that populist culture may also be the legitimate subject of state intervention, using state power and influence to avoid social exclusion. Though relevant to it, this does not in itself, however, resolve the question of how equal access to media output must be.

To a limited extent, comparisons can be drawn with the regulation of privatised utilities, where Universal Service Obligations (USOs) have been utilised (see Prosser 2005) to seek to avoid some of the potential consequences of the free play of market forces in terms of 'cherry-picking' and social exclusion. Crucially, to support even a minimum standard of equality of access to media output, and therefore information necessary to permit participation as a citizen, an adequate range of media must be available to all at an affordable cost. As McQuail (1992: 4) notes, even the liberalising Peacock Committee (1986) 'endorsed the importance of public service purposes, especially in respect of providing universal service'.

Despite the promise of new technology providing the potential for an unparalleled number of channels and services becoming available, 'without regulatory intervention the broadcasting market is likely to provide *fewer* radio and television programmes and services free at the point of use' (Collins and Murroni 1996: 79, original emphasis). As Charlesworth and Cullen state (1996: 31), citizenship issues may easily be marginalised if not provided for explicitly when basic USO requirements are drawn up.

In Keane's terms (1991: 176), 'Democracy requires informed citizens. Their capacity to produce intelligent agreements by democratic means can be nurtured only when they enjoy equal and open access to diverse sources of opinion.' With the new technology for delivering the multi-channel future, however, comes also the facility to restrict access in ways impossible with conventional, analogue broadcasting. Digitalisation means that those receiving broadcasts must do so via decoding equipment, with the possibility of incorporating facilities for charging, either on a subscription or pay-per-view basis, therefore being readily available. The 'public good' characteristic of conventional broadcasting and the practical difficulty of allocating charges to individual recipients do not therefore apply to digital broadcasting. In addition, if technological gateways are not kept open, undue power to control who can transmit (and what, and when) will be handed to those corporate interests controlling the gateways. Here, as is the case under the EU's New Regulatory Framework discussed in Chapter 6, something akin to the 'essential facilities' doctrine may be called in aid and applied in areas such as CASs. It should be apparent, however, that regulation founded exclusively on economic rationales is unlikely to be enough, in itself, to guarantee the meeting of citizenship expectations.

However, it is still necessary to offer some response to the question of how equal access must be to offer effective guarantees that equality of citizenship is furthered or protected. In McQuail's terms (1992: 21), the difficulties here

> stem mainly from disagreements about what features of mass communication are essential (many are clearly not) and about whether special arrangements, interfering in the free market, are needed at all to secure a fair and efficient provision of those services which are agreed to be essential.

To some extent, these issues relate to substantial differences in definition of PSB (Price and Raboy, 2003). In the final analysis, it seems impossible to draw a clear 'line in the sand' on this issue, not only because of inherent difficulties in determining which aspects of media output are and are not prerequisites of citizenship, but also because of the rapid and unpredictable nature of ongoing technological development. Collins and Murroni (1996: 81) are undoubtedly right to seek to ensure the continuation of what they term 'community service obligations' via 'the continued existence of publicly funded services and notably the BBC', 'must-carry requirements for the services [PSB] which conform to positive (and negative) programme requirements on alternative delivery systems', and 'the granting of priority access to networks of limited capacity to services which are free at the point of use'. Some of these principles have clearly found a place in the regulatory mechanism applied to DTT, discussed in Chapter 4.

Yet we are not seeking to argue here that all elements of the historical settlement for regulating PSB should be carried forward. Certainly, it is right to have concerns where some apparently important principles and practices are departed from. As we observed in Chapter 4, trends in relation to Channel 3, following the Carlton/Granada merger, already appear to be challenging one element of 'community service' in this context, namely a reduction in locally focused and produced programming, which, historically, has served to reflect regional identity and culture. Likewise, imposing minimum requirements for amounts of other specific programme genres such as children's television will require a great delicacy of touch and careful research and monitoring on the part of Ofcom, given the post-2003 practice of regulating such matters across the public service sector as a whole rather than in relation to any particular channel. There may well be a case to argue that, rather than attempt to prescribe precise programme limits or quotas based on specific examples of output which will inevitably be transient and are likely to be arbitrary, it does seem sensible to grant regulators sufficient discretion to take action in this area, but with the discretion structured by reference to the fundamental long-term principle informing the overall regulatory agenda. Reflecting broadly the terms of Ofcom's recent PSB Review, the question which regulators must consider and give reasoned justifications for the answers they reach is whether their decision will lend support to the maintenance of availability to all of a wide and high-quality range of media products (as a prerequisite of citizenship). This allows, and indeed requires, the regulator, quite properly, to reflect on the media as a whole as opposed to any particular media sector. It allows the regulator, subject to the rigorous accountability mechanisms indicated below, the flexibility to determine new cases in light of current circumstances and foreseeable future developments. It does not bind regulators, nor does it permit regulators to bind themselves, to considering an issue in a narrow context. In these circumstances, the substance of the regulators' decisions are legitimated by reference to the fundamental, citizenship justification for intervention, while requirements of transparency and accountability ensure the legitimacy of the procedures they should be required to adopt.

At the time the first edition of this book was written in the late 1990s, specific, procedural and substantive developments were cause for concern in relation to the example of the licensing regime introduced in connection with the then forthcoming DTT service. The introduction of Oftel, the specialist telecommunications regulator with experience of regulating telecommunications against USO requirements, into the arrangements for licensing CASs could then be seen as a positive step forward, and the degree of alertness shown to the potential threat posed by a *BSkyB* interest in a consortium seeking multiplex licences was a hopeful sign in terms of regulating media markets. The arrival of Oftel on the media scene appeared to suggest the likelihood of an appropriately increased emphasis on behavioural measures as telecommunications and the media converge. It also appeared to offer support for proposals for a single media/communications regulator, positioned to take an overview of the field as a whole. That said, the fact that control of key features in the digital infrastructure was not factored into the calculations of limits on cross-media ownership demonstrated an ongoing weakness in the system. While the focus of the Broadcasting Act 1996 provisions on cross-media ownership comprised an attempt to limit the growth of such empires, the failure to incorporate into such calculations and thresholds control of crucial technological gateways indicated a somewhat blinkered approach to the modern cross-media context. Media cannot be regulated meaningfully in isolation and, in assessing the degree of concentration in the market as a whole, control over gateways and pinch-points in the technological infrastructure (such as CASs and EPGs) needs weighing alongside control over newspapers and broadcasting corporations. In this sense, the creation of Ofcom must be welcomed, establishing a body able to take the necessary overview of the media industries.

The recent growth in uptake of digital television, especially via DTT, which we noted in Chapter 4, seems likely to continue or indeed increase further in the build-up to analogue switch-off. In this sense, the regulatory framework for DTT takes on additional significance, and thus it is especially welcome to note some positive elements in the regulatory structures and systems in place in relation to this delivery mechanism. However, the positive developments as have been seen in relation to DTT do nothing to reduce the need for a general acknowledgement of the purpose of regulation: to further the public interest in terms of the affordable and widespread availability of a range of quality media products. As competition for viewers from an increasing number of pay-television broadcasters grows, the greater the need for protection of those aspects of PSB that are valued most. The BBC and Channel 4 in particular, but also the ITV regional companies, should continue to play an important part in the mixed economy of broadcasting, ensuring the continuation of a range of quality output which the market alone is unlikely to deliver. Pay-television is likely to extend usefully the range of broadcasting at the margins, creating and filling new niche markets, but is not likely to offer the core of high-quality, innovative, informative, educative and entertaining programming that public service broadcasters have traditionally provided, given the lack of commercial prospects in this area. With this in mind, the BBC must be relegitimised by reference to its central democratic function but, if necessary, governments could legitimately bolster its funding beyond the licence fee, ensuring its future success by providing a financial safety net in much the same way as Channel 4 was protected in its early years. On this occasion, however, it might be more reasonable to impose such provisions on niche satellite and cable companies, exempted from the panoply of public service requirements, rather than the ITV regional companies with which BBC is very much in competition. Such 'play or pay' type provisions are perfectly consistent with the legitimising justification of furtherance of citizenship which underpins PSB.

The foregoing has largely examined issues of regulation of media markets rather than media content, though the emphasis on range and quality of programming implies an acceptance of the advisability of overtly 'content-biased' policies as suggested by Marsden (1997b). It must be accepted that it is rather far-fetched to expect the imposition on individual newspapers of the kind of balance requirements that public service regulation applies to broadcasters. However, the public interest justification for media regulation, as defined above, appears to permit or indeed encourage intervention to prevent political or cultural homogeneity in the press just as much as anywhere else in the media. Though it is only proper and consistent with the line espoused here that the press must be viewed in the context of the wider media, to the extent that a lack of diversity existing in the press sector distorts the balance of views in the media as a whole intervention targeted at the press is perfectly justifiable. While it would seem unlikely that the present government, or any likely successor, would be keen to intervene to offer press subsidies to newspapers representing minority interests (and therefore not commercially viable) in the way that Humphreys (1996: 92–3) refers to in Scandinavia, to introduce guarantees of journalistic and/or editorial independence, thus restricting the potential influence of newspaper owners (Gibbons 1992), would not necessarily offend the spirit of the age.

It seems that the post-Diana revision to the PCC code of conduct, taking effect in January 1998, served to take the heat out of the privacy issue. Meanwhile, the Human Rights Act's impact on the UK's law of privacy seems to have been less than far-reaching, leaving the self-regulatory system for the press largely untouched – 'The Last Chance Saloon' appears still to be open and serving. However, as is evidenced by the example of the ASA, under a self-regulatory or now 'co-regulatory' system, the question of who regulates is not necessarily as important as whether they do so effectively and accountably, though in the case of self-regulatory regimes, a clear collective self-interest, seemingly absent from the newspaper industry, appears to be crucial.

The so-called 'self-regulatory alternative' is, however, as Prosser (1997: 271) indicates, something of a misnomer, confusing the techniques of self-regulation with the 'prescription for overall institutional design'. As any study of the PCC and ASA will indicate, self-regulation is neither to be necessarily wholeheartedly embraced or deprecated. It is merely a technique which may be adopted to achieve regulatory objectives. Provided that it is accountable and effective, and Curran and Seaton's proposal (1997: 369) to link its use with a greater 'professionalisation' of the media appears useful in this respect, it is no more or less problematic than any other mode of regulation. But to be effective and legitimate, it must operate accountably within an overall institutional design which is premised upon clear regulatory rationales and objectives. The use of self-regulation, or its very similar modern manifestation in co-regulatory structures, is not an acceptable alternative to the establishment and articulation of such institutional goals.

Self-regulation, however, also raises questions of more general application to media regulators, of accountability in the exercise of regulatory power. This is no constitutional or legal nicety but fundamental to establishing the democratic legitimacy of regulatory regimes.

A perennial concern in relation to regulatory activity generally is the risk of regulators exercising unnecessarily wide and unstructured discretion without meaningful checks on the exercise of their powers. In our particular context, historically a major focus of concern related to government ministers who were seen to exercise wide-ranging discretion over newspaper acquisitions and, to have the ability to exert both formal power and informal influence over broadcasters and, via powers of appointment, the regulators; for an organisation such as the BBC, the claim of real independence from government, in such circumstances, has on occasion been severely challenged. In the past, it was undoubtedly the case that regulators such as the ITC could act in pursuit of only the vaguest public interest tests, without a clear idea of underpinning values or future objectives and subject to review by the courts only if they err significantly in procedure or commit the most egregious substantive errors. They were under minimal duties to give reasons. All of these bodies were distanced from the public, run by government appointees and rarely engaged in wide-ranging or open consultation. In this respect, they had much to learn from regulators of the utilities, such as Oftel, whose consultation processes appeared by comparison innovative, wide-ranging, meaningful and transparent (Prosser 1997; Graham 2000).

In terms of clarity and simplicity, there is much to be said for Ofcom having subsumed and combined the relevant functions of, among others, the DCMS, ITC, BSC, Oftel, DTI and the MMC, especially given the context of technological overlap and convergence. Despite this greater degree of regulatory tidiness resulting from the 2003 Act, significant issues remain unresolved. In particular, an ongoing risk remains of regulatory capture by the industries it is intended to regulate. The risk might be presumed to be proportionately greater in the case of a single regulator and therefore requirements of transparency are still more important.

This latter feature of institutional design also seems crucial in contributing to ensuring that an 'independent' regulator such as Ofcom does indeed remain independent of government influence. Here, the role and position of Ofcom is by no means wholly novel. The increased role of a semi-independent Bank of England in relation to interest rates and the creation of the independent Food Standards Agency (Feintuck 2004: 73–94) suggest that the government understands the potential advantages of independence for agencies in public interest areas.

To return to the image used earlier, the outstanding question is whether Ofcom has been built on sufficiently strong conceptual foundations to allow it to rise above and survive the inrushing tide of developments in the media industries. As things stand, it is hard to offer a conclusive answer. On the one hand, widespread consultation and the publication of detailed findings arising out of the PSB Review look promising. On the other hand, board meetings held in private, the relaxing of programming requirements on ITV companies and a lack of clarity as regards its relationship with the BBC may be thought to raise questions over the regulator's role and likely effectiveness in relation to PSB.

From the point of view of the public lawyer, but more generally from the point of view of democracy and constitutionalism, a key issue in the reform of the media regulation regime is the development and application of hard-hitting requirements of accountability. Legitimacy in the exercise of power requires it to be limited, and thus media regulators should be subjected to requirements of transparency in their operation that should lead to both greater clarity in the decision-making process and a greater sense of legitimacy for regulators in their actions.

The introduction of the FOIA may offer some marginal benefits here. That said, availability of information on demand does not achieve as much as the automatic publication and widespread dissemination of information. Greater public representation on regulatory bodies is probably desirable, though not in principle a necessity, given that whoever is making the decisions should be rendered subject to public scrutiny and accountability, though transparency in the appointments process is clearly appropriate. Widespread consultation by regulators beyond directly interested parties and extending to the general public is certainly indicated as necessary, and in this respect there are some hopeful signs in relation to Ofcom. That said, an important issue in determining the effectiveness of consultation processes and the like is their timeliness in relation to the decision-making process. If consultation is to be meaningful, it needs to take place at an early enough stage to influence the range of options ultimately to be chosen from, that is to say before certain options have been foreclosed. An example of the latter issue arose in the pre-Ofcom era but typifies the problems. The consultation exercise by the DCMS and RA in relation to DTT (DCMS 1998a), launched in February 1998, was certainly welcome, being accompanied by the publication of a study on the predicted economic impact of the government's policies (DCMS 1998b) but it came awfully late in the day, and long after a clear decision had been taken by the Major government, and endorsed by Blair's, to opt for DTT as opposed to other delivery mechanisms as the chosen future mainstream platform for delivering television. In many ways, such late consultation typifies the approach of treating citizens as consumers, with the limited rights and interests that entails, rather than as citizens, which would involve expectations of informed consultation and involvement at the formative stage of policy-making. An important benchmark against which Ofcom may be judged will be whether it can improve on such practices.

By way of contrast with current norms in regulatory practice, meetings of regulatory bodies should be widely publicised and open to the public and the media, except only where particularly sensitive material (and not all commercial material is confidential) is being discussed, and in such defined exceptions detailed justifications must be provided. In this respect, as we noted in Chapter 4, Ofcom's practice, as commented on by the DCMS Select Committee, is a cause for concern. Most important of all, however, regulators must be required to give reasons for their decisions, identifying why one option has been preferred over others, and justifying their chosen course of action in terms of the public interest criteria of citizenship and the range and quality of media output.

There is nothing particularly innovative or unusual in these recommendations within public law scholarship. In particular, anyone familiar with Harden and Lewis (1986) or indeed Keane (1991) will recognise their basis in US public law, in the provisions of the constitution, in the Administrative Procedure Acts and 'Government in the Sunshine' legislation and in the judicially developed 'hard-look' doctrine. Though ever wary of 'legal transplants' and conscious of the underlying constitutional, social and political differences between Britain and the US, ongoing issues in relation to the accountability of regulators, touched on in Chapter 5 indicate the desirability of equivalent measures in Britain. Though the ultimate success or failure of such measures will inevitably depend to some degree upon their interpretation and development by the judiciary, it is to be hoped that the advent and bedding-down of the Human Rights Act will encourage British judges to develop a more principle-oriented approach to public law, and in any event, the presence of a clearly articulated citizenship orientation for the reformed media regulation regime would provide a relevant focus for review activity.

The issues and requirements outlined above are intended primarily to improve the quality and legitimacy of decision-making. However, were measures to be introduced that require decision-makers to operate transparently and to justify decisions against the objective of maximising the universal availability of a wide-ranging media output, a side-effect of such reforms would be likely to be more meaningful standards of judicial review of regulatory activity. Judicial process would enjoy greater purchase than where those exercising discretion do so in the absence of developed or articulated criteria, and the existence of such principle would also help in turn to structure judicial discretion.

The public interest in furtherance of citizenship via universal access to a diverse range of quality media products demands and justifies much more than structural regulation. It justifies regulation of output, in terms of the imposition on broadcasters of positive programme requirements and perhaps the imposition of 'play or pay' levies to support PSB, on those broadcasters exempted from such comprehensive requirements. It justifies also regulation of carriage, in terms of open access through gateways or essential facilities, and the imposition of must-carry requirements in relation to PSB transmissions. It also justifies behavioural regulation, especially in terms of addressing the abuse of dominant positions, and, perhaps, the need to guarantee journalistic independence so as to reduce the influence of either private owners or government. It may even justify public subsidy of media not otherwise economically viable, along the lines suggested by Curran and Seaton (1997) in relation to 'Civic Media' or already seen in Scandinavia (Humphreys 1996). It is clear that versions of some of these principles, though by no means all, have now been adopted in the UK under the framework established by the Communications Act 2003.

As should be apparent, there is no neat single answer to how the media regulation regime should be reformed. There is a place for structural regulation, given the contingent relationship between concentration in media ownership and lack of diversity in output. There is a place for behavioural regulation, in terms of restricting the ability of those controlling gateways to exercise undue influence, especially given that behavioural regulation may link more closely than structural regulation to the ultimate objective of achieving diversity in output. Clearly, a multi-track approach is indicated, utilising the market-oriented mechanisms of competition where appropriate but resorting without shame or hesitation to citizen-oriented public interest interventions when necessary. However, we would continue to argue that, to be effective, regulation must be focused upon a single organising principle, and if universal availability of diverse media output is adopted, then both structural and behavioural regulation must be viewed properly as merely surrogates for direct 'imperative' content regulation which focuses more clearly on the central issue and offers a more direct route to diversity.

This book has revolved around two central issues: conflicts between different rationales for media regulation, and a degree of concern regarding the use of discretion and accountability in its exercise. However, it is clear that both these tensions can be used to creative ends if activity is channelled towards a clear goal, and if the exercise of discretion is rendered accountable by making its exercise transparent and ensuring that it is properly 'confined, structured and checked'. In resolving these tensions, conceptual clarity is of the utmost importance.

The general trends identified by Hoffmann-Riem (1996: 340 *et seq.*), from cultural to economic emphasis, from freedom of communication to freedom of entrepreneurship in broadcasting, from comprehensive to limited regulatory responsibility and from programming-oriented (content) to allocation-oriented (licensing) regulation, form part of what he identified ten years ago as a paradigmatic shift in media regulation policy. Certainly, all these trends can still be observed in British regulation and in the reforms undertaken in the 1990s and in the Communications Act 2003. Though the legislative history may appear somewhat piecemeal and reactive, there is no doubt that these measures can now be seen in their totality to represent a fundamental change of emphasis in the regulatory machine, away from regulation for public service values and towards regulation of economic activity.

The changed view of the state and the extent of its legitimate activity brought about during the Thatcher and Major years and now accepted by the Blair government has introduced significant additional complications to an already confused agenda regarding media regulation. To borrow Osborne and Gaebler's terms (Osborne and Gaebler 1992), in many areas of public life, public bodies have moved away from 'rowing' (meaning the actual provision of services) to 'steering' (meaning control over the direction such services will take). But steering implies direction, and in the absence of clear objectives arising from a developed and articulated vision of value and principle, reform of the regulatory structure in this environment, even on as grand a scale as the introduction of Ofcom, might ultimately appear to be comparable with rearranging the deckchairs on *The Titanic* – it may provide a comforting impression of orderly activity and tidiness but will do nothing to avert impending disaster. In this sense, not only is the media not being rowed by public bodies, it may not even be steered on a safe and prudent course.

Reflecting in particular the fourth 'law job' identified in Chapter 1, Ranson and Stewart (1989: 12) state that:

> The public domain has to determine which activities are essential to maintain and develop the 'common-wealth'. It may be defending the boundaries of the realm, developing an efficient infrastructure for private transactions, or more actively pursuing the public purpose of an active citizenship.

Yet it is increasingly difficult to get a hearing for such arguments, and still harder to get such policies pursued by the government on behalf of the nation's people. The ideological predisposition of the New Labour governments has reflected the ongoing hegemony of the Thatcher/Reagan economic perspective, and even the quiet acceptance of a legacy summed up by Thatcher's classic reference to there being 'no such thing as society'. Indeed, modern social and political policy in Britain has increasingly confirmed a vision focused on individual interests and, more specifically, individual economic interests. In practice, the process is encapsulated in a symbiotic relationship between what Marquand (2004) discusses in terms of the decline of the public domain and Monbiot (2000) identifies as 'the captive state'. As the state has withdrawn from certain roles and activities in thrall to the power of the market, so powerful private corporate interests have come to dominate activities and functions once unarguably within the public domain. In such conditions, it becomes increasingly important, but simultaneously increasingly difficult, to argue for the legitimacy of state intervention as regards the outcomes of the exercise of corporate power.

In such a context, not only are tensions heightened between competing visions of public service and commercialism in broadcasting, but also a vigorous and robust regime of media regulation becomes more and more unlikely. Yet the idea of a legitimate public sphere must remain central both to the activities of the media, operating as a public resource, and to media regulators, whose activities are legitimated by reference to these purposes. Citizenship and democracy will not be protected if effective regulation of the media and meaningful accountability of the media and their regulators is not achieved, and this will not be achieved without the adoption and application of a clear, organising conceptual framework. Thus both substantive and procedural reform is indicated, but such reform must take into account a clear conceptual basis.

While it might be expected that constitutional values would provide such foundations, comparative evidence is somewhat inconclusive. In some countries, such as Germany and Italy, constitutions and statements from the respective constitutional courts appear at times to promise much but in practice they have failed to halt wholesale concentration of ownership in commercial media. In the US, there is even a sense in which the constitution appears to have served as an obstacle to intervention relating to the achievement of diversity in output, the constitutional guarantee of free speech, intended to protect the individual against the potential mighty power of the state, being called in aid by corporate media giants to resist regulation of their activities (Feintuck 2004: 141–52). This is what McChesney (1999) has powerfully described as the 'Commercialized First Amendment'. In Britain, the relevant constitutional values remain hopelessly ill-defined. However, while neither the existing arrangements nor the constitutional reform programme which the Labour government has undertaken provide straightforward answers to this problem, it can still be argued that both constitutional values and legal concepts may yet provide some limited assistance.

Discussing regulation of the airwaves in the US, McQuail notes that 'there is no doubt that the legislation, in the name of the "public interest", and in return for the grant of a licence to operate was intended to place the broadcaster in a position of public *trustee*' (1992: 50, original emphasis). Hoffmann-Riem (1992b: 46) states that the German Federal Constitutional Court 'apparently does not believe that private, market-oriented broadcasting can in the long run serve as a trustee for all societal interests and protect vulnerable values sufficiently, and it has therefore taken great pains to ensure such a lasting, trusteeship role for public broadcasting to provide sufficiently broad, high-quality programming for all sections of the population'. Elsewhere, Hoffmann-Riem (1996: 77) specifically attributes a concept of 'trusteeship' to the activities of the BBC and broadcasting regulators in Britain, though he describes (1996: 340) the recent paradigmatic shift in media regulation as being essentially away from the trustee model to a market model. The language of trusteeship is very pervasive and persistent in relation to PSB.

Curran and Seaton (2003: 367) quote the 1926 Crawford Report referring to the BBC in terms of 'a public corporation acting as trustee for the national interest'. Coming right up to date almost eighty years on, when launching the Charter Review Green Paper proposing the reformed governance structure for the BBC (discussed in Chapter 2), the Secretary of State Tessa Jowell stated that 'A BBC Trust will be the custodian of the BBC's purposes, the Licence Fee and the public interest' (DCMS Press Notice, 2 March 2005).

Though it has to be expected that none of the above statements necessarily intended the concept of 'trusteeship' to be understood in the peculiar sense attributed to it in English law, it is interesting to compare the implications of their statements with the meaning of legal trusteeship, which is very different to 'ownership' as generally understood.

Under a trust, a legal or natural person, a 'settlor', will grant property to trustees who will then hold this property *for the benefit of others*, specified in the trust deed as beneficiaries either individually or as a group. The trustee, by virtue of the fiduciary duties associated with the position, will be responsible to the beneficiaries for the maintenance of the value of the asset held and for payment to them of benefits as prescribed by the terms of the trust. Though essentially a private law concept, it is also applied in situations such as charitable and educational trusts, where large numbers of potential beneficiaries exist, and who will receive benefits as and when they come forward and are approved as being within the valid class of beneficiary as identified by the trustees or, in the case of dispute, the courts.

Examples of legal trusteeship do exist within the British media, most notably the Scott Trust, established in 1936 by the family of the former owner of the *Manchester Guardian*, to run what is now *The Guardian* and since its acquisition *The Observer*. In essence, the trust mechanism operates to preserve a degree of passivity in proprietorship, avoiding the degree of interference with editorial line sometimes associated with ownership (see Gibbons 1992).

However, the legal essence of a trust is that property is held *for the benefit of others*, the property subject to the trust being held by a body of trustees who exercise some though not all of the 'incidents of ownership' (Honoré 1987), and the legal concept of a trust is therefore difficult to apply in the context of the media as a whole. In relation to privately owned media, a legal trust will only occur if the existing owner chooses, voluntarily, to hand over property to trustees for the benefit of others; they cannot be forced to become unwilling settlors. Even in relation to a 'publicly owned' body such as the BBC, however, the legal concept of the trust is not readily applied, as the duties of the Board of Governors do not extend to the delivery of specific benefits to an identifiable group of specific individuals. The individualistic private property-based concept of the trust does not transfer easily into the context of public resources such as the media.

Though, therefore, the legal concept of trusteeship is not widely applicable in this context, the principle of exercising power over property for the benefit of others manifests itself also in a second concept: 'stewardship'. This appears to be hinted at by Gibbons (1992: 279), when argues that

> the special status of freedom of the press is based on its association with editorial autonomy and that, whatever grounds owners may have for resisting regulatory intervention, it will not be sufficient for them to assert their property rights. Indeed, it may be that the only way to protect freedom of the press is to limit those interests.

In the concept of 'stewardship' may be found an answer which avoids the legal complexities of trusteeship while emphasising the media's function as a public resource and the resultant public interest values. It acknowledges the 'right' of media owners to benefit from their private property while simultaneously pursuing Keane's agenda that 'communications media should be for the public use and enjoyment of all citizens and not for the private gain or profit of political rulers or businesses' (Keane 1991: 127).

In discussing the concept of stewardship, in the context of a discussion of theory of property in relation to the finite and non-renewable resource of land, Lucy and Mitchell (1996: 584) state that

> an abstract account of stewardship maintains that the holder, or steward, has some control and rights over the resource, but that control must in the main be exercised for the benefit of specific others. Since the steward's control must *in the main* be exercised in favour of others, it is not the case that he must be completely selfless, an island of altruism in a sea of self-interest. (Original emphasis)

The task of regulating the media has already been compared with that of managing a public asset considered unique, or at least finite and non-renewable, such as a National Park. In Britain, landowners in National Parks are placed under what amounts to a limited duty of stewardship, supervised by a planning authority whose explicit duty is to manage the potential conflicts of interest between those who own land in the area, those who want recreational access to the area and the conservation of the area's outstanding natural features for future generations. National

Park planning authorities in Britain are not granted ownership of all land in the area, but rather, in the interests of those of present and future generations who wish to use the area for recreation, powers to restrict the activities of those who do own the land, replacing what in Honoré's terms are the full set of 'incidents of ownership' with a more limited set of incidents of stewardship. Thus planning controls on building and industry are strictly enforced in such areas, while efforts will also be made to prevent or repair damage done to the area by the many visitors who will come each year.

The explicit objective of such a planning authority is to resolve the conflicts of these competing interests. The extent to which such conflicts are successfully resolved can be debated on a practical, technical, legal or theoretical level (for example, in relation to access to land see Barker 1994, and Barker and Lucy 1993), though there can be little doubt that the result better serves the perceived public interest than would a total absence of regulation, abandoning all to the unrestricted commercial property rights and interests of the landowner. Similarly, while the application of stewardship principles to the media would not resolve all existing challenges to regulation, it might assist substantially in breaking the contingent link between ownership and output.

Arguably, the media are at least as important to democracy and citizenship as conservation of our wild and open spaces and maintenance of access to them. As the mixed media economy appears to tend to privilege unduly the commercial and marginalise the public interest elements, it therefore seems necessary to reclaim some of this territory for the legitimate public interest. It is impossible, given the ongoing non-interventionist rhetoric of government, to imagine the present or any foreseeable government taking steps to nationalise or renationalise sectors of the economy in pursuit of public interest claims. However, it is possible to envisage a government, with citizenship explicitly at the centre of its agenda (or at least its rhetoric), imposing stewardship arrangements in relation to national assets that form essential aspects of citizenship and democracy.

Though digital technology has ended any scarcity of resources in the media, especially ended the frequency shortage justification for regulation, to argue for stewardship is not to revert to this argument. Rather, it is to recognise that in certain areas of media activity, for example technological gateways in DTT, the resource is effectively unique and finite, but also that, *as a whole*, the media form a unique democratic resource in which public interest as well as private property rights deserve recognition. We are all stakeholders in both National Parks and the media.

Though 'stewardship' is not a 'black letter' legal concept in English law, it is clearly embodied, in the context of National Parks, in the activities of planning authorities and the restrictions upon landowners enforced by them. In a sense it can also be seen in relation to the regulation of privatised utilities, where the activities of regulators serve to limit the freedom of companies to act entirely in pursuit of commercial interests. It can also be embodied in relation to more general restrictions on corporate governance of companies, suggested by some versions of 'corporate social responsibility' where the primary profit-maximisation duty of directors to shareholders can be tempered by measures demanding of the management of the company a degree of responsibility to the broader public (Whitehouse 2003).

It has been argued consistently in this book that the power and democratic significance of the media justify its regulation in the public interest. It can now be seen that there is nothing unique in this proposition which can also be applied to other large businesses:

> The reason large companies should be viewed as social enterprises relies, it is suggested, on a political theory about the legitimacy of private power. That theory holds that the possession of social decision-making power by companies is legitimate (that is, there are good reasons for regarding its possession as justified) only if this state of affairs is in the public interest. Since the public interest is the foundation of the legitimacy of companies, it follows that society is entitled to ensure that corporate power is exercised in a way that is consistent with that interest. To describe companies as social enterprises is thus to make a claim about the grounds of their legitimacy, and its practical significance is to hold that the state is entitled to prescribe the terms on which corporate power may be possessed and exercised. (Parkinson 1993: 23)

In relation to the media, the recognition of 'stewardship' obligations by those who regulate, and their enforcement on those who own and control, though it may appear a flimsy basis on which to regulate (having no hard legal foundation), serves precisely the function which has been identified as necessary throughout this book and reflects closely the social responsibility model of Siebert *et al.* (1956). It simultaneously acknowledges the rights of media owners to make profits, thereby avoiding any significant blight on entrepreneurship, while limiting their rights of ownership in pursuit of citizenship-related objectives such as universal access and diversity of output. It promotes the decommodification of the media and protects against the risks to citizenship, and therefore democracy, posed by exclusive ownership of key aspects of the public communication mechanisms. In the application of measures such as the essential facility doctrine in relation to gateways and bottlenecks in the digital infrastructure, as in the EU's New Regulatory Framework, and via the likes of must-carry requirements restricting the nature of private proprietorial power, the spirit of stewardship is already present in media regulation. Though introduced specifically in pursuit of market objectives, their origins (Feintuck 2004: 16–17), the genetic inheritance of these measures, perhaps relate closely to a vision of public interest very similar to that adopted in this book.

Stewardship-type duties can also be found in other aspects of regulatory activity in relation to the media, for example in the enforcement on licensed commercial broadcasters of positive programming and other licence requirements. There are, of course, problems which have already been identified in relation to the practical exercise of these powers; however, what is more important from the point of view of a stewardship-type agenda is that the remit is extended to apply to the media as a whole rather than discrete aspects of it.

Thus regulators, in enforcing a stewardship agenda, must be empowered to ensure that ownership, whether of broadcasting or print or both, in so far as it impacts on diversity of output, is not allowed to run counter to citizenship interests. In this sense, the strategic position and broad brief granted to Ofcom positions the regulator well in terms of undertaking such a task. However, and here is where Ofcom's brief may appear much less satisfactory, it also requires an acknowledgement that the public interest in the airwaves and other media demands at least as much recognition as commercial interests, and that the property rights of those who develop and own new technology must be limited by reference to the public interest in the media's role as a public resource. Again, the failure to prioritise sufficiently these interests among Ofcom's many and various objectives, duties and powers may be thought to render the regulator's foundations weak in relation to protecting such public interest concerns.

The principle of stewardship appears to offer a coherent foundation for the exercise of regulatory power in pursuit of citizenship-related public interests in the media. It helps to give effect to underlying constitutional values and fills a gap in the existing conceptual framework of law.

Those regulating to further stewardship of the media might legitimately be empowered to require corporate bodies to divest themselves of assets where their ownership of them is deemed to run counter to interests of citizenship, or to require the implementation of effective guarantees of editorial or journalistic independence from proprietorial interference, or, in order to support those broadcasters that continue to provide the full range of public service output, to impose financial levies on those who do not offer a full range of programme services or do not make them universally available. The regulators might also be permitted to allocate public funds to subsidise new or existing media which serve to extend the range of media output.

All of this presupposes, however, the acknowledgement and adoption of citizenship as the logical, legitimate, central organising principle for the democratic endeavour of media regulation. In more concrete terms, this would require spelling out, via the imposition on regulators of a primary and predominant duty to act in pursuit of, and justify their actions in terms of, the furtherance of universal access to a diverse range of media output. At the same time, it must be accepted that ownership of the media, so essential a part of the fabric of democracy, must not be subject to the full power of private ownership, but rather to a stewardship model, reflecting the public interest. While such reform might appear revolutionary, it does not require the total abandonment of all existing regulation, but merely a refocusing of the entire mechanism onto the clear and unambiguous objective of citizenship. In this sense, the potential of a public interest principle which is premised directly upon expectations of citizenship may serve, as suggested in Chapter 3, as an 'interpretative principle', making connections between regulatory practice and the democratic value-base, and re-establishing a regulatory focus on underlying but often under-enforced constitutional norms (Sunstein 1990; Feintuck 2004, 188–94). In the absence of clarity regarding these fundamental values, regulation will remain unfocused and essentially reactive to technological change and commercial development, resulting in uncertainty and *ad hoc* responses which confirm rather than challenge the hegemony of market forces.

Unfortunately, it may be that the opportunity offered in the course of the passage of the Communications Act 2003, opened up especially by the Puttnam Report, has now been missed, at least at the statutory level. While the opportunity to enshrine such values in legislation will almost certainly not present again for some considerable time, this is not to say that Ofcom could not develop such a position for itself. Within its statutory brief, it seems perfectly possible for the regulator to develop policies which absorb and reflect such an approach, which embody a meaningful vision of public interest. While the omens do not look good in such a respect given the dominance of market-driven perspectives, a truly independent regulator may yet choose to resist on appropriate occasions. Only time will tell.

In the first edition of this book, it was argued that the then present circumstances, of ongoing revolutionary change in the media and the degree of constitutional change occurring in Britain, appeared to form precisely the conjunction of events identified by Blumler and Gurevitch (1995: 204) as representing the opportunity for a fundamental overhaul of regulatory arrangements and the replacement of ill-suited and poorly structured, historically contingently designed institutions with a new generation of regulator appropriate to the modern context and equipped with a clear overarching philosophy. The law, like other aspects of media regulation, had developed in an incremental and pragmatic fashion, and the potential it offered for providing procedural and substantive fairness and support for fundamental constitutional and democratic principles had hardly begun to be harnessed.

While the ongoing media revolution did in 1999, and still does in 2006, offer the conditions in which it is possible for change to be 'captured' by the state and forced into the service of the public interest or of citizenship, the absence in Britain of a developed concept of the state, and therefore public law (Prosser 1982) or even public service (Prosser 1997: 287), forms a major obstacle to this task, given the significant relationship noted by Humphreys (1996) between media regulation and historical, constitutional tradition. Prior to 2003 we argued that the move to a single, unified media/communications regulator, even assuming its operation to be adequately transparent and accountable, along the lines suggested by Collins and Murroni would be unlikely to be of assistance, unless it was accompanied by a fundamental reappraisal of the conceptual basis for regulation. In this sense, the Communications Act 2003 came very close to delivering, but ultimately looks to have fallen short of our hopes and expectations. While offering supportive words to the public interest in citizenship, it does not guarantee protection for these values via law. It does not exclude regulatory intervention in pursuit of such objectives, but unfortunately the realities suggest that the economics of the market will be prioritised and citizenship values marginalised.

In 1999 the first edition of this book concluded by arguing that:

> The opportunity must be taken now, to reinvest the media regulation process with purpose and legitimacy, via overt recognition of the public interest in the universal provision of a wide range of quality media output. In pursuit via regulation of citizenship objectives, however, it is crucial to ensure that the regulatory process meets the highest standards of transparency and accountability. If this opportunity is missed, there can be little doubt that the last remnants of diversity in the press, and what remains of the uniquely valuable, PSB

tradition in Britain will be lost to future generations, and along with them will be lost a crucial element of democracy.

There would be little satisfaction to be had from being proved right in this respect. Unfortunately, it is probably fair to conclude now that the PSB tradition, and the values of citizenship and democracy which it served, are no safer now than they were before the Communications Act 2003.

References

Abel, R. (1994) *Speech and Respect*. London: Sweet & Maxwell.

Ainsworth, L. and Weston, D. (1995) 'Newspapers and UK Media Ownership Controls', *Media Law and Practice*, p. 2.

Amato, G. (1997) *Antitrust and the Bounds of Power*. Oxford: Hart Publishing.

Annan Report (1977) *Report of the Committee on the Future of Broadcasting*, Cmnd 6753. London: HMSO.

Areeda, P. (1990) 'Essential Facilities: An Epithet in Need of Limiting Principles', *Antitrust Law Journal*, vol. 58, p. 841.

Ariño, M. (2004) 'Digital War and Peace: Regulation and Competition in Digital Broadcasting', *European Public Law*, vol. 10, p. 135.

Ayers, I. and Braithwaite, J. (1992) *Responsive Regulation: Transcending the Deregulation Debate*. Oxford: Clarendon Press.

Bagdikian, B. (2004) *The Media Monopoly*. Boston: Beacon Press.

Baldwin, R. (1995) *Rules and Government*. Oxford: Clarendon Press.

Baldwin, R. and Cave, M. (1999) *Understanding Regulation*. Oxford: Oxford University Press.

Baldwin, R. and Hawkins, K. (1984) 'Discretionary Justice: Davis Reconsidered', *Public Law*, p. 570.

Baldwin, R. and McCrudden, C. (1987) *Regulation and Public Law*. London: Weidenfeld & Nicolson.

Baldwin, R., Scott, C. and Hood, C. (eds) (1998) *A Reader on Regulation*. Oxford: Oxford University Press.

Barbalet, J. (1988) *Citizenship*. Milton Keynes: Open University Press.

Barber, N. W. (2005) 'The Limited Modesty of Subsidiarity', *European Law Journal*, vol. 11, p. 308.

Barbrook, R. (1995) *Media Freedom: The Contradictions of Communications in the Age of Modernity*. London: Pluto Press.

Barendt, E. (1985) *Freedom of Speech*. Oxford: Clarendon Press.

Barendt, E. (1991) 'The Influence of the German and Italian Constitutional Courts on Their National Broadcasting Systems', *Public Law*, p. 93.

Barendt, E. (1995) *Broadcasting Law: A Comparative Study*. Oxford: Clarendon Press.

Barendt, E. M. and Hitchens, L. P. (2000) *Media Law: Text, Cases and Materials*. London: Longman.

Barker, F. (1994) *'Private Property, Public Access – A Critique of the Legal Framework Governing the Enforcement and Exercise of Public Rights of Access to Land'*. Unpublished PhD thesis, University of Hull.

Barker, F. and Lucy, W. (1993) 'Justifying Property and Justifying Access', *Canadian Journal of Law and Jurisprudence*, p. 287.

Bartosch, A. (1999) 'The Financing of Public Broadcasting and EC State Aid Law: An Interim Balance', *European Competition Law Review*, vol. 20, p. 197.

Bavasso, A. F. (2002) 'Public Service Broadcasting and State Aid Rules: Between a Rock and a Hard Place' *European Law Review*, vol. 23, p. 340.

Bavasso, A. F. (2003) *Communications in EU Antitrust Law: Market Power and Public Interest*. The Hague: Kluwer.

BBC (2003) *BBC Goes in the Clear on Digital Satellite*. London: BBC. Available at: http://www.bbc.co.uk/pressoffice/pressreleases/stories/2003/03_march/12/digital_sat.shtml (last accessed 30 December 2005).

BBC (2004a) *Annual Report and Accounts 2003/2004*. London: BBC.

BBC (2004b) *Building Public Value: Renewing the BBC for a Digital World*. London: BBC.

BBC (2004c) *Consultation on the Regulation of Electronic Programme Guides: BBC Response*. London: BBC. Available at: http://www.ofcom.org.uk/consultations/responses/epc/responses/bbc.pdf (last accessed 20 May 2005).

BBC (2005) *Annual Report and Accounts 2004/2005*. London: BBC.

Bell, J. (1993) 'Public Interest: Policy or Principle?', in Brownsword, R. (ed.), *Law and the Public Interest* (Proceedings of the 1992 ALSP Conference). Stuttgart: Franz Steiner.

Bergman, M. A. (2001) 'The Role of the Essential Facilities Doctrine', *The Antitrust Bulletin*, vol. 46, p. 403.

Better Regulation Task Force (BRTF) (2003) *Independent Regulators*, London: BRTF.

Birkinshaw, P. (1993) ' "I Only Ask for Information" – The White Paper on Open Government', *Public Law*, p. 557.

Birkinshaw, P. (1994) *Grievances, Remedies and the State*, 2nd edn. London: Sweet & Maxwell.

Birkinshaw, P. (2001) *Freedom of Information: The Law, the Practice and the Ideal*, 3rd edn. London: Butterworths.

Birkinshaw, P. (2003) *European Public Law*. London: LexisNexis.

Birkinshaw, P. (2005), *Government and Information: The Law Relating to Access, Disclosure and Their Regulation*. Haywards Heath: Tottel Publishing.

Birkinshaw, P., Harden, I. and Lewis, N. (1990) *Government by Moonlight: The Hybrid Parts of the State*. London: Unwin Hyman.

Bishop, S. and Walker, M. (2002) *The Economics of EC Competition Law*, 2nd edn. London: Sweet & Maxwell.

Black, J. M. (1996) 'Constitutionalising Self-Regulation', *Modern Law Review*, vol. 59, p. 24.

Black, J. M. (2000) 'Proceduralizing Regulation – Part I', *Oxford Journal of Legal Studies*, vol. 20, p. 597.

Black, J. M. (2001) 'Proceduralizing Regulation – Part II', *Oxford Journal of Legal Studies*, vol. 21, p. 33.

Black, J. M. (2002) *Critical Reflections on Regulation*, Centre for the Analysis of Risk and Regulation Discussion Paper No. 4. Available at: http://www.lse.ac.uk/collections/CARR/pdf/Disspaper4.pdf (last accessed 30 December 2005).

Blom-Cooper, L. and Pruitt, L. R. (1994) 'Privacy Jurisprudence of the Press Complaints Commission', *Anglo-American Law Review*, p. 133.

Blumler, J. (ed.) (1992a), *Television and the Public Interest: Vulnerable Values in West European Broadcasting*. London: Sage.

Blumler, J. (1992b) 'Introduction: Current Confrontations in West European Television', in Blumler, J. (ed.), *Television and the Public Interest: Vulnerable Values in West European Broadcasting*. London: Sage.

Blumler, J. and Gurevitch, M. (1995) *The Crisis of Public Communication*. London: Routledge.

Blumler, J. and Madge, J. (1967) *Citizenship and Television*. London: PEP.

Bollinger, L. (1990) 'Freedom of the Press and Public Access', in Lichtenberg, J. (ed.), *Democracy and the Mass Media*. Cambridge: Cambridge University Press.

Bork, R. H. (1978) *The Antitrust Paradox: A Policy at War with Itself*. New York and London: Free Press.

Born, G. and Prosser, T. (2001) 'Culture and Consumerism: Citizenship, Public Service Broadcasting and the BBC's Fair Trading Obligations', *Modern Law Review*, vol. 64, p. 657.

Borrie, G. (2005) 'CSR and Advertising Self-Regulation', *Consumer Policy Review*, vol. 15, no. 2, p. 64.

Bratton, W. *et al.* (1996) 'Introduction: Regulatory Competition and Institutional Evolution', in Bratton, W. *et al.* (eds), *International Regulatory Competition and Co-ordination*. Oxford: Clarendon Press.

Briggs, A. (1985) *The BBC: The First Fifty Years*. Oxford: Oxford University Press.

Broadcast Committee of Advertising Practice (BCAP) (2005a) *Television Advertising Standards Code*. London: BCAP. Available at: http://www.asa.org.uk/NR/rdonlyres/89548571-FA23–4642-B04D-8812C58D9FF3/0/BCAP_Television_Advertising_Standards_Code.pdf (last accessed 30 December 2005).

Broadcast Committee of Advertising Practice (BCAP) (2005b) *Advertising Guidance Notes 1–6*. London: BCAP. Available at: http://www.asa.org.uk/NR/rdonlyres/0FE76E96-E485–4775-B12B-E860C7CCCCD7/0/BCAP_Advertising_Guidance_Notes.pdf (last accessed 30 December 2005).

Broadcasting Policy Group (2004) *Beyond the Charter: The BBC After 2006*. London: Premium Publishing.

Calcutt, D. (1990) *Report of the Committee on Privacy and Related Matters*, Cm. 1102. London: HMSO.

Calcutt, D. (1993) *Review of Press Self-Regulation*, Cm. 2135. London: HMSO.

Carter, E. J. (2001) 'Market Definition in the Broadcasting Sector', *World Competition*, vol. 24, no. 1, p. 93.

Cartlidge, H. and Mendia Lara, F. (2005) 'End of Season for the Premier League?', *New Law Journal*, vol. 155, p. 1881.

Cary, A. (1993) 'Subsidiarity – Essence or Antidote to the European Union', in Duff, A. (ed.), *Subsidiarity in the European Community*. London: Federal Trust.

Cave, M. (2002) *Review of Radio Spectrum Management*. London: Department of Trade and Industry.

Cave, M., Collins, R. and Crowther, P. (2004) 'Regulating the BBC', *Telecommunications Policy*, vol. 28, p. 249.

Channel 4 Corporation (C4C) (2004) *Channel 4 Television Corporation Report and Financial Statements 2004*. London: C4C.

Charlesworth, A. and Cullen, H. (1996) 'Under My Wheels: Issues of Access and Social Exclusion on the Information Superhighway', *International Review of Law, Computers and Technology*, vol. 10, no. 1, p. 27.

Charny, D. (1991) 'Competition Among Jurisdictions in Formulating Corporate Law Rules', *Harvard Journal of International Law*, vol. 32, p. 423.

Clark, B. (1940) 'Towards a Concept of Workable Competition', *American Economic Review*, vol. 30, p. 241.

Coad, J. (2003) 'The Press Complaints Commission: Some Myths about Self-Regulation', *Entertainment Law Review*, vol. 14, p. 211.

Coad, J. (2005) 'The Press Complaints Commission: Are We Safe in its Hands?', *Entertainment Law Review*, vol. 16, p. 163.

Coase, R. H. (1959) 'The Federal Communications Commission', *Journal of Law and Economics*, vol. 11, p. 1.

Coleman, F. and McMurtrie, S. (1995) 'Red Hot Television: Domestic and International Legal Aspects of the Regulation of Satellite Television', *European Public Law*, vol. 1, no. 2, p. 201.

Collins, H. (1999) *Regulating Contracts*. Oxford: Oxford University Press.

Collins, H. (2003) 'Introduction: The Research Agenda of Implicit Dimensions of Contracts', in Campbell, D. et al. (eds), *The Implicit Dimensions of Contract: Discrete, Relational and Network Contracts*. Oxford: Hart Publishing.

Collins, R. (ed.) (1996) *Converging Media? Converging Regulation?* London: IPPR.

Collins, R. and Murroni, C. (1996) *New Media, New Policies*. Cambridge: Polity Press.

Committee on Standards in Public Life (CSPL) (2005a) *The Seven Principles of Public Life*. London: Committee on Standards in Public Life. Available at: http://www.public-standards.gov.uk/about_us/seven _principles.htm (last accessed 22 December 2005).

Committee on Standards in Public Life (CSPL) (2005b) *Getting the Balance Right: Implementing Standards of Conduct in Public Life – Tenth Report*, Cm 6407. London: Stationery Office. Available at: http://www.public-standards.gov.uk/10thinquiry/report/Graham%20Tenth%20Report.pdf (last accessed 30 December 2005).

Congdon, T., Graham, A., Green, D. and Robinson, B. (1995) *The Cross Media Revolution: Ownership and Control*. London: John Libbey.

Cox, B. (2004) *Free For All? Public Service Television in the Digital Age*. London: Demos.

Craufurd-Smith, R. (2001) 'State Support for Public Service Broadcasting: The Position under European Community Law', *Legal Issues of Economic Integration*, vol. 28, p. 3.

Craufurd-Smith, R. (2004) 'Community Intervention in the Cultural Field: Continuity or Change?', in Craufurd-Smith, R. (ed.), *Culture and European Union Law*. Oxford: Oxford University Press.

Craufurd-Smith, R. and Böttcher, B. (2002) 'Football and Fundamental Rights: Regulating Access to Major Sporting Events on Television', *European Public Law*, vol. 8, p. 107.

Criscuolo, A. (1998) 'The "TV Without Frontiers Directive", and the Legal Regulation of Publicity in the European Community', *European Law Review*, vol. 23, p. 357.

Culture, Media and Sport Committee (2005) *A Public BBC: Volume II – Oral and Written Evidence*, HC 82-II. London: HMSO.

Curran, J. and Seaton, J. (1997) *Power Without Responsibility: The Press and Broadcasting in Britain*, 5th edn. London: Routledge.

Curran, J. and Seaton, J. (2003) *Power Without Responsibility: The Press, Broadcasting and New Media in Britain*, 6th edn. London: Routledge.

Dahlgren, P. (1995) *Television and the Public Sphere: Citizenship, Democracy and the Media*. London: Sage.

Daintith, T. (1979) 'Regulation by Contract: The New Prerogative', *Current Legal Problems*, p. 41.

Daintith, T. (1994) 'The Techniques of Government', in Jowell, J. L. and Oliver, D. (eds), *The Changing Constitution*, 3rd edn. Oxford: Clarendon Press.

Davis, K. C. (1971) *Discretionary Justice: a Preliminary Inquiry*. Urbana, IL: University of Illinois Press.

Day, P. and Klein, R. (1987) *Accountabilities*. London and New York: Tavistock.

De Búrca, G. (1998) 'The Principle of Subsidiarity and the Court of Justice as an Institutional Actor', *Journal of Common Market Studies*, vol. 36, p. 217.

De Witte, B. (1995) 'The European Content Requirement in the EC Television Directive – Five Years After', in Barendt, E. M. (ed.), *The Yearbook of Media and Entertainment Law*. Oxford: Clarendon Press, vol. 1, p. 101.

Department of Culture Media and Sport (DCMS) (1996) *Guide to Schedule 2, Broadcasting Act 1996*. Available at: http://www.culture.gov.uk/m1.htm.

Department of Culture, Media and Sport (DCMS) (1998a) *Television: The Digital Future*. Available at: http://www.culture.gov.uk/CONS.htm.

Department of Culture, Media and Sport (DCMS) (1998b) *A Study to Estimate the Economic Impact of Government Policies Towards Digital Television*. Available at: http://www.culture.gov.uk/NERA.htm.

Department for Culture, Media and Sport (DCMS) (2003) *Copy of the Amendment dated 4th December 2003 to the Agreement of 25th Day of January 1996 (as amended) Between Her Majesty's Secretary of State for Culture, Media and Sport and the British Broadcasting Corporation*. London: Department of Culture, Media and Sport. Available at: http://www.bbc.co.uk/info/policies/charter/pdf/agreement_amend.pdf (last accessed 30 December 2005).

Department of Culture, Media and Sport (DCMS) (2004a) *A Guide to Digital Television and Digital Switchover*. London: DCMS.

Department of Culture, Media and Sport (DCMS) (2004b) *Digital Television Action Plan – Version 12*, London: DCMS.

Department of Culture, Media and Sport (DCMS) (2005) *Review of the BBC's Royal Charter: A Strong BBC, Independent of Government*, Green Paper. London: DCMS.

Department for Education and Skills (2005) *Higher Standards, Better Schools For All*, White Paper, Cm 6677. London: HMSO.

Department of National Heritage (DNH) (1995a) *Media Ownership: The Government's Proposals*, White Paper, Cm. 2872. London: HMSO.

Department of National Heritage (DNH) (1995b) *Privacy and Media Intrusion*, White Paper, Cm. 2918. London: HMSO.

Department of National Heritage (DNH) (1995c) *Digital Terrestrial Broadcasting: The Government's Proposals*, White Paper, Cm. 2946. London: HMSO.

Department for National Heritage (DNH) (1996) *Copy of the Agreement Dated the 25th January 1996 Between Her Majesty's Secretary of State for National Heritage and the British Broadcasting Corporation*. London: Department for National Heritage. Available at: http://www.bbc.co.uk/info/policies/charter/pdf/agreement.pdf (last accessed 30 December 2005).

Department of Trade and Industry (DTI) (1996) *Spectrum Management: Into the 21st Century*, White Paper, Cm. 3252. London: HMSO.

Department of Trade and Industry (DTI) (2004) *Enterprise Act 2002: Public Interest Intervention in Media Mergers*. London: Department of Trade and Industry. Available at: http://www.dti.gov.uk/ccp/topics2/guide/ukmediaguide.pdf (last accessed 30 December 2005).

Doherty, B. (2001) 'Just What Are Essential Facilities?', *Common Market Law Review*, vol. 38, p. 397.

Dougan, M. (2000) 'Minimum Harmonization and the Single Market', *Common Market Law Review*, vol. 37, p. 853.

Dovey, J. (1995) 'Access Television', in Dowmunt, T. (ed.), *Channels of Resistance: Global Television and Local Empowerment*. London: Channel 4/BFI.

Dowmunt, T. (ed.) (1995) *Channels of Resistance: Global television and Local Empowerment*. London: Channel 4/BFI.

Doyle, G. (1997) 'From "Pluralism" to "Ownership": Europe's emergent policy on Media Concentrations Navigates the Doldrums', *Journal of Information, Law and Technology*. Available at: http://elj.warwick.ac.uk/jilt/commsreg/97_3doyl/.

Doyle, G. (2002) *Media Ownership*. London: Sage.

Drijber, B. J. (1999) 'The Revised Television Without Frontiers Directive: Is It Fit for the Next Century?', *Common Market Law Review*, vol. 36, p. 87.

Dryzek, J. (2000) *Deliberative Democracy and Beyond: Liberals, Critics, Contestations*. Oxford: Oxford University Press.

Ehrlich, E. (1922) 'The Sociology of Law', *Harvard Law Review*, vol. 36, p. 130.

Eldridge, J., Kitzinger, J. and Williams, K. (1997) *The Mass Media and Power in Modern Britain*. Oxford: Oxford University Press.

Elliot, M. (1981) 'Chasing the Receding Bus: The Broadcasting Act 1980', *Modern Law Review*, p. 683.

Estella, A. (2002) *The EU Principle of Subsidiarity and Its Critique*. Oxford: Oxford University Press.

Esty, D. C. (2000) 'Regulatory Competition in Focus', *Journal of International Economic Law*, vol. 3, p. 215.

Esty, D. C. and Geradin, D. (2001) 'Regulatory Co-Opetition', in Esty, D. C. and Geradin, D. (eds), *Regulatory Competition and Economic Integration: Comparative Perspectives*. Oxford: Oxford University Press.

European Audiovisual Observatory (2004) *Transfrontier Television in the European Union: Market Impact and Selected Legal Impacts*. Strasbourg: European Audiovisual Observatory. Available at: http://www.obs.coe.int/online_publication/transfrontier_tv.pdf.en (last accessed 30 December 2005).

European Commission (1992) *Pluralism and Media Concentration in the Internal Market: An Assessment of the Need for Community Action*, Com. (1992) 480.

European Commission (1994) *Follow-up to the Consultation Process Relating to the Green Paper on Pluralism and Media Concentration in the Internal Market – An Assessment of the Need for Community Action*, Com. (1994) 353.

European Commission (1997) *Towards an Information Society Approach*. Available at: http://www.ispo.cec.be/convergenceg.

European Commission (2002a) *Commission Guidelines on Market Analysis and the Assessment of Significant Market Power under the Community Regulatory Framework for Electronic Communications Networks and Services*, [2002] OJ C 165/06.

European Commission (2002b) *Must-Carry Obligations under the 2003 Regulatory Framework for Electronic Communications Networks and*

Services. Brussels: Commission of the European Communities. Available at: http://europa.eu.int/information_society/topics/telecoms/regulatory/digital_ broadcasting/documents/onp_dbeg_doc_re_must_carry.pdf (last accessed 30 December 2005).

European Commission (2003) *Fourth Report of the Commission to the Council, The European Parliament, The European Economic and Social Committee and the Committee of the Regions on the Application of Directive 89/552/EEC – 'Television Without Frontiers'*, COM (2002) 778. Brussels: Commission of the European Communities.

European Commission (2004a) *Communication from the Commission: A Pro-Active Competition Policy for a Competitive Europe*, COM (2004) 293. Brussels: Commission of the European Communities.

European Commission (2004b) *Sixth Communication from the Commission to the Council and the European Parliament on the Application of Articles 4 and 5 of Directive 89/552/EEC 'Television Without Frontiers', as amended by Directive 97/36/EC, for the Period 2001–2002*, COM (2004) 524. Brussels: Commission of the European Communities. Available at: http://europa. eu.int/eur-lex/lex/LexUriServ/site/en/com/2004/com2004_0524en01.pdf (last accessed 30 December 2005).

European Commission (2004c) *Commission Staff Working Paper: Annex to the European Electronic Communications Regulation and Markets 2004 (10th Report)*, SEC (2004) 1535. Brussels: Commission of the European Communities.

European Commission (2005a) *Issues Paper for the Liverpool Audiovisual Conference: Cultural Diversity and the Promotion of European and Independent Audiovisual Production*. Brussels: Commission of the European Communities. Available at: http://europa.eu.int/comm/avpolicy/revision-tvwf2005/ispa_cultdiv_en.pdf (last accessed 30 December 2005).

European Commission (2005b) *Issues Paper for the Liverpool Audiovisual Conference: Rules Applicable to Audiovisual Content Services*. Brussels: Commission of the European Communities. Available at: http://europa.eu. int/comm/avpolicy/revision-tvwf2005/ispa_scope_en.pdf (last accessed 30 December 2005).

European Commission (2005c) *Community Framework for State Aid in the Form of Public Service Compensation*. Brussels: Commission of the European Communities. Available at: http://europa.eu.int/comm/competition/state_aid/ others/public_service_comp/en.pdf (last accessed 30 December 2005).

European Parliament (2003) *Report on Television Without Frontiers*, Document A5-0251/2003. Brussels: European Union.

European Parliament (2005) *Report on the Application of Articles 4 and 5 of Directive 89/552/EEC, as amended by Directive 97/36/EC, for the Period 2001–2002*, Document A6-0202/2005. Brussels: European Union.

Feintuck, M. (1994) *Accountability and Choice in Schooling*. Buckingham: Open University Press.

Feintuck, M. (1995) 'Good News for the Media? Developments in Regulating Media Ownership in Britain and Europe', *European Public Law*, vol. 1, no. 4, p. 549.

Feintuck, M. (1997a) 'Regulating the Bogey Man', *Utilities Law Review*, p. 29.

Feintuck, M. (1997b) 'The UK Broadcasting Act 1996: A Holding Operation?', *European Public Law*, vol. 3, no. 2, p. 201.

Feintuck, M. (1997c) 'Regulating the Media Revolution: In Search of the Public Interest', *Journal of Information, Law and Technology*. Available at: http://elj.warwick.ac.uk/jilt/commsreg/97_3fein/.

Feintuck, M. (2003) 'Walking the High-Wire: The UK's Draft Communications Bill', *European Public Law*, vol. 9, no. 1, p. 105.

Feintuck, M. (2004) *The 'Public Interest' in Regulation*. Oxford: Oxford University Press.

Feldman, D. (ed.) (2004) *English Public Law*. Oxford: Oxford University Press.

Fenwick, H. and Phillipson, G. (2000) 'Breach of Confidence as a Privacy Remedy in the Human Rights Act Era', *Modern Law Review*, vol. 63, p. 660.

Ferguson, M. (ed.) (1990) *Public Communication: the New Imperatives*. London: Sage.

Fletcher, R. (2002) 'Good Faith or a Contagious Disease of Foreign Origin?', *Business Law Review*, p. 5.

Føllesdal, A. (1998) 'Survey Article: Subsidiarity', *Journal of Political Philosophy*, vol. 6, p. 190.

Footer, M. E. and Beat-Graber, C. (2000) 'Trade Liberalization and Cultural Policy', *Journal of International Economic Law*, vol. 3, p. 115.

Fordham, M. (2004) *Judicial Review Handbook*, 4th edn. Oxford: Hart Publishing.

Foster, R. (1992) *Public Broadcasters: Accountability and Efficiency*. Edinburgh: Edinburgh University Press.

Fried, C. (1982) *Contract as a Promise: A Theory of Contractual Obligations*. Cambridge, MA: Harvard University Press.

Gamble, A. (1994) *The Free Economy and the Strong State: The Politics of Thatcherism*. Basingstoke: Macmillan.

Garzaniti, L. J. H. F. (2003) *Telecommunications, Broadcasting and the Internet: EU Competition Law and Regulation*, 2nd edn. London: Sweet & Maxwell.

Gibbons, T. (1991) *Regulating the Media*. London: Sweet & Maxwell.

Gibbons, T. (1992) 'Freedom of the Press: Ownership and Editorial Values', *Public Law*, p. 279.

Gibbons, T. (1996) 'Commentary on the Broadcasting Act 1996', *Current Law Statutes Annotated*. London: Sweet & Maxwell.

Gibbons, T. (1998) *Regulating the Media*, 2nd edn. London: Sweet & Maxwell.

Goh, J. (1997) *European Air Transport Law and Competition*. Chichester: Wiley.

Goldberg, D. and Verhulst, S. (1997) 'Legal Responses to Regulating the Changing Media in the UK', *Utilities Law Review*, p. 97.

Golding, P. (1990) 'Political Communication and Citizenship: The Media and Democracy in an Inegalitarian Social Order', in Ferguson, M. (ed.), *Public Communication: the New Imperatives*. London: Sage.

Graham, C. (1994) 'Self-Regulation', in Genn, H. and Richardson, G. (eds), *Administrative Law and Government Action*. Oxford: Clarendon.

Graham, C. (2000) *Regulating Public Utilities: A Constitutional Approach*. Oxford: Hart.

Graham, C. and Prosser, T. (eds) (1988) *Waiving the Rules: The Constitution Under Thatcherism*. Milton Keynes: Open University Press.

Grantham, B. (2004) 'Cultural "Patronage" versus Cultural "Defence": Alternatives to National Film Policies', in Moran, L. J., Sandon, E., Loizidou, E. and Christie, I. (eds), *Law's Moving Image*. London: Glasshouse.

Grimm, D. (1995) 'Does Europe Need a Constitution?', *European Law Journal*, vol. 1, p. 282.

Hall, S., Chritcher, C., Jefferson, T., Clarke, J. and Roberts, B. (1978) *Policing the Crisis: Mugging, the State, and Law and Order*. Basingstoke: Macmillan.

Hamelink, C. (1995) 'The Democratic Ideal and Its Enemies', in Lee, P. (ed.), *The Democratization of Communication*. Cardiff: University of Wales Press, pp. 15–37.

Hancher, L. and Moran, M. (1989) 'Organising Regulatory Space', in Hancher, L. and Moran, M. (eds), *Capitalism, Culture and Economic Regulation*. Oxford: Clarendon Press.

Harcourt, A. (1996) 'Regulating for Media Concentration: the Emerging Policy of the European Union', *Utilities Law Review*, p. 202.

Harcourt, A. J. (2005) *The European Union and the Regulation of Media Markets*. Manchester: Manchester University Press.

Harden, I. and Lewis, N. (1986) *The Noble Lie: The British Constitution and the Rule of Law*. London: Hutchinson.

Harlow, C. and Rawlings, R. (1997) *Law and Administration*, 2nd edn. London: Butterworths.

Hatzopoulos, V. (2000) 'Recent Developments in the Case Law of the European Court of Justice in the Field of Services', *Common Market Law Review*, vol. 37, p. 43.

Helberger, N. (2002) *Access to Technical Bottleneck Facilities: The New European Approach*. University of Amsterdam: Institute for Information Law. Available at: http://www.ivir.nl/publications/helberger/C&S2002.html (last accessed 1 August 2005).

Helberger, N., van Eijk, N. A. N. M. and Hugenholtz, P. B. (2000) *Study on the Use of Conditional Access Systems for Reasons Other than the Protection of Remuneration, to Examine the Legal and the Economic Implications within the Internal Market and the Need of Introducing Specific Legal Protection*. Amsterdam: Institute for Information Law. Available at: http://www.ivir.nl/publications/other/ca-report.pdf (last accessed 1 August 2005).

Held, V. (1970) *The Public Interest and Individual Interests*. New York: Basic Books.

Herman, E. and McChesney, R. (1997) *The Global Media*. London: Cassell.

Herold, A. (2003) 'European Public Film Support in the WTO Framework', *IRIS Plus*, issue 2003–6. Available at: http://www.obs.coe.int/oea_publ/iris/iris_plus/iplus6_2003.pdf.en (last accessed 10 December 2005).

Hertz, N. (2002) *The Silent Takeover: Global Capitalism and the Death of Democracy*. London: Arrow Books.

Hitchens, L. (1994) 'Media Ownership and Control: A European Approach', *Modern Law Review*, p. 585.

Hitchens, L. (1995a) ' "Get Ready, Fire, Take Aim". The Regulation of Cross Media Ownership – An Exercise in Policy-Making', *Public Law*, p. 620.

Hitchens, L. (1995b) 'Fit to Broadcast? Fit to Decide?', *Media Law and Practice*, vol. 16, no. 3, p. 115.

Hoffmann-Riem, W. (1992a) 'Defending Vulnerable Values: Regulatory Measures and Enforcement Dilemmas', in Blumler, J. (ed.), *Television and the Public Interest: Vulnerable Values in West European Broadcasting*. London: Sage.

Hoffmann-Riem, W. (1992b) 'Protecting Vulnerable Values in the German Broadcasting Order', in Blumler, J. (ed.), *Television and the Public Interest: Vulnerable Values in West European Broadcasting*. London: Sage.

Hoffmann-Riem, W. (1996) *Regulating Media: The Licensing and Supervision of Broadcasting in Six Countries*. New York: Guilford Press.

Hogan, D. (1997) 'The Logic of Protection: Citizenship, Justice and Political Community', in Kennedy, K. (ed.), *Citizenship Education and the Modern State*. London: Falmer.

Holmes, J. (2004) 'European Community Law and the Cultural Aspects of Television', in Craufurd-Smith, R. (ed.), *Culture and European Union Law*. Oxford: Oxford University Press.

Home Affairs Committee (1988) *Third Report of the Home Affairs Committee's Inquiry into The Future of Broadcasting*, HC Paper 262, Session 1987–88.

Home Office (1997a) *Rights Brought Home: The Human Rights Bill*, White Paper. Cm 3782. London: HMSO.

Home Office (1997b) *Your Right to Know: Freedom of Information*, White Paper. Cm 3818. London: HMSO.

Hondius, F. (1988) 'Regulating Transfrontier Television: The Strasbourg Option', *Yearbook of European Law*, vol. 8, p. 141.

Honoré, A. (1961) 'Ownership', in Guest, A. G. (ed.), *Oxford Essays in Jurisprudence: A Collaborative Work*. Oxford: Oxford University Press.

Honoré, A. (1987) *Making Law Bind*. Oxford: Clarendon Press.

Humphreys, P. (1994) *Media and Media Policy in Germany: The Press and Broadcasting Since 1945*. Oxford: Berg.

Humphreys, P. (1996) *Mass Media and Media Policy in Western Europe*. Manchester: Manchester University Press.

Humphreys, P. (1997a) *Power and Control in the New Media*. Paper presented at the ECPR Workshop, New Media and Political Communication, Berne, 27 February to 4 March.

Humphreys, P. (1997b) 'Media Concentration and Policy in Germany'. Unpublished paper presented at University of Manchester Workshop, Directions in the Regulation of Media Ownership, 17 October.

Humphreys, P. and Lang, M. (1998) 'Regulating for Media Pluralism and *Standortpolitik*: The Re-Regulation of German Broadcasting Ownership Rules', *German Politics*, vol. 7, p. 176.

Hutton, W. (1995) *The State We're In*. London: Jonathan Cape.

Hutton Report (2004) *Report of the Inquiry Into the Circumstances Surrounding the Death of Dr. David Kelly C.M.G.*, HC 247. London: HMSO.

Independent Television Commission (ITC) (1997) *ITC Announces Its Decision to Award Multiplex Licences for Digital Terrestrial Television*, news release. Available at: http://www.ofcom.org.uk/static/archive/itc/latest_news/press_releases/release.asp-release_id=610.html.

Independent Television Commission (ITC) (2002) *The ITC Programme Code*. London: ITC. Available at: http://www.ofcom.org.uk/tv/ifi/codes/legacy/programme_code/itc_pc.pdf (last accessed 30 December 2005).

Itzin, C. (1995) 'Pornography, Harm and Human Rights – The European Context', *Media Law and Practice*, p. 107.

Johnson, G. W. (1988) 'Introduction: Is the United States Supreme Court Ready for the Question?', *Brooklyn Law Review*, vol. 54, p. 729.

Jones, A. and Sufrin, B. (2004) *EC Competition Law: Text, Cases and Materials*, 2nd edn. Oxford: Oxford University Press.

Jones, T. (1992) 'Judicial review of the ITC', *Public Law*, p. 372.

Jowell, J. (1994) 'The Rule of Law Today', in Jowell, J. and Oliver, D. (eds), *The Changing Constitution*, 3rd edn. Oxford: Oxford University Press.

Jowell, J. (2000) 'Beyond the Rule of Law: Towards Constitutional Judicial Review', *Public Law*, p. 671.

Jowell, J. and Cooper, J. (eds) (2000) *Understanding Human Rights Principles*. Oxford: Hart Publishing.

Kahn-Freund, O. (1974) 'On Uses and Misuses of Comparative Law', *Modern Law Review*, p. 1.

Keane, J. (1991) *The Media and Democracy*. Cambridge: Polity Press.

Kennedy, K. (1997) *Citizenship Education and the Modern State*. London: Falmer.

Klingler, R. (1996) *The New Information Industry: Regulatory Challenges and the First Amendment*. Washington DC: Brookings Institute Press.

Koenig, C. and Röder, E. (1998) 'Converging Communications, Diverging Regulators? Germany's Constitutional Duplication in Internet Governance', *International Journal of Communications, Law and Policy*, vol. 1, Summer. Available at: http://www.ijclp.org/1_1998/rtf/ijclp_webdoc_1_1_1998.rtf (last accessed 20 November 2005).

Lawson-Cruttenden, T. and Addison, N. (1997) *Blackstone's Guide to the Protection From Harassment Act 1997*. London: Blackstone Press.

Le Grand, J. (1991) 'Quasi-markets and Social Policy', *Economic Journal*, vol. 101, p. 1256.

Lee, P. (ed.) (1995) *The Democratization of Communication*. Cardiff: University of Wales Press.

Leigh, I. (1999) 'Horizontal Rights, The Human Rights Act and Privacy: Lessons from the Commonwealth', *International and Comparative Law Quarterly*, vol. 48, p. 57.

Lenaerts, K. and Van Nuffel, P. (1999) *Constitutional Law of the European Union*. London: Sweet & Maxwell.

Lester, A. (2004) 'Human Rights and the British Constitution', in Jowell, J. L. and Oliver, D. (eds), *The Changing Constitution*, 5th edn. Oxford: Oxford University Press.

Lewis, N. (1975) 'IBA Programme Contract Awards', *Public Law*, p. 317.

Lewis, N. D. (1996) *Choice and the Legal Order*. London: Butterworths.

Leys, C. (2001) *Market-Driven Politics: Neoliberal Democracy and the Public Interest*. London: Verso.

Libertus, M. (2004) *Essential Aspects Concerning the Regulation of the German Broadcasting System. Historical, Constitutional and Legal Outlines*, Institute for Broadcasting Economics, Cologne University, Working Paper No. 193. Available at: http://rundfunkoek.uni-koeln.de/institut/pdfs/19304.pdf (last accessed 20 November 2005).

Lidbetter, A. (1994) 'The Advertising Standards Authority, the Committee of Advertising Practice and Judicial Review', *Media Law and Practice*, p. 113.

Lipsey, R. G. and Chrystal, K. A. (1999) *Principles of Economics*, 9th edn. Oxford: Oxford University Press.

Lloyd, J. (2004) *What the Media Are Doing To Our Politics*. London: Constable.

Longley, D. (1993) *Public Law and Health Service Accountability*. Buckingham: Open University Press.

Lucy, W. and Mitchell, C. (1996) 'Replacing Private Property: The Case for Stewardship', *Cambridge Law Journal*, p. 566.

Majone, G. (1997) 'From the Positive to the Regulatory State: Causes and Consequences of Changes in the Mode of Governance', *Journal of Public Policy*, vol. 17, p. 139.

Marquand, D. (2004) *Decline of the Public*. London: Polity Press.

Marsden, C. (1996) 'Judicial Review of the Channel 5 Licence Award', *Nottingham Law Journal*, p. 86.

Marsden, C. (1997a) 'Structural and Behavioural Regulation in UK, European and US Digital Pay-TV', *Utilities Law Review*, p. 114.

Marsden, C. (1997b) 'The European Digital Convergence Paradigm: From Structural Pluralism to Behavioural Competition Law', *Journal of Information, Law and Technology*. Available at: http://elj.warwick.ac.uk/jilt/commsreg/97_3mars/.

Marsden, C. (2004) 'Co- and Self-Regulation in the European Media and Internet Sectors: The Results of Oxford University's Study www.selfregulation.info', *Communications Law*, vol. 9, p. 187.

Marshall, T. (1964) *Class, Citizenship and Social Development*. New York: Doubleday.

Mason, R. (2005) *The Tender Process for a Public Service Publisher*. London: Ofcom. Available at: http://www.ofcom.org.uk/consult/condocs/psb3/tender.pdf (last accessed 30 December 2005).

Matsushita, M., Schoenbaum, T. J. and Mavroidis, P. (2004) *The World Trade Organization: Law, Practice and Policy*. Oxford: Oxford University Press.

Mazzoleni, G. (1992) 'Is There a Question of Vulnerable Values in Italy?', in Blumler, J. (ed.), *Television and the Public Interest: Vulnerable Values in West European Broadcasting*. London: Sage.

McChesney, R. W. (1999) *Rich Media, Poor Democracy: Communications Politics in Dubious Times*. New York: New Press.

McGonagle, T. (2002) 'Co-Regulation of the Media in Europe: The Potential for Practice of an Intangible Idea', *Iris Plus – Legal Observations of the European Audiovisual Observatory*. Available at: http://www.obs.coe.int/oea_publ/iris/iris_plus/iplus10_2002.pdf.cn (last accessed 30 December 2005).

McGonagle, T. and Richter, A. (2004) 'Regulation of Minority-Language Broadcasting', *Legal Observations of the European Audiovisual Observatory*, Issue 2. Available at: http://www.obs.coe.int/oea_publ/iris/iris_plus/iplus2_2004.pdf.en (last accessed 20 May 2005).

McGonagle, T., Davis Noll, B. and Price, R. (eds) (2003) *Minority-Language Related Broadcasting and Legislation in the OSCE*. Amsterdam: Institute for Information Law. Available at: http://www.ivir.nl/publications/mcgonagle/minority-languages.pdf (last accessed 20 May 2005).

McQuail, D. (1992) *Media Performance: Mass Communication and the Public Interest*. London: Sage.

Minor, W. S. (1962) 'Public Interest and Ultimate Commitment', in Friedrich, C. J. (ed.), *Nomos V: The Public Interest*. New York: Atherton Press.

Monbiot, G. (2000) *The Captive State: the Corporate Takeover of Britain*. London: Macmillan.

Monti, M. (2003) *Competition and Regulation in the Telecom Industry – The Way Forward*, SPEECH/03/604, given at the ECTA Conference, Conrad Hotel, Brussels on 10 December. Available at: http://europa.eu.int/rapid/pressReleasesAction.do?reference=SPEECH/03/604&format=HTML&aged=0&language=EN&guiLanguage=en (last accessed 1 August 2005).

Moran, L. J., Sandon, E., Loizidou, E. and Christie, I. (eds) (2004) *Law's Moving Image*. London: Glasshouse.

Moreham, N. A. (2001) '*Douglas and others v. Hello! Ltd* – the Protection of Privacy in English Private Law', *Modern Law Review*, vol. 64, p. 767.

Moreham, N. A. (2005) 'Privacy in the Common Law: A Doctrinal and Theoretical Analysis', *Law Quarterly Review*, vol. 121, p. 628.

Motta, M. (2004) *Competition Policy: Theory and Practice*, Cambridge: Cambridge University Press.

Munro, C. (1991) 'Press Freedom – How the Beast was Tamed', *Modern Law Review*, p. 194.

Munro, C. (1997) 'Self-regulation in the media', *Public Law*, p. 6.

Munro, C. (2003) 'The Value of Commercial Speech', *Cambridge Law Journal*, vol. 62, p. 134.

Murray, A. and Scott, C. (2002) 'Controlling the New Media: Hybrid Responses to New Forms of Power', *Modern Law Review*, vol. 65, p. 491.

Negrine, R. (1994) *Politics and the Mass Media in Britain*, 2nd edn. London: Routledge.

Nihoul, P. and Rodford, P. (2004) *EU Electronic Communications Law: Competition and Regulation in the European Telecommunications Market*. Oxford: Oxford University Press.

Nolan, D. (1997) 'Bottlenecks in Pay Television: Impact on Market Development in Europe', *Telecommunications Policy*, vol. 21, p. 597.

Norton, P. (2004) 'Regulating the Regulatory State', *Parliamentary Affairs*, vol. 57, no. 4, p. 785.

O'Donnell, G. (1999) 'Horizontal Accountability in New Democracies', in Schedler, A. et al. (eds), *The Self Restraining State: Power and Accountability in New Democracies* Boulder, CO and London: Lynne Rienner Publishers.

Ofcom (no date a) *Freedom of Information Act 2000: Ofcom's Publication Scheme*. London: Ofcom. Available at: http://www.ofcom.org.uk/about/cad/foiindex/foi_act_pub_scheme/ (last accessed 30 December 2005).

Ofcom (no date b) *Ofcom's Regulatory Relationship with the BBC*. London: Ofcom. Available at: http://www.ofcom.org.uk/about/accoun/bbc (last accessed 30 December 2005).

Ofcom (no date c) *The Ofcom Content Board: Functions and Role*. London: Ofcom. Available at: http://www.ofcom.org.uk/about/csg/ocb/functions_role/ (last accessed 30 December 2005).

Ofcom (no date d) *The Content Sanctions Committee: Terms of Reference*. London: Ofcom. Available at: http://www.ofcom.org.uk/about/csg/ocsc_index/ocsc_tor2/ (last accessed 30 December 2005).

Ofcom (2003) *How Will Ofcom Consult? A Guide to Our Consultation Process*. London: Ofcom.

Ofcom (2004a) *Ofcom Review of Public Service Television Broadcasting: Phase 1 – Is Television Special?* London: Ofcom.

Ofcom (2004b) *Ofcom Review of Public Service Television Broadcasting: Phase 2 – Meeting the Digital Challenge*. London: Ofcom.

Ofcom (2004c) *Ofcom Review of Public Service Television Broadcasting: Phase 3 – Competition for Quality*. London: Ofcom.

Ofcom (2004d) *The Regulation of Electronic Programme Guides*. London: Ofcom. Available at: http://www.ofcom.org.uk/consult/condocs/epg/epg/condoc_150104.pdf (last accessed 29 December 2005).

Ofcom (2004e) *Statement on Code on Electronic Programme Guides.* London: Ofcom. Available at: http://www.ofcom.org.uk/consult/condocs/ epg/statement_archived/statement.pdf (last accessed 29 December 2005).

Ofcom (2004f) *Code of Practice on Electronic Programme Guides.* London: Ofcom. Available at: http://www.ofcom.org.uk/tv/ifi/codes/EPGcode/241557 (last accessed 29 December 2005).

Ofcom (2004g) *Adjudication of Ofcom Content Sanctions Committee – Auctionworld Limited.* London: Ofcom. Available at: http://www.ofcom. org.uk/tv/obb/adv_comp/aw.pdf (last accessed 29 December 2005).

Ofcom (2004h) *Adjudication of Ofcom Content Sanctions Committee – Auctionworld Limited (in Administration).* London: Ofcom. Available at: http://www.ofcom.org.uk/tv/obb/adv_comp/aw2.pdf (last accessed 29 December 2005).

Ofcom (2004i) *Adjudication of Ofcom Content Sanctions Committee – Digital Television Production Company Limited (XplicitXXX).* London: Ofcom. Available at: http://www.ofcom.org.uk/tv/obb/ocsc_adjud/adj_20040727.pdf (last accessed 29 December 2005).

Ofcom (2004j) *Memorandum of Understanding between Ofcom and the ASA(B) and BCAP and BASBOF.* London: Ofcom.

Ofcom (2004k) *Promoting Effective Self-Regulation: Criteria for Transferring Functions to Co-Regulatory Bodies.* London: Ofcom.

Ofcom (2004l) *Draft Listed Events Code and Regulations.* London: Ofcom.

Ofcom (2004m) *New Voice Services: a consultation and interim guidance.* London: Ofcom.

Ofcom (2005a) *Digital Television Update – Q4 2004.* London: Ofcom.

Ofcom (2005b) *Digital Television Update – Q1 2005.* London: Ofcom.

Ofcom (2005c) *Digital Television Update – Q2 2005.* London: Ofcom.

Ofcom (2005d) *Ofcom Broadcasting Code.* London: Ofcom.

Ofcom (2005e) *Review of the BBC's Royal Charter: Ofcom Response to the Green Paper.* London: Ofcom.

Ofcom (2005f) *Radio Communications Market 2005.* London: Ofcom.

Ofcom (2005g) *Digital Dividend Review.* London: Ofcom.

Ofcom (2005h) *Annual Report on Core Activities 2004/5.* London: Ofcom.

Ofcom (2005j) *Statement on the Ofcom Broadcasting Code.* London: Ofcom.

Ofcom (2005k) *Ofcom Broadcast Code Guidance.* London: Ofcom. Available at: http://www.ofcom.org.uk/tv/ifi/guidance/bguidance/ (last accessed 29 December 2005).

Ofcom (2005l) *Ofcom Broadcast Bulletin – Issue No. 46 (24 October 2005).* London: Ofcom. Available at: http://www.ofcom.org.uk/tv/obb/prog_ cb/ pcb49/issue46.pdf (last accessed 29 December 2005).

Ofcom (2005m) *Adjudication of Ofcom Content Sanctions Committee – Playboy TV UK/Benelux Limited.* London: Ofcom. Available at: http://www.ofcom.org.uk/tv/obb/ocsc_adjud/adj-playboytv.pdf (last accessed 29 December 2005).

Ofcom (2005n) *Adjudication of Ofcom Content Sanctions Committee – Channel U*. London: Ofcom. Available at: http://www.ofcom.org.uk/tv/obb/ocsc_adjud/Achannelu.pdf (last accessed 29 December 2005).

Ofcom (2005o) *Adjudication of Ofcom Content Sanctions Committee – Piccadilly Radio, in respect of its service 'Key 103' FM*. London: Ofcom. Available at: http://www.ofcom.org.uk/tv/obb/ocsc_adjud/key103.pdf (last accessed 29 December 2005).

Office of the Commissioner for Public Appointments (OCPA) (2005) *Code of Practice for Ministerial Appointments to Public Bodies*. London: OCPA. Available at: http://www.ocpa.gov.uk/publications/pdf/codeofpractice.pdf (last accessed 30 December 2005).

Oftel (1997a) *Submission to the ITC on Competition Issues Arising from the Award of Digital Terrestrial Television Multiplex Licences*. Available at: http://www.ofcom.org.uk/static/archive/oftel/ind_info/broadcasting/dtt.htm.

Oftel (1997b) *Oftel Publishes Advice to ITC on Bids for Digital Terrestrial Television Licence*, press release. London: Oftel.

Oftel (1997c) *The Regulation of Conditional Access for Digital Television Services. Oftel Guidelines*. Available at: http://www.ofcom.org.uk/static/archive/oftel/ind_info/broadcasting/conacc.htm.

Oftel (2002) *Terms of Supply of Conditional Access: Oftel Guidelines*. London: Oftel.

Ogus, A. (1994) *Regulation: Legal Form and Economic Theory*. Oxford: Clarendon Press.

O'Malley, T. (2005) *Keeping Broadcasting Public*. London: Campaign for Press and Broadcasting Freedom.

O'Malley, T. and Soley, C. (2000) *Regulating the Press*. London: Pluto Press.

O'Neill, O. (2004) 'Accuracy, Independence and Trust', in Runciman, W. G. (ed.), *Hutton and Butler: Lifting the Lid on the Workings of Power*. Oxford: Oxford University Press.

Osborne, D. and Gaebler, T. (1992) *Reinventing Government*. New York: Addison-Wesley.

Page, A. (1987) 'Financial Services: The Self-Regulatory Alternative?', in Baldwin, R. and McCrudden, C. (eds), *Regulation and Public Law*. London: Weidenfeld & Nicolson.

Palzer, C. (2002) 'Co-Regulation of the Media in Europe: European Provisions for the Establishment of Co-Regulation Frameworks', *Iris Plus – Legal Observations of the European Audiovisual Observatory*. Available at: http://www.obs.coe.int/oea_publ/iris/iris_plus/iplus6_2002.pdf.en (last accessed 30 December 2005).

Parkinson, J. (1993) *Corporate Power and Responsibility: Issues in the Theory of Company Law*. Oxford: Oxford University Press.

Parkinson, J. (2003) 'Legitimacy Problems in Deliberative Democracy', *Political Studies*, vol. 51, p. 180.

Peacock Report (1986) *Report of the Committee on Financing the BBC*, Cmnd 9824. London: HMSO.

Peak, S. and Fisher, P. (1996) *The Media Guide 1997*. London: Fourth Estate.

Posner, R. A. (2001) *Antitrust Law*, 2nd edn. Chicago and London: University of Chicago Press.

Press Complaints Commission (no date) *The Evolving Code of Practice*. London: PCC. Available at: http://www.pcc.org.uk/cop/history.html (last accessed 30 December 2005).

Press Complaints Commission (2005) *Press Complaints Commission Code of Practice – 13 June 2005*. London: PCC. Available at: http://www.pcc.org.uk/cop/cop.asp (last accessed 30 December 2005).

Price, M. E. and Raboy, M. (eds) (2003) *Public Service Broadcasting in Transition: A Documentary Reader*. The Hague: Kluwer.

PriceWaterhouseCoopers (2005) *Economic Analysis of the TV Advertising Market*. London: Ofcom.

Programme for Comparative Media Law and Policy (PCMLP) (2004) *Self-Regulation of Digital Media Converging on the Internet: Industry Codes of Conduct in Sectoral Analysis*. Oxford: PCMLP.

Prosser, T. (1982) 'Towards a Critical Public Law', *Journal of Law and Society*, p. 1.

Prosser, T. (1994) 'Regulation, Markets and Legitimacy', in Jowell, J. and Oliver, D. (eds), *The Changing Constitution*, 3rd edn. Oxford: Oxford University Press.

Prosser, T. (1997) *Law and the Regulators*. Oxford: Clarendon.

Prosser, T. (1999) 'Theorising Utility Regulation', *Modern Law Review*, vol. 62, p. 196.

Prosser, T. (2000) 'Public Service Law: Privatisation's Unexpected Offspring', *Law and Contemporary Problems*, vol. 63, p. 63.

Prosser, T. (2005) *The Limits of Competition Law: Markets and Public Services*. Oxford: Oxford University Press.

Puttnam Report (2002), *Report of the Joint Committee on the Draft Communications Bill*, HL Paper 169-I: HC 876-I, 25 July.

Ranson, S. and Stewart, J. (1989) 'Citizenship and Government: The Challenge for Management in the Public Domain', *Political Studies*, p. 5.

Regulatory Impact Unit (2004) *Code of Practice on Consultation*. London: Cabinet Office. Available at: http://www.cabinetoffice.gov.uk/regulation/consultation/documents/pdf/code.pdf (last accessed 20 December 2005).

Reich, C. (1964) 'The New Property', *Yale Law Journal*, vol. 73, p. 733.

Robertson, G. and Nicol, A. (1992) *Media Law*, 3rd edn. London: Penguin.

Robertson, G. and Nicol, A. (2002) *Robertson & Nicol on Media Law*, 4th edn. London: Sweet & Maxwell.

Rudenstine, D. (1996) *The Day the Presses Stopped: A History of the Pentagon Papers Case*. Berkeley, CA: University of California Press.

Runciman, W. G. (ed.) (2004) *Hutton and Butler: Lifting the Lid on the Workings of Power*. Oxford: Oxford University Press.

Sadler Report (1991) *Inquiry into Standards in Cross Media Promotion*, Cm 1436, London: HMSO.

Scanlon, T. M. (2000) *What we Owe to Each Other*. Cambridge, MA and London: Belknap.

Schiller, H. (1996) *Information Inequality*. New York: Routledge.

Scott, C. (2001) 'Analyzing Regulatory Space: Fragmented Resources and Institutional Design', *Public Law*, p. 329.

Scott, C. (2002) 'The Governance of the European Union: The Potential for Multi-Level Control', *European Law Journal*, vol. 8, p. 59.

Selznick, P. (1985) 'Focusing Organisational Research on Regulation', in Noll, R. G. (ed.), *Regulatory Policy and the Social Sciences*. Berkeley, CA: University of California Press, quoted in Ogus, A. I. (1994) *Regulation: Legal Form and Economic Theory*. Oxford: Clarendon Press.

Seymour-Ure, C. (1996) *The British Press and Broadcasting Since 1945*, 2nd edn. Oxford: Blackwell.

Siebert, F., Peterson, T. and Schramm, W. (1956) *Four Theories of the Press*. Urbana, IL. University of Illinois Press.

Skouris, W. (ed.), (1994) *Advertising and Constitutional Rights in Europe*. Baden-Baden: Nomos Verlagsgesellschaft.

Smith, G. and Wales, C. (2000) 'Citizens' Juries and Deliberative Democracy', *Political Studies*, vol. 48, p. 51.

Stewart, P. and Gibson, D. (2003) 'The Communications Act – A New Era', *Communications Law*, vol. 8, no. 5 p. 357.

Stewart, R. B. (1983) 'Regulation in a Liberal State: The Role of Non-Commodity Values', *Yale Law Journal*, vol. 92, p. 1537.

Stroux, S. (2004) *US and EC Oligopoly Control*. The Hague: Kluwer.

Sunstein, C. R. (1990) *After the Rights Revolution: Reconceiving the Regulatory State*. Cambridge, MA: Harvard University Press.

Tehranian, M. and Tehranian, K. (1995) 'That Recurrent Suspicion: Democratization in a Global Perspective', in Lee, P. (ed.), *The Democratization of Communication*. Cardiff: University of Wales Press, pp. 38–74.

Teubner, G. (1993) *Law as an Autopoietic System*. Oxford: Blackwell.

Teubner, G. (1987) *Juridification of Social Spheres*. Berlin: Walter de Gruyter, extracts in Baldwin, R., Scott, C. and Hood, C. (eds) (1998) *A Reader on Regulation*. Oxford: Oxford University Press.

Teubner, G. (1999) 'Legal Irritants: Good Faith in British Law or How Unifying Law Ends Up in New Divergences', *Modern Law Review*, vol. 61, p. 11.

Thomas N. (1995) 'Linguistic Minorities and the Media', in Lee, P. (ed.), *The Democratization of Communication*. Cardiff: University of Wales Press, pp. 173–82.

Tunstall, J. and Palmer, M. (1991) *Media Moguls*. London: Routledge.

Ungerer, H. (1995) *EU Competition Law in the Telecommunications, Media and Information Technology Sectors*. Speech to the Fordham Corporate Law Institute, 22nd Annual Conference on International Antitrust Law and Policy, Fordham University School of Law, New York City, on 27 October 1995. Available at: http://europa.eu.int/comm/competition/speeches/text/sp1995_041_en.pdf (last accessed 20 May 2005).

Ungerer, H. (2004a) *Legal Framework to Secure Open Media Markets and the Independence of the Press – The Role of EU Competition Law*. Speech given at the Conference on Democracy and Human Rights in the EU, Opole, Poland. Brussels: Commission of the European Communities. Available at: http://europa.eu.int/comm/competition/speeches/text/sp2004_009_en.pdf (last accessed 30 December 2005).

Ungerer, H. (2004b) *Regulating Tomorrow's Information Society and Media*. Speech given at the International Institute of Communications, Berlin. Brussels: Commission of the European Communities. Available at: http://europa. eu.int/comm/competition/speeches/text/sp2005_008_en.pdf (last accessed 30 December 2005).

Ungerer, H. (2005) *Broadcasting or Broadbanding? Speech to the International Institute of Communications Conference on Regulating Tomorrow's Information Society and Media*, Berlin, 14 April 2005. Available at: http://www. europa.eu.int/comm/competition/speeches/text/sp2005_008_en.pdf (last accessed 10 December 2005).

Van Hecke, S. (2003) 'The Principle of Subsidiarity: 10 Years of Application in the European Union', *Regional and Federal Studies*, vol. 13, p. 55.

Van Loon, A. (2004) 'The End of the Broadcasting Era: What Constitutes Broadcasting and Why Does it Need to be Regulated?', *Communications Law*, vol. 9, p. 172.

Varney, E. C. (2005) 'Winners and Losers in the Communications Sector: An Examination of Digital Television Regulation in the United Kingdom', *Minnesota Journal of Law, Science and Technology*, vol. 6, p. 645.

Varney, M. (2004) 'European Controls on Member State Promotion and Regulation of Public Service Broadcasting and Broadcasting Standards', *European Public Law*, vol. 10, p. 503.

Varney, M. (2004/2005) 'Must-Carry Obligations in the New European Regulatory Framework for Communications: A True Guardian of Pluralism and Diversity?', *Utilities Law Review*, vol. 14, p. 68.

Varney, M. (2005) 'The Roles of Private Property, the "General Interest" and Stewardship in the Regulation of the Digital Media'. Unpublished PhD thesis, University of Hull.

Veljanovski, C. (1987) 'Cable Television: Agency Franchising and Economics', in Baldwin, R. and McCrudden, C. (eds), *Regulation and Public Law*. London: Weidenfeld & Nicolson.

Veljanovski, C. (1989) *Freedom in Broadcasting*. London: Institute of Economic Affairs.

Verhulst, S. (1997) 'Public Service Broadcasting in Europe', *Utilities Law Review*, p. 31.

Vick, D. (1995) 'The First Amendment Limitations on Broadcasting in the United States after *Turner Broadcasting v FCC*', *Media Law and Practice*, p. 97.

Viscusi, W. K., Vernon, J. M. and Harrington, J. E. (2000) *The Economics of Regulation and Antitrust*, 3rd edn. Cambridge, MA and London: MIT Press.

Wacks, R. (1995) *Privacy and Press Freedom*. London: Blackstone Press.

Wallace, R. and Goldberg, D. (1989) 'The EEC Directive on Television Broadcasting', *Yearbook of European Law*, vol. 9, p. 175.

Whish, R. (1993) *Competition Law*, 3rd edn. London: Sweet & Maxwell.

Whish, R. (2003) *Competition Law*, 5th edn. London: LexisNexis.

Whitehouse, L. (2003) 'Corporate Social Responsibility as Citizenship and Compliance', *Journal of Corporate Citizenship*, vol. 11, p. 85.

Wilkinson, A. (2003) 'The Nature of the Beast', *Marketing Week*, vol. 26, no. 42, p. 23.

Wring, D. (2005) 'Politics and the Media: The Hutton Inquiry, the Public Relations State, and Crisis at the BBC', *Parliamentary Affairs*, vol. 58, p. 380.

Index

accountability, 8, 38, 50, 66, 169
  definition, 171
  of regulators, 126, 158–9, 170–6,
    191–3, 196, 198, 199, 259, 262,
    264–7, 269
Advertising Standards Authority
    (ASA), 34, 67, 127, 170, 191,
    195–9, 202, 204, 241–2, 264–5
analogue switch-off, 24, 28, 43, 69,
    80, 145, 148, 152–3, 263
Annan Report, 77, 79, 135
applications programming interface
    (API), 147, 223, 228–9

Bagdikian, B., 20, 72, 129, 238,
    251–2
Barendt, E., 11–13, 16, 32, 38, 51,
    57, 79, 80, 81, 87, 100, 107,
    136, 144, 181, 184, 202, 209,
    215, 233, 237
behavioural regulation, 28, 68, 71,
    90, 93, 104, 127, 251, 269
Berlusconi, S., 20, 40, 72
Black, J., 173, 202–3, 204–5, 207,
    240, 242
Blair, T., 37, 108, 112, 197, 250, 267,
    269
Blumler, J., 1, 4, 17, 54–5, 64, 66,
    278
British Board of Film Classification
    (BBFC), 10, 34, 67, 81, 169
British Broadcasting Corporation
    (BBC), 1–2, 27–8, 40–2, 43–4,
    50, 55, 64, 67, 77, 79, 82, 84–5,
    111, 120, 146, 151–2, 155–7,
    163, 178, 182, 186, 188, 203,

    225, 225–6, 239, 255, 261,
    263–6, 271–2
  Charter, 2, 39, 42, 44–54, 60, 64,
    67, 79, 120, 155, 157, 177, 181,
    183–5, 231, 255, 272
  duopoly with ITV, 2, 25, 40, 41,
    83, 136
  Governors, 45, 50–4, 78, 166,
    176–7, 185, 273
  licence fee, 42, 44, 83, 157
Broadcasting Acts, 38, 79, 127
  Broadcasting Act 1980, 135, 178
  Broadcasting Act 1981, 181
  Broadcasting Act 1990, 51, 70,
    128, 130, 135–8, 147, 179–81,
    184, 189, 203
  Broadcasting Act 1996, 51, 75, 80,
    95, 128, 130, 135, 139–40,
    142–5, 146–8, 154, 161, 164–5,
    166–7, 184, 189, 263
  see also Communications Act
    2003; Television Act 1963
Broadcasting Standards Commission,
    51, 81, 112, 184–5, 186–7, 189,
    266
Broadcasting Standards Council, 67,
    155, 166
BSkyB, 4, 18, 25, 43, 84–5, 136,
    145–6, 149, 151, 165, 225, 226,
    236, 262

cable, 25, 69, 72, 84, 93, 146, 164,
    176, 246
Calcutt Reports, 191–2
Carlton Television, 94, 95, 151, 155,
    161–5, 244, 262